SOUND OF DRUMS

SOUND OF DRUMS

Selected Writings of
SPENCER B. KING
from his
Civil War Centennial Columns
Appearing in the Macon (Georgia)
Telegraph-News, 1960-1965

with a foreword by
HENRY Y. WARNOCK

MERCER

ISBN 0-86554-107-8

Sound of Drums
Copyright ©1984 by
Mercer University Press, Macon GA 31207
All rights reserved
Printed in the United States of America

All books published by Mercer University Press
are produced on acid-free paper that exceeds
the minimum standards set by the National Historical
Publications and Records Commission.

Library of Congress Cataloging in Publication Data
King, Spencer Bidwell, 1904-1977
Sound of drums.

1. Georgia—History—Civil War, 1861-1865—Addresses,
essays, lectures. 2. Macon Region (Ga.)—History—
Addresses, essays, lectures. I. Title.
E559.9.K56 1984   973.7'09758   84-6631
ISBN 0-86554-107-8 (alk. paper)

· CONTENTS ·

FOREWORD

By HENRY Y. WARNOCK

On Sunday, 11 December 1960, the *Macon Telegraph and News* began to run a weekly article commemorating the centennial of that worst of American conflicts—the Civil War. The newspaper had asked Dr. Spencer King, chairman of the department of history at Mercer University, to write the series, and he had agreed. Thus began a long and remarkable journey into our tragic past—a journey that was not to end until 1965. Dr. King's dedicated work was truly a labor of love, for he never accepted any remuneration for the hundreds of columns that he contributed over a period of more than four years.

Precisely how the project originated does not appear to be known. Very likely it was suggested by *Telegraph and News* staff members, a number of whom were friends of Dr. King. If such was the case, the public was and is truly indebted to them, for Dr. King's prolonged excursion into the murky waters of Civil War history was a highly successful effort to bring readers into intimate contact with the realities of war and wartime life. Indeed, I am increasingly convinced that these journalistic efforts, now collected into book form, will emerge as Dr. King's best and most enduring work, a judgment with which he would probably be quite pleased.

The evidence suggests that the series was not necessarily intended to run a specified length of time, but the fact that it continued the full run of the centennial celebration is further indication of its wide acceptance. Dr. King himself apparently had to examine the propriety of celebrating a lost cause at all; but having resolved his own doubts, he set to work with vigor. We cannot eliminate history, he noted in one place, and further reminded his readers that we were to "commemorate" rather than "celebrate" the war. The haunting "unspoken question" apparently never ceased to bother him, but Southerners a century ago found comfort even in defeat, "and some of that comfort is claimed today by their descendants," he wrote.

In 1970 Dr. King organized a selection of the articles into book form and ran ten Xerox copies. It is this collection that Mercer University Press is now making available to the public. The organizational plan, both topical and chronological, is the work of Dr. King himself.

The writing plan, as originally conceived, was twofold in nature: the articles were to deal largely with commonplace daily life and events as reflected in sources such as diaries, letters, and newspaper accounts; second, the locale and scope were to be limited for the most part in some way to Middle Georgia and the people of that area. On both counts a better choice than Dr. King as author could not have been made. Already an expert on Georgia history, Dr. King expanded his knowledge of local history to encyclopedic dimensions, and Middle Georgia names and designations flowed from his pen with consummate ease. Local events and people were then skillfully connected to the larger crisis that loomed over Southern lives for so long. Nevertheless, the focus was essentially local rather than monumental, so that the reader could readily identify with both citizen and soldier as recognizable people rather than as a remote *dramatis personae* in some long-forgotten conflict. The result was to rivet the reader's attention to events often small in scale but nonetheless moving and revealing.

The use of letters, diaries, and other documentary sources reinforced the technique already suggested above. Dr. King's knowledge of manuscript sources was astonishing; indeed, one can only wonder where he unearthed most of the rich lode of original source material from which he drew. The effect is truly noteworthy. We are told not only *about* fear and pain and despair and joy and hunger, but the participants and victims themselves tell us in their own words *what* life was like. We are thus exposed to the full power of human emotions, often expressed in horrendous English but made more poignant by the lack of erudition. The characters speak, and in doing so they tell us more than a shelf of textbooks could ever convey.

All this is not to say that Dr. King did not from time to time ponder the larger issues at stake in the fierce conflict of 1860-1865, since occasionally he reflected on slavery, secession, states' rights, and other related topics. For the most part, however, he left this sort of historical speculation to be treated elsewhere and instead led his readers into nooks and crannies of Civil War history all too often left unexplored by professional historians.

Discrete journalistic pieces, as these are, do not lend themselves to a unified, coherent thematic development or thesis. If there is an underlying theme that runs through the whole series, it is the theme of tragedy—war as a bitter exercise in horror that neither North nor South should have had to endure. To this extent Dr. King was truly objective, lamenting the bloodshed on both sides of the battlefield, often citing Northern gallantry as well as Southern heroism. Yet the reader will soon discover that the point of view is decidedly Southern. Outsiders may read his words, but they should be warned in advance that these essays were written by a dedicated Southerner for the home folks, the people who historically endured not only tragedy but also the humiliation of defeat and the pain of conquest. Dr. King achieved what may be described as "objective partisanship," a fair presentation without rancor or polemics but withal unabashedly Southern.

Whatever Dr. King may have done in these articles, it is to his lasting credit that *one* thing he most certainly did not do: he never apologized for the South and what it did between 1860-

1865. Like any Southerner who has given the matter thought, Dr. King knew that his and other grandfathers and grandmothers of the South were neither villains nor traitors, but were instead men and women willing to make a bold strike for their independence, and pledging their lives and fortunes to the effort. He is thus not embarrassed to evoke notions of pride, heroism, endurance, and the like, terms often today considered out of fashion and even naive. Such uncomplicated faith is especially refreshing in view of the fact that modern day historiography is more often than not hostile and unfriendly to the nineteenth-century South, especially the white South. It is therefore quite within the logic of the articles, for example, that Dr. King should defend Captain Henry Wirz of Andersonville.

These writings should not be used as reference materials or read as a comprehensive survey of the Civil War. Dr. King was the first to admit that errors crept in here and there, and his give-and-take with his readers no doubt sparked additional interest. The articles should be read without pressure, mused upon, and—if one may use such a word in conjunction with suffering—enjoyed. At the end, the reader will know a great deal about Middle Georgia, the South, and the Civil War, and he will know a great deal about the joys and sorrows of people playing their appointed roles in a gigantic tragedy.

Spencer Bidwell King, Jr., was born in Birmingham, Alabama, in 1904, but in every sense of the word he was a Georgian, with his roots going back to the area of Americus. As the son of a Baptist minister, however, he learned to accept movement as a way of life. He graduated from Mercer University in 1929 and later received the Ph.D. degree from the University of North Carolina, where his major professor was Ray Newsome. At that university he also came under the influence of Professor Fletcher Green, a prominent Southern historian, and the two men remained friends throughout their lives.

After a teaching stint at Mars Hill College, Dr. King came to Mercer in 1946 as head of the history department, a post he held until 1970. As a teacher he possessed the rare ability to arouse students' intense interest in the Old South and the Civil War, and no doubt that fascination is still carried by dozens of

Mercer University alumni. Dr. King's teaching colleagues grew quite used to seeing students bring him letters, diaries, mementos, and Civil War artifacts, which doubtless were of some help to him. But even more important as a source of knowledge was his disciplined work schedule, quite the envy and terror of those who shared nearby offices. Over the years the hard work resulted in numerous articles and books dealing mostly with Georgia history.

Some months before his death it was discovered that Dr. King had developed an inoperable brain tumor. He died in 1977 and is buried in the family cemetery at Americus, a few short miles from the Andersonville Cemetery and the monument of Captain Wirz.

The third floor of the restored Mercer University Administration Building has been dedicated to Dr. King's memory. Here may be found his portrait and a display case of King mementos and publications. At each June graduation, the Spencer B. King, Jr., Distinguished Professor Award is presented to a member of the faculty of the College of Liberal Arts of Mercer University.

Editor's Note: Dr. King's original style has been preserved as much as possible, except for some standardization of terms, abbreviations, and the like, contained in the series. The original spelling and grammar of the primary sources also have been retained.

• I •

SECESSION

MACON TOOK HOLIDAY TO HEAR ALEX STEPHENS AND "LITTLE GIANT"

Among Middle Georgia boys interested in the sectional crisis at the close of the year 1860 was George W. Scattergood of Macon. His diary, which records commonplace happenings that occurred when he was a student in Benjamin Mitchell Polhill's school, gives us an insight into the movement of Georgia to secession and the increasing interest in military drills at the Fair Grounds.

As early as 24 April 1860, George had gone down to see the Macon Volunteers drill. "Just before the Volunteers left the Fair Grounds the Honorable Thomas Hardeman came out there; the soldiers cheered him, and tried to get a speech out of him, but could not succeed."

George was a faithful pupil, mastering his Cicero and Horace. Frequent entries in his diary indicate his pleasure at his accomplishments. On 23 Oct. he had a bad cold; but, "notwithstanding this obstacle," he said all of his lessons went "pretty well."

Alexander H. Stephens and Stephen A. Douglas, "the little giant," both spoke in Macon on 30 Oct. Mr. Polhill gave a "holy day." George, after "being pushed about a good while," finally found a spot where he could hear. Stephens, supporting the

Douglas-Johnson ticket, spoke first. He "proved to the people that he was still alive in body as well as sentiments." He spoke for about two hours. George didn't think when he began that he could speak as long as he did; he was so frail. "Judge Douglas followed, who I do not think, is as eloquent as Mr. Stephens."

On 8 Nov. George wrote: "Mr. Clisby (Joseph Clisby, editor of the *Telegraph*) in yesterday's column stated that seven towns in Connecticut had gone for Lincoln with twenty-one hundred." Georgia states' righters cast over 51,000 for Breckenridge, the unionists cast over 42,000 for Bell, and the regular Democrats numbered less than 12,000 for Douglas.

But Lincoln was elected, as George had feared, and the young pupil observed the "Minute Men" marching to the Court House on the evening of 28 Nov. Other companies met them there and they all marched to Concert Hall where they were addressed by Clifford Anderson and Phillip Tracy, who "were very strongly in favor of secession." On the last day of the month Mr. Polhill "taught without giving any time at noon so that he could parade with the Macon Volunteers."

Polhill let his pupils out at 9 o'clock on 4 Dec. so that they could go down to Concert Hall and hear Robert Toombs speak for Breckenridge and states' rights: "It was a very good speech, and he was applauded from time to time by the pleased audience." George went down to hear Thomas R. R. Cobb, another extreme secessionist, speak on 10 Dec. "I think there were a great many things he could have left out," he opined.

The last entry in George Scattergood's diary was made on 12 Dec. 1860. Mr. Polhill gave a holiday that day, and George went to the fair. The legislature was there. Several military companies came also and "presented to the eye a grand spectacle."

George had received a good classical education under the discipline of that very fine teacher, B. M. Polhill, but his education was not for living. On 1 May the year following his studies with Mr. Polhill, he joined the Floyd Rifles [Company C, Second Battalion, Georgia Infantry], Maj. Thomas Hardeman, commanding, and went off to Virigina to defend Richmond. He was killed in battle at Petersburg on 22 June 1864.

[The Scattergood diary is owned by Miss Ruth English of Powersville.]

THE TELEGRAPH SECEDES

Joseph Clisby seceded from the Union sometime in November after Lincoln won the election of 1860. I do not mean the well-known school in Macon but the man for whom the school was named. In 1855 Mr. Clisby assumed the editorship of the *Telegraph* which Myron Bartlett had established in 1826 and made it a permanent daily in 1860. He shifted the editorial policy of the paper from mere irritation of federal encroachment on states' rights to a final and definite call for secession, as we shall see.

In 1850, when the South had to swallow a bitter pill in the form of the admission of California as a free state and when students of Mercer University up at Penfield, Georgia, were ready to draw the line, the editor asked, "Must we pocket every indignity and insult the Free States may see fit to heap upon us?" Union sentiment was strong enough in 1850 to hold Georgia loyal, and Georgia was strong enough to persuade the neighboring states not to take the course South Carolina was urging. The Georgia Platform that submitted to the admission of California on the proffered bargain of an enforced fugitive slave law saved the Union for ten more years.

After the South had decided for union in 1850, the *Telegraph* became less bellicose. Phillip Tracy, who preceded Clisby as editor, had refused to follow the extremists that early. When the South Carolina congressman, Preston Brooks, caned Senator Charles Sumner of Massachusetts in 1856 for his vilification of Brooks's uncle, the aged Senator Andrew Pickens Butler, also of South Carolina, many admiring friends of Brooks sent him canes—enough to bash in the heads of all Abolitionists. But the *Telegraph*, now under Clisby, went along with other conservative papers of the South in deploring the regrettable and unwise attack by the hot-headed South Carolinian.

The secession fire of the *Telegraph* had died down to glowing embers during the 1850s. But with the election approaching in the fall of 1860 and with Lincoln's victory appearing more and more certain, editor Clisby began to fan the embers again into flame. Not immediately, but steadily. On 9 Nov. following the announcement of Lincoln's election, the editor emphasized the "equal necessity of calmness and vigilance." However, he thought Lincoln's election presented "no other alternative than a political revolution on the one hand or a social revolution on the other—slow it may be but as inevitable as fate itself." He favored a convention and would entrust to it the final decision between secession and union.

On the 10th he urged the people to commit the subject to the delegates and then as patriots, as Georgians, "stand by the decision of the Convention." The fire-eaters, Thomas R. R. Cobb and Robert Toombs, addressed the legislature in Milledgeville on the 12th and 13th, urging secession. Stephens followed with an urgent plea for moderation. "I am for exhausting all that patriotism demands before taking the last step," said Little Alex. He urged the "united cooperation" of all the Southern states. "Then in the face of the civilized world," he continued, "we may justify our action." In commenting on this speech of Stephens, editor Clisby said, "The time then for the South to move for her own protection is the time when she is the most united . . . the most alive to danger."

The *Telegraph* had definitely joined the secessionist papers by 22 Nov. when it endorsed the *Augusta Constitutionalist* in saying, "The antagonism of the two sections, North and South, is radical and incurable. The South should take care of herself by establishing a government of her own." The following month, on 20 Dec., South Carolina took the lead and passed an ordinance of secession. Georgia followed over a month later.

Answers to readers' Centennial questions:

To. L. W.—Your father's birthday, 21 March 1861, was not the day Gen. Beauregard captured Ft. Sumter to start the Civil War [12 April] nor was it the day the *Star of the West* was forced out of Charleston Harbor [9 Jan.] but it was the first day of spring.

CHRISTMAS LETTER: 1860

Secession sentiment was stronger in southwest Georgia in December 1860 than it was in eastern North Carolina, judging from Ellen King's letter from Fayetteville, North Carolina, written on Christmas Day to her father in Americus. Ellen had married Sampson P. Boone, of Fayetteville, and was visiting his family at the time.

Fayetteville
Dec. 25th, 1860

My Dear Father,

I have been thinking ever since I have been in Fayetteville of writing to you and the inclination was so strong this morning that I could not resist even if it was Christmas and about a half a dozen voices going on around me.

I wish you, Ma and all the rest, a Merry Christmas. The day is very dull and rainy but it is very pleasant in the house. Every one seems a little excited. I have heard more "Christmas Gift" than I have in some time before, but I guess the hard times and the rumor of war keeps a good many from enjoying themselves that would otherwise do so. Some of the Ladies here are very much excited and in Wilmington the Ladies are attending night meetings. That I think is carrying things too far.

Most of the people are for Union here. I believe that this family is almost converted to the disunion faith. What is funny to me is that it is the American Party that is so opposed to disunion. Their cry is "wait and see." We went out to a Paper Mill yesterday and as we came home we passed through the little village of Rock Fish. There had been a target shooting there in the morning. They were at dinner when we passed. Some of Mr. Boone's friends were there and told us if Disunion sentiments were spoken there they would be mobbed. One of them was to speak. He begged him to flavor it with some [secession talk], but he would not agree to do it. They were not at work at the mill but we went in and saw the Machinery. Mr. Boone explained it to me so I could understand it.

I saw something that I never saw before, it was a Bridge that covered two different creeks and I don't suppose it was more than 30 feet long, if that. It is a beautiful place now and I guess it must be more so in the Summer.

I have not been out much. I went to Church Sunday, heard a very excellent sermon. The Ladies don't dress here like they do in Georgia, but they look very nice. Sunday night I heard a Lecture from Mr. Hunter on Sunday Schools. Emma, I expect, remembers him. She heard him in Atlanta. I was very much pleased and as a deranged man said, he "discoursed like a young thunder." This is quite a large place. The business streets look very like a city, and one would suppose that there was a good deal of business done, but they say there is not.

There is such a clatter of tongues that I can't write any more. I don't know how many of the Grand children have come. I would be very much pleased if you would answer this. But I did not write expecting you to answer because there is enough there that have more time to write than you. But please write if you have time. Have you thought of us today?

I would not be surprised if we were at home week after next, but I will write again and let you know for certain. Mr. Boone sends his love to all. I am anxious to get him home for one thing and that is to let you all see what a kind good husband and man he is. But all the family are good clever people and I think a good deal of them and they act as if they did of me. They are so kind to me.

Give my love to all. We are quite well and have been since we left. Good bye.

Hoping to hear from you soon,

I remain your
Affectionate
Ellen

Tell Ma just imagine that I have caught her Christmas Gift.

My Christmas Wish: For all my friends and especially the Civil War buffs: I shall not try to "get you Christmas Gift" as Ellen King would because our mother taught us children that was not polite. Instead I shall wish you, in the words of Bell Wiley's Johnny Reb, the usyul grismus cher, deer frens, and pertak lightly of that O Bea Joyful or else yo'all will bea shoutin' Hale Columbya insted o'prazin Jef Davis.

South, Right or Wrong

South Carolina had seceded five days before the Christmas of 1860. Joseph E. Brown, Georgia's governor, was sure which course his state would take two weeks ahead of its secession convention in Milledgeville, the state capital. He went to Savannah and ordered Col. Alexander R. Lawton to take possession of Pulaski, the Federal fort there. This fort, which Robert E. Lee had helped to build, guarded the city at the mouth of the Savannah River. Col. Lawton took possession of it on the morning of 3 Jan. Since no Federal troops garrisoned it at the time, the spark that set off the Civil War was not to be struck until the capture of Ft. Sumter in April.

The week before Col. Lawton took Pulaski, on Christmas Day while some folks were celebrating the birth of Christ, a large crowd of citizens of Fort Valley gathered at Armory Hall to hear Prof. T. B. Russell and Hon. Samuel Hall, a visitor from Macon County, deliver "eloquent and patriotic" secession speeches. Then they resolved, unanimously, "that in the opinion of this meeting, Georgia should secede from the Union previous to the 4th of March." Two Fort Valley Companies, the Georgia Rifles and the Governor's Guard, offered to hold themselves "in readiness to move at a moment's warning to our state to assist in defense of her sovereignty, her honor, her altars and fireside."

Editor Joseph Clisby, of the *Macon Telegraph*, looked back on the old year and forward to the new in his editorial of 1 Jan. 1861. South Carolina was already out of the Union. Mississippi, Florida, and Alabama would declare their independence on the 9th, 10th, and 11th, respectively. Yet, Clisby would start the new year "with a light heart." Thus it was with the South. It started with a light heart on a long road that would wind over the land and sea for more than four years, a road marked by 2,261 battles and 618,000 deaths, more than all other American war deaths combined.

After reviewing past events, editor Clisby said,

> But the great event of the age is the disruption of this Republic, and instead of any longer keeping step to the music of the Union, all intelligent men proclaim that "Illium fuit." The causes that have produced this unavoidable result are all but too well known to every intelligent man in the country. South Carolina has already proclaimed herself an independent sovereignty—Alabama, Florida, and Mississippi have wheeled into line, and is it too much to say that the old Empire State, the keystone of the arch, will come forward and stand side by side, shoulder to shoulder, in defense of our section—our section right or wrong. We owe it to our mechanical interests, we owe it to our educational institutions, and we owe it to our love of liberty, to cut loose from the fanatical horde who are ever asserting that this is a "land where genius sickens and fancy dies."
>
> In conclusion, may the great Southern Confederacy take her place among the nations of the earth, and march fearlessly onward to the high destiny that awaits her, alike regardless of the threats from without and timid remonstrances from within. With grateful feelings to an All-wise Creator for the many privileges which our people have enjoyed, we bid an affectionate farewell to the old year, and start our annual journey anew, with a light heart [and perhaps a light pocket] wishing one and all A Happy New Year.

My New Year Wish: May 1961 have much more of the elements of happiness than 1861, with less strife and more concord, not only for a united nation but also for a united world.

Toombs's Five Demands

Robert Toombs delivered his farewell speech to the United States Senate on 7 Jan. 1861. Soon after, he and Sen. Alfred Iverson and all the Georgia representatives in the United States Congress were "out of the Union." Toombs had not favored separation of his state from the Union during the controversy over the admission of California back in the year 1850, but after the election of Lincoln in November 1860, he became one of the strongest secessionists of the South. I have mentioned previously his strong fire-eating speech before the Georgia legislature in Milledgeville on the night of 13 Nov. One of the clearest statements of the position of the South at this time was that of Toombs in his last words spoken in the Senate chamber on 7 Jan. In this farewell speech he made it quite clear what the South wanted.

> Senators, my countrymen have demanded no new government. They have demanded no new Constitution. The discontented States have demanded nothing but clear, distinct constitutional rights, rights older than the Constitution. What do these rebels demand? First, that the

people of the United States shall have an equal right to emigrate and settle in the territories with whatever property they may possess.

Second, that property in slaves shall be entitled to the same protection from the government as any other property, leaving the State the right to prohibit or abolish. Third, that persons committing crimes against slave property in one state and flying to another shall be given up. Fourth, that fugitive slaves shall be surrendered. Fifth, that Congress shall pass laws for the punishment of all persons who shall aid and abet invasion and insurrection in any other State. We demand these five propositions. Are they not right? Are they not just? We will pause and consider them; but mark me, we will not let you decide the questions for us. I have little care to dispute remedies with you unless you propose to redress our wrongs. But no matter what may be our grievances, the honorable senator from Kentucky says we cannot secede. Well, what can we do? Submit? We will stand by the right; we will take the Constitution; we will defend it with the sword, with the halter around our necks. You can not intimidate my constituents by talking to them of treason.

You will not regard Confederate obligations; you will not regard your oaths. What, then, am I to do? Am I a free man? Is my State a free State? We are free men. We have rights. I have stated them. We have wrongs. I have recounted them. I have demonstrated that the party now coming into power has declared us outlaws and is determined to exclude thousands of millions of our property from the common territory; that it has declared us under the ban of the Union and out of the protection of the laws of the United States everywhere. They have refused to protect us from invasion and insurrection by the Federal power and the Constitution denies to us in the Union the right to raise fleets and armies for our own defense. All these charges I have proven by the record; and I put them before the civilized world and demand the judgment of today, of tomorrow, of distant ages and of heaven itself upon the justice of these causes. We have appealed time and time again for these constitutional rights. You have refused them. We appeal again. Restore to us those rights as we had them; and your court adjudges them to be; just as our own people have said they are. Redress these flagrant wrongs—seen of all men—and it will restore fraternity and unity and peace to us all. Refuse them and what then? We shall ask you: Let us depart in peace. Refuse this, and you present us war. We accept it and inscribing upon our banners the glorious words, "Liberty and Equality," we will trust to the blood of the brave and the God of battles for security and tranquility.

On the next day Macon's military companies, the Volunteers, the Guards, the Jackson Artillery, and the Floyd Rifles, commanded by Captains Robert H. Smith, L. M. Lamar, Theodore M. Parker, and Lt. W. H. Ross, respectively, paraded through the streets in their gay uniforms "eliciting" many complimentary remarks from the ladies "despite the muddiness of the streets."

The Union Is Dissolved

The convention that met at the state capitol in Milledgeville to determine the course of Georgia in the crisis of 1861 began its deliberations on 16 Jan. Three days later Georgia declared herself once again a "free and independent State." On 14 Jan. the *Macon Telegraph* had published a letter from Thomas Hardeman, Jr., congressman from this district, advising "immediate secession."

Among the conservative element at the convention were Alexander H. Stephens, Benjamin H. Hill, and Herschel V. Johnson. They did not want Georgia to take independent action, but urged cooperation with other states in the hope of compromise. Among the leading secessionists were Robert Toombs and Thomas R. R. Cobb. Judge Eugenius A. Nisbet, of Macon, moved rather suddenly into the secessionist camp and found himself chairman of the committee named to prepare the Ordinance of Secession. The committee was made up of the three conservatives and the three secessionists named here. Though the committee was balanced, the convention was heavily weighted with those who favored immediate independence.

The selection of Judge Nisbet for the chairmanship of this important committee gave proof of his standing in the state. He had served in both houses of the Georgia General Assembly, had served his state in the United States Congress, and had been one of three justices to serve on the first Supreme Court of Georgia. His affiliation with the Ocmulgee judicial circuit dated back to 1823 when he was only twenty years of age. He was so young it took a special act of the legislature to admit him to the bar.

Judge Nisbet drafted the ordinance; it is said he wrote it in his Macon home, the eight-columned house which can still be seen at 1034 Georgia Avenue. This second declaration of Georgia's independence was finally adopted by an unanimous vote of the convention and signed by all except six delegates who protested the action of the majority. However, these six yielded "as good citizens" and pledged their "lives, fortunes, and sacred honor" to the defense of their state.

The delegates who favored secession carried the motion to adopt the ordinance by a vote of 208 to 89 at 2:00 P.M., 19 Jan., and by that vote the convention had declared "That the Union now subsisting between the State of Georgia and other States, under the name of the United States of America, is hereby dissolved, and that the State of Georgia is in the full possession and exercise of all those rights of sovereignty, which belong and appertain to a free and independent State." A burst of artillery fire announced to the waiting crowd on the Capitol grounds the "glad tidings and the bells of the city pealed forth a joyous welcome to the new-born Republic."

Of interest to the people of Macon and its environs are the names of the delegates from Bibb and neighboring counties who signed the ordinance. From Bibb there were Judge Nisbet, Washington Poe, John B. Lamar; from Monroe, Hiram Phinazee, Robert L. Rodney, John T. Stephens; from Jones, James M. Gray, Peyton T. Pitts; from Baldwin, Lucilius H. Briscoe, A. H. Kenan; from Twiggs, John F. Fitzpatrick, Stephen L. Richardson; from Houston, John Mason Giles, B. W. Brown, Daniel Franklin Gunn; from Macon [County], William H. Robinson, Joseph J.

Carson; from Crawford, W. C. Cleveland and Isaac Dennis. Peach County was not laid out until 1924.

A. L. Hull, in his fascinating book, *Annals of Athens*, described the way the folks up his way received the news of secession:

> The Troup Artillery fired a salute of a hundred guns. A great unrest pervaded the community; nobody knew exactly what to expect. Some predicted war, others scouted the idea . . . yet the people began to gather themselves together, and the military companies began to drill.

MACON HAILS SECESSION

Georgia became an independent republic on 19 Jan. Anticipating it, the Macon "Minute Men" met the night before and planned a grand parade to celebrate the secession of the sovereign state of Georgia from the federal union. Clifford Anderson was chosen to be the chairman for the occasion. The citizens were requested to light up their homes and places of business on the night of the proposed jubilee. Monday, 21 Jan., was chosen.

Lou Burge, Wesleyan student, wrote in her diary:

> Macon is illuminated in honor of the secession of Georgia. Every city street is illuminated. College looks beautiful. We had a fine time fixing up our room. . . . We had two flags, bearing Georgia and Florida upon them, floating from the windows. The torchlight procession came by the college. The boys hollered for the Wesleyan girls; 'twas an exciting time. All the companies were out; also the Minute Men.

The planners, meeting at Concert Hall, arranged the procession. The Jackson Artillery was to march first. It was to be followed by the Macon Volunteers, then, in order, the Macon

Guards, the Floyd Rifles, companies A, then C, then B of the "Minute Men," the Fire Department, the Mayor and Aldermen, and finally the citizens.

According to the *Telegraph*, the "City was one sea of light." The description of the celebration given here is taken verbatim from the issue of 22 Jan. 1861.

> At 8 P.M., the immense crowd, at the firing of the signal gun, moved from the Court House and marched up Mulberry Street until they arrived opposite the Lanier House where they halted and listened to the singing of a patriotic ode by a choir of thirty young ladies who were repeatedly cheered by the enthusiastic multitude.
>
> The singing was admirably done, and reflects much credit upon the singers who had but a day or two to prepare. If the dead man who corresponds with the *Tribune* has any regard for his readers he will warn them to keep on the other side of Jordan, for people who shout like the men, women and children shouted last night for liberty and equality, can never be conquered.
>
> After the singing, the procession moved on until they arrived at the residence of Honorable James Nisbet, where another halt was ordered, for what we knew not, but a few moments sufficed to dissipate all doubts as to the nature of our detention, for the order was given to advance upon a bowl of of punch [the bowl was about the size of a barrel], generously provided for the occasion by our worthy host, who well knew the wants of the poor soldier and the generous fireman.
>
> The lubricator must have been excellent as some whose physical [condition] would hardly warrant it, were very ambitious.
>
> Each dwelling was brilliantly illuminated along the whole route of the procession, and our limited space prevents an extended notice. The College and the Asylum for the Blind were noticeable features along the route, and the long, loud, hearty shouts that went up in response to the waving handkerchiefs from the College, will long be remembered by those who passed that way.
>
> Another halt was made at the Brown House, where Misses Barnes and Wright, of Atlanta, electrified the vast concourse of people with appropriate songs, containing many local hits, which were received with such shouts as only Macon men can give.
>
> At the residence of Col. John B. Lamar, the Hon. Howell Cobb, after repeated calls, came out and made a soul-stirring speech, after which, the procession moved to Mulberry Street, and were dismissed.

Col. Lamar's House stood on Walnut Street. It was later converted into the Macon Clinic. The Lamar Infantry, which was organized in September 1861, was named for Col. Lamar. The colonel's sister was the wife of Maj. Gen. Howell Cobb who commanded the Georgia Reserves and the Georgia Militia. His headquarters was Macon toward the end of the war, and he lived in this house from April 1864 until his death in 1868. His wife had inherited it from her brother who died in the second year of the war.

RALLYING TO THE COLORS

Robert Toombs did not occupy his seat in the United States Senate after 4 Feb. 1861. He had returned to his own Washington, Georgia, and thence to the Montgomery convention. Soon after Toombs withdrew, Sen. Alfred Iverson returned to his home in Columbus, having left bitter words ringing in the Senate chamber: "Sir, disguise the fact as you will, there is an enmity between the northern and southern people that is deep and enduring, and you can never eradicate it—never!"

On 23 Jan., five days before Sen. Iverson resigned, Georgia's eight congressmen withdrew and came back to their homes— Peter Love to Thomasville, Martin Crawford to Columbus, Thomas Hardeman, Jr., to Macon, Lucius Gartrell to Atlanta, John Underwood to Rome, James Jackson to Athens, Joshua Hill to Madison, and John Jones to Waynesboro.

Thomas Hardeman, Jr., born in Eatonton and educated at Emory, came back to Macon to command the Floyd Rifles which he first commanded in 1854. This company had been organized in 1840 by Samuel R. Blake. Benjamin F. Ross followed Blake as captain in 1843. Company headquarters was at the Floyd House, a hotel at the corner of Mulberry and Third streets. The company was named for Gen. Charles R. Floyd.

When South Carolina seceded and trouble was brewing around Ft. Sumter, the Floyd Rifles telegraphed their captain, then representing his district in Congress, and advised him that they had offered to go to the aid of their neighbor state. According to Mary Callaway Jones, the best living authority on Macon's history, Capt. Hardeman wired in reply a terse reference to Holy Scripture: "Ruth 1:16."

Later, when companies were needed in Virginia, the Floyd Rifles, led by Capt. Hardeman, volunteered along with the Macon Volunteers, the City Light Guards of Columbus, and the Spalding Grays of Griffin. Robert A. Smith was captain of the Volunteers, Peyton H. Colquitt was captain of the Columbus Guards, and Leonard L. Doyal was captain of the Spalding Grays. They left by train on Saturday, 20 April 1861. And, as Mrs. Jones expressed it, "the old car shed on Fourth street witnessed the anguish of the goodbyes as the boys left for Portsmouth, Virginia." Lou Burge, a Wesleyan student, noted in her diary that the girls were "almost all crying." When the four companies arrived at Camp Georgia they were organized into the Second Georgia Battalion. They elected Capt. Hardeman their commander with the rank of major. Sgt. George W. Ross was made captain of the Floyd Rifles. Maj. Hardeman later became colonel of the 45th Georgia Infantry, C. S. A.

Toward the end of the war Col. Hardeman returned to Georgia and served as Speaker of the House of Representatives. He lived to return to the United States Congress in 1883. He served until 1885. When he died in 1891 he was buried in Macon's Rose Hill Cemetery on the hill that overlooks the city where he drilled his Floyd Rifles in the gay days before the war clouds gathered.

It was entirely fitting and proper that in 1951, when another chapter of the United Daughters of the Confederacy was born to work alongside the Sidney Lanier Chapter, the name of Capt. Thomas Hardeman, Jr., should have been chosen for it. And in addition to the illustrious name of Thomas Hardeman is that of his wife, Jane Lumsden, who was the first president of the Ladies Memorial Association, which had the remains of local Confederate dead placed in neat rows of marked graves in Rose Hill where they are honored every year on Memorial Day.

CONFEDERACY IS FORMED

Texas seceded from the Union on 1 Feb. 1861, and three days later a convention of seven states met in Montgomery to unite, first into a provisional government, then, on 11 March, into the full-fledged Confederate States of America. Georgia leaders, both extreme secessionists and conservatives who had wanted cooperation all along, took leading roles in the drama being enacted in the Alabama city. The delegates at Montgomery—the number varied from 41 to 50—were, in the opinion of E. M. Coulter, "the best the South had to offer." Georgia had the largest delegation, but as the delegates voted by states the number didn't matter. Nine of the ten Georgia delegates elected attended the convention; the other one, Augustus Romaldus Wright, of Rome, went instead to the nation's capital to join others in a futile effort to find a way to heal the breach.

Two of the strong possible candidates for president of the Confederacy were among the Georgia delegation. They were Robert Toombs, of Washington, and Howell Cobb, of Athens.

Cobb was elected president of the convention by acclamation and was the choice of some for the highest office in the Confederacy. Delegates from adjacent states, however, did not share the Georgians' enthusiasm for Cobb, and the Georgia group itself could not unite on Toombs. An opinion crystallized in favor of Jefferson Davis, of Mississippi. Alexander Hamilton Stephens, of Crawfordville, was proposed for the office of vice-president. Stephens was nominated by Augustus Holmes Kenan, of Milledgeville, seconded by Eugenius Aristides Nisbet, of Macon. Davis was on his way to Montgomery from the Mississippi delta when Stephens was inaugurated on 11 Feb. The president's inauguration followed on 18 Feb. President Davis appointed Toombs to the office of secretary of state.

Benjamin Harvey Hill, of LaGrange, was, like Stephens, more represenative of the conservative element in the convention. In a sense, the "father" of the Confederate Constitution was Thomas Reade Rootes Cobb who, like his brother Howell, lived in Athens. Francis Stebbins Bartow, of Savannah, one of the hottest of the fire-eaters, was made chairman of the military committee. There might, by chance, be war if the Federal government would not let them go in peace.

The 10th and remaining delegate to the Montgomery convention was Martin Jenkins Crawford, of Columbus. During the provisional period the convention acted in the capacity of a legislative assembly. This provisional Confederate Congress authorized the president to appoint a commission to go to Washington to negotiate for peaceful relations between the two nations. Crawford was one of the three men given this important job. When the United States refused to have official meetings with them they prepared a statement addressed to William H. Seward, secretary of state, which declared that "the people of the Confederate States will defend their liberties to the last against this flagrant and open attempt at their subjugation."

Two who defended their liberties to the death were Col. Francis Bartow, killed at Bull Run, the first battle of the war, and Thomas Cobb, killed on 13 Dec. 1862, the month after he was promoted to the rank of brigadier general.

THE REPUBLIC OF GEORGIA

In the short interval between the secession of Georgia and the formation of the Confederacy, Gov. Brown enjoyed the distinction of being the chief executive of the sovereign and independent republic of Georgia. That he exercised that power to the fullest extent there is no doubt. We have already seen how he seized Ft. Pulaski. Before the end of January 1861, he had ordered the United States Arsenal at Augusta seized and had taken possession of the Oglethorpe Barracks and Ft. Jackson at Savannah. The Georgia flag now waved over almost all of the state. This flag had a field of white and bore the seal of the state, surmounted by set stars to represent the six states then out of the Union. At the top of the flag was an eye. The stars were all deep red except the one representing Georgia, which was blue. One place this flag did not fly was Jasper, in Pickens County. Some wanted the governor to order troops to cut down the Stars and Stripes which the Unionists hoisted in defiance of the secessionists, but he waited patiently until the people themselves decided to exchange it for the new flag.

There were several ways in which Gov. Brown showed the independence of his state, such as the seizures of Federal property mentioned above and his sending Thomas Butler King to represent Georgia in European capitals in an effort to negotiate trade relations. But the one which interests me most was the commissioning of John Kell to purchase a ship and command it. This Kell did before Commodore Josiah Tatnall took command of the "mythical Georgia navy" for the purpose of coastal defense.

John McIntosh Kell was well prepared for the life he was to lead during a war that was fought on the seas as well as on land. He had been educated at the Naval Academy at Annapolis. He had seen service in the Mexican War and had gone with Perry to Japan on his famous door-opening expedition in 1853. Sea-roving Kell holds special interest for the people of Macon and Middle Georgia. Though born in Darien, he and his wife Julian Blanche, the daughter of Nathan Monroe of Macon, lived at Sunnyside, a plantation near Griffin. They were neighbors of Mary Day and her folks. Mary, you will remember, married Sidney Lanier. The Macon home of Nathan Monroe can be seen today on Rogers Avenue facing Ralph Small's home. The Ralph Small house was the home of the Skelton Napiers in the happy antebellum days when Blanche roamed the wide expanse between the two houses before they were moved to face each other on a city street.

At the time of Lt. Kell's appointment the Georgia navy had only one ship afloat, the steamer *Savannah*. He served on this ship in coastal defense until May 1861, then he reported to Raphael Semmes for duty on the *Habana*, later renamed the *Sumter*. The *Sumter* was Semmes's flagship until it was succeeded by the *Alabama*. Kell was Adm. Semmes's executive officer on the *Alabama* when it was attacked and destroyed by the *Kearsarge* in the English Channel on 19 June 1864. Monroe d'Antignac, of Griffin, the grandson of John Kell, has the telegram which John sent to Blanche telling her of his safety and the rescue of the other officers and most of the crew. The *Alabama*'s loss was 9 killed, 21 wounded, and 10 drowned. After the sinking of the *Alabama*, Kell was given command of the ironclad *Richmond* doing patrol duty on the James River. After the war he became the adjutant general of Georgia.

With the birth of the Southern Confederacy, the so-called Georgia navy was no longer independent. Nor was any other part of the government for that matter—except of course Joe Brown. But more of this anon.

WHY GEORGIA LEFT UNION

With Georgia out of the Union—having become once again a free, sovereign, and independent state on 19 Jan. 1861—we should pause and reflect on the reasons why she followed South Carolina, Mississippi, Florida, and Alabama in such a move. The Hundred Years' War of words on the controversy of what caused the Civil War is now entering its second century. The war followed as an inevitable and natural consequence of secession, but what really caused secession?

Basic to the problem, of course, is the economic factor. The commercial and industrial free labor system of the North was in conflict with the plantation slavery system of the agricultural South. That factor was very evident 30 years before in the tariff issue. The constitutional question has been de-emphasized by some of our national historians, but we cannot escape the states' rights philosophy that rang optimistically then. The moral issue grew more tense after 1830, and it is that question I wish to deal with here.

None should deny the evil of slavery any more than he should challenge the present-day Negro's equal right to "Life, Liberty, and the Pursuit of Happiness," but we must see the Old South's position in the frame in which it was then set. We must understand the problem in the light of the prevailing philosophy of that day. That philosophy was clearly expressed by Judge Nisbet, the author of Georgia's Ordinance of Secession, when he declared in Neal v. Farmer [1851]:

> The Negro and his master are but fulfilling a divine appointment. Christ came not to remove the curse; but recognized the relation of master and servant, he prescribed the rules which govern, and the obligations which grow out of it, and thus ordained it as an institution of Christianity.

The South's contention that all slaves were happy is weakened by the fact that many of them ran away. But our story here concerns a Negro slave who having run away, found his Bibb County plantation home more desirable than a Columbus, Ohio, prison. He belonged to Col. Leroy Napier, of Macon. Col. Napier, a wealthy planter who subscribed $58,000 to the Confederate cause in 1861, sent six sons to fight for that cause. He lived in a Greek Revival house fronted by six fluted Doric columns, with inverted laurel wreaths on the frieze. It stood on the hill where the Lanier Senior High School now stands. It was later moved down the hill and now faces Napier Avenue.

The colonel's slave boy, Leroy, alias Covey, wrote to his former master in November 1849, begging him to come and get him out of jail and take him home.

> *Dear Kind master you are now addressed by your runaway that left you about 2 years ago and now wish to return and if you will come and take me home I will be a good boy and serve you faithful. I am now confined in the Ohio Penitentiary at Columbus Convicted for receiving a stolen horse to keep over night valued at $150 and dear Master I hope that these things will be a warning to me when I return home . . . If you cannot remember me do not let it prevent your coming after me for I belong to you. If you have a bill of sale bring it with you if not take the description which I have given go before a magistrate swear to the same then get some of your friends to sign, it will answer just as well . . . Dear master I wish to come home.*

The original letter is in the Hardeman Library at Mercer University. I do not know whether Leroy wrote the letter or had someone write it for him, neither do I know whether or not Col. Napier brought him home. A note penciled on the letter by William Greene states, "I think Col. Napier let the Negro stay where he was."

THE CONFEDERATE COLORS

One hundred years ago yesterday, Abraham Lincoln was inaugurated president of what was left of the United States. But 4 March 1861 was not a Saturday, according to my trusty Goodykoontz's Manual; the day was Monday. As we all know, by that time, seven states had withdrawn from the federal union, their leaders declaring they could not endure a president who would destroy slavery, their "peculiar institution." Lincoln's words, "I have no purpose directly or indirectly to interfere with the institution of slavery in the states where it exists," were not taken at face value, and the Montgomery convention deliberately chose the day of Lincoln's inauguration to raise the "Stars and Bars" of the Southern Confederacy.

The *Telegraph* gave full coverage to the Lincoln inaugural address. It appeared in full on 4 March, ran in a one-sheet extra the same day, and was printed again in full the next day. In reporting on the speech, editor Clisby had this to say: "He has manifested his want of perception of the 'special sacredness' of States by leaving them out of his political system altogether." Our Wesleyan diarist, Lou Burge, thought Lincoln's message "the poorest thing I ever read." Then she went on to say, "Who could expect more of one who spent his life in the West, first as a rail-splitter and then as a boatman on the Ohio?"

Soon after the Southern delegates convened at Montgomery they turned their attention to the matter of choosing a flag, a seal, a coat of arms, and a motto for the new government. William Porcher Miles, of South Carolina, was chosen chairman of the committee charged with this responsibility. The final decision on the flag, after many suggestions had been made, was a design of three bars—red, white, and red—with a blue field containing a circle of seven white stars.

It had been the intention of the Montgomery delegates to hoist the flag at precisely the time Lincoln was making his inaugural address in Washington, but there was a delay. Finally, in mid-afternoon the ceremony took place and the flag was raised on the capitol dome. President Tyler's granddaughter was given the honor of raising the new flag. The bands played, and a seven-gun salute was fired. This set off a great celebration in the Alabama city. Soon the Stars and Bars was waving in towns and cities all over the Deep South, and companies of soldiers were following that emblem as they drilled and marched through the streets to the accompaniment of martial airs and the approving smiles of their ladies.

But no one, in city, town, or village, was quicker to make a flag than the Vineville ladies at Macon, and no flag bearer could present the Confederacy's emblem sooner than the Floyd Rifles. The Rifles, remember, was Capt. Thomas Hardeman's company. And it was Capt. Hardeman's wife, Jane Lumsden, who sat up all night with other ladies of the neighborhood to have it ready the day after learning its design.

How could they learn so quickly about the adoption of the flag? And how could they know the design of it? The answer lies in the ingenuity of a Macon man who went to Montgomery to observe the work of the convention and to report back to his hometown the events which had taken place. That man was John Campbell Butler, and he was the superintendent of the Georgia-Alabama division of the Magnetic Telegraph Company. Just as soon as he learned the details of the flag design he telegraphed a description of it to Capt. Hardeman. The Vineville ladies gathered at the Hardeman home and lost no time in making the flag for the company that was soon to carry it to Virginia to defend their homeland from that front.

John Butler tells the story himself in his interesting *Historical Record of Macon and Central Georgia* (p. 257). According to Butler, it was the first flag of the Confederacy to wave over the state, and the Floyd Rifles was the first Georgia company to fire a salute "in honor of the Confederate colors." After they raised their new flag, they paraded in full dress uniform through the town—before breakfast!

JOINING THE NEW NATION

The Montgomery convention adopted the "permanent" constitution of the Confederate States of America on 11 March 1861,
and the Georgia convention, which had moved from Milledgeville to Savannah, ratified it unanimously on 16 March. Since
19 Jan. Georgia had moved out of the United States into a new
nation.

It might be assumed from the above statement that the new
union of Southern states—seven in number—might be tightly
bound together in their common cause, even as the American
colonies of the British Empire drew their bonds of union tighter
in opposition to the Mother Country. But such was not to be the
case. Gov. Brown, who had led Georgia in her crisis of secession
and into the Confederacy, was to show just about as much independence as he had shown in the interval between secession
and the formation of the Confederate government. In fact, the
theory of states' rights was spelled out more clearly in the Confederate Constitution than in the Federal document, and Brown

never overlooked that. In later installments of this series I shall point out examples of Gov. Brown's independent attitude and behavior.

I cannot help reminding my rabid states' rights friends who still talk of interposition that all this happened a hundred years ago. Though the states may not have realized it at the time, state sovereignty was surrendered at the constitutional convention of 1787. The Civil War merely confirmed it. Some of us Southerners have a hard time recognizing the fact that the Civil War is past history. There are many people today of whom it can be said in the words of Faulkner, as I remember them, "the past is not dead—it is not even past."

Let us take a look at the constitution that Georgia ratified as she joined her neighboring states in what they all thought would be a "permanent" Confederacy. For the sake of expediency, not wishing to offend moderate states which might join them, and because of the need for haste so that they could get a government functioning before the Republicans took over in Washington, the convention delegates used the Federal Constitution as a model. After all, they were not revolting against the Constitution as the Founding Fathers—many of them Southerners— had written it. They were simply rebelling because of the way, as they saw it, the North had twisted the original document. Needless to say, the Confederate Constitution safeguarded slavery as well as states' rights. Also, this constitution would not permit the Confederate Congress to protect and favor industry through high tariff and bounties.

Then, there were improvements among the changes made in the Federal Constitution. Some of the new, liberal features were as follows: the president was to be limited to one six-year term; he was to enjoy the privilege of vetoing separate items in an appropriation bill, that is, he did not have to accept a bad appropriation which had been linked to a good one; members of the president's cabinet were to have seats in Congress without the privilege of voting—this follows the British system; an executive budget system was adopted; and new states could not be added by a simple majority, but would require a two-thirds vote of Congress for admission. Such improvements grew out of the formative years of experience. The seceding states had seized on the opportunity to make innovations that the federal union, bound by tradition, would have had difficulty in instituting.

On the very day of Georgia's ratification of the Confederate Constitution, the *Macon Telegraph* announced that the offer of the Independent Volunteers to serve the new nation had been accepted. Some of the citizens offered to collect funds to purchase uniforms for those who were unable to buy them. Editor Clisby wondered if the ladies could not "present this gallant corps with an appropriate flag?" Readers of last Sunday's column will remember that the Vineville ladies had already made one for the Floyd Rifles. Some people had the idea that war might result from this division of one nation into separate governments.

· II ·

THE WAR

RENDEZVOUS AT MACON

Early in April 1861, Robert Toombs told the Wilkes County people the chances for peace were better than war. Nevertheless, Macon's Camp Oglethorpe, located at the east end of Oglethorpe Street, became the rendezvous spot for companies from near and far. The coastal areas were to be defended. Of special concern to the Independent Regiment of Georgia Volunteers being organized here was Ft. Pickens at Pensacola. It, like Ft. Sumter, was still in Federal hands. Capt. Patton and Lt. Atkinson went on a "professional" tour of southwest Georgia to enlist all who were "patriotically inclined." A thousand men, 80 to a company, poured into Macon in the first days of April. Their destination was Ft. Pickens, their purpose, "the extermination of the Lincoln rats" that infested that fort. The Macon companies acted as hosts and the ladies of the city as hospitality committees. The ladies contributed meats and delicacies, scarfs and home-knitted socks. The visiting soldiers were so greatly impressed that they published many resolutions in the local paper.

Capt. Pickard brought his Quitman Guards from Forsyth into camp so quietly on the evening of 1 April that the local companies did not have time to prepare a welcome. But they made up for it during the next few days as they received hundreds of new volunteers at Camp Oglethorpe. Joining the Macon companies to form the regiment were Capt. Harvey's Newnan Guards, Capt. Willkin's Southern Guards of Columbus, Capt. Larey's Etowah Infantry, Capt. Evans's Southern Independents of Bainbridge, Capt. Sprayberry's Ringgold Infantry, Capt. Ezzard's Gate City Guards of Atlanta, Capt. Jones's Washington Rifles of Sandersville, Capt. Houser's Southern Rights Guards of Perry, and Capt. Camp's Walker Light Infantry and Capt. Clark's Oglethorpe Light Infantry, both from Augusta. From Macon were the Brown Infantry, under Capt. Smith, and the Independent Volunteers, under Capt. Aderhold. These were the companies forming the first regiment for Pensacola. So many men came that some were turned away as companies reached their quota of 80 men. The 20-man staff of the *Macon Telegraph*, from "sweep and errand boy to the Boss of all," seemed to want to join up. Nine of them did.

The new soldiers were busy doing the work of expanding a camp to meet the needs of 1,000 men and more. Some were busy pitching tents according to the plan of the streets which had been laid out. Some were digging latrine trenches. Raw mess sergeants, one of them admitting very frankly that his cooking would be a mess, were trying to work out the problems incident to preparing the meals. As soon as the necessary work was done, the Oglethorpe Light Infantry marched up to to R. L. Wood's Photography Gallery and posed at attention in front of the place to have a picture made of the company, "in sections."

An election was held: Lt. J. N. Ramsey, of the Southern Guards of Columbus, was elected colonel of the regiment; Capt. J. O. Clark, of the Oglethorpe Light Infantry, was made lieutenant colonel; and Capt. G. H. Thompson, of the Georgia Army, was chosen major. At the same time, Capt. Larey of the Etowah Infantry, was elected major of the Independent Battalion.

Gov. Brown came over from Milledgeville and reviewed the troops. He made a speech to the newly formed regiment. The streets leading to the camp ground "were filled with pedestrians, gents on horseback, and carriages." The drilling of the companies "was an exciting scene to witness, and sometimes their sudden wheeling was the cause of great confusion as they would march full upon some unsuspecting crowd of spectators." The governor ended his remarks with these words: "Go then and may the God of battles go with you, and lead, protect and defend you, till the last foot-print of the invader shall be obliterated from the soil of our common country."

Then came the time to board the cars and wave goodbye to the mothers, sisters, sweethearts, and friends swarming around the train. One Irish mother bade farewell to her son, too young for anything but an aide, with these words:

> Well, Jimmy, goodbye to yez, arrah me poor divil, I'm afraid I'll nivir see yez agin, for bad luck to me Jimmy, but ye'll sthale every divil a thing from the solgers, and I'm sure they'll hang yez before ye get back!

Zeilin and Hunt's Drug Store advertised "Henry's Extract of Ginger" to prevent the bad effects of change of weather, water, and diet and guaranteed the departing soldiers it would be a sure preventive of dysentery, cholera, and diarrhea.

THE FIRST SHOT IS FIRED

The shore batteries at Charleston opened fire on Ft. Sumter at 4:30 A.M. on 12 April 1861. The attack was made under the command of Gen. Pierre G. T. Beauregard. The garrison at the Federal fort was under the command of Maj. Robert Anderson.

An interesting question for the experts and the buffs is as old as the war itself: Who committed the overt act? Some historians, James C. Randall among them, deny that Lincoln maneuvered the Confederacy into the role of the aggressor. Yet he did, by attempting to provision the fort, cause the Confederates to fire the first shot. The *New York Tribune,* as early as the 5th, feared that at "any moment" the news would come that Sumter had been assaulted. A dispatch issued from Washington at 10:00 P.M. on 9 April stated that Beauregard had been notified of the Federal government's intention to supply Anderson "and that in the event the vessels performing that duty were fired upon,

Anderson would open his batteries, and the Government would sustain him at every hazard."

Mrs. Roger A. Pryor, whose husband went in the company of others at Gen. Beauregard's direction to demand the surrender of the fort, thought the overt act "for which everybody looked" was the reinforcement of the fort by Federal troops. Whether you take the view that the South drew "first blood" in this bloodless engagement or whether you put the blame on the Federal government for attempting a ruse under the guise of provisioning the fort, the fact remains that the war which had become inevitable had started.

The "magnetic" telegraph line brought the news of the fall of Ft. Sumter quickly to Macon. Among those recording their feelings upon hearing of the attack was Anne, the ten-year-old daughter of Simri Rose. This family was one of the original families of Macon. Simri Rose had settled at Ft. Hawkins in 1819 and built his home on Beall's Hill, adjacent to the place where Mt. De Sales Academy now stands. Little Anne kept a diary for a few short entries, until her mother took it away from her for confiding romantic sentiments to it. On the evening of Friday, the very day of the beginning of the attack, Anne made the following entry: "This morning the news came of the bombardment of Ft. Sumter by the Confederate troops. Heaven defend the right." And the next day she wrote, "Sumter is taken and the stars and bars wave over it. Hurrah! Unto God be the praise." On the following Tuesday the Columbus Guards passed through Macon. Anne went down to see Johnny. "God bless the boy," she wrote. Lou Burge, at Wesleyan, recorded the historic event: "The Stars and Bars now float over Sumter. All honor to our brave Gen. Beauregard!"

Gov. Brown authorized the notice which ran in the Milledgeville *Federal Union* on 9 April to the effect that "no more volunteers were wanted" at that time. The *Macon Telegraph* commented, "Before another issue of the *Federal Union* three thousand additional volunteers will be summoned to the field by the Governor."

The Macon paper reported the capture of Ft. Sumter in an "Extra" on the 13th.

> Fort Sumter is unconditionally surrendered to the Confederate States.
> This great and glorious event has just taken place. Not one of our soldiers
> is killed or wounded. Anderson's force is supposed to be dreadfully cut
> up. Hurrah for the Confederate States of America.

Actually, Anderson suffered only one casualty, and that when a cannon exploded as a salute was fired.

The prediction of the *Macon Telegraph* concerning the need for additional volunteers was true. Immediately following the attack on Sumter, Lincoln issued a call for 75,000 men to crush the "rebellion." Davis and the Southern governors retaliated with calls for even more volunteers. Virginia had already recognized the Confederacy as "an independent power." Now, Lincoln's decision to suppress the "rebellion" with force drove Virginia out of the Union. Three more states followed, and North and South pushed forward their preparations for war.

OFF TO WAR IN VIRGINIA

Virginia, upon hearing that Lincoln planned to suppress the "insurrection" that blazed up at Ft. Sumter, decided on 17 April 1861 to join the Confederacy. The Macon paper proclaimed the news in an extra edition. At Griffin a new flag with the eighth star was hoisted amid the firing of guns, ringing of bells, and shouts of "Welcome! Old Dominion."

In response to President Davis's call for Georgia troops on the 19th, Gov. Brown ordered companies from Macon, Griffin, and Columbus to entrain for Virginia. They were the Floyd Rifles, the Macon Volunteers, the Columbus Light Guards, and the Spalding Grays. These companies were formed into the Second Georgia Battalion when they reached Norfolk. Thomas Hardeman, Jr., captain of the Floyd Rifles, was elected major and placed in command of the battalion.

On Saturday night, 20 April, a great crowd of citizens gathered at the station house to bid farewell to the soldiers. The train left at 10:00 P.M. carrying Capt. Hardeman and his 80 Floyd

Rifles, Capt. R. A. Smith and his 66 Volunteers, and Capt. P. H. Colquitt and his 85 Columbus Guards. The Spalding Grays would board the train at Griffin.

Lou Burge wrote, "Em Bellamy spent nearly the whole evening in my room crying about the war and John H. Ross, who leaves tonight." Lou apparently had no sweetheart, but she was kept busy looking after the girls who were "almost all crying." Em and Fannie Perkins went down to tell John Ross goodbye. Lou observed: "Between her and Cousin Emma Ward crying about Ed Guinn, I have had a time of it."

The battalion formed at the Lanier House. Marianna Cobb, Howell's daughter, gave the Volunteers a company flag. Her brother, Lamar, a private in the company, presented it to Capt. Smith, who accepted it graciously. The battalion, escorted by the Bibb Cavalry and Jackson Artillery, and a band, marched slowly to the depot. "Hardly a word was spoken" as the large assemblage marched along with the soldiers the short distance from the Lanier House on Mulberry Street, up Cotton Avenue to Forsyth Street, and to the depot.

The depot was then located in the vicinity of the present St. Paul's Episcopal Church. According to reports, thousands of local citizens milled around the depot to say goodbye to the departing soldiers, dressed in a varied assortment of uniforms. Finally, the long train pulled out of the station "bearing away the hope and pride of many sad hearts."

No sooner had the Rifles and the Volunteers left for Virginia than a Home Guard was formed. It consisted of 115 men and was under the command of Capt. B. F. Ross, who had once commanded the Floyd Rifles. Also the young boys were not to be ignored. Fifty youngsters, ranging from twelve to sixteen years of age, had been organized under the name of Volunteer Cadets. The Macon Volunteers had left them armed with flint and steel rifles. Editor Clisby expressed a hope: "Long may the Volunteer Cadets wave."

Nor was a Home Guard and a young cadet corps thought to be sufficient protection for the citizens of Macon. The young ladies felt that they should contribute to the security of the community, at least to the extent of protecting their teacher who remained behind, apparently, to see that their education was not neglected. In behalf of the girls, one of them wrote the following letter to the editor.

> Mr. Clisby—I wish to introduce to your good graces a Military Company just now forming, who have styled themselves, "Branham's Riflemen." Not willing to see their most estimable instructor exposed to the ruthless hand of the merciless foe, with no protection but his own brave self, while all our "gallant men" are absent defending our Forts and common interests, they have organized this heroic corps of girls, pledging themselves to defend him till their last apron is more holey than righteous . . . May we depend on you?

To which the editor replied, "We are ever a firm ally of the ladies."

South Georgia Enlistees

Gov. Brown answered the Confederacy's April 1861 call for an additional 3,000 volunteers with a letter on the 11th to Leroy P. Walker, secretary of war. In it he said he feared "no difficulty in procuring a sufficient number to fill the requisition" and agreed to "exert all possible effort to provide them with tents and equipment made at the Georgia penitentiary." But as the month closed he advised Walker that he did not think it possible to readily equip the companies with tents, knapsacks, and other accoutrements. He reminded the secretary that he had sent most of his "best-drilled companies to Virginia," but that he would do all in his power to help him.

Reports of companies' being formed all over Georgia were reaching the governor's ears at the state capitol in Milledgeville. Many of the men who enlisted knew nothing of military science, but they were willing to learn. Practically every one of them was handy with a rifle, having spent many hours stalking game in the swamps and woodlands and often hitting the eye of a squirrel sitting in the top of a tall pine tree. And being free men, unaccustomed to military discipline and unaccountable to any military hierarchy, they organized their companies in good democratic fashion by electing their officers.

Typical of the many letters received by the governor is the following one from Theodore L. Guerry, a citizen of Georgetown, situated down on the Chattahoochee River in southwest Georgia. In this letter the newly elected captain offered the services of the "Quitman Grays" to their state, and to the Confederacy if needed.

April 29, 1861

Governor Brown

Dear Sir:

This will introduce you to my friend M. P. Jordan who brings to you the returns of an election for officers of a Military Company formed or completed Saturday, 27th inst., in this County. It numbers 74 men good and true with a prospect of increasing it to 80 or more. It was raised for the pressing emergency that is upon us and composed mainly of raw recruits totally ignorant of military drill or discipline. I have, as you will find, been honored with the command of the Company and profoundly ignorant as I am of Tactics or military science, I shall assume the responsibility under the apprehension that the "Time may need even such defenders." Unskilled and unprepared as they necessarily are in the art of war, the "boys" are eager for active service and pledge themselves to be ready to march in ten days or as soon thereafter as possible to any point you may assign them or their services may be required.

I may remark that the company numbers within its ranks a large proportion of the best material both physical and moral that our little County affords. You are referred to Mr. Jordan for further details if needed. Any courtesies rendered to Mr. Jordan during his stay in Milledgeville will be duly appreciated. It is superfluous to assure you that your sagacity, firmness, and propitutude in the fearful crisis through which we are passing meet not only the warmest approval, but universal admiration.

Wishing you continued health and strength adequate to the labors and responsibilities that may yet await you.

I am sincerely your friend,

T. L. Guerry

Lewis P. Dozier was elected first lieutenant of the "Quitman Grays," Francis M. Bledsoe, second lieutenant, and Osborn R. Smith, third lieutenant. Guerry was later made lieutenant colonel, commanding the 11th Georgia Volunteers, and Bledsoe was made captain of the company, which was designated Company "I" in this regiment.

ARRIVAL AT CAMP NORFOLK

Maj. Thomas Hardeman's Second Georgia Battalion which left Macon on 20 April 1861 for Virginia arrived at Portsmouth on the evening of the 23rd. The journey by rail through Augusta, Wilmington, and Goldsboro had been without mishap and with good speed, considering the development of steam locomotive transportation up to that time.

Robert A. Smith, captain of the Macon Volunteers, sent back news of the journey. His report was published in the *Telegraph*. The journey had been "delightful." The soldiers had had "enough of everything except sleep." A "thousand ladies" had waited at the Wilmington depot three hours for the train to arrive. Fathers brought their daughters and introduced them to the Georgia boys in their shining gray uniforms. All the company commanders except Capt. Smith made speeches, and Roger Pryor bade the battalion Godspeed as the troops boarded the train to continue their journey to Virginia. Capt. Smith said he was "better employed" at Wilmington than those who were making speeches. As he put it, "the Volunteers said as they could not kiss the girls themselves, they would do it all by proxy, and told the girls to kiss their Captain." And they went at it, if we can believe the captain, "in good style." He must have had a busy time of it, for he said, "I kissed all under 17 years who presented themselves, until the train started."

It was the same story at Goldsboro when the battalion stopped for supper. Here again, the captains made speeches to encourage the North Carolina Rebels. All through that state the Georgia boys found the Confederate flags flying and heard cheers for the Confederacy ringing in their ears. The Seminary girls at Winston-Salem, North Carolina, sang "Dixie's Land" for the troops, but here, it seems, Capt. Smith's offer to kiss the college girls was discouraged—perhaps by the dean. Thus, denied the kissing privilege, Capt. Smith made a speech.

The Georgia battalion, consisting of Macon, Columbus, and Griffin troops under Maj. Hardeman, was soon joined by other Georgia companies and also by companies from other states. There were approximately 2,000 troops at the Navy Yard at Portsmouth by 9 May.

The troops were expecting an attack on the two cities, Portsmouth and Norfolk. These twin cities were separated by the Elizabeth River which divided the Navy Yard on the Portsmouth side from Norfolk on the opposite side. Fortifications were being thrown up along the river and cannons were being put in place. The river below Norfolk was blockaded. The Southern Rifles could see a gun boat they thought to be the *Pocahontas* in the distance. There was much activity as old ships were being made ready for service. Maj. Hardeman's battalion was given an extremely important and dangerous assignment. It was to march to Tanner's Cross Roads to hold a bridge in case of attack. The bridge was in the line of march from Fortress Monroe. The battalion was only about two and a half miles from the fort at Old Point Comfort, which commanded the entrance to the Chesapeake Bay and Hampton Roads.

On 15 May, the battalion paraded before "a large crowd of ladies and gentlemen from Norfolk." After the parade the spectators visited "Camp Georgia." There was "music and mirth" on that evening, but the next morning orders came to march out of camp. Editor Clisby, of the *Telegraph*, did not console the tearful girls left behind in Macon when he published the following note concerning the arrival of the troops in Norfolk. The communication read,

> Our bold soger boys are getting so endeared to Norfolk that some of them threaten to secede and join some of the belles of that fair city if they are ordered away. It is much to be feared that, while the Macon lassies are crying their eyes out when they think of their Charleys and Willies gone to the wars, the soger boys are not doing the corresponding things, by any manner of means.

Nevertheless, the "soger boys" had not entirely forgotten their sweethearts back home, as many letters from Virginia will testify. We shall quote some of those letters in due time. Some of the boys were getting homesick far away up in Virginia as they gathered around the camp fires in the evenings, and some were getting concerned about the possibility of snipers in the trees in the shadowed rim just beyond the circle of light.

THE FIRST TASTE OF FIRE

Though First Manassas, or Bull Run [21 July 1861], was the first big battle of the Civil War, there were some engagements before that time, and soldiers were dying—some in battle, some of pneumonia, and one, the first casualty, quite by accident. The first death of the war was not caused by musket fire, but by the accidental drowning of Noble Leslie De Votie on 12 Feb. 1861. De Votie, one of eight founders of the Sigma Alpha Epsilon fraternity at the University of Alabama in 1856, had graduated at the top of his class. Now, he was the chaplain of the Governor's Guards, and they were disembarking at Mobile for Virginia. The young chaplain slipped at the wharf and fell among the pilings where the high waves pounded his body until his companions recovered it, too late to revive him.

A part of the Federal strategy was to seize Confederate seaports all the way from Norfolk, Virginia, around the Atlantic to Brownsville, Texas, on the Gulf. The Confederates began a concentration of troops around Norfolk as soon as Virginia seceded.

Two months before First Manassas there was an engagement at Sewell's Point. The engagement at Big Bethel Church [10 June] is usually considered the first battle of the war, but there was enough fighting at Sewell's Point to give one soldier an opportunity to write home from Camp Lee on 21 May saying he thought a few were killed.

The engagement at Sewell's Point began before the Confederates had finished constructing a fort at the mouth of the James River, just opposite Fortress Monroe. They named it Ft. Beauregard. Before any guns could be mounted at the fort, the Federal gunboat, *Monticello*, opened fire, scattering about 150 Negroes working on the fort in about as many different directions.

The next day being Sunday, an order from Maj. Thomas Hardeman, Jr., interrupted divine worship at Camp Lee. Capt. Colquitt moved his company out toward Sewell's Point fifteen minutes after the order was received. Other companies followed, marching with full packs through hard rain. The next morning, they were ordered to march back before they could prepare breakfast.

It is difficult to say where or when the first soldier died, but some of the Georgia boys who died defending Fortress Monroe were in the Macon County Volunteers. On hearing of the death of some of the Volunteers, an Americus citizen, who signed her name "Hallie," wrote the following poem honoring those who died. It appeared in the *Telegraph* on 1 June, ten days before the battle at Big Bethel Church. This is proof that there were casualties before the "first battle."

> *Strangers, your graves are far away,*
> *On distant Southern shores;*
> *There cold your gallant forms now lay,*
> *Your smiles shall beam no more.*
>
> *Not a rude sound shall reach your ears—*
> *Sweet peace to you is given;*
> *While fall for you our moanful tears,*
> *Your resting place is Heaven.*
>
> *Ah, when you left your home and friends,*
> *Virginia's soil to tread,*
> *The thought ne'er came which hearts now rends*
> *Your lives should soon be sped.*

But heroes, rest on Southern soil,
Virginia guards your sleep;
Though soldiers, now ye're free from toil,
Yet still for you we weep.

Magnolia's breeze shall never fan
Your noble brows again,
Nor shall you in the battle's van,
Your country's cause maintain.

O stranger friends, bring sweetest flowers,
And strew them o'er their graves—
For far they lie from Georgia's bowers,
Where love's sweet blossom waves.

Farewell, each noble Georgian son,
Our hearts for you still sigh—
While freedom's triumph shall be won,
Your names shall never die.

THE BATTLE AT BIG BETHEL

The fight at Bethel Church on the York Peninsula, 10 June 1861, is generally considered to have been the first battle of the Civil War worthy of the name. The Battle of Big Bethel occurred more than a month before First Manassas. The Confederates won both engagements.

Mary Boykin Chesnut was at Camden, South Carolina, on 10 June. "Colonel Magruder has done something splendid on the Peninsula," she wrote in her diary. "Three hundreds of the enemy killed, they say." Later the news reached Forsyth, Georgia, where Julia Stanford was teaching at the Monroe Female College. Julia had heard the report of the battle but now the number of Yankee casualties had grown to "four thousand." Julia's interest was divided between thoughts of the Confederate soldiers, especially one whom she would marry later, and concern for the young ladies in her care who were "in trouble for being escorted by young men—violation of gallantry laws."

Bethel was hardly a sufficient preparatory battle for Manassas, soon to follow, but raw soldiers on both sides began to learn more about the art and horror of war. Mrs. Chesnut was perplexed because she could not reconcile war with Christianity. When a "poor young soldier" was found dead at Bethel with a bullet in his heart and a Bible in his pocket inscribed "From the Bible Society to the defender of his country," she asked, "If the Bible can't prevent war, how is it to stop a bullet?"

Col. J. Bankhead Magruder listed by name only one Confederate soldier as killed in the day's fighting. He was Henry L. Wyatt, of the 1st North Carolina, commanded by Col. D. H. Hill. Wyatt was one of four to volunteer to move up to and burn a blacksmith shop shielding the enemy. A bullet in the head stopped him. Col. Hill was justly proud of his regiment which had performed so well—only about 300 Confederates were engaged against about a half dozen enemy regiments numbering over 3,000. "Their conduct," he said, "has furnished another example of the great truth that he who fears God will ever do his duty to his country." Ten Confederates were wounded. The total Union loss was 76, of which 18 were killed.

Magruder left his cavalry at Big Bethel under the command of Maj. E. B. Montague and marched his other force back to Yorktown. Maj. Montague pursued the Union troops for five miles to New Market Bridge. Magruder had North Carolina and Virginia regiments at Big Bethel. The Georgia companies which marched to Sewell's Point the month before were not in the fight.

For those not engaged in the battle, camp life had something of a social atmosphere. Wives of some of the officers and even some of the privates were visiting their husbands at Fairfax Station, near Manassas Junction. One soldier wrote, "Their tents gave unmistakable evidence of care and taste." The men were conscious of the fact that ladies were there. They attempted to go about in full dress and "all who come upon the parade ground have their hair combed."

A sympathetic note that recurred at intervals throughout the cruel war was sounded in Col. Magruder's report when he said,

Our means of transportation were exceedingly limited, but the wounded enemy were carried with our own wounded to farm houses in our rear, where the good people, who have lost almost everything by this war . . . received them most kindly and bound up their wounds.

Query Dept. To H. B.—Let us hope the citizens of your town will clean up the Confederate monument in the public square and that other towns will follow. William Jordan Bush, of Fitzgerald, died on 11 Nov. 1952, at the age of 107, the last Confederate in Georgia. Of the remaining six, John B. Salling died at Kingsport, Tennessee, on 16 March 1959 at the age of 112, and Walter Williams, who claimed he was a member of Hood's Texas Brigade, died at Houston on 19 Dec. 1959, at the age of 117. By this time all old Union soldiers had died. Thus the Confederate veterans could claim the final victory over the G.A.R.

A Prelude to Bull Run

Before the Federal general McDowell and the Confederate commanders Beauregard and Johnston brought their armies together in battle at Bull Run, there was fighting in western Virginia around Rich Mountain, Laurel Hill, and Beverly. Confederate general Robert S. Garnett had been sent into the area to defend it against Union troops pouring in with increasing strength.

During the second week of July 1861, Georgia troops, as well as regiments from Tennessee and the Carolinas, aided the Virginians in this first campaign of the war. The Union general George B. McClellan sent about 9,000 Union troops from Philippi, where Confederates had already been routed, in the direction of Beverly. There were 3,381 Confederates at Laurel Hill, 859 at Rich Mountain, and only 375 at Beverly. Fighting started near Bilington on 7 July. Gen. W. S. Rosecrans dislodged Col. John Pegram's Confederates, now strengthened to about 1,300, from their entrenched position at Camp Garnett on Rich Mountain, and Gen. T. A. Morris forced Gen. Garnett from Laurel Hill. "They have not given me an adequate force," Gen. Garnett had complained. "They have sent me to my death."

McClellan planned to push his forces to Beverly and cut Gen. Garnett's line of communication between Bilington and Staunton. Rosecrans and Morris had executed that plan successfully, but not without stubborn opposition. Gen. Garnett was reinforced by the 1st Georgia Infantry regiment under the command of Col. J. M. Ramsey. A reporter who signed his name "Ned" wrote to the *Macon Telegraph* saying that Col. Ramsey's "gallant First Georgia relieved at daybreak Col. Taliaferro's Twenty-Third Virginia which had been under fire all night, and succeeded in killing about six and capturing one lieutenant." Firing was still going on at the time of his writing [noon, 9 July]. "Ned" observed that the Yankee troops were "poorly clad" and appeared to be "of the lowest class of humanity, who, it seems, it would be doing the world a blessing to relieve of."

Gen. Garnett was shot from his horse on 13 July in the Cheat River Valley. The riderless horse dashed to the rear carrying a wordless message that the first Confederate general had fallen. Union forces took possession of the body; but later, "with tokens of respect" from Gen. McClellan, it was delivered to the Garnett family for burial.

Confederate observers claimed the retreat from Laurel Hill "was conducted in so skillful a manner as to amount to almost a victory." On the contrary, McClellan telegraphed Washington a glowing report of Union victory. McClellan lost 13 killed, 40 wounded, and claimed 200 Confederates killed and 1,000 taken prisoners. Confederate reports indicate that McClellan claimed twice the number of prisoners as were actually taken. Union general J. D. Cox thought McClellan's claim "curious" when he compared the official report with the actual campaign as he knew it to be.

GEORGIA'S "BRAVE BOYS"

In July 1861 Northerners believed their army under the command of Gen. Irvin McDowell was ready to march to victory, and they demanded action. "On to Richmond" was their cry, and they thought this first big battle of the war would be the last. They named the battle Bull Run, after a little creek that ran northeast of Manassas Junction. If you were born and bred in the South, you would know they meant Manassas.

Manassas, Virginia, was a railroad junction which needed to be cut if the Union troops were to get to Richmond. By popular demand McDowell moved his army, more like a parade than a military movement, into battle. He hoped to cut the railroad and roll on over Beauregard's army to the Confederate capital.

Northern newspapers had carelessly revealed McDowell's plans, and the Confederate generals were ready with raw but determined Rebels who, meeting the enemy, drove him back to Washington in utter confusion. McDowell, his army, members of official Washington, and even citizens went out to see the

grand spectacle. To their surprise they found that Gen. Joseph
E. Johnston had been able to bring a formidable army to Manassas, after leaving enough men in the Shenandoah Valley to
impede the progress of Patterson. Johnston, with Gen. Bernard
Bee's brigade, joined Beauregard on the morning of 20 July.
Thomas J. Jackson—the next day Bee would name him "Stonewall"—brought his brigade up, and two regiments, the 7th and
8th Georgia of Col. Francis S. Bartow's brigade, reached the field
that evening.

I am particularly interested in the 8th Georgia, commanded
by Col. William M. Gardner after Bartow, its first colonel, was
given command of the brigade. The reason for my interest is
that Company C of the regiment was the Macon Guards, whose
captain was Lucius M. Lamar. Mrs. Lamar, it will be remembered, had left hurriedly the week before from Macon to be with
her husband and "her brave company" in the event of a battle.
This brings First Manassas very close to the hearts of Macon
people.

On the evening of the battle, 21 July, the 7th and 8th Georgia
regiments were ordered to join Bee's brigade at Stone Bridge,
where the Federal attack was expected to be concentrated. When
it was learned that the Federal column on the Sudley road had
attacked Col. N. G. Evans, Bee and Bartow went to his assistance. At about 11:00 A.M. Beauregard ordered Bartow to place
the 7th and 8th in a pine thicket to the right and front of Evans.
The fighting here was "fierce and destructive." Bee, Evans, and
Bartow fought an unrelenting battlestorm for an hour.

The 8th suffered heavily. Col. Gardner was severely
wounded. The Macon Guards fought gallantly, less than a score
of them came out of the battle unscathed. As the tired men of
the 8th Georgia marched back toward Richmond after their exhausting chase of the Federals, Gen. Beauregard lifted his hat,
as they passed by, saying, "Eighth Georgia, I salute you." And
in Richmond the populace cried, "There goes the Eighth Georgia—what brave boys!"

Tired as they were, they found strength in the exhilarating
thrill of victory. Yet little joy was shown; they had lost their
brigade commander. Francis S. Bartow, the fiery secessionist

from Savannah, had defied his governor in offering himself and
his Oglethorpe Light Infantry for the defense of Virginia. Gov.
Joseph E. Brown had protested. He needed the Savannah troops
to defend the coast, but Bartow had replied, "I go to illustrate,
if I can, my native state." On the eve of battle he had warned:
"Remember, boys, battle and fighting mean death." His horse
was shot under him and he died at the nearby Henry house. His
last words were "They have killed me, but never give up the
fight." He did not realize that they had turned the grand Union
parade into an unorganized and disorderly retreat.

Mary Boykin Chesnut tells how Bartow's widow received the
news of her husband's death from Mrs. Jefferson Davis. She was
lying on her bed when the president's wife knocked. When she
saw who it was "she sat up ready to spring to her feet." But
there was an expression on her visitor's sad face that "took the
life out of her."

The look gave her the answer to the dread question that so
many wives were asking and would continue to ask. She sank
back upon the bed and "covered her face with her shawl." Capt.
Lamar's wife did not have the same tragic experience, but there
was much work to do for "her brave company," the Macon
Guards, for the anticipated conflict with the "Hessians" had resulted in pain and death for many of them.

MACONITES AT MANASSAS

When reports of casualties resulting from the battle at Manassas Junction began to arrive in Macon, Mrs. Lucius Lamar's neighbors feared that her husband, captain of the Macon Guards, had been killed. She had gone to Virginia to be near him on the eve of the battle. As it turned out, it was Pvt. Leonidas Lamar, the captain's cousin, who was killed, leaving his wife and little son to weep for him. Mrs. Lucius Lamar's Macon friends were relieved to know she would not come back a widow, but were saddened to read the casualty list which included, in addition to Leonidas, four other members of the Guards who were killed that day. They were Walter C. Allen, W. F. Garey, W. M. Jerry, and William M. Jones.

The Macon Guards—Company C of the 8th Georgia—as was mentioned in the previous installment, had been in the forefront of the attack at Manassas. They had fought valiantly and had suffered heavily. Eighteen men of the company had been wounded. The casualty list included Andrew McKenna, W. B. Ainsworth, William M. Bearden, William F. Blue, C. R. Caldwell, T. R. Christian, E. J. Collins, W. C. M. Dunson, Charles

Gamble, John Gamble, James M. Goff, F. B. Green, M. A. Malsby, George F. McLeod, Henry J. Peter, William C. Poe, C. P. Wilcox, and W. D. Woods. An observer was impressed by the behavior of this company.

> The Guards have won a proud historical fame, which will be cherished by every citizen of the town they so gloriously represented on the battlefield. The first blood shed by the Confederates at Manassas flowed from their corps, and no company on the battlefield saw harder service or performed it more gloriously.

The news of the victory heartened the Macon citizens but the thought of the men killed and wounded sobered them, and they began to plan at once to do their part in caring for the wounded. Citizens from all over the county gathered at the City Council Chamber to make plans for raising money to meet the expenses of nurses and surgical supplies. Mayor M. S. Thompson, who had equipped a whole new company—the "Thompson Guards"—took an active interest in the project, and with him on the committee to provide the funds were Capt. B. F. Ross, I. C. Plant, Capt. George A. Dure, and Ovid G. Sparks. The ladies were anxious to lend what assistance they could, and through their Soldiers' Relief Society they promised aid in sending boxes of carded lint, cotton, and bandages.

In the words of Joseph Clisby, the Manasssas victory grew upon the Macon people in "completeness and magnitude." He understood the significance of the victory with remarkable insight. In the first place, he correctly thought it would "infuriate the Black Republican war party" to the "highest pitch of frenzy and desperation." But he was certain that in the end "its backbone will be broken." In the second place, he felt sure the Confederate victory would strengthen the peace party in the North. He said it illustrated "the character of the resistance to be met, the terrible nature of the undertaking, the awful sacrifice of human life it will involve, [and] the hopelessness of the object to be obtained." As for the South, he thought it would "stimulate our enthusiasm and confidence at home." And, finally, he believed it would practically assure the Confederacy recognition by Britain and other European powers. But in this he was mistaken.

Every war has had it humorists, and the South has produced its share of them. The Georgia writer known as "Bill Arp," who has been quoted before in this series, was still teasing President Lincoln the following winter about his proclamation ordering the Southern rebels to disperse within twenty days. Now, months having passed since the presidential proclamation, we find Bill Arp still needling Lincoln about his order.

> The spring has shed its fragrance, the summer is over and gone, the yellow leaves of autumn have covered the ground, old Winter is slobbering his froth on the earth, but we have not been able to disperse as yet.

Then, in the cocky Southern attitude resulting from the big Confederate victory the previous July at Manassas Junction, he said,

> Me and the boys started last May to see you personally, and ask for an extension of time, but we got on a bust in old Virginny about the 21st of July and like to have got run over by a parcel of fellows running from Bull Run to your city.

Lincoln, however, had no time to take notice of Bill Arp. He was too busy moving his generals about, like pieces for a huge chess board, and girding the Union for a very real and brutal war.

MORE ABOUT MANASSAS

The Macon paper continued to praise the Macon Guards for their part in the glorious victory at Manassas which put the Federals on the run and caused much rejoicing all over the South. Much space was given in the columns of the *Telegraph* to the battle and especially to the Guards under the command of Capt. Lucius C. Lamar. One unidentified writer said the men of this company had worked as hard "as our slaves" and had shown themselves "willing to sacrifice all on the altar of their country's honor and liberty." They had "crowned themselves with glory" and had "won their laurels in this desperate conflict with a merciless enemy." The captain was due some praise also: "During the battle Capt. Lamar, not content to remain in the rear and give his orders, rushed forward and in a firm voice called to his brave boys to follow."

More recruits were badly needed to fill the gaps in the ranks left by the dead and wounded. Capt. Lamar issued a call for volunteers and Joseph Clisby, editor of the *Telegraph*, said, "Let our young heroes come forward. It will be an honor to say at the close of this war 'I was one of the Macon Guards.' "

Not only did the Guards need more men but the company was also short of clothing and equipment, especially shoes. The unknown writer quoted above said he had seen a letter from a member of the company which stated that "nearly all" were without shoes. He urged the Macon people who had already generously helped to outfit the company to make further contributions. And the next day the paper carried a notice saying that because of the efforts of the ladies of the Soldiers' Relief Society "in procuring a new supply of shoes for our brave Macon Guards ... the corps will soon receive a new and complete outfit."

Souvenir hunters and trophy collectors swarmed over the battlefield as soon as the fighting ceased. One of the Macon men who had been sent to Virginia to look after the wounded returned with a fair amount of relics from the first big battle of the war. Among his treasures were flattened musket balls, fragments of shells, a gunner's jacket, and the spear of a flagstaff. The most gruesome thing he brought back was a Zouave's cap "ventilated with a bullet hole directly through it just above the visor." He also had with him some letters that he had gathered from the pockets of dead Yankees. One was from a Connecticut girl to her soldier sweetheart. In it she said she was sick of war and wondered if her lover "has any proper business in Virginia or will get home alive."

There were other vultures hovering over Manassas, too, those with wings. An eyewitness reported, "It was a sad sight—the battlefield that day. The enemy's dead still lay scattered in every direction, and the silent vultures had begun to circle above them." He described how they looked in death.

> Nearly all of them lying upon their backs, some of them with their legs and arms stretched out to the utmost. Many had their feet drawn up somewhat, while their arms, from the elbows, were raised and the hands rather closed after the fashion of boxers. It was a singular and prevailing attitude. . . .

A YEAR OF SIGNIFICANCE

Now before the year grows any older, let us take a look at some of the important events which will claim our attention during the coming months as we observe the centennial of that very significant year, 1862. And what an important year it was! Some historians say the tide turned in favor of the Union in '62. This thinking is not based on clear-cut Northern victories in major battles for, actually, some of the bigger battles were either indecisive or resulted in Confederate gains. Rather, it is based on such factors as the strengthening of the Northern blockade along the South Atlantic and Gulf coasts, Grant's successful invasion of Tennessee, and Lee's failure to launch an offensive in Maryland at the battle of Antietam. There was some activity, too, in the trans-Mississippi region, but it had less bearing on the final outcome than the blockade or the campaigns east of the river.

No one could tell Johnny Reb and his officers that the advantages gained by the Yankees in '62 would spell out their lost cause by '65. It was not until the next year that Vicksburg and Gettysburg convinced them the tide had turned. Even then, knowing how the struggle would ultimately end but not knowing when, the Confederates fought stubbornly, hopelessly on.

The one big land battle of the previous year was fought at Manassas Junction in Virginia, near a creek called Bull Run, but seasoned veterans and raw recruits would witness many big ones in '62. In Tennessee the Federals captured the river forts, Henry and Donaldson, in the cold month of February. By April, Grant had moved on to Shiloh. Here Albert Sidney Johnston lost his life, and Beauregard retreated to Corinth. McClellan began a spring campaign through the Peninsula toward Richmond. With Lincoln juggling his generals, Lee and Jackson defeated John Pope at Manassas in August. Lee's failure at Antietam resulted in a victory for the abolitionists who persuaded Lincoln that it would be good diplomatic strategy to emancipate all slaves in Rebel territory. At year's end the big battle at Fredericksburg gave Lee a victory over Burnside, thus renewing the hopes of a disheartened army, just a little while before they scattered up the Shenandoah Valley.

All the excitement in '62 was not confined to big land battles. In March the *Monitor* fought it out with the *Merrimac* at Hampton Roads to inaugurate war between ironclads.

As I follow in chronological order the events of the year, I shall try to keep in sight the Macon companies, see where they go, keep up with their camp life, and follow them in battle. Some men will be carried wounded to Richmond and other places for hospitalization; some will die fighting. A few will return home on furlough, but there was little time for home visits. Because they were no different from other soldiers, it will be found that some took advantage of the termination of their enlistment— until conscription got them—that others reenlisted, and that still others deserted. But for all, soldiers and home folks alike, it was a hard year, one in which the full force of Northern invasion and blockade was felt mightily.

The month of April was especially important for the state of Georgia. It was the month of Andrews's Raid which brought about the Great Locomotive Chase between the *Texas* and the

General. Look for a reenactment of this as a part of the Centennial observance. Of greater significance to Georgia and the Southern cause was the capture of Ft. Pulaski on 11 April. This, too, will be on the centennial calendar of 1862.

PENINSULAR CAMPAIGN

The Second Georgia Battalion, as well as other units that contained Bibb County companies, had spent a comparatively quiet winter in Virginia, but the spring of 1862 brought renewed activity. The people of Norfolk had been kind to the soldiers from Middle Georgia, according to the *Macon Telegraph*, and the time had been spent in parades and mock battles with snowballs. Monotony had also been relieved by the arrival of new troops and, in some cases, visits from friends and home folks. Only four men had died—these as a result of measles and pneumonia. Now, the battalion was looking forward to returning to Macon, but with the coming of spring Bluecoats began to appear in the Peninsula as Gen. McClellan began preparations for his push toward Richmond.

The Peninsula Campaign was fought on land and water. The Confederate ironclad *Virginia* [*Merrimac*], having fought a drawn battle with the *Monitor* on 9 March, returned to Norfolk for repairs. The *Virginia* kept the Federal fleet in Hampton

Roads for a while, preventing it from approaching Richmond up the James River, but finally her commander, Josiah Tatnall, set the ship on fire to prevent her capture when Norfolk fell on 10 May.

We get something of the feel of the Peninsula Campaign from a letter written by Capt. Edward F. Hoge to his sweetheart, "Miss Gene." It was dated 23 March and was written at a camp two miles west of Orange Court House. Hoge's company was the "LaFayette Volunteers," Company G, 9th Georgia. This captain became a full colonel on 1 March 1864 and was reported disabled by wounds on 3 March 1865. The Gen. Jones who ordered Hoge's arrest for shooting a partridge was Brig. Gen. Samuel Jones, a Virginian whose brigade included four Georgia regiments, the 1st, 8th, which included the Macon Guards, 9th, Hoge's regiment, and the 11th.

> *Miss Gene,*
>
> *Your very interesting and most welcome letter reached me a day or two before we left winter-quarters else you would have heard from me sooner.*
>
> *On the afternoon of the 7th inst orders were received to be ready next morning for a march. Every man was immediately put in light marching order: three days rations of hard bread and salt meat was issued, everything except a change of clothing and two blankets to each man was burned and every other necessary preparation speedily made. Early in the morning of the 8th inst we reported according to orders on the turnpike leading from Centreville to Warrenton; here we remained till 10 o'clock on the day following in order to give the wagons of the army an opportunity to get in advance of the army. . . . We stayed within a mile of the town of Culpepper for four days and have been here three days. The day before we got here I was somewhat "taken down." We had been halted about 3 o'clock to remain till morning in a beautiful piece of woodland. The boys were cutting wood, building fires, preparing supper and making themselves comfortable generally when a partridge flew up on a limb a few yards above my head; the boys holloed "shoot it" and I fired at it with my repeater just once! For this terrible offence I was ordered by Genl Jones to consider myself under arrest, and threats were made of Court-marshall. The next day, however, Jones sent an order releasing me. I suppose he saw plainly that he had acted the part of a fool and a tyrant. . . .*
>
> *Where we are to rest at the end of our march is not given to us to know. . . . I suppose there is no one of lower grade than a Major Genl*

that knows our destination. I am satisfied, nevertheless, that we will not halt permanently till we reach the city of Richmond. A great many took up the idea that Gordonsville was the place, but no preparations for defense are being made there whereas they are strongly fortifying Richmond; the larger stationary pieces that were received from our admirable works at Manassas instead of being planted at Gordonsville are sent on to Richmond. I understand that General Ewell's brigade is fortifying the near bank of the Rappedan, only four miles from us, between us and the enemy; this does not signify a stand at all, for Genl Johnston, old Joe, old long-headed-eagle-eyed matchless Genl Joseph E. Johnston, had a thousand hands at work on the fortifications at Manassas for a week before we left there. We built a Rail Road from Manassas to Centreville all just to fool the enemy. Spies, no doubt, were thick amongst us there and the enemy knew all that was going on, and just when they were ready with their thousands to attack him front and rear and by both flanks the aforesaid Joseph very calmly and easily turned his army and left them "with their fingers in their mouths."...

I am indebted to Maconite John Black, Jr., for discovering Capt. Hoge's letter. He found it in Dalton in the possession of Mrs. Eugenia Jarvis, the daughter of the recipient of the letter quoted above.

PREPARATIONS AT PULASKI

The month of April 1862 was, like all Aprils during the war years, a full and active month: McClellan advanced toward Richmond from the Peninsula; Jackson, with 18,000 troops, kept more than twice that many Federals busy in the Shenandoah Valley; Albert Sidney Johnston was killed at Shiloh, and the Union forces pressed on Corinth; Farragut occupied New Orleans; and the *Texas* chased and caught the *General* just five miles below Chattanooga. But in Georgia, more than Andrews's Raid, attention was focused on Savannah where Ft. Pulaski was to fall on the very same day [11 April] as the "Great Locomotive Chase."

Savannah citizens had been anticipating an attack for several months. In fact, they were within earshot of the guns that thundered the previous November in the Battle of Port Royal, South Carolina. They were in a state of discouragement and disorganization as Robert E. Lee came down to assume command of the Military Department of South Carolina, Georgia, and Florida. But the winter passed without a Federal attack on Ft. Pulaski, Savannah stronghold on Cockspur Island at the mouth of the Savannah River. Sgt. William Mosely had written home from Savannah on 2 Jan., "Some thinks we will all be discharged before long but I don't think so."

Lt. Theodorick W. Montfort had volunteered to leave Virginia for the defense of the Georgia coast, and his Georgia company, the Wise Guards, of Macon County, had volunteered to go with him. He reached Savannah in time to write his wife at Lanier on 12 Feb. He said,

> *I volunteered to come here, because it was considered a point of danger, and because other companies in the 3 Regts. refused to come I felt that having volunteered to aid in the protecting the confederacy, Ga. and our homes, that it was our duty to volunteer. . . . I therefore advised our company to volunteer and am proud to say that they, with a full knowledge of all the facts that we probably would have to fight soon . . . volunteered.*

But on 1 March, William W. Head wrote his wife in Milner as follows:

> *Every thing in this country [Savannah] continues without any material change. The enemy stays at a safe distance, and our troops are in fine spirits. We are ready for them whenever they choose to land. Savannah is safe, I confidently believe.*

By 15 April, however, Montfort was certain the battle was about to begin. He wrote a lengthy letter on that date to his wife and children. He was inside the fort at the time, as, indeed, he had been since 12 Feb.

> *A battle is inevitable. Fight we must and fight we will. Yesterday was the day we were to have been attacked but from some cause it has been delayed—which we were all glad of as we would be glad to have about three days more to complete and finish strengthening our position. We expect to continue our labours day and night until the same is finished. Not even will circumstances permit us to be idle tomorrow [Sunday]. We must prepare for an unequal and unjust struggle and conflict forced upon us by our Yankee enemy. They are about fifty to our one, with superior arms, vessels, etc. Their heavy cannon and mortars are frowning upon us from some seven Batteries and an innumerial quality of boats—all intended for our destruction—the destruction of men that have never wronged them or sought to devest them of a right. What a comment upon this enlightened and Christian age. . . .*

I think the Garrison is determined without regard to the superior number of the enemy to strike until the walls of our Fort is battered down or to fall. If the Fort is taken we want them to find nothing to take but crumbled and ruined walls and mangled corpse. Yet amidst all of our vindictive feelings and bitter hatred to our enemy there is something sad and melancholy in the preparation for battle. To see so many men preparing for the worst by disposing of their property by Will, to see the surgeon sharpening his instruments and whetting his saw to take off when necessary those members of our body, that God has given us for our indispensible use, to see men engaged in carding up and preparing lint to stop the flow of human blood from cruel and inhuman wounds is awful to contemplate.

The Casements are cleared; nothing is allowed to remain that is combustible or would be in the way during the engagement—listen—the floor is covered around each gun with sand not for health or cleanliness but to drink up human blood as it flows from the veins and hearts of noble men, from the hearts of those that love and are beloved, that is necessary to prevent the floor from becoming slippery with blood so as to enable the men to stand and do their duty.

I have but little apprehension but what I shall survive the present threatening conflict as well as all others that duty may call me to face and that I shall live to see this war ended and our people free and independent as well as to meet you, my wife, and children and be quiet and happy once more at home. . . .

Montfort did survive that battle, as we shall see. And he survived imprisonment which followed the battle. In fact, he lived to be released and sent home. But he died at his mother's home in Butler a few days after his return.

April 8, 1962

THE IMPENETRABLE FORT

"They will make it pretty hot for you with shells, but they cannot breach your walls at that distance." The tall, straight, graceful speaker was Gen. Robert E. Lee. He was at Ft. Pulaski on his last inspection tour of the fort which he had built thirty years before as a young lieutenant of the army engineers. The time was Spring 1862.

He had every reason to believe the truth of his statement, and Col. Charles Olmstead, 24-year-old commander of the fort defending the city at the mouth of the Savannah River, was confident, too, that Gen. Lee was right. The walls were seven and a half feet thick, and the heavy artillery which the Federals had placed on Tybee Island were almost a mile away. The military experts agreed that those big guns could not breach the thick masonry walls with their shells at more than 800 feet, and they were more than twice that far away. Furthermore, the gunboats dared not get close enough for good shots because the fort was protected with big cannons manned by a garrison of 385 men, some of them skilled bombardiers.

Lt. Theodorick W. Montfort, of the Wise Guards, was one of those who had faith in those big guns, and, though the enemy mortars "frowned" upon Pulaski, he knew Pulaski's guns were as strong as they were clean and shiny. The men treated their cannon with great care, even gave pet names to the big monsters. Montfort wrote home about it.

> I really feel attached to my guns, and so do the men. My guns feel to me as part of my family. You would be really amused to hear the endearing epithets and see the tender care and consideration that is paid to them. I love them on account of my frequent and almost hourly association with them. I love them because they are willing and submissive instruments in my hands, to protect myself and my country. I love them because it is human and natural to love and pet something. I love them because the names reminds me of home and my wife, my mother, my friends. And I love them because the names act as an incentive to stimulate me to acts of bravery.

He was in command of three large ones. The 64-pounder he named "Addie Elizabeth" for his mother; the 53-pounder he called "Sarah" in honor of Mrs. Samuel Hall, a Macon County neighbor; and the 32-pounder he dubbed "Louisa" for his wife.

But with all the confidence Col. Olmstead and the Confederates had in their "pets," the Federals had a weapon with a striking power then unknown to the attacker or defender. It was the rifled cannon invented by Adm. John A. Dahlgren. When Col. Olmstead made his bold reply to the surrender order which Lt. James H. Wilson delivered to him—"I am here to defend the fort not to surrender it"—he knew he was outmanned and that the mortar batteries were ready to belch fire and the gunboats were ready to strike, but he did not know what the rifled cannon could do. Neither did Capt. Quincy A. Gillmore, who was ready to give them their chance, but he would soon find out.

Firing began at 7:40 A.M. on 10 April, about two hours after Olmstead had rebuffed Lt. Wilson. More than 5,000 shells were hurled from Tybee Island. A Yankee corporal wrote a message on the first one. It read, "A nutmeg from Connecticut; can you furnish a grater?" This same corporal told how a shell broke the flagstaff on the parapet and the colors fluttered down amid cheers from the attackers. In a little while two members of the garrison had sprung upon the parapet under "a perfect shower of shot and shell" to raise it again on a makeshift staff mounted on a gun carriage.

By noon Gillmore was sure his rifled cannon would breach the wall. A newspaper reporter thought he saw a gleam of sunlight through the wall at sunset. Then firing practically ceased during the night. At 7:00 the next morning the batteries opened up again and kept up a terrific rate until 2:00 P.M. when the garrison flag went down and the white flag of surrender was hoisted. "The outer wall of two casements was entirely down," Olmstead explained to his wife, "while those terrible rifle projectiles had free access to the brick traverse protecting our magazine door." He did not know at what moment they might all be "blown in the air."

Two weeks later Louisa Montfort received a letter from Governor's Island, New York.

My Dear Wife [she read], We are all here and well, situated between and in full view of the Cities of N.Y. and Brooklin. I am without a dollar and half naked. Prince [his Negro slave] has left me. Our parole covers some 50 acres. Send me the Daguereotype of yourself and each one of my children, including my Baby. Have them all taken together if convenient. All letters sent me will be read. . . . All things will have an end, be of good cheer. I shall be at home some day. May heaven bless you all, farewell.

RETURN OF 2ND BATTALION

April 1862 was a very important month for Georgia. Down at Savannah, as the last two essays have shown, a great excitement prevailed with the fall of Ft. Pulaski. Up above Atlanta, on the Western and Atlantic Railroad a thrilling locomotive chase took place. You have been seeing much about that in the papers, and next week I shall tell you about it. But Macon, too, marked the month as one to be remembered. That was the month of the arrival of the Second Georgia Battalion. The two Macon companies in the battalion, which had left for Virginia in April the year before, finally returned. The town had looked for them for some time. A basket dinner had been planned and postponed, but now the dinner could be served.

A total of 23 combat organizations from Bibb County served in various places and in various ways during the war. Two companies of cavalry, the Bibb County Cavalry, Capt. Samuel S. Dunlap, and the Ocmulgee Rangers, Capt. Thaddeus G. Holt, Jr.; 3 companies of artillery, the Jackson Artillery, Capt. Theodore W. Parker [first captain], the German Artillery, Capt. F. Burghard, and the Napier Artillery, Capt. Leroy Napier [first captain]; and 18 infantry companies were this county's contribution to the defense of Georgia and the Southland.

But interest centers more on the Second Battalion for several reasons. For one thing, the Second Battalion was the first in the state to go to Virginia. Then the Floyd Rifles were commanded first by Thomas Hardeman who had already won distinction as a member of the United States Congress. Hardeman was raised to the rank of major and given command of the battalion at the time of its organization. Another thing that gives the battalion prestige is the fact that Sidney Lanier was a member of the Macon Volunteers under Capt. Robert A. Smith. This company won honors in the Seven Days' Battles around Richmond and, later, at Fredericksburg.

The Second Battalion was temporarily disbanded at the end of the one-year enlistment period, but, as the Goldsboro [N.C.] *Tribune* put it, they were "determined to reenlist to a man." And they did, when the battalion was reorganized at Wilmington in May, serving all the way to Appomattox.

Besides the Rifles and the Volunteers, the other infantry companies from Macon, as listed in the History Edition of the *Macon News* [1929], were as follows: Brown Infantry, Capt. George A. Smith, Co. C, 1st Georgia; Independent Volunteers, Capt. J. W. Aderhold, Co. A, 1st Georgia; Central City Blues, Capt. J. G. Rogers, Co. H, 12th Georgia; Lochrane Guards, Capt. Jackson Barnes, Co. F, Infantry Battalion, Phillips Legion; Ross Volunteers, Capt. Jones, Co. D, 30th Georgia; Lamar Infantry, Capt. T. W. Brantley, Co. A, 54th Georgia; Rutland Guards, Capt. J. W. Stubbs, Co. B, 27th Georgia; Sparks Guards, Capt. J. B. Comming; Thompson Guards, Capt. J. A. Van Valkenburg, 10th, 12th, and 61st Georgia Regiments; Macon Guards, Capt. Lucius M. Lamar, Co. C, 8th Georgia; Gresham Rifles, Capt. M. R. Rogers, Co. A, 45th Georgia; Mangham Infantry, Capt. Charles J. Williamson; Scott Infantry, Capt. T. J. Pritchett, Co. B, 64th Georgia; and Lockett Infantry, Capt. Charles J. Harris, Co. K, 59th Georgia.

The Second Battalion was in Virginia when winter broke. The Floyd Rifles were ordered to Tanner's Creek Crossroads where they were to throw up temporary works to secure the Confederate position on 16 March; then they were ordered to Sewell's Point. On the 19th they were ordered to Goldsboro. By that time their term of enlistment had ended. Maj. Hardeman had already gone to Macon. Later, as colonel he was placed in command of the 45th Georgia Infantry. Maj. L. T. Doyal succeeded Col. Hardeman as commander of the battalion. Doyal was a Baptist minister, and he must have been a good influence upon his men. The Goldsboro paper said there was "not a dissipated man in the battalion." The *Tribune* was impressed by the decorum and discipline of the men.

Macon was justly proud of her returning soldiers, and the *Daily Telegraph* said they appreciated "this demonstration of esteem and honor." The basket dinner which had been so long planned and postponed was a huge success, as reported in the *Telegraph* on 3 April. There were speeches of welcome and many happy homes in the community, for a little while—but only for a little while. Soon they were off again to Virginia and the defense of Richmond. Finally they were forced to travel the road to Appomattox.

THE TEXAS AND THE GENERAL

As a boy I watched many Western movies and was thrilled every time the cowboys on their broncos outran and caught a train. If you and I had been living at Big Shanty [Kennesaw] up above Atlanta a hundred years ago and had happened to be around the Lacy Hotel on the morning of 12 April 1862, about 6 o'clock, we would have seen three men running to catch their own train, the *General*, which had been stolen from them right under their eyes when they stopped for a 20-minute breakfast. The men were William A. Fuller, conductor of the train, Jeff Cain, the engineer, and Anthony Murphy, foreman of the Western and Atlantic shops. And, though then unknown to the pursuers, the thieves were Capt. James J. Andrews, a Kentucky Unionist spy, and his 21 soldiers in disguise. They had boarded the train at Marietta and started off toward Chattanooga at full speed when the crew and passengers detrained for breakfast.

This sensational incident, often told in song and story, and finally in a movie, *The Great Locomotive Chase*, was reenacted recently with much glamour and ballyhoo when the Louisville and Nashville ran the *General* once again over the track between Atlanta and Chattanooga. This trip, made a hundred years after the famous "Andrews Raid," was a full dress affair with politicians, newspaper men and women, prominent citizens, and at least one expert, Wilbur Kurtz of Atlanta, who probably knows more about that incident than any living person. The L & N spent months and an unannounced sum of money preparing the *General* for this run and the many more it will make as it goes on tour over the country. One major difference is that now the engine will get its steam from oil rather than wood as it did in the old wood-burning days.

Union general O. M. Mitchell believed the best way to defeat the Confederacy was to disrupt its transportation system. On 11 April, he brought a large force into the little town of Huntsville, Alabama, and destroyed the Memphis and Charleston, the trunk line of the Confederacy. Then, under his orders, Andrews and his disguised soldiers stole the *General* and attempted to destroy the Western and Atlantic between Atlanta and Chattanooga. But William Fuller and his associates outran the *General*, catching her at the Tennessee line, but they did not run all the way on foot! Here is the story.

It was a misty and drab morning on 12 April; rain fell intermittently during the day. Because the trestles and bridges on the Western and Atlantic were wet, and because Fuller and the pursuers were determined to catch the thieves, this supply line of the Confederacy was saved for the time being. The next year [3 May 1863], another attempt to destroy this line was also thwarted, that time by the help of a brave girl. But that is another story, which will be told at the proper time.

Fuller and his men did not run far before they came upon a handcar. Impressing it and its crew, they increased the speed of the chase. For some distance the grade was downward, but finally their handcar had to be propelled upgrade. When they reached the Etowah River, 12 miles beyond the town of Kingston, the pursuers changed to a still more worthy vehicle for pursuit. It was the engine *Yonah*. Fuller, who had been only four minutes behind Andrews at Kingston, lost a little time in getting the

Yonah underway. He loaded it with soldiers and away they went. Southbound trains were a handicap for Andrews and his raiders. At Adairsville they met one. Andrews again tried the trick of asking the southbound train to take a siding so that he could rush "powder to Gen. Beauregard at Corinth." It worked again!

The raiders would stop from time to time and rip up crossties, or drop them off the back of the train. With the tracks torn up in front of him, Fuller and his posse left the *Yonah* and started out again on foot. After a while they encountered the southbound train that Andrews had tricked at Adairsville. It was the *Texas*. Fuller impressed it into service and running it backwards, sometimes a mile a minute, he came in sight of the *General* between Calhoun and the Oostenaula River. Andrews dropped two cars, one at a time, from the train to stop the *Texas*, but the *Texas* caught the loose cars and roared on. Andrews set a boxcar on fire on a covered bridge over the Chickamauga River, but the timber was too wet to burn. The *Texas* caught the *General* at the Tennessee line.

Andrews and his men fled into the woods, but all were caught. Seven of them, including their leader, were executed. The others were put in prison. Some of these were exchanged, others escaped.

The raid brought fear to Georgians. "The mind and heart shrink back appalled at the . . . contemplation" of the possible consequences of this bold adventure, was the opinion of the *Southern Confederacy*, an Atlanta newspaper. Every precaution was taken to protect the railroad from another such raid. Militia guarded the roads day and night and sentries stayed alert watching its 16 bridges.

CONFEDERATE SUCCESSES

Unreconstructed Rebels—are there any left?—will be pleased at the timing of my resumption of Civil War essays since it marks the centennial of a Confederate victory. As August turned into September in 1862, the Confederates were rejoicing over the victory they had won at the Second Battle of Manassas. They had the Union troops on the run again in Virginia. It was not to last long, however, for Lee's invasion of Union territory was thwarted at Antietam on 17 September.

The *Macon Daily Telegraph* reported an "active stampede of the enemy" in both Virginia and Tennessee at the end of August. Gen. Pope was falling back and being "hotly" pursued by the Confederate troops. The advancing Confederates could see them striking their tents, and they found abandoned stores and equipment all along the route. In Tennessee the Federals scurried out of camp "in three hours notice in panic." The *Telegraph* thought perhaps Buell was falling back to effect a junction with Rosecrans in order to join forces and make a stand somewhere below

Nashville. The Macon paper was informed by some unknown source that "Tennessee and Kentucky will be abandoned by the enemy without a blow."

News from all quarters gave the *Telegraph* the impression that "our army near Rappahannock is pushing the enemy with vigor." The Lynchburg *Republican* had reported that intelligence from Gordonsville revealed the fact that the Yankees had retreated from Culpepper and were being pushed back across the river.

The following letter, which was loaned to me by Mrs. Eugene Humphries of this city, throws some light on the conditions and activity during the first week of September 1862. The letter was written by Sgt. Humphries to his wife. The sergeant was a cavalryman in Company A of Phillips's Legion, Drayton's Brigade, Longstreet's Division. The letter was written from Gordonsville, Virginia, on 7 Sept. 1862. It is copied here in full.

Dear Wife

This leaves me well at this time and I hope this may reach you all enjoying the same good blessings.

We have stopped at this place today for the purpose of giving our horses a little rest as we have put them through since we have left Richmond. I sent you a short letter from there by Mr. Prosser. I would have written you a longer one but I had so much to do that morning that I did not have time. As for when I will ever get one from home, I cannot tell as I don't have any idea.

I suppose it is some ninety or a hundred miles from here before we get to the Legion. It is currently reported about here that our army is over on the other side of the Potomac river. How true it is I cannot say as there is always some report going through the camps. I expect it is so as I saw them carrying a train load of boats from Richmond on out that way somewhere.

We have got in sight of the mountains once more. I was in hopes that I would never see another mountain as long as I live, but it seems my fate to have to pass through them once more, and I hope it may be my fate to get out. It is our cry now, Ho: for Washington and I am in hopes that we will not be in as bad luck as the Yankees were when they got in three miles of Richmond and was so confident of getting it. If we ever get in three miles of Washington City, we will have it or make a heap of death come. The country from here to Richmond is very poor looking country to me. There is not much of anything planted. In fact nothing but a little corn that is very sorry. You must excuse bad writing and all such as I had to make Adam clean the bread pan to get it to write on. I am now sitting down flat on the ground with the bread pan on my knee, bottom upward and writing on the bottom. I have written to Pa and Buck from Richmond. Did they get them [?] and to Priss all along the road before I got there. I suppose she did not get any as she never answered them. Give my love to all and excuse this letter as I have no news that would interest you. Write to me whenever you get a chance or a little oftener. As ever,

Sergt. E. J. H.

QUIET IN THE MOUNTAINS

While Sgt. Humphries was trudging through the Virginia mountains, as he said in his letter quoted last Sunday, Pvt. William Hampton Hill from Tennille was marching through the Cumberland Mountains in Tennessee. With Buell moving toward Nashville to make a juncture with Rosecrans in the western part of the state, Confederate generals Kirby Smith and Bragg were moving toward Kentucky through eastern Tennessee. Pvt. Hill, of Company E, 12th Georgia Battalion, was in Jacksboro, Tennessee, just ten miles from the Kentucky line at a spot in the Cumberland Mountains northwest of Knoxville.

Whatever activity these armies might or might not have had in September, Pvt. Hill's company was taking things easy at the time he wrote the following letter. It was written at Jacksboro (sometimes spelled Jacksborough) on 6 Sept. 1862. Luther R. Underwood, of this city, is to be thanked for bringing this letter from his family collection into the light of day.

Dear Jane:

As I have not wrote you in several days and Mr. Kitridge is going home I thought I would write you a few lines informing you that I am in good health and hope this will find you enjoying the same kind of health. There is nothing new going on here. Things are very still. The Army that we was with when we left here is now about two hundred miles from us so I don't think there is much danger of us going any farther this way but we will know in a few days as Major Capers is at Knoxville on his way back to his Battalion and it is thought very strong that we will go to Georgia or South Carolina. If we do I shall come by home if I can. Our Battalion is in very good health. We have 3 or 4 sick men. Mac Mathis and Buford Mathis has got the typhoid fever and Ed Martin has been very low with it but is getting better. We have only lost three men out of our company yet. Hut Wood, John Cumming and old man Green Kitridge has been detached to do Government work at Macon. John and Jim is both well. Will is about like he was. I am trying to get him a discharge.

I eat so much at dinner I cannot hardly set to write. I had a stew made out of back bones and spare ribs. You may know that was good. We are living like fighting chickens but the Guard duty is pretty heavy. I am off two days and on one. There has been no rain here yet. . . .

The Government has raised our wages. My wages now is about 20 dollars per month. Tell Miss Liza that George gave Joe his letter. He is well but I expect she knows as much about him as I do for I don't see him once a week hardly. I am now at a man's house by the name of Lovet about one mile from camp. I was down here on picket and the shower came up and I came down to the house. He has got two daughters here with one child each and their husbands [are] in the Yankee Army. I have been cooking for two week. You ought to see me making up biscuits and frying fritters. I tell you I am hard to beat. I made one of the shashingest pies the other day your ever read of. We have plenty of rye, coffee & sugar to go in it and now and then we get brandy enough to get drunk on but very seldom. I would like to have a drink now very well.

I will send you the twenty dollars by Kitridge if I don't forget it. I recon we will be paid off again soon but I don't know, when they get ready and not before. Wait 2 or 3 days after you get this and if you don't hear any more from me I want you to write me again.

The letter quoted last Sunday and this one quoted today indicate a quietness in Virginia and Tennessee following Second Manassas and other engagements at the end of August. Lee's army, however, was moving toward the bloodiest day of the whole war—17 Sept. Next week this column will have something to report concerning the outcome of that great Battle of Antietam, or, as the Confederates called it, Sharpsburg.

ANTIETAM: BLOODIEST DAY

Today we are on the eve of the centennial of the bloodiest day of the Civil War—17 September 1862. The confidence and optimism that resulted from Second Manassas were high for the first two weeks of September, but the battle at Sharpsburg, Maryland, which is called Antietam in the present-day history books, turned Lee's advance toward the Federal capital into a disappointing retreat and gave Lincoln the encouragement he needed to announce his Proclamation of Emancipation.

The *Macon Telegraph* was puzzled at the claims of Union victories in the face of steady Confederate advances into Maryland. The Macon paper editorialized sarcastically,

> We are forcibly struck with the fact that . . . the Grand Union Army has been pitched neck and heels out of Virginia, by an almost unbroken series of Union victories, from Richmond to the Potomac. They have never yet met with a fair and square defeat, according to their own testimony. We think it a puzzle intricate enough to confound the most astute Yankee, to reconcile the grand result with the process.

Jackson won a victory at Harper's Ferry on the 15th, capturing its garrison of 11,000 troops and much equipment. This increased hopes among the Rebels that they would be successful in carrying the war far into Union territory, not only into Maryland but also into Pennsylvania. The Union capital was also an objective. But McClellan caught the Confederates near Sharpsburg. There were 70,000 Union and 40,000 Confederates engaged. The statistics tell the story: 2,100 Union dead, 2,700 Confederates; more than 9,000 wounded on each side.

It took a little while for the news to reach the Deep South and even longer for the significance of the failure of the invasion to be comprehended. Actually, the battle was a draw, but McClellan could claim a technical victory as Lee withdrew into Virginia the day after the battle. It was five days later before the *Telegraph* carried any news of it. The announcement read as follows: "A terrible battle has been fought at Sharpsburg, in which we have lost three generals and four have been wounded. . . . " The paper carried a dispatch from the Richmond *Enquirer* saying, "The fight was resumed on Thursday, and the enemy routed and driven nine miles." But the end result for Lee was failure and disappointment.

The result for the Union? Renewed confidence and a boldness reflected in Lincoln's Preliminary Emancipation Proclamation [23 Sept.]. The effect on Britain and France was such that those two nations, until then on the verge of recognizing the Confederacy, hesitated and moved away from recognition.

The tragic news of the loss in dead brought sorrow to many homes and knowledge of the thousands wounded brought sympathy and response, especially from the ladies of the Soldiers' Relief Society. The Macon paper published an appeal from this society in its issue of 26 Sept. which read:

> In consequence of the multiplied battles that have recently transpired on our Northern border, the ladies of the Soldiers' Relief Society again Petition the benevolent and philanthropic to unite with them in their efforts to administer to the comfort and alleviate the sufferings of the sick and wounded.
>
> An opportunity again affords itself for us to indicate our gratitude and appreciation to these who have fought and bled for the protection

of our rights, and the generous impulses of our hearts should gush forth in a united stream towards this common center of sympathy and interest. . . .

We earnestly appeal to "all" interested in the welfare of our brave defenders, to cooperate with us in sending Hospital stores for their relief.

Turn in the War's Tide

The battle fought at Antietam Creek, though considered to have been a draw, had far-reaching implications. As was pointed out in this column last week, it gave Lincoln the victory feel even if it did not give the Union a clear-cut victory; it gave the president a psychological advantage which he capitalized on by announcing his plan to free all the slaves in Rebel territory. It also determined the course of the British and French governments. The United States could now turn them against the Confederacy just about the time that government had begun to expect recognition and aid. It showed the Confederacy the futility of a Northern invasion—a lesson not remembered the next year when Lee went to Gettysburg. Therefore, 17 Sept. 1862 cost the Confederacy more than just its 2,700 killed and 9,029 wounded. In a sense, that day marked the turning of the tide for the Confederacy, as some historians see it.

It is not hard to see the logic of this view, though I consider the real turning point to have been July 1863, when Grant cut the Confederacy at Vicksburg and Meade turned Lee back at Gettysburg. Looking at the war in retrospect, one could very well say, however, that Antietam marked the beginning of the end. Of course, the Rebels could not see the hopelessness of the struggle then. They only saw the inevitable defeat after July 1863, yet a year away. Even then, after they knew the cause was hopeless, they fought on as though they were certain of final victory. But this was simply a foolhardy and stubborn, unconquerable spirit in conflict with common sense and reason which told them the cause was destined to end in failure.

In reflecting on this I often think of Winston Churchill's comment. This fighting on against impossible odds after the fate of the Confederacy was sealed was to him "one of the enduring glories of the American people." As late as October 1863, months after Gettysburg and Vicksburg, Josephine Habersham of Savannah, could write in her diary:

> Things look brighter for our beloved Country. Mississippi is coming out finely. The enemy has a great drain with all the little armies it has to keep there! The loss of Vicksburg has produced nothing very beneficial for them. . . . So things look bright, thank God.

At war's end John T. Trowbridge, a roving reporter from Boston, visited the battlefield at Antietam Creek and found much evidence of the fierce battle that had been fought there. Trees were riddled with bullets; farmers frequently plowed up skulls and bones in their fields. On the crest of a hill near a log house he was shown an abandoned well where 57 Confederates had been buried together. The owner of the place had been offered a dollar a head for burying them and had saved himself the trouble of digging separate graves by throwing the bodies into his well. Long after the battle, according to the Boston reporter, people exploring the woods around the Sharpsburg battle area would find the remains of soldiers in ravines and behind logs where they had dragged themselves when wounded, there to die in their loneliness, and there to remain until some explorer found them.

Trowbridge visited the ground which had been purchased for a national cemetery. Work on it had not begun when he was there, and the big question for the authorities was whether or not to bury the Rebel dead with the Union dead. Many were opposed to bringing them together in death, but Trowbridge said he did not object. He wanted the Johnny Rebs properly buried, in deep graves like the Union men. He thought hogs rooting in the fields might turn up skeletons of the Rebels if they were thrown into shallow trenches; and that, to him, was "not a sight becoming a country that calls itself Christian."

So, the philosophical reporter thought the dead should be buried together, "they of the good cause and they of the evil." In his opinion, "neither was the one cause altogether good nor was the other altogether bad." Yet he had strong notions that the Union cause looked toward "liberty and human achievement" and the Southern cause looked back to "barbarism and the Dark Ages." He was willing to concede that the "holier one" was clouded by much "ignorance and selfishness," and that the "darker one" was "brightened here and there with glorious flashes of self-devotion."

FIGHT AT FREDERICKSBURG

"Jeb" Stuart's bold cavalry raid around the Union army into Pennsylvania near Gettysburg in October 1862 and Gen. McClellan's hesitancy to move against Richmond after Lee had successfully "escaped" from Antietam caused Lincoln to decide again to shift generals. He replaced McClellan with Maj. Gen. Ambrose E. Burnside. The *New York Herald* complained of the displacement of McClellan by Burnside and was unhappy and dismayed to announce to the public (which must have been useful intelligence to the Confederate army, since this was five days before the battle of Fredericksburg) that the planned advance upon Richmond by way of Fredericksburg was "impracticable" because of the "impossibility of subsisting a Federal army at a distance of more than two or three days march [say 30 miles] from a water base!"

The *Macon Daily Telegraph* observed three days after the battle, which was fought on the 13th, that this should "open the eyes of the North to the hopeless character of their present undertaking." The result: the Union lost 1,284 killed and 9,600 wounded of their 113,000 troops; the Confederacy lost 595 killed and 4,061 wounded of the 75,000 under Lee and his lieutenants. Is it any wonder that Lincoln again shifted generals and placed Joseph Hooker in command?

Georgia troops fought bravely at Fredericksburg and many Georgia families mourned the deaths of their sons. Georgians were especially active in two important phases of the battle, in holding the line of A. P. Hill's division and in the assault upon Marye's Heights. Gen. Hill commended all his brigades. He said Gen. Thomas's 45th Georgia "was not recalled from the position it had so gallantly won in the front line." The Macon company called the "Gresham Rifles" was Company A of this regiment. Such praise was pleasant to the ears of its captain, M. R. Rogers. The 45th suffered 48 casualties. Pvt. Welborn J. Willis of the "Gresham Rifles" was among those killed.

In addition to the "Gresham Rifles," Capt. Jackson Barnes's "Lochrane Guards" and Capt. H. N. Ellis's Macon Artillery were in the battle. J. A. Van Valkenburg's "Thompson Guards" may have been engaged in the fighting also. This company was moved from the 10th Georgia to the 13th and, finally, to the 61st. The 61st Georgia lost 100 killed and wounded. The heaviest Georgia casualties were suffered by the 14th regiment with 22 killed and 83 wounded.

The "Lochrane Guards" were in Phillips's Legion [Company F]. This brigade was under the command of Brig. Gen. Thomas R. R. Cobb, who took it from his older brother Howell. The most famous incident of the battle was the charge he led at Marye's Heights. Union troops swarmed up to Cobb's brigade. Confederate artillery poured hot lead into the charging mass of Bluecoats, but they pressed up to the stone wall behind which the Confederates were fortified. They were swept back time after time. In all, they made six brave charges, but were finally beaten off by Cobb's troops.

Gen. Cobb was directing his brigade from behind a barn near the stone wall that protected his troops, but in the fury of the battle he must have ventured too far into the open, because a musket ball from the enemy fire caught him in the calf of the leg. He was carried off the field, but died in a very short time.

Thomas R. R. Cobb, of Athens, had been one of the leaders in the secession movement. At the Montgomery convention, he had figured prominently in the writing of the Confederate Constitution which launched the new government on its way. He was not content to carry his state out of the Union nor simply to serve the Confederacy in a civil capacity. His sacrifice of devotion was to bleed to death with Welborn Willis, the Macon boy, and hundreds of others like him. "The whole state will mourn his untimely but glorious death," said the *Macon Telegraph*. Editor Clisby believed there was "no man of greater, and very few of equal, promise" as this brave officer. Gen. Lee considered him to be "one of the South's noblest citizens and the army's bravest and most distinguished officers."

The death of their general was a sad thing, but the victory that came to Cobb's Legion after a three-day march through the snow was some consolation to the battle-weary soldiers. And it was such courage and fortitude as this that made possible Lee's victory at Fredericksburg. Of course, J. R. Cooke's North Carolinians played their heroic role, too, and many others; but the Georgians were there to get their share of the glory—and death. And while the Confederates were turning the Federals on their left, Jackson was turning them on his right. The failure of the Union troops at Fredericksburg brought Northern spirits about as low as they had been.

The battle, as usual, was nauseating in its bloody messiness. Henry King, Company C, 10th Georgia Battalion, was roaming over the battleground three weeks after it was over and found horses "scattered over the field unburied" and saw dead Yankees half buried, "with their hands and feet sticking out and their caps lying about . . . with brains in them."

SOUTH'S COSTLIEST VICTORY

2 May 1863 was one of the grandest, and at the same time one of the saddest, days during the entire tragic drama of the Civil War. It was Jackson's supreme moment of glory and death; it was Lee's costliest victory. The place was Chancellorsville.

Chancellorsville lay about ten miles west of Fredericksburg, where that previous December, Lee and his lieutenants had won another victory. Since that time Lee had held strong positions below the Rappahannock, but Hooker crossed the river on 27 April with 130,000 men to attack Lee's army, which numbered less than 60,000. Lee divided his forces. Jackson would go through the wilderness and strike Howard on the Union right, while Lee would advance upon the Union center and left.

Jackson's flanking movement was perhaps the greatest in all of military history. Surely, it is the most talked about in Confederate military history. Dr. Hunter McGuire, Jackson's physician described it.

Never can I forget the eagerness and intensity of Jackson on that march
to Hooker's rear. His face was pale, his eyes flashing . . . he leaned over
the neck of his horse as if in that way the march might be hurried. . . .
Every man . . . knew that we were engaged in some great flank movement,
and . . . pressed on at a rapid gait.

On the morning of 3 May, Lee, with mixed emotions, sent a
dispatch to President Davis:

Yesterday Gen. Jackson penetrated to the rear of the enemy and drove
him from all his positions from the Wilderness to within one mile of
Chancellorsville. He was engaged at the same time in front by two of
Longstreet's divisions.

   This morning the battle was renewed. He [the enemy] was dislodged
from all his positions around Chancellorsville, and driven back toward
the Rappahannock, over which he is now retreating. . . . We have again
to thank Almighty God for a great victory. I regret to state that Gen.
Paxton was killed and Gen. Jackson severely and Gen. Heath and A.
P. Hill slightly wounded.

The tragedy of Jackson's fatal wound was even more melancholy news to Lee when he heard how the great tactician had
been struck down by a volley fire, not by the enemy, but by
soldiers of the 18th North Carolina. Beginning about 5:00 P.M.
on the evening before, which was Saturday, Jackson's men, with
a "wild rebel yell," had rushed upon Howard's corps. The Federals fled in dismay along the turnpike toward Chancellorsville,
two miles away. As darkness began to blur the trees of the
tangled forest, Jackson's own men became disorganized, and
their commander ordered a halt.

About midnight Jackson and his staff rode forward to determine whether a body of troops in the distance was friend or foe.
The North Carolina regiment took them for Union officers and
opened fire. Jackson and Maj. Crutchfield were wounded. The
enemy moved in and captured some of the staff, but failed to see
the wounded officers on the ground. Jackson and Crutchfield
were taken to the field hospital at Wilderness Old Tavern. With
Dr. McGuire in charge, the surgeons amputated Jackson's left
arm after removing a ball from his right hand. Lee sent Jackson
a message: "Tell him he has lost his left arm, but I have lost my
right arm."And earlier he had dictated another message: "Could

I have directed events, I should have chosen for the good of the country to be disabled in your stead."

Down in Georgia and throughout the South, people waited anxiously for more cheerful news about the condition of their hero. Said the Savannah *Republican*,

> No man has a deeper hold on the confidence and affections of the Southern people. . . . The death of Jackson would be a serious blow to the cause, and spread mourning throughout the land. With painful apprehensions all will await the result.

Macon citizens were concerned about "Stonewall," but they also searched the *Telegraph* for the list of dead and wounded of the Floyd Rifles and the Macon Volunteers.

As Sunday morning began to wane, Jackson told Dr. McGuire he had a pain in his right side. It proved to be the beginning of pneumonia. Finally, on Sunday the 10th, Gen. Jackson crossed "over the river," where he could "rest under the shade of the trees."

So, Jackson was dead. But he died with the knowledge that he had performed a remarkable feat by routing a superior force, confident that he had faithfully served his God and country to the best of his ability. And that, to Lt. Col. G. F. R. Henderson of the British Staff College, was a best without equal. "No general ever made fewer mistakes," he said. "No general so persistently outwitted his opponents."

WHEN THE TIDE TURNED

As the crow flies, less than fifty miles separate two great battlefields that ran red with blood a hundred years ago, but the battles were separated in time by nearly ten months. The Battle of Antietam was fought just beyond the Potomac in Maryland on 17 Sept. 1862, and the Battle of Gettysburg, in Pennsylvania, ended on 3 July after three days of fighting and heavy losses on both sides. Antietam had been the bloodiest day of the entire war, but blue-clad and gray-clad soldiers killed one another for three days at Gettysburg, and the statistics ran higher.

We have just passed the centennial of Gettysburg, and out west on the Mississippi River, a century ago, the long siege of Vicksburg ended with Pemberton surrendering to Grant. July 4th was the day agreed upon for the convenience of Yankee celebrations. Josephine Habersham, of Savannah, did not know why Union gunboats were celebrating off the Savannah coast, but she had a few reflections of her own concerning that Independence Day. Said she,

The insolent Yankees in our neighborhood are firing their guns in honor of the day! Little do they know or appreciate the precious boon of Liberty left us by our father on that glorious day, 1776! God grant that we Southerners, as a nation, may yet show the world an example of a refined and Christian nation who, having dearly bought this priceless boon, may know how to enjoy and value it!

As has been pointed out previously in this column [see *Telegraph-News*, 23 September 1962], there are those who consider Antietam to have been the turning point of the war, and it well might have been, in a sense. As heretofore mentioned, Antietam gave Lincoln the "victory feel" and a psychological advantage which he used in announcing the Emancipation Proclamation, thus turning the tide of British and French sentiments away from the Confederacy. All of this is true, and if the Confederates could have analyzed the situation correctly, as can now be done with a hundred years' perspective, they might have considered Antietam the turning point. But to tell Johnny Reb that his cause was hopeless in 1862 would be like telling Harriet Beecher Stowe that Uncle Tom didn't live in a cabin. The Confederates were too stubborn even in 1863 to stop fighting for what was then clearly a lost cause. Nevertheless, the real turning point was July 1863, when Meade turned Lee at Gettysburg and Grant cut the Confederacy in two at the Mississippi River by taking Vicksburg.

Many Georgia boys were at Vicksburg and many more at Gettysburg. Josephine Habersham's oldest son, Joe Clay, was with Johnston who was trying to get through to relieve Pemberton, but Sherman was in his way at Jackson. By 8 July Josephine had learned the fate of Vicksburg, but was still muddled about the Battle of Gettysburg. "It seems impossible," she said of Vicksburg's fall, "after the repeated assurances that Pemberton's sustenance would last much longer." But she went on to say, "Against this, we hear that Lee has fought with Meade [Hooker's Army] and beat and captured 40,000 prisoners! Pity they hadn't just happened to chance to get killed instead."

Pvt. John Oliver Andrews, a Butts County boy of the "Jeff Davis Rifles," which was Co. I, 14th Georgia, told of his experiences at Gettysburg in the following manner.

I was wounded the afternoon of the 3rd in Pickett's charge [. I] laid on the battlefield in a wheat field until 11 o'clock that night and was carried by Alex Holsenback to the field hospital. I laid there on the ground with no blanket or anything in the way of cover until one of my company, Yelverton Thaxton, split his blanket open and put half of it over me. A deed of this kind can never be forgotten.

Early the next morning, July 4th, orders came to load all the wounded in ambulances, wagons, etc. and start back to cross the Potomac River into Virginia. I was placed in an ambulance on my back and had to lie there for two days and nights, it requiring that time to get back to Winchester, Va. where we were taken out and placed in a hospital. The good ladies of that city gave every attention possible, but we were there only three days, when we were placed in fruit cars and sent to Richmond, Va. They kept us there in Winder Hospital until September 17th, when I was given a sixty day furlough home. I was sure glad to get back home where my dear Mother was prayerfully waiting my return. It seemed that the next sixty days were the happiest time of my life and the shortest.

AT BLOODY CHICKAMAUGA

The Indian name for Chickamauga Creek is "River of Death," and it was there on 19-20 Sept. that 4,000 soldiers died one hundred years ago. The Indians who gave it this appropriate and ominous appellation had reddened its waters many times with the blood of warriors, but never before had Chickamauga Creek been so bloody or its banks so littered with dead men as it was on that early fall morning after the first day's fighting.

It was a glorious but costly victory for the Confederate general Braxton Bragg, aided by Hill and Longstreet. Gen. William S. Rosecrans was forced to retreat to Chattanooga, leaving the Rebels in possession of north Georgia, but not before Gen. George H. ("Rock of Chickamauga") Thomas had held Snodgrass Hill all during the second day of The Big Battle. Col. Peyton H. Colquitt was wounded and carried to Atlanta to die, and Gen. John B. Hood was also wounded, but lived to fight again.

On 21 Sept., as Rosecrans retreated to Tennessee, destroying his stores and abandoning his dead on the march, a dispatch was sent from the battlefield at 11:00 A.M. which read: "The enemy retreated from our front . . . last night. Our victory is complete. . . . The army is in fine spirits and ready and eager for vigorous pursuit."

The *Macon Telegraph*, which received and published the above mentioned dispatch on the 24th, was a little bit cautious the previous day when the editor said, "Let us not raise the shout of triumph and thanksgiving 'til the struggle is over." The editor thought that if Rosecrans was defeated it would be "the grandest achievement of the war." But he warned, "Let us reserve comments until we are clear of the woods."

Many of the 30,000 wounded soldiers of both armies—about equally divided between the Blue and the Gray—were carried to Atlanta for hospitalization. Some passengers coming to Macon by train from Atlanta reported that the city resembled a battlefield. The Union prisoners, they said, were "far more crestfallen than any which have been heretofore brought through the place."

Appeals for aid appeared in the Macon papers. The ladies of the Relief Society were asked to meet at "The Cutting Room" to prepare "lint and bandages." Their president reflected their optimism when she said, Chickamauga

> has freed the land from a proud, vindicative, and remorseless invader.
> It may be . . . the precursor of independence and peace. It has protected
> our sex from insult and outrage and guaranteed to us the security and
> happiness of our homes.

The sick and wounded overflowed the hospitals in Atlanta, and several hundred of them were sent to other cities. Of those sent to Macon, about 150 were quartered at the City Hall. Citizens were urged to send them food immediately, "in time for breakfast." Mayor O. G. Sparks said, "We will nurse the sick and wounded, but proper food is indispensable."

The full force of the drama enacted on Chickamauga Creek a century ago is vividly portrayed by that masterful story teller, Ambrose Bierce.

> By the banks of that "River of Death" a little six-year-old boy, fright-
> ened by a rabbit on that September morning, suddenly found a crawling
> mass of soldiers, more like animals, crawling toward the stream that
> might quench a parched tongue or bathe a bloody face. With his wooden

sword the boy led that grotesque army of crawling wounded men to the water's edge. Some were carrying others, some were dragging themselves; some had shell-torn faces; and some dragged themselves with one arm, the other simply a bloody mass of flesh in a torn coat sleeve. Some drank from the stream; others fell exhausted into it, never to rise again. The boy crossed on stones over the shallow creek only to see his home in flame on the other side. Stumbling toward the flaming ruins he came upon his mother lying in the grass, a jagged hole in her forehead—"the work of a shell." The little boy made "wild, uncertain gestures." He gave a "series of inarticulate and indescribable cries." He was a deaf mute.

"Storms and Troubles"

The year 1863 closed, as did the year 1963, on a melancholy note. This was true no less of the weather than of politics and war. Editor Joseph Clisby of the *Macon Daily Telegraph* wrote his farewell to 1863 with the rain "pouring down in torrents" outside his window. "The lightning's flash shoots athwart the dark horizon almost every moment," he said, "and peal on peal of heaven's artillery, but for the coolness of the atmosphere, which a feeble fire in the grate is vainly endeavoring to combat or mitigate, would convey the idea of an August storm."

Macon people will long remember the ice, sleet, and snow that marked the transition from 1963 to 1964. But we are told that what appeared to be the "lightning's flash" and "heaven's artillery" were really balls of fire from "hot" wires and broken transformers and the "thunder" of falling trees and heavy limbs breaking off.

The year 1863 was one of "storms and troubles," in editor Clisby's words, and if 1963 had nothing other than the assassination of our president to mar it, this year, too, would go down in history as a tragic and significant one.

The military defeats suffered by the Confederacy were particularly bad for the South. The tide had definitely turned at Gettysburg, and the Confederacy had been split by Grant's capture of Vicksburg, both of which had occurred in July. But war weariness was making its mark on Northerners also. Politically, the year 1863 would bring its troubles and storms to the Union, as the year 1964 will do. The transition today from the old year to the new has much in common with the same time a century ago, with one very obvious difference, for which all thinking Americans are grateful. That is, the nation is united. That was far from true in 1864. Neither the political battles of this election year of 1964 nor the social and economic conflicts within the country will really divide us. And should threats from outside become more dangerous, they would only bind us more closely together.

But signs of national healing were not to be seen in the year that Lincoln stood for reelection. The Confederacy, though all reason protested against it, was stubbornly holding to a vain hope. This attitude can be found in diaries and letters of the period as well as in Southern editorials. With all the setbacks of the previous year, the editor of the Macon paper reflected a note of optimism in his New Year's editorial on 1 Jan. 1864.

> As the heavy pall of clouds disappears before the rising sun, so may the clouds which lower around our fate as a people begin to disperse with the military and political events of the incoming year. Why should they not? Everyone must have observed, during the progress of this mighty struggle, how almost without perceptible reason, and sometimes apparently against the current of military events, the horizon has lighted up and men's hearts become buoyant and hopeful.

The key to hope for a successful new year in the field of battle lay, as the editor thought, in agricultural production from the fields of the farmers. He deplored the heavy conscription policy that put men "too old for soldiers" into the ranks of the armies and took them away from their fields when they were "in the very prime of their experience and capacity as agricultural producers."

> Let the next three months be spent in active preparation of men, munition, and supplies for the spring campaign and believe the attempt of the enemy to penetrate the interior of the South will result in proving to him that it is an enterprise which must be abandoned; and as the experience of the past six months has led us from over confidence to comparative despondency, so that of the next six months shall restore us to a full assurance of ultimate success.

Such confidence was unwarranted, and six months later Sherman was well on his way to Atlanta. Perhaps the editor knew why he was whistling in the dark, as did many a Johnny Reb in the camps and on the battlefield. But the remarkable thing is that the Southern spirit that struggled on against insurmountable odds, with food and supplies dwindling constantly, would not admit defeat. Defeat was a certainty, but the Southern people found it hard to give up a struggle for a way of life that they wanted so badly to keep, not realizing than an even better way of life would someday rise out of the ashes of despair.

SHERMAN IS COMING!

"What momentous days are these in the history of the Confederate States!" Not even editor Joseph Clisby of the *Macon Daily Telegraph* knew just how momentous the days of May 1864 were to be, not only for the Confederacy but for Georgia. By the time the month had run its course, the editor's comment was, as he well knew, an understatement.

An unidentified traveler from Dalton arrived in Macon and was interviewed by the editor of the *Telegraph*. It was the Dalton man's opinion that fighting would begin in the vicinity of Dalton within 48 hours. He said the Union forces were coming on in heavy strength and the Confederate troops were moving forward to meet them.

Sherman was in command of the Union forces which numbered about 100,000 men. He had received instructions from Grant, now the commander of all Federal forces and busy himself with plans to move against Lee in Virginia. Grant's orders to Sherman were to penetrate as far as possible into Georgia. To do this, Sherman used his able generals. James B. McPherson commanded the Army of the Tennessee, George H. ("The Rock of Chickamauga") Thomas led the Army of the Cumberland, and John M. Schofield headed the Army of the Ohio.

Joseph E. Johnston, one of the South's ablest generals, had replaced Braxton Bragg as commander of the Army of Tennessee. (Note: Union armies were named for rivers, Confederate armies for states.) Johnston's arrival revived the drooping spirits of the Georgia, Alabama, Carolina, and Tennessee boys who made up the bulk of the Army of Tennessee. They knew now they had a general who would save his army if at all possible and as long as possible. He had to conserve his strength, for he had only 60,000 to pit against Sherman's superior force—superior only in numbers, not in leadership. Johnston's soldiers would concede to no one greater ability than their commander's.

The *Telegraph* quoted the Atlanta *Reveille* as substantiating the traveler from Dalton. That paper said, "The enemy are concentrating heavily at Ringgold and Cleveland, and are gradually advancing. A battle is expected at an early date. Look out for stirring news."

Editor Clisby concluded that the Federals were contemplating a flank movement by way of Rome because the Dalton man told him the Union forces were massing at Gunter's Landing and Larkin's Ferry. He was not sure whether the enemy was in motion for a fight or feint, but he was sure north Georgia was about to see bloody action soon. And he was right. But because of Johnston's Fabian tactics of parry and thrust, a great major battle costing thousands of lives was averted for the month of May. Nevertheless, a number of small battles, skirmishes, and engagements were to be fought before the big battle of Kennesaw Mountain. Some of these engagements, such as Resaca and New Hope Church, proved Johnston's ability to wear down and harass the enemy. Johnston was able to do this without losing a large number of fighting men. Spring rains helped slow down the enemy, but the Army of Tennessee found the muddy roads as much a handicap as did the Army of the Tennessee.

The confidence that Johnston's men had in their commander is seen in a letter which Willie Habersham wrote to his mother in Savannah. He assured her, "There can be no doubt we shall be victorious." (Quoted in *Ebb Tide*, Athens, University of Georgia Press, 1858.) A whippoorwill's song reminded Willie of his home at White Bluff, but seemed strange in his surroundings where the whistle of bullets through the air was more common than bird calls.

Rendezvous at Dalton

Every available man and officer would be needed if Gen. Johnston was to slow down Union forces under Sherman in north Georgia. Confederate forces were moving toward the Dalton area as rapidly as possible. Soon the Army of Tennessee would reach its maximum strength of 60,000. Evidence of the fact that officers and men were traveling the muddy roads of Georgia in the wet month of May to augment Johnston's forces is seen in the unpublished diary of Capt. George A. Mercer, son of Gen. Hugh W. Mercer. Gen. Mercer's brigade had been assigned to Gen. W. H. T. Walker's division, and George was on his father's staff.

George left Savannah 30 April, at 5:20 P.M. to be exact. He carefully jotted down the time of his departure in the little pocket diary which he carried with him. (This diary was later copied by his wife in a more legible fashion and is now preserved in the Southern Historical Collection at the University of North Carolina.) Traveling with the 54th Georgia, he reached Dalton on 2 May. During the next few days he "fixed up" his quarters.

At this point it would be well to summarize the activity and trace the movement of the Union and Confederate troops. The campaign against Atlanta is dated 1 May through 8 Sept. Though there was not a great deal of open fighting in mass and no engagement worthy of the name battle until 14-15 May at Resaca, there were many skirmishes prior to that time. There was a skirmish at Stone Church on 1 May and a series of minor skirmishes during the first week of that month at Tunnell Hill, Chickamauga Creek, Red Clay, and Varnell's Station.

No one knew exactly where or when the enemy would strike. The pattern of movement was clear to Sherman and his officers only. If Johnston had any notion of the intentions of his adversary he never let his subordinates into his confidence. Willie Habersham, in a letter to his mother, wrote of him, "If his coat knew his plans he would throw it away!" An unidentified brigadier general was doing his best to let the people know, but all he could say, as quoted in the *Macon Telegraph* (4 May 1863), was that he believed the fight would be at Dalton,

> yet this amounts to nothing only as an opinion of a brigade commander who knows but little more than the men he commands. This much I do know: that the troops in the Army of Tennessee were never in a better condition to contend for their homes at the deadly cannon's mouth.

One can follow Gen. Walker's division at the end of that week by reading Capt. Mercer's diary. On Saturday (7 May), the troops were ordered "under arms." Cannon and musketry were heard towards the north. The evening before, George had participated in serenading the ladies at Gen. Walker's headquarters and did not get to bed until midnight. Friday afternoon had been given over to a dress parade of the 16th South Carolina and 46th Georgia at Gen. S. R. Gist's headquarters. There was heavy firing for several hours during Saturday morning, presumably on the Ringgold road.

Orders were received at noon to break camp and march west of Dalton. The brigade, in a state of "considerable excitement," started at 1:30 and "reached rendezvous half an hour before the time fixed." They bivouacked at 5:30 that afternoon, after "a hot, dusty march."

On the way, Gen. Walker had communicated to them the "news of victory in Virginia." George wrote, "The regiments received the news with great enthusiasm." They were all in "fine spirits." That night the troops bivouacked in the woods.

Union troops demonstrated against the Confederates at Rocky Face Ridge from the 8th to the 11th and at Resaca from the 8th to the 13th. Contact between opposing forces was made at Sugar Valley and a demonstration was made on Dalton between the 9th and the 13th. The battle of Resaca occurred on 14-15 May.

The brigadier general quoted above wrote,

> You need not be troubled as to whether Richmond or Atlanta will be attacked. Only continue to impress the people at home with the importance of confidence in our leaders, and urge them to make every preparation in time for the relief of the wounded and disabled.

THE BATTLE OF RESACA

On the opening day of the two-day battle at Resaca (14-15 May 1864), the *Macon Daily Telegraph* carried a description of the terrain above Atlanta and the location of the troops in that area. "Ora," as he identified himself, a special correspondent of the *Montgomery Advertiser*, wrote the piece for his newspaper and it was copied by the Macon paper.

On Johnston's front lay Ringgold and Tunnel Hill. Those places were seven miles northwest of Dalton. On the right, a dirt road ran from Cleveland to the East Tennessee & Georgia Railroad, two miles from Varnell's Station. The enemy was "in force" there and was reported advancing. On the Confederate left lay the Chattanooga, or Rocky Face, Mountains running north and south and enclosing Dalton. Hooker's corps was thought to be in the vicinity between Red Clay and Lee and Gordon's mills. Red Clay was on the East Tennessee & Georgia Railroad, 22 miles east of Chattanooga, and the mills were on the West Chickamauga Creek, on the road to Lafayette.

The Union forces could make a flank movement on Resaca
by advancing from Lee and Gordon's mills. Resaca was situated
16 miles south of Dalton. To flank Johnston by way of Rome,
Sherman would have to send Hooker's corps up the Lafayette
road by way of Summerville, 30 miles north of Rome. That route
was the old line of march attempted by Rosecrans at the Battle
of Chickamauga (19-20 Sept.). But he attempted in vain, as
Bragg drove him back to the Chattanooga. "Ora" closed his description with a petition to Heaven: "God grant that the enemy
may find another 'River of Death' in his advance on Dalton."
But it was not to be.

Johnston had sent Hood, along with Hindman, Cleburne, and
Walker, to Resaca, but when he learned that McPherson had
pulled back, he changed his orders and strengthened his position
at Dalton. Wheeler defeated Stoneman's cavalry at Dalton on
the 12th.

The Battle of Resaca opened on the 14th. Hooker's corps ad-
vanced the next day and was "bravely met" by Hindman's line
and repelled them, according to Confederate historian Joseph T.
Derry. Willie Habersham, writing to his mother, said he thought
Johnston would ultimately succeed in his efforts to wear down
Sherman's forces and make citizens as well as soldiers grow tired
of war. As to the outcome of the Atlanta campaign, Willie said,
"There can be no doubt we shall be victorious."

Following Resaca, there was action at Ley's Ferry on the
Oostanaula River and skirmishes around Rome, Calhoun, and
Floyd's Springs. There was an engagement at Adairsville on the
17th and another thrust at Rome at the same time. There was
some action at Kingston and Cassville on 18-19 May and at
Cartersville on the 20th. Skirmishing continued in and around
all these places for several days.

The month of May closed with fighting around Dallas. The
most significant battle was at New Hope Church (25-28 May).
But here again Johnston proved too clever to let Sherman draw
him out for possible mass destruction by superior forces. The
odds were too great for Johnston to risk a general assault there.
The big battle at the end of the next month would be Kennesaw
Mountain (27 June).

Capt. George Mercer made the following entry in his diary on 23 May: "Monday. At 10 A.M. marched towards Atlanta,very hot and dusty. Thunder shower at noon, reached bivouac after march of about seven miles, at 4 P.M." Six hours to travel seven miles! The rains were getting worse and the roads were becoming more and more difficult to travel. "The mud is actually up to our knees," wrote Willie Habersham to his mother on 5 June. Willie's 54th Georgia regiment moved only three miles during the whole night of 4 June.

THE ATLANTA CAMPAIGN

This column naturally leans heavily on Southern diaries and Confederate accounts of battles and war conditions, but beginning today and continuing in the next installment I shall turn to a Union soldier's reminiscences for a report on the Atlanta Campaign. His name was Mitchell Alexander Chandley. He was a Southerner, from western North Carolina, but he joined up with the Union army, as did so many of the men from the southern Appalachian Mountains region. Tennessee had 56 regiments and other units in the Union army, North Carolina had 8, Alabama had 6, South Carolina had 5, and Georgia had 1.

For the use of Chandley's reminiscences, I am indebted to his great great granddaughter, Mrs. William H. Barbee, whose husband is on the mathematics faculty of Mercer University.

"On the 21st day of July, 1863," the Union soldier began, "I left my father's house, in Madison County, North Carolina, to make my way to the Union armies in the state of Kentucky, having previously enlisted to be a soldier in the army of the

United States." With some difficulty Chandley and others were able to get through the Confederate lines and reached London, Kentucky. On 11 August 1863, he and his companions got to Camp Nelson and were mustered into Company K of the 8th Tennessee Volunteer Infantry of the United States. After two or three days his regiment was ordered back into Tennessee.

During the winter of 1863-1864, while the spring drive into Georgia was being planned, the Union soldier was in Knoxville. His story follows, uninterrupted, just as he told it.

> The next morning the Confederates were all gone and about 10 o'clock Gen. Sherman and his staff rode into Knoxville. I saw them. They sure did look good to us. We knew they were friends—and friends that could and would help us. After the siege was over it did not seem that we did much that winter. We would advance until we would come upon the enemy and then skirmish with it until night and then retreat toward Knoxville. We did not retreat all the way to Knoxville and the enemy did not seem to follow us. We advanced and retreated the same way about all winter. It seemed that neither side was willing to risk an engagement. We had gone up to Bull's Gap, however, when spring came and on the 27th day of April, 1864, we left Bull's Gap for Georgia and went by way of Dalton, Georgia, and joined or became a part of Sherman's army.

> The first skirmish we got into in Georgia was at Buzzard Roost and after we had advanced a good piece we were ordered to retreat, which we did in regular order. That is, No. 1 would retreat about fifteen paces and face the enemy, then No. 2 would retreat the same distance and face the enemy. We retreated alternately this way until we left the enemy entirely. We thought then, or some did, that we were going to do just as we did in East Ten., but we were mistaken. That was the last time we were ordered to retreat in Georgia. It was go forward all of the time after that and we went forward unless repulsed by the enemy and it was a very few times that we were repulsed, but we were repulsed a few times, but we did not retreat far when repulsed.

> From Buzzard Roost we marched to Resaca, where we were in the first general engagement we were in [in] Georgia. There were two or three lines [of] soldiers in front of the line I was in, and when we got to a little ravine we were ordered to halt while the lines in front of us went on. Just at that time a staff officer galloped up and asked if our regiment had been engaged and when informed that it had not been engaged he ordered that it march by the left flank up the ravine. It was but a little way till we got into the woods where the Confederate artillery was dropping the limbs from the trees fearfully. It was but a little ways until we were ordered to front face and just at that time Co. B on the extreme left

became badly exposed and some were shot down and we were about to become demoralized. Just then a staff officer that we called Lieutenant Tracy galloped up, jumped off his horse, and ordered us to line up and seeing our Colonel among the wounded, holloed at him to right oblique and draw them out of that dangerous place.

The staff officer ordered us to take the ridge and we charged to the top of the ridge, when he ordered us to lie down and to kill the last one of the enemy if they came on us. In a few minutes another line of men came up and passed over us and captured the enemy's works in front of us.

THE SIEGE OF ATLANTA

Mitchell Chandley's account of the Atlanta Campai‚ n, which started last Sunday, is concluded here. The narrative continues beyond the Battle of Atlanta, however, and takes Chandley and his regiment back to Tennessee as they pursue Hood's army. Hood had moved out of Atlanta in the hope of making Sherman follow with his entire force. But Sherman sent Thomas after Hood and kept the bulk of his army in Georgia, as is well known. The interesting document from which the account of the Atlanta Campaign is extracted relates Chandley's experiences, even after the war had ended, but I have used it here only to relate the Atlanta Campaign as Chandley tells it. In this passage the Union soldier tells about the long siege of Atlanta and his concern about his health. He suffers from a bad case of mumps at Decatur.

After the Battle of Resaca it was a continuous skirmish every day, if not a general fight, until we reached the vicinity of Atlanta. During one week of the time our regiment guarded the ammunition train of wagons, and was not in the fighting. It seemed to be General Sherman's aim to close up on the front of the enemy without bringing on a general engagement and then fortify all the front and having some more men than the enemy, proceed to flank them out,

On the sixth day of August 1864 we charged the enemy at a place called Utoy Creek and we were badly repulsed. I happened to be on the skirmish line which was greatly to my advantage, I think, but my company did not suffer nearly so bad as others did, but one man of our company was killed on the skirmish line and he fell right by me. There were two of our company killed that were not on the skirmish line and only one wounded and he got well. To show how bad it was, Co. E of our regiment went into the battle with thirteen men, and a lieutenant and five of them were killed and five of them were wounded, some of whom died, and the lieutenant was wounded. Other companies fared nearly as bad.

Along toward the last of the siege of Atlanta we were swung away down to the right to a place called Jonesboro, where an awful battle was fought. We were not in the fight, but immediately after the battle passed over the battle ground. It was an awful slaughter. I saw many arms and legs of men lying about promiscuously as well as dead and wounded men. That night we heard the Confederates blowing up and destroying everything in Atlanta. The Atlanta campaign was over and each side, no doubt, was anxious to take a much needed rest.

Our regiment went to Decatur, Georgia, and stayed there about a month. I had the mumps and was feeling very badly, and answered the sick call. The doctor named Snodgrass looked at me and cursed me and said I had the mumps and that I was excused.

After two or three weeks we were ordered to march and I went to the doctor and told him that I felt quite well but that he had scared me up and I had come to see him about it. He examined me and said for me to go but if I got to feeling bad to let him know at once but I kept on going and did not have to call on him on account of the mumps any more.

I will just remark here that our regiment never did get into the city of Atlanta but we sure did surround it.

We left Decatur and traveled North and we soon had a forced march to get to Allatoona Pass, where the Confederates had sent a force to capture our supplies. We did not get in the fight there but we kept the Confederates from retreating South. There again we saw the awfulness of war. The Confederates left three doctors here after the battle to care for their wounded and Oh! what groaning and taking on of the wounded. It was enough to make us all wish for sense enough to keep out of war. Why haven't civilized people got sense enough to live together in peace?

The Confederates here thought they had sufficient force to crush the Union forces at once which they set in to do and failed. It was surely one of the cruelest conflicts of the war. I saw wheelbarrow after wheelbarrow rolled out loaded with arms and legs of men. There were piles of arms and legs lying all about and in the lot near the hospital there was a hole larger than one ordinary grave nearly full of arms and legs and in one chimney corner I saw a great pile of arms and legs. It looked many times worse to me than to see dead human beings. It has been many years since I saw the horrors of the Battle of Allatoona Pass and I have no desire to ever see such an awful thing again. I would rather never think of it but it was such a scene as to never be forgotten while life lasts.

The primary interest for the next few weeks will be action in the region between Allatoona and Atlanta.

KENNESAW REVISITED

Military operations around Marietta and Kennesaw Mountain crowded the war calendar from 10 June to 2 July, with the general assault on Kennesaw Mountain occurring on 27 June. The battle at Kolb's Farm was fought on 22 June. Hood, who was involved in a bloody fight with Hooker and Schofield, compelled the Union forces to withdraw with a loss estimated at 1,000 men. The next day Sherman observed that the lines were very close together and that the fighting was furious. Willie Habersham got a taste of excitement there. He wrote his mother that he and a companion were within six or eight yards of a nest of Yanks. They fired briskly at the Bluecoats, forcing them to "change their quarters." There was a great deal of artillery fire also. The Northern commander said, "As fast as we gain one position, the enemy has another ready." George Mercer wrote in his diary, "Heavy cannonading between Yankee Batteries and our Batteries on Kennesaw Mountain. Enemy shelling Batteries on our front at 4 P.M." Casualties in his father's brigade up to that time numbered 435. Twenty-nine of those were counted among the dead, some were killed in close hand-to-hand fighting. That afternoon Hood attacked the enemy on the left and drove him from his entrenchments and thus secured the Powder Springs Road. After a quiet morning on the 23rd, George rode to Marietta where he heard "furious cannonading all afternoon."

On the 24th a severe attack was repelled by Hardee's corps. The Second Georgia Battalion sharpshooters held the rifle pits on Walker's front against repeated attempts of the enemy to break it. It was at this time that Sherman decided to try a direct frontal assault on Johnston's line. Perhaps he had been needled into this attack which proved to be so costly. A correspondent at Dalton whose pen name was "Max" had written on 10 May in such a way as to tease the Union general out of his flanking tactics. Did the general read the piece which was quoted in several papers? (See *Macon Telgraph*, 14 May 1864). It is doubtful that Sherman had read it, but the general did show something of a retaliatory mood when he said, "The enemy and our own officers had settled down to a conviction that I would not assault fortified lines. All looked to me to outflank."

Max had this to say.

> Did it ever occur to you that the Yankee General is an ingenious ass? Well, sir, such is the fact. . . . His policy seems to be that of a random, haphazard kind, which hopes the lightning may strike, but has neither purpose nor method. . . . If Sherman really means to fight why doesn't he come on? . . . You must be patient with Sherman. He means well, but is, as I said, an ass . . . He is beating about among the rocks and woods, like the blundering deer stalker and the first thing he knows will stumble into some trap or another of his own making.

And that is just what Sherman did do on the 27th. He allowed three days for preparations. He then ordered McPherson to move forward at Little Kennesaw and Thomas to assault the mountain about a mile farther south. Both Thomas and McPherson failed miserably in their efforts. The 63rd Georgia engaged in hand-to-hand fighting with the 53rd Ohio. The 63rd had been trained to the point of perfection in the use of bayonets and they "made splendid use of their knowledge on this occasion," according to Confederate historian Joseph T. Derry. Derry relates how

One little Irishman encountered a tall, stout Federal soldier, who seized his gun by the barrel. The two had quite a struggle for the prize, when Pat, perceiving that the Federal soldier was about to get the best of him, with the exclamation, "To hell with you and the gun!" gave his opponent a sudden shove which threw him to the ground; and then taking to his heels made his escape. (*Confederate Military History*, 6, Georgia, 319).

This was Sherman's greatest mistake. It cost him 3,000 men. He admitted his error in judgment, but rationalized with philosophic resignation. "It produced good fruits," he said, "as it demonstrated to General Johnston that I would assault and that boldly." But the Union general had learned his lesson, and he resumed his flanking tactics as he ordered McPherson and Schofield to move their lines toward the Chattahoochee. Atlanta lay ahead, a coveted prize.

According to Gen. Johnston, the heaviest attack had been upon Cheatham's division and Cleburne's left. Hardee's corps lost 286 killed, wounded, and missing. The Episcopal bishop, Gen. Leonidas Polk, was killed at Pine Mountain and his command was taken over by Maj. Gen. William Wing Loring. The corps, in addition to losing its beloved fighting bishop, lost 236 killed, wounded, and missing. After the battle, the Confederates carried the bishop's body, along with a number of others, down to Atlanta for a funeral at St. Luke's.

THE BATTLE OF ATLANTA

If we should turn the calendar of time back one hundred years tonight and drop in on Mary Gay at her home in Decatur we would experience the almost unbearable tension that had been building up in that community ever since Sherman's armies had crossed the Chattahoochee River. Wheeler's Cavalry, which had been a source of comfort and strength for the Decatur people, suddenly vanished, and the next morning "Distant roar of cannon and sharp report of musketry spoke in language unmistakable the approach of the enemy, and the rapidity of that approach was becoming alarming." It was the Battle of Peachtree Creek.

Two days later, the Battle of Atlanta would force Hood to settle down to the long hard siege which would extend from the Battle of Ezra Church (28 July) through the Battle of Jonesboro (21 Aug.-1 Sept.).

Telitha, the deaf Negro servant girl in the Gay home, could speak only a few incoherent words. On seeing the Federals riding into Decatur, she came running and mumbled the words "Yank!

Yank!" She ran to get a blue garment to show her mistress the
color of their uniforms. That was the way the arrival of Schofield's men was announced to Mary Gay. "If all the evil spirits
had been loosed from Hades and Satan himself had been turned
loose upon us," the Rebel girl said, "a more terrific, revolting
scene could not have been enacted."

Knowing the fear which their arrival engendered, some of
the soldiers took advantage of the situation and played the role
of monstrous beast for the pure pleasure of frightening the ladies
whom they knew were expecting to be treated in that fashion.
Mary Gay said she was relieved of her fear when she observed
that no "personal violence" was intended. But such antics as was
exhibited by one Yankee soldier must have caused consternation
in the Gay household. Mary and her mother locked the doors
and took their stand with the Negroes in the yard, hoping in
vain that the invaders would not batter their way into the house.
"One of the beasts got down on his all-fours and pawed up the
dust and bellowed like an infuriated bull," she said. He must
have been the "king's fool," she continued, "and was acting in
collusion with the house pillagers sent in advance of the main
army to do their dirty work, and to reduce the people to desti-
tution and dependence."

While the "infuriated bull" was cavorting around in the yard,
"a horde of thieves were rummaging the house, and everything
of value they could get their hands upon they stole—locks and
bolts having proved ineffectual barriers to this nefarious work."
When their work was finished they had "killed every chicken
and other fowl upon the place, except one setting hen." Suffering
a similar fate were "a fine cow and two calves, and twelve hogs."

For some time Mary and her mother, with their two faithful
servants, Telitha and Toby, were afraid to return to the house,
but the officers gave them assurance that they would be safer
indoors than out, and they got up enough courage to return.
Emmeline, a Negro girl whom they had hired out in Decatur,
had been discharged by her employer and had returned, but she
did not prove to be "so faithful as her kith and kin, and was soon
on familiar terms with the bummers." Mary Gay could not find

the words to describe the sight that met her eyes when they reentered the house.

The several acres of land adjacent to the Gay house served as a camp ground for the cavalry. "Soon what appeared to us to be an immense army train of wagons commenced rolling into it," Mary wrote. (The incidents related here are taken from her *Life in Dixie During the War* [Atlanta, 1897].)

> In less than two hours our barn was demolished and converted into tents, which were occupied by privates and noncommisioned officers, and to the balusters of our portico and other portions of the house were tied a number of large ropes, which, the other ends being secured to trees and shrubbery, answered as a railing to which at short intervals apart a number of smaller ropes were tied, and to these were attached horses and mules, which were eating corn and oats out of troughs improvised for the occasion out of bureau, washstand, and wardrobe drawers.
>
> Men in groups were playing cards on tables of every size and shape; and whisky and profanity held high carnival. Thus surrounded we could but be apprehensive of danger; and, to assure ourselves of as much safety as possible, we barricaded the doors and windows, and arranged to sit up all night, that is, my mother and myself.

MACON UNDER FIRE

For more than three years Macon could hear the drums roll in Virginia and out on the Mississippi only by way of the imagination. Then, with Sherman pushing Johnston down the valleys of north Georgia and across the Etowah and Chattahoochee rivers, the citizens of this Middle Georgia city could almost hear the rattle of drum and musket less than 100 miles away. Finally, at the end of July 1864, they could hear the roll of the kettle drums and see fire spitting from the muskets and cannons.

The war came close to the little city on the Ocmulgee every time another company sallied forth to fight in Virginia, Tennessee, Alabama, or wherever, or every time the casualty list appeared in the *Telegraph*, or whenever a train load of prisoners arrived to fill the crowded hospitals. But three times the war—the shooting war with its thunder of cannon, its crack of rifles, its dust and din and its rebel yell—came to the homes of Macon. We call the first time Stoneman's Raid, which took place exactly one hundred years ago, at the end of July 1864. The second time the drums beat loudly and the zing of minnie balls could be heard through the trees was the fight at Griswoldville on 22 November of that same year. The third and last time was when Gen. James H. Wilson with his more than a 1,000 mounted men approached the city in April 1864. The first two times are the ones we prefer to remember, for they were the glorious battles of victory when gallant Confederates kept the enemy east of the river and thus saved Macon from capture and perhaps destruction. The third time is the story of the end, but the telling of it can wait. There were to be several months of stubborn fighting before the final collapse of the Confederacy and the surrender of Macon. The time has now come for the telling of the first assault, Stoneman's Raid.

On 30 July the Macon paper reported that scouts had met the advance of Stoneman's troops, or a detachment of them. They had ridden out of Atlanta, some by way of Griffin and Forsyth, and Stoneman and the remainder by way of McDonough and Milledgeville. The Confederate scouts, under the command of Capt. Samuel S. Dunlap, met an advance guard about five miles beyond Clinton and exchanged shots with them. Stoneman's columns were moving toward Macon from the east, down the Milledgeville road. "The excitement in town is considerable," said the *Telegraph*, "and the people are gathering up their weapons to meet the foe."

Stoneman disregarded Sherman's orders, which were to make a "concentration with Gens. McCook and Garrard near Lovejoy['s]" station. They were to destroy the Central Railroad there and move on to Macon and capture the city. After that they were to move down to Andersonville and release the thousands of Union prisoners. Two important factors unknown to Stoneman were the fact that on the evening of the 29th, Maj. John H. Nisbet arrived in town with 600 Tennesseeans on the way from Andersonville to Atlanta and that Gen. Joseph E. Johnston, the able general who had been removed from command of the Army of Tennessee before the Battle of Atlanta, was in Macon at that moment. Another thing he didn't know was that Gov. Brown, who was also in the city, was able to persuade every able-bodied man and boy of this community who could get a gun to rally in companies under the command of Gen. Howell Cobb in defense of their homes. Col. J. B. Cumming commanded the Macon forces on the Clinton Road; Maj. Edwin Taliaferro's battery was on a hill beyond Ft. Hawkins, and Lt. Col. Findlay's Georgia Reserves were between him and Cumming. On the west side of the river were Capt. B. F. Ross's Volunteers and firemen, convalescents from the hospitals, and the Silver Grays, a company of old men who were stationed on the Vineville road.

John C. Butler, who witnessed the bombardment of Macon, tells how

> All the militia at this place were immediately ordered under arms. Brown, being in the city, issued a proclamation, calling upon every man, citizen or refugee, who had a gun of any kind, or could get one, to report to the courthouse, with the least possible delay, to be formed into companies to aid in the defense of the city.

The Macon paper said "The citizens responded promptly, and by 7 o'clock on Saturday morning (30 July) several thousand of our men were drawn up in line of battle on Walnut Creek." Gen. Johnston had been requested to assume command of all the forces, with Gen. Cobb as his second. By the time Stoneman mounted his big artillery pieces on Dunlap Hill the defenders had made "all the necessary preparations" to meet the foe.

BATTLE OF DUNLAP HILL

Stoneman, who had failed to concentrate his forces at Love-joy's station and destroy the Central railroad tracks above Macon, did send one column to attack "several undefended points" on that road near Macon, "tearing up the track and burning the bridges over Walnut Creek and the Oconee River; destroying cars and locomotives at Gordon and Griswoldville." But of even greater concern to the residents of Macon were the artillery pieces that were sitting on top of the hill at the Dunlap farm. (The location is the present home of the superintendent of the Ocmulgee National Park.)

The Federals tore down Mrs. Dunlap's stables and erected a temporary entrenchment across the yard. Officers who occupied the Dunlap house directed the attack on Macon from that point. The Confederates had erected earthworks to the rear of the house (they have been preserved) to protect Macon from troops advancing from the direction of Clinton and Milledgeville, but were unable to hold the hill. The Federal battery opened fire and, according to the *Macon Telegraph*, several homes and buildings were struck by shells which were hurled across the Ocmulgee River.

One of the houses which were struck was the home of Judge Asa Holt on Mulberry Street. This house, now known as the Cannonball House, is preserved by the Lanier Chapter of the United Daughters of the Confederacy. It is open to the public, and the ladies who act as hostesses will tell you how the ball struck the sand sidewalk, glanced up and through an upper corner of the front parlor into the hall, and landed on the floor of the hallway.

The Macon defenders answered the fire of the artillery from Dunlap's Hill with the fire of their own cannon, directed by Maj. Taliaferro. The Macon paper stated, "As soon as our artillery opened, our shells commenced falling around the house, and one passed through the building, compelling the inmates to leave." The Yankees retreated "precipitately" to the creek. As they left, however, they "took away all of the Negroes" belonging to Mrs. Dunlap.

Butler, the Macon historian (*History of Macon and Central Georgia*, Macon, 1879), describes how Stoneman and his men retreated from Macon on the evening of 30 July and were met by a portion of Wheeler's cavalry at Sunshine Church, near Clinton, on 1 Aug. Gen. Alfred Iverson was in command of the Confederate cavalry which engaged the Federals and, "after a short battle," captured Stoneman and 500 of his troops.

On 2 Aug. the *Macon Telegraph* carried the "Glorious News" of the surrender of Stoneman. The paper announced,

> At noon yesterday a courier arrived in Macon with the following dispatch: "Our scouts from the battlefield, eight miles beyond Clinton, report Stoneman and his entire force captured, and he will be in Macon this evening or tomorrow morning."

The claim that the "entire force" had been captured was, of course, an error. As Butler says, "The main body of the enemy was not in the battle at Sunshine and succeeded in making their escape."

On Wednesday morning, 3 Aug., the *Telegraph* announced
that Stoneman, the "Yankee celebrity," had arrived "here on
Monday evening, accompanied by his staff and escorted by a
guard of Confederate cavalry." He was confined at Camp Oglethorpe, "where he will be able to reflect, for a few days, on the
vicissitudes of fortune, and to regret that he was mad enough
to go so far from home."

The editor had great praise for Gen. Iverson who made the
capture. The 500 prisoners were also brought into the city the
next morning. Gen. Johnston praised Gen. Cobb and especially
commended the men and boys of Macon who defended their city
so successfully. He said,

> With them, and as many of the workshops and volunteers of the town
> as he could find arms for, in all fifteen or eighteen hundred, General
> Cobb met the Federals on the high ground east of the Ocmulgee, and
> repulsed them after a contest of several hours, by his own courage and
> judicious disposition, and the excellent conduct of his troops, who heard
> hostile shot for the first time.

Grateful Macon citizens were planning a tribute dinner for Gen.
Iverson, but his command was ordered away before it could be
held.

FIGHT AT GRISWOLDVILLE

This column took a long vacation after it last appeared on 2 Aug. of this year. We now resume and will run a short time— go into winter quarters, you might say—then conclude the series in the spring. It has been a long while since we began way back in December 1960, and many significant days are marked on both the nineteenth and twentieth century calendars. But the end of the series is in sight. We shall watch the war drag wearily on to Appomattox and see it terminate right here in our own city with the ex-president of the Confederacy a prisoner of the Federals at the Lanier Hotel.

Much has happened since August on our hundred-year-old calendar. By September Sherman had taken possession of Atlanta and made it a military post, driving the citizens out of their homes. Some chose to go south as Sherman permitted them to do, but some chose to go north under the protection of the Union. All had to leave the city. Sherman's capture of Atlanta six weeks after his victory over Hood in July was of great value to Lincoln and the Republican party, which needed a military victory before the presidential election of 1864 in order to keep McClellan and the Peace Democrats from winning on a stop-the-war platform.

The middle of the month of November on our 1864 calendar saw the departure of Sherman from the smoking ruins of Atlanta, and in a month's time his right wing under Howard and his left under Slocum converged near Savannah. These two wings were comprised of four corps of infantry numbering 60,000 plus Kilpatrick's cavalry numbering 5,500. Hardee, a Savannah native, was in general command of the Chattahoochee, but in more direct contact with Howard's right were G. W. Smith and Alfred Iverson who were covering the Federal advance at Lovejoy. Sherman himself left Atlanta with Jeff C. Davis's corps on 16 Nov. and moved directly through Covington and Milledgeville. Cobb at Macon had a very small force, but units of Wheeler's and Smith's commands joined him on the 19th.

The city, and, indeed, the whole of Middle Georgia, was in a state of anxiety. Nevertheless the people had a determination to withstand if possible and, if not, to endure whatever fate was in store for them. "This is no time for weak and timid men," the *Macon Telegraph* editor thought. "He who thinks of fleeing at the approach of his adversary is unworthy of the name of man," he wrote. Gov. Brown issued a statement at Milledgeville saying, "Death is to be preferred to loss of liberty. All must rally to the field for the present emergency."

Hardee took personal command at Macon and sent Wheeler to Clinton where his escort was able to repulse a Federal cavalry command. On the 22nd, Howard, as he approached Gordon, sent one division and Kilpatrick's cavalry toward Macon for a second demonstration against the city. Wheeler's men captured a Federal picket post which cost the enemy about 60 men. A vigorous cavalry fight followed at Griswoldville. Walcutt's Federal brigade held its ground in spite of the fact that Walcutt himself was wounded. But the affair at Griswoldville, like Stoneman's Raid earlier, was celebrated by the Macon people as a victorious effort to repulse the invader. Macon, then, was spared and the Union army, after some fun and frolic at Milledgeville, where they held a mock session of the state legislature, foraged its way to Savannah.

The Macon paper was well pleased with the outcome of the battle at Griswoldville. One could hardly call it a clear-cut victory—Confederate victories were beginning to be very scarce—but there was a feeling of confidence that the defenders of Macon had shown courage and had won some honors. Editor Clisby, of the *Telegraph*, said, "The result was highly creditable to our troops." He was also pleased at the behavior and spirit of the citizens. He said, "The city is remarkably quiet and the people cool and confident."

This was the last unsuccessful attempt of the Federal forces to capture Macon—though they would probably deny that it was a serious attempt. The next thrust at our city resulted in its capture in April 1865. The spirit of Macon in November 1864, as Sherman's troops moved away toward Savannah, is seen in the following comment from the *Macon Telegraph*.

> We think . . . that the Yankees are satisfied with their experience of that portion of our forces they encountered at Griswoldville, and have become satisfied that the road to Macon is indeed "hard to travel."

YANKEES AT COVINGTON

Sherman's left wing, which numbered 27,000 troops, was composed of A. S. Williams's XX Corps, which went through Social Circle and Madison, and J. C. Davis's XIV Corps. These two corps of the left wing, commanded by Slocum, converged at Milledgeville.

The best account by a citizen of the arrival of the Federals at Covington is the well-known journal of Dolly Lunt Burge of that town. The portion of her journal covering the Yankee invasion was edited by Julian Street in 1927, and the full journal has recently been edited by James I. Robinson, Jr.

Mrs. Burge lived a lonely life on her dead husband's plantation with her little twelve-year-old daughter, whom she called Sadai. Another daughter, Lou, had died at nineteen years of age. Lou was a student at Wesleyan when the war started. Her diary gives us a good insight into the mood of the Wesleyan girls when the Macon boys marched off to war—"The girls are almost all crying!" But Lou did not live to welcome the returning soldiers.

Dolly Burge's burdens grew heavier and her troubles began to increase when on 16 Nov. she learned that "the Yankees were coming!" She was returning from shopping in Social Circle when she met a man who told her that "a large force was at Stockbridge" and that the Covington Home Guard had been alerted.

Dolly admitted to her diary on the 18th that she "slept very little last night." When she arose she could see in the distance "large fires like burning buildings," but she knew she was "in the hands of a merciful God who has promised to take care of the widow and the orphan." She sent two of her mules off in the night with neighbors to be hidden in the woods, and she buried a barrel of salt for which she had paid $200. That night she slept in her clothes, having heard that the Yankees had searched a neighbor's house, "drank his wine, [and] took his money."

The XIV corps encamped just east of Covington that night and the next day Sherman and the men of Davis's corps filed by all day long.

All day, as its sad moments rolled on were they passing, not only in front of my house, but they came up behind, tore down my garden palings, made a road through my back yard and lot field, driving their stock and riding through, tearing down my fences and desolating my home. . . .

As the Federals came "filing up," Dolly hastened back to her frightened servants and told them

they had better hide and then went back to the gate to claim protection and a guard. But like Demons they rush in! My yards are full. To my smoke-house, my Dairy, Pantry, Kitchen and Cellar, like famished wolves they come, breaking locks and whatever is in their way. The thousand pounds of meat in my smoke-house is gone in a twinkling, my flour, my meat, my lard, butter, eggs, pickles of various kinds, both in vinegar and brine, wine, jars and jugs, are all gone. My eighteen fat turkeys, my hens, chickens, and fowls, my young pigs, are shot down in my yard and hunted as if they were the rebels themselves. Utterly powerless I come to appeal to the guard.

But the guard could not help her—"it is the orders."

After the army had passed on, Mrs. Burge recorded her relief in her diary. "I feel so thankful," she wrote, "that I have not been burned out." The day was Sunday, and Mrs. Burge and

Sadai went to a neighbor's house where they ate "dinner out of the oven . . . some stew, no bread."

RUDE YANKEE CONDUCT

While Sherman was moving toward Milledgeville, the state capital, via Covington and Eatonton, some of Howard's men who were in Sherman's right wing were passing through Butts County on their way toward Macon. They shifted direction east of the Central of Georgia Railroad so that they passed through Jackson rather than Griffin. Nevertheless, citizens of Spalding County and all along the Central's tracks south of Lovejoy were in a state of alarm. Some fled to Macon and on beyond to southwest Georgia, some went east only to run into Yankees, and others stayed stoically at home to take whatever fate had in store for them.

Among those who fled eastward, and into trouble, was Emma Manley who lived near Griffin. She was a young woman "just out of college," and her parents fearing for her safety sent her to Mrs. Asa Buttrill's, her sister's home at Sylvan Grove near Jackson, to get her out of the path of the Federals. This made it possible for her to be with her niece and college mate, Mary

Buttrill. But there her luck ended, for no sooner had she arrived than her sister decided that the girls must refuge to Macon. Emma's brother, Manson, was stationed in Macon, and he and some other scouts had been sent up to see how Sherman's army was advancing. The scouts spent the night of 16 Nov. at Sylvan Grove.

The next morning they started out at daybreak. Two large wagons loaded with food, valuables, and comforts for the refugees had already gone ahead of them. Ben Drake, a wounded soldier, drove the girls, Emma and Mary, in a "handsome phaeton." They drove rapidly to the Ocmulgee River which they crossed into Jasper County at Roach's Ferry. When they reached Stephen Johnson's home about a mile from the river they stopped at his well. Suddenly they saw a "blue cloud of Yankee Soldiers coming over the hill." Emma's brother Manson and her nephew, Taylor Buttrill, mounted their horses, and Ben Drake jumped into the phaeton and the boys all dashed off "at a great speed for Macon."

Quickly a "hundred or more Blue Coats on fast horses came up" and found Emma and Mary and their maids at the well. Here is the way Emma remembered it as she described it to her friends in Griffin in 1921.

> The Yankee soldiers yelled out, "Where are those damn Rebs that were with you?"
> We said, "Gone." Manda, one of the maids, ran up the left road screaming, "Come back Marse Taylor and give up. These Yankees will kill you."
> She mislead them; they ran for miles and came back cursing furiously for our boys had taken the right hand road to Macon.

The Union soldiers took the girls to Gen. George E. Spencer's tent. The general then took them to a small log cabin farm house, the home of a Mrs. Fear. He told Mrs. Fear to take them in "or I'll burn your house damn quick."

He then put a guard around the house and, according to Emma, personally attended to the girls' needs. She said he brought nice meals to them and their maids three times each day. But occasionally an "impudent Yank" would come into the house. "One took my hands," she said, "and looked at my rings." And another time, "One rough man came in and asked to the old lady sitting in the corner of the cabin, 'You look damn happy setting on that stool smoking your pipe.' 'Yes,' said the old lady. 'We Southland people are like a goose. Pick us as clean as you please, but we will feather out next spring.' "

Gen. Spencer stayed with the girls at the cabin for three hours after the army had passed. He then left them food and gave them a horse to get them home. Emma had letters from him after the war had ended. In Mary's opinion, the general "was smitten."

When they got back to Emma's sister's home they found the house standing, but the "palings, fences, gin-house, cotton, cows, chickens, horses and mules were all gone." Everything in the house except her sister's bedroom furniture was destroyed. They sat up by the open fire each night for a week, having no bedding to keep them warm. They lived on parched corn and roasted potatoes, and had no dishes or cooking vessels.

Gen. Blair and his staff occupied Mrs. Buttrill's parlor for a little while. Emma gave an indication of his character when she said Gen. Blair would kick out a window pane when he wanted to shout an order to a soldier outside. Further indication of rude Yankee conduct is seen in Emma's testimony when she said,

> One windy morning during the Yank's stay my sister looked out her window and said " 'twas snowing." She said the "faithful colored woman" sitting nearby replied, "No, Missus, these men are ripping open your feather beds and pillows to see the feathers fly."

Emma concluded by saying,

> Six months after the war Ben Drake drove up to Sylvan Grove with the carriage and horses. Had I remained at my own home in Spalding County, I would not have seen a single Yankee.

YANKEES AT TURNWOLD

"Turnwold" was the name of Joseph Addison Turner's plantation near Eatonton. Turner was a man with varied interests. First, of course, he was a planter. But he, like many other planters, tried to make his plantation self-sufficient. He even manufactured hats. His hats were in such demand that he did a retail business. However, he would not condescend to peddle them in Eatonton, but advertised in his own private paper, *The Countryman*, that anyone wanting a hat must come and get it. His paper, which provided an apprenticeship for a young man named Joel Chandler Harris, was the only plantation newspaper in existence.

In the 6 Dec. issue of *The Countryman* for the year 1864, Turner tells of the coming of the Yankees to his place. His first encounter with Sherman's soldiers was when two "bummers" came one night, a little after midnight, posing as Confederates. "They soon agreed their object to be whiskey." Turner's neighbor, Bradley Slaughter, had sent them to his house, but he

got a bottle of whiskey, and, after our two guests drank, they begged
us so hard to let them have some, that we poured out about two-thirds
of the whiskey (mean sorghum) into a canteen of one of them. They both
left, thanking us, and insisting on paying us. But we told them no, and
they thanked us again, and said they were going to cross the river, and
report to the nearest commandant of a military post. Next morning,
their horses' tracks were followed, and it appeared that they returned
towards the Yankee camp at Park's Bridge.

Sam Reid, a neighbor, went off with his own mules and slaves
on Sunday, 20 Nov., to hide them in the swamp. Turner sent his
also. After lunch four or five Yankees came, "professing they
would behave as gentlemen." But Turner observed that "These
gentlemen, however, stole my gold watch, and silver spoons,
besides whiskey, tobacco, and a hat or two, apiece." About the
middle of the afternoon four more came and "got a few hats, and
one fiddle, and some whiskey. About night, two dutchmen came,
and got some whiskey, a few hats," and other things.

The Yankees camped at Denham, about three miles from
Turnwold, on Sunday night. The next morning they burned the
tannery. Twenty or more came and got mules, horses, and two
slave boys, Jack and Tom. Firing was heard in the direction of
Milledgeville that night. It was Slocum's XX Corps at Denham.
They had passed as though going to Sparta, but turned in the
direction of Milledgeville.

On Thursday, 24 Nov., Turner rode over to see neighbor
Aleck Eakin. He drove "old Dinah" hitched to his buggy, "using
plough gear for harness." Dinah was so poor and "no account"
that "the Yankees would not have her." After dinner he rode to
Denham. "What a wreck I found—smoking ruins, and private
papers scattered all over." He called at his mother's and found
that the "Yankees did not get to her house at all."

He thought he heard the "din of battle" and the flashing of
guns on Friday morning (25 Nov.) about 3 o'clock. It turned out
to be the burning of Mrs. Johnson's gin house, and what he
thought was the flashing of guns was "the flames of that
burning." But he did hear artillery in the distance.

Turner's journal, as published in *The Countryman*, for the three days from 26 Nov. through 28 Nov. is quoted here without editing.

Sat. 26th—Various Negroes, who went off with the yankees, are returning. None of mine have done so. These negroes report that Macon was captured by the yankees, on tuesday, and that the firing heard here, on friday morning, was a salute to Sherman, who then arrived in Milledgeville. They report Milledgeville uninjured, and the yankees going directly to Augusta. Negroes report J. M. Bonner, and J. A. Davis killed— B. F. Adams wounded in the hand, and one of his sons wounded. Their tale is an improbable one.

Sun. 27th—The tales the negroes told yesterday, ascertained to be untrue. The yankees did not go to Macon at all, but are fleeing towards the coast—Wheeler on their right flank, Hampton on their left, and our forces gathering in front. Gen. Bragg has arrived in Augusta with 10,000 or 15,000 troops. Got the Constitutionalist, *of 25th, and* Chronicle & Sentinel, *of 24th. The latter patriotic as ever—the former filled up with fault-finding of the confederate administration.*

Mon. 28th—On last tuesday, there was a battle fought at Griswoldville. Mr. Prudden, in a note of today, gives me the following items:

"Killed—Dr. J. A. Davis, A. S. Moseley, Paul Wheeler, and J. M. Bonner.

"Wounded—C. Caswell, mortally; J. Middleton, severe, in arm; Ralph Jones, slight, in foot; A. Martin, side; W. Hawkins, severe, in hip; H. Baldwin, neck; J. Bowdoin, slight, in foot; W. A. Gatewood, severe, in leg, near the thigh.

"About eighty were killed, and some four hundred wounded, in the militia.

"The yankees crossed at Milledgeville, and, when last heard from, were in the neighborhood of Sandersville.

"Macon was not attacked.

"The state troops have started for Savannah, via Albany, and Thomasville.

Respectfully,
S. G. Prudden"

FALL OF MILLEDGEVILLE

As the last months of 1864 were fading the weather grew ever colder, as though foretelling the death of the year. November of that year is said to have been one of the coldest on record. That may partially explain the fact that Sherman's men burned so much property, even church pews. They tried in every way possible to keep themselves warm, finding very little warmth in the hospitality of the Georgia people. Even Gov. Brown, in evacuating Milledgeville, was so thoughtless as to forget to leave Sherman any bed clothes, or even a bed for that matter, as he left the state capital along with the legislators who fled from the approaching enemy. Sherman, who occasionally occupied the governor's mansion, had to improvise a bed and eat on a table made of planks laid across camp chairs because the governor had removed the furniture.

The reference to destruction of property should not be taken to imply that Sherman deliberately burned private homes as a part of his total war in Georgia. According to J. C. Bonner, a well-known Georgia historian whose home is in Milledgeville, the burning of residences was a rare exception. Bonner does tell how the general, on finding himself quartered on one of Howell Cobb's plantations, ordered its "complete destruction." But he says there were only two residences destroyed on the approach to Milledgeville and only two in the city itself. The planned destruction by fire was that of public buildings and equipment that might be used against the Union forces if left intact.

Sherman did not have to fight his way into Milledgeville. Actually, there was only one fatality. One of the two plantation homes burned as the Federals approached Milledgeville was that of William A. Jarrett. The other was the property of Judge Iverson L. Harris. Patrick Kane, Jarrett's caretaker, was so zealous in his defense of the place that he was shot and killed, and the property he tried to defend was burned.

According to Bonner, the most dramatic incident in Middle Georgia was Rufus Kelly's one-man stand against Sherman's right wing at Gordon. That wing was commanded by Gen. Oliver O. Howard. Gen. Wayne had ordered his battalion of 600 to avoid contact with Howard's 30,000 troops. Kelly, who had already lost a leg in reckless fighting in Virginia, stood alone against the whole right wing and caused so much consternation that Howard was delayed for awhile at Gordon.

But it was Sherman's left wing, under the command of Gen. Henry W. Slocum, that was "headed directly for the state's capital." Bonner says the first to arrive in Milledgeville were some of Hugh Judson Kilpatrick's cavalry corps, numbering 5,000 horsemen. Young Kilpatrick—he was only 26 years of age—was, in Sherman's eyes, "a hell of a damned fool." But that was the kind of men he said he wanted to do the job he had in mind. A total of 30,000 Federal troops were the unwelcomed visitors that began to arrive at Georgia's capital city on 20 Nov. Nor were the 30,000 troops all. Sherman had to move, in addition, a "wagon train of seven hundred vehicles, 30 artillery pieces, 12 thousand horses and mules, and approximately 5,000 head of cattle."

The main body of troops arrived in the city on 23 Nov. It was then that "some of the younger officers" engaged in a bit of horseplay by staging a mock session of the legislature during their stay in Milledgeville. Bonner says they were "apparently from the 3rd Wisconsin and the 107th New York regiments."

The "burlesque performance" turned into wholesale bedlam when the Yankees, playing the role of Georgia legislators, fled at the approach of Union troops. The Union officers were a little confused in their history as they combined the secession convention with a session of the legislature, but they had the maximum of fun from the experience. They also debated a motion to repeal the Ordinance of Secession. The motion passed, of course.

The red-headed general enjoyed the report of the mock legislative session when it was brought to his attention. After the war was over the incident had impressed itself so strongly upon his mind that the told about it in his memoirs. Here is the way he told the story.

> Some of the officers (in the spirit of mischief) gathered together in the vacant hall of Representatives, elected a Speaker, and constituted themselves the Legislature of the State of Georgia! A proposition was made to repeal the ordinance of secession, which was well debated, and resulted in its repeal by a fair vote! I was not present at these frolics, but heard of them at the time, and enjoyed the joke.

The "joke" became more serious when soldiers ransacked the entire building, including the state library. The books were thrown out the windows and an eyewitness stated that he saw a "cavalryman . . . walk his horse back and forth over the books to trample them in the mud."

SHERMAN IN SAVANNAH

This is the saddest Christmas that I have ever spent and my only pleasure during the day has been in looking forward to spending my next Christmas in the Confederacy.

This was the way Fanny Cohen, a young Jewish girl in Savannah, began her daily entry in her diary on 25 Dec. 1864. Fanny was the 24-year-old daughter of Octavus Cohen, a well-to-do Savannah commission merchant and cotton exporter. She and all her friends of the young set in that port town were downcast and uneasy that Christmas because Sherman with his more than 60,000 Yankees arrived at their seacoast destination in time for the general to give the city to President Lincoln as a Christmas present. The long month's march had ended with the Federal corps of the left and right wings at Pooler, on the outskirts of Savannah, by the middle of December. Then, after the fall of Ft. McAllister, which made it possible for Union boats to supply his army, Sherman accepted the surrender of the city from Maj.

Richard D. Arnold with the promise that he would not destroy
it.

Gen. Hazen, who had led the Federals in the capture of Ft.
McAllister, shared the Octavus Cohen home during his stay in
Savannah. Hazen himself did not disturb Fanny's thoughts, but
with stories of the wild and reckless young Gen. Kilpatrick cir-
culating around town, Fanny and her friends had cause to be
worried.

Gen. Hazen had been a personal friend of the Cohens before
the war and a guest in their home in happier days. But when
Fanny had to receive a Union officer in her parlor alone one day
she was considerably relieved when he finally took his leave.
She had not offered him a seat and after standing for some
moments "he remarked that he should call again as he wished
to become personally acquainted by my father." "I gave him no
answer," she said, "but opened the front door for him and he
walked out like a well-bred dog." She hoped, "from the bottom
of my heart," that he had paid his last visit.

The fears of the citizens were unfounded. Sherman, who
found the atmosphere in Savannah entirely different from that
of Atlanta, was in no mood to destroy the lovely city of colonial
culture, and he kept his promise to Maj. Arnold. Writing to Grant
at the end of the month, he said,

> The people here seem to be well content, as they have reason to be, for
> our troops have behaved magnificently; you would think it Sunday, so
> quiet is everything in the city day and night.

Something of the spirit of Christmas must have gotten into
the general who had made a month of hell for Georgia. He softened his harsh words, which threatened to deny the destitute
people of food, with kind deeds by ordering that captured provisions be returned to the people, and he arranged for captured
rice to be sold in Northern markets to provide money to purchase
food for them.

Fanny began her diary on 21 Dec., the day Sherman's troops
entered the city, and stopped writing it on 3 Jan. 1865. It ends
abruptly. The Federals remained in Savannah about two more
weeks before beginning their march through the Carolinas. Why

Fanny stopped so suddenly no one knows. In editing her journal for the *Georgia Historical Quarterly* (December 1957), I speculated on the reasons.

Were the precious sheets of paper used up? Was she too busy darning her stockings, mending her dresses, and putting her hands to unaccustomed house work? Whatever the reason, it is evident that she found herself in a different world now.

The remainder of her entry for 25 Dec. follows:

This morning my uncle Mr. Myers and his daughter Mrs. Yates Levy came to see us and told us of a party given the evening before by the Negroes at Gen. Geary's Hd. Qrts. where the Gen. went into the kitchen and desired an introduction to the ladies and gentlemen there assembled. After the introduction he asked who were slaves and who were free. There was but one slave present and a servant girl of my Aunt's who acknowledged the fact. This elegant gentleman enquired into her private history and finding that she was a married woman begged an introduction to her husband Mr. Valentine. He then presented Mr. Valentine, as a Christmas gift, with a free wife. The girl was so much amused having always been a favorite servant and treated like one of the family that she told it to her mistress as a good joke. In the afternoon we had a rebel meeting. Dr. R. [deliberately blotted out], Fanny Levy, Dr. B. [deliberately blotted out] and our own family forming the party. We abused the Yankees to our hearts' content and congratulated ourselves upon once more being together. Dr. R. told me of a news paper that had been issued, called "The Loyal Georgian" with this Motto "Redeemed, regenerated and disenthralled—the Union must and shall be preserved." This of course created great merriment, the first time I had a hearty laugh since the Goths had been among us. Dr. B—spent the evening with us. We are beginning to improve in spirits; we did not retire until 10 o'clock.

FIGHTING IN ALABAMA

The early signs of spring in the Deep South in 1865 may have stirred the fighting blood of the Yankee soldiers, but it must have caused the Confederates to have a deep longing for peace, to wish for an end to the long marches and fierce battles, the weariness, exhaustion, and actual hunger. Johnny Reb would have much preferred to go home and break ground for spring planting. It is true he was willing to sign a resolution pledging his regiment "to battle to the end . . . to not lay down our arms until independence is secured," but his heart was not really in it.

The old Rebel defiance would express itself occasionally in such resolutions, and the boys in gray would quote Patrick Henry's famous words, "Is life so dear, or peace so sweet as to be purchased at the price of chains and slavery? Forbid it, Almighty God!" Nevertheless, the stubborn courage was ebbing away as food, equipment, clothing, and ammunition diminished.

Lee was being encircled by Grant's forces around Petersburg and Richmond. Joe Johnston, who had been put back in command of what was left of his old army, was being pursued through the Carolinas by Sherman. Hood was being hounded by Thomas in Tennessee after having been whipped by him at Nashville the previous December. Taylor was being hard pressed by Canby around the mouth of the Alabama River, near Mobile. And Nathan Bedford Forrest was playing hide-and-seek with Gen. James Wilson farther up the river in the vicinity of Selma.

Soon Wilson would begin his famous raid from Selma, Alabama, to Macon, the last major campaign of the war. By the time it was completed on 20 April, Lee would have already surrendered his Army of Northern Virginia at Appomattox and Joe Johnston would be within six days of surrender at Durham, North Carolina. But before Wilson could begin what became the longest cavalry raid of the war at Selma, he had to capture that city. Forrest knew the value of Selma to the Confederacy. It was the Pittsburgh of the South, the major ordnance center of the Confederacy. Without the production of the foundries there, the Rebel armies would be helpless. So, a race for Selma began between Forrest and Wilson. It began on 22 March, when Wilson's cavalry corps of the Military Division of the Mississippi, numbering 12,500, left the Tennessee River at Chickasaw, Alabama.

Twenty miles from Selma, at Pleasantville, in what is recorded as the Battle of Ebenezer Church, Forrest personally encountered the mounted saber battalion of Col. Frank White's 17th Indiana. Gen. Emory Upton, young, efficient, with a fresh wound in his leg, was in command of the 4th Division which included the 17th Indiana. Wilson recalled in his memoirs how Upton "turned Forrest's rules of war against him by getting there first with the most." This left That Devil Forrest no alternative but to "curse and fight," and he did that with "characteristic energy."

One of Col. White's young officers, a Capt. Taylor, matched the bold Forrest with equal daring in close combat. Their horses were flank-to-flank. The boy captain inflicted a saber wound upon Forrest, nipping him in the arm before the general could get his horse free to turn for a pistol shot. The boy fell dead from his saddle. Gen. Forrest, in telling about it a few days later, his arm still in a sling, said, "If that boy had known enough to give me the point of his saber instead of the edge, I should not have been here to tell you about it."

E. N. Gilpin, 3rd Iowa Cavalry, a clerk at Gen. Upton's headquarters during the Alabama and Georgia campaign, recorded in his diary how the men of the 4th Division were captivated by the youthful but skillful commander. Upton was only 36. Gilpin said,

> When the fighting was hottest, he was right there by their side, and they know he is a brave man and a skillful general. Their hearts are with him. He came here a boy—and he has whipped Forrest and they all want to yell when they see him riding down the line.

Gilpin, whose diary will help us follow Gen. Wilson on his campaign from Selma to Macon, was "so full of the day's excitement" that he "could not sleep." In the next room he heard Gen. Upton tossing in his bed. He, too, was having difficulty getting to sleep. In his dreams, the general "was fighting the battle over again."

THE BATTLE OF SELMA

On Sunday, 16 April 1865, George A. Mercer, son of Gen. Hugh W. Mercer, wrote in his diary: "We are now passing through a period of deep depression. Our vindictive enemies seem successful on every hand, and God appears to smile upon their cause."

The discouragement of George Mercer was shared now by all Confederates everywhere, soldiers and civilians alike. Johnny Reb wanted nothing more than to put his tired legs under his mother's dining table again. The table, likely, would not be loaded with a great variety of delicious food, but it would seem great to a boy whose day's ration was a handful of corn.

George Mercer had heard that Lee had abandoned Richmond, but did not know he had surrendered. He wrote,

> *Genl Lee is now in a very critical position. Johnston is confronted by Sherman's large and victorious army. The enemy is penetrating every part of our land with their raiding parties, burning and destroying.*

One of these raiding parties was Wilson's Cavalry Corps which had already captured Selma and Montgomery by this time.

Selma, an Alabama city upon which civil rights has recently focused attention, was the goal of both Confederate general Nathan Bedford Forrest and of Union general James Harrison Wilson, as was mentioned in this column last Sunday. The importance of that manufacturing city was also pointed out. Forrest got to Selma "fustest"—but not with the "mostest"—and dug in, expecting an attack momentarily. The odds against him were two to one.

The day was Sunday, 2 April. Gen. Wilson was determined to make the attack under cover of darkness. He announced his plan to his officers. Upton was to take his 4th Division in on the left hand road, and Long, with the 2nd Division, was to take the right. Upton, with 300 picked men, was to cross Bench Creek Swamp to assault Forrest's works at the weakest point. The signal for the assault was to have been "a single shot from Rodney's guns," but an unexpected movement in Long's rear caused the officers to move quickly without further orders from Wilson.

Gen. Wilson records in his memoirs how, at 5:00 A.M. , Long pushed the dismounted troops forward "straight at the rebel works" 600 yards away. The men soon reached the glacis in the face of "a galling fire of musketry" from Armstrong's brigade at the parapets. With Minty, Vail, and Kitchell leading, the men "clambered over each other's shoulders like boys playing leapfrog." They were met by brave Rebels in a "sharp hand-to-hand fight," but the spirit of the Union soldiers was "irrestible and soon gave them a complete victory."

Upton, having heard the noise of battle on his right, made his way across the swamp, "carrying the works in his front with little loss." Long had not been so fortunate. He himself had been hit and had lost 4 officers and 38 men, plus 270 wounded.

Wilson mounted his favorite horse, Sheridan, and led the 4th Regulars into the thick of the battle. The horse was hit in the breast and sank to the ground. His rider, seeing the wound was slight, remounted him and sounded the rally. He rode the wounded gray horse until 11 o'clock that night. Sheridan survived that battle, but received a fatal wound at Columbus and died at Macon.

Gen. Wilson was generous in the credit he gave to his opponents: "Forrest, Buford, Armstrong, and Adams exerted themselves as they never did before to stem the tide of defeat, but all their efforts were futile." The Union victory was complete, and the Confederate officers and men retreated from Selma in confusion. Some left without their horses, not having time to locate them. As they departed they fired a large cotton warehouse to keep the enemy from getting the bales stored there. The fire spread to the barracks and to ammunition storehouses, causing shells to explode. Pandemonium followed. Excitement was everywhere. Rebels who had taken time to find their horses and mount jumped them over the bluffs into the river. The Union cavalry followed them closely slashing away with their sabers. Women and children rushed to and fro, crying as they went.

"Of all the nights of my experience," wrote E. N. Gilpin, Gen. Upton's clerk, "this is most like the horrors of war—a captured city burning at night, a victorious army advancing, and a demoralized one retreating." He closed his diary that night with the following observation:

> The soldiers, over-powered by weariness, wrapped in their blankets, sunk to rest about the streets; the citizens, exhausted by excitement and fear, the cries of their children hushed at last, snatching a troubled sleep; the wounded, lulled by opiates into forgetfulness of their amputated legs and arms; the dead, in their last sleep, with white faces upturned to the sky; for the passion, cruelty, bitterness and anguish of war, this Sunday night now nearly gone, will be remembered. If there is a merciful God in the heavens, He must be looking down upon this scene in pity.

SOUTHERN HOSPITALITY

If one had been able to read simultaneously the dispatches from Richmond and Selma on Sunday evening, 2 April 1865, one would have realized the full significance of that day for the dying Confederacy. But that would have been impossible because the wires were not carrying the news very fast. Gen. Wilson commented on the meaning of that day years later when he was writing his memoirs. Not only had he captured the "most complete set of fortifications in the South, covering the most important Confederate depots of manufacture and supply," but Grant had at the same time taken Richmond. These two events were "practically the end of the war for the Union."

Within a few days after the capture of Selma, Wilson began to map his campaign. It would include attacks on Montgomery, Columbus, and Macon, but he did not pull the main body of his 12,000 horsemen out of Selma until detachments had scouted the area between that city and Montgomery and he had measured the strength of his adversary. During the interval and before he ordered the burning of all Confederate stores and munitions, his soldiers were free to take a close look at the people they had subdued.

If there be any thought in anyone's mind that Southern hospitality was dead when the enemy moved into the city, let him observe what Gen. Upton's clerk, E. N. Gilpin, had to say about the matter. On 9 April—an important day up in Virginia at a place called Appomattox Courthouse—Gilpin made the following entry in his diary.

Business in the office finished, went out in the city in search of amusement. Went to one of the best looking houses in the neighborhood, sat down on the porch and began a conversation with Mr. M——. Told him who I was, and the current news at headquarters, and got the old gentleman interested, I suppose. He asked me to dinner; I declined, but said I would come and take supper with him. He seemed a little surprised, but quickly recovering said, "Yes, and spend the evening, and I'll have my girls sing and play for you." While we were talking, I saw two girl faces peeping from behind the curtain, so I thought I would ask Thornton to come too. At the appointed time we appeared at the residence; I, in a blue jacket and gilt saber-belt, gray trousers above my cavalry boots, and wearing a Secesh cap. Thornton is a handsome fellow, and in any uniform would take a girl's eye.

The old gentleman introduced us to his affectionate daughters the Misses Erminie and Kate. Thornton was at once struck with Miss Erminie. We walked in the garden, picked flowers, and talked of the beautiful in nature, and all that. A sweet-faced, elderly lady announced supper, and made us welcome, saying that her son was a soldier too, pointing to a portrait on the wall, a handsome military figure in gray uniform, her eye resting with motherly pride on his features. I noticed that they were like her own.

After supper we were invited to the parlor, and what was begun as a piece of soldierly bravado, was likely to end in a civilized social call. Waverly novels, handsomely bound, were with other books on the table. "There is no more romance in these days, or I might call you Flora McIvor," I said to Miss Kate. She had pictured how she and Miss Erminie used to gallop up the river with a gay cavalcade, to where the Pearl and Swiftwater joined, and have their picnics in the woods. "That," she said, "was before Brother Henry took all our horses and joined Forrest." Miss Erminie played "The Bonny Blue Flag," and other Southern songs, and then Miss Kate, to her sister's accompaniment, sang, "Tis But an Hour Since First We Met." Both girls were little Rebels to the finger tips, and said they hoped we "would be taken prisoners." I told them of a pretty black-haired little Rebel, who sat smiling innocently and fishing, her Capitola hat thrown carelessly beside her, while our command was marching past; but she was counting every company, to report our numbers to General Price, and we all narrowly escaped capture. At this Miss Kate laughed and clapped her hands and said, "That's what I'd like to do!"

Perhaps it was because I had on Secesh clothes that I was so drawn to her; but she was a beautiful girl, and wore the rose I had given her, and when she sweetly sang, "When This Cruel War Is Over," she had to promise to write the words. At the doorstep she gave me her hand and said, "If they take you prisoner, I will have my brother see that they treat you well." She turned quickly away, for she knew I was reading her face.

On the way to camp I kept humming the refrain, "Hopes and Fears How Vain," and trying to recall the tones of her voice. Next morning a parcel came, tied with a dainty pink ribbon, and the song written in a fine girlish hand, with "suit of gray" for "suit of blue," as it runs in the Northern version, the words "hoping that we meet again" underscored, which made the recipient so sentimental that he was unfit for duty all the rest of the day. We have met again, and I found, what I knew I should find, a sweet sincerity added to her girlish beauty; but even you, my curious little journal, shall not know what words were said.

MARCH ON MONTGOMERY[1]

After a week spent in and around Selma, Gen. Wilson ordered his lumberjacks who comprised the 4th Michigan to construct a pontoon bridge 850 feet long over the Alabama River. Most of the 12,000 troops filed all day and night across the rickety improvised bridge. Croxton's men, who comprised the 1st Brigade of McCook's division, were operating against Forrest somewhere beyond the city. Wilson did not know just where, but under a flag of truce he held a conference with Forrest in a vain effort to get an exchange of prisoners, and though failing in that, he did learn from Forrest of Croxton's whereabouts. Croxton, with about 2,000 troops, continued to harrass Forrest and do mopping

---

[1]Editor's note: Dr. King's original title for the previous article, "Southern Hospitality" (21 March 1965), was "Surrender at Selma." The article "March on Montgomery" is also dated 21 March 1965. This second article was inadvertently omitted when the series was printed in the *Macon Telegraph and News*. Dr. King restored this essay to its proper place when he compiled his collection of the articles.

up work until, after 30 days of riding, he rejoined McCook's division in Macon.

The floating bridge held together fairly well during the march. The rear guard passed over it on the 9th. The bridge was then destroyed, and the long column of mounted troops started toward its immediate objective, Montgomery. The gun factories and ammunition plants, including any and all ordnance which could possibly be used by the Confederates had been burned, the railroad lines torn up, and even old and useless horses had been burned by the departing Yankees. Yet, Wilson had left his own surgeons in the town to attend the wounded of both sides.

A correspondent of the *Macon Telegraph and Confederate*, writing from Montgomery, estimated Wilson's troops marching toward the city to have been 6,000. His dispatch, dated 8 April, indicated that the fear of an attack had subsided. Gen. Forrest had ordered Gen. Buford, in command of the local defenses, to move toward Selma from the east to intercept the enemy, while he, Forrest, would "visit Selma from the western side."

Four days later, Wilson arrived at Montgomery and found, to his great surprise, that the city was undefended. The mayor and some citizens met him on the outskirts of the city with a flag of truce and surrendered "without terms or conditions." The Corps Commander described his arrival as follows:

> *Naturally both officers and men were at once notified that the city had surrendered and that there would be no fight. It is but the truth to add that they were disappointed. They had not thought it possible that Montgomery, after having given such proud defiance at the outbreak of the Rebellion . . . would surrender without even a show of resistance. But when they became convinced that such was the case, they consoled themselves with making the best possible preparations for a triumphal march through the principal streets to their designated camp beyond.*

The conquerors then paraded through the streets of the city where the Confederate government had begun so auspiciously. Gen. Wilson wrote,

> *Five brigades, not far from twelve thousand troopers, were in that column passing in review, as it were, before the ladies and gentlemen of the city. Many witnessed it from the windows, doorsteps, and sidewalks with silent respect, which showed clearly that the great Rebellion was at an end.*

Gilpin, Gen. Upton's clerk, described the scene.

> There before us was the State capital, the first capital of the Confederate
> states; now, from the dome, floated the "old flag!" In a moment every hat
> and cap flew off, and three cheers, loud and long, were given! The town
> took up the echoes as old familiar sounds; and the people seemed to live
> as of yore, under the "Stars and Stripes!"

Wilson "accepted the hospitality" of a Col. Powell, one of the
leading citizens. The colonel and his family

> were people of education and refinement, who knew how to be polite even
> to unwelcome guests. They had seen no Union soldiers except prisoners
> of war, but, fearing that those in arms . . . would be violent and predatory,
> the colonel had, as a precautionary measure, emptied his wine cellar and
> broken the bottles on the curbstone. Many of his neighbors had followed
> his example.

When Wilson arrived the gutters were "red with running wine."
He went on to say,

> When it was seen that not a trooper left his place in the ranks, that there
> were neither marauders nor drunken men, and that perfect order pre-
> vailed, a feeling of silent awe seemed to spread to the features of those
> worthy people. More than one lady expressed her surprise and gratifi-
> cation at the perfect behavior of our men, while all concerned declared
> their regret at the waste of wines and liquors which had been poured
> into the gutters to make certain that the Yankee troopers should have no
> opportunity for drunkenness.

CAPTURE OF COLUMBUS

Gen. Wilson recognized the importance of Columbus, "the door to Georgia," in measuring the success of his long cavalry raid from Selma to Macon. As the Yankee neared the city on the Chattahoochee River, 400 miles from the place where the raid originated, the defenders of Columbus began to tighten their muscles for one final effort to stop the victorious horsemen. Years later, in his memoirs, Wilson said the assault on Columbus was the "last real battle of the war."

The people of Macon, who had heard the guns roar and the drums roll twice before, would soon hear them again. The Macon paper, on 14 April, received information on the whereabouts of Wilson's corps. According to reports, the troops were at Line Creek headed toward Columbus. Gen. Howell Cobb, in command of the Georgia troops, returned to Columbus that morning to put the defenses "in the best possible condition to make a successful resistance." The Macon paper was certain of "our ability to repel the enemy" and hold the city.

The fortifications at Columbus had not been fully completed at that time. News of the approach of the enemy spurred the city to greater efforts to strengthen them. According to D. W. Standard (*Columbus, Georgia, in the Confederacy*, 1954), the fortifications consisted of "a two-mile line of trenches and gun emplacements on the crest of the ridge on the Alabama side of the Chattahoochee River."

The Federals went through Tuskegee, a town made significant by the Negro institute established there by Booker T. Washington. Gen. Emory Upton's clerk, E. N. Gilpin, whose diary fills in much detail of our narrative, told how the

> principal citizens came out and surrendered the town, and their good ladies and daughters came thronging out to see us and were quite friendly, surprised and thankful that we did not charge upon them with our sabers, yelling and swearing, as they expected us to do from all reports.

Evidence that the morale of the Union troops was high is seen in Gilpin's comment made on the 15th. "We are camping tonight on a fine plantation owned by an old Confederate. Plenty to eat, drink, and make merry over." Standard, pointing out that Montgomery—"the Cradle of Secession"—was "the victim of a week of burning and pillaging," said, "the forces still felt the flush of this victory as they approached Columbus."

The battle started at 8:00 on the evening of 16 April and lasted until 11:00 that night. The defenders, outnumbered by more than two to one, were no match for the seasoned Federals. The Yankee cavalrymen dismounted and began a "determined" assault upon the Confederate line. They were driven back by "confused firing in the dark." Twice more they assaulted. After two hours of "continuous firing," the news spread that one company had broken the line and was "in possession of the bridge over the river to Columbus." A final cavalry charge drove Cobb's forces out of the city—all that is, who were not captured. Gen. Wilson said the most "conspicuous" man killed was Charles A. L. Lamar, Savannahian remembered for his connection with the famous slave ship *Wanderer*.

Destruction of all stores and supplies which would in any way aid the Confederacy was the pattern all the way from Selma to Columbus. Cotton was, somehow, considered a fit commodity for destruction. Gen. Wilson tells in his memoirs of the cotton men coming to him pleading that he take for his own use what he desired, "on the sole condition that I should spare the remainder." His comment on that was, "This, of course, made the destruction all the more certain."

According to Standard, the day following the battle most of the people "closeted themselves in their homes and left the city to the mercy of the invaders." One of those invaders, Gilpin, was up early the next morning looking about the city. He found the forts full of prisoners. He was proud of the compliment Gen. Wilson paid his superior, Gen. Upton. He shared the opinion of the officers that Upton was deserving of the credit he received, that he had the confidence of the men as well as the officers, and that "he strikes quickly and surely." Upton told his commander that he could now take his division and "march through the South in any direction." Gilpin proudly asserted that Gen. Upton "is not given to boasting, and as a military man, is sure of what he says. We are masters of the situation."

MARCHING ON MACON

As Sherman had done the previous fall in Georgia, Wilson was doing in the spring of 1865 in Alabama and Georgia. Each had done as complete a job as possible in destroying Confederate war supplies and public property. Sherman was now pursuing Joseph E. Johnston through the Carolinas, and James H. Wilson, with his Cavalry Corps of the Military Division of the Mississippi, was destroying all he could on his 500-mile raid from Selma to Macon.

Gen. E. F. Winslow was given the job of destruction at Columbus. The record was 20,000 sacks of corn, 15 locomotives, 250 freight cars, 2 bridges, machine shops, roundhouses, railway supplies, 1 naval armory and shipyard, 2 rolling mills, the government arsenal and niter works, 2 powder magazines, 2 ironworks, 3 foundries, 10 mills and factories, 100 rounds of artillery ammunition, and "immense quantities of small arms, military accoutrements, and army clothing of which no account could be taken." Winslow was dedicated and his men inspired in their work. Wilson said,

> The destruction of the last factories, depots, and warehouses of the Confederacy was as complete as fire would make it, and of itself must have been the deathblow to the Confederacy, even if it had been able to keep its armed forces together for a further struggle.

George Mercer, writing in his diary on the very day of the battle of Columbus, sensed the economic victory of the North as he came face to face with the fact of Union victory in the clash of arms. He said,

> *Our Rail Road connections are all being severed and many think we can no longer feed large armies in the field, and that we must resort to the guerilla system. On the other hand the North does not appear to feel the war at all: all these indicate wealth and comfort: imigration far more than repairs the loss in battle and it is boasted that the recent discoveries of petroleum alone will create wealth enough to pay off this war debt.*

But he showed something of the indefatigable spirit which, though weaker, was still characteristic of the fighting South. He said,

> *I cannot believe that a just God will permit us to be overwhelmed, and utterly cast down. While there is life there is hope: we must continue the good fight, and leave the rest to Heaven.*

Wilson had divided his forces before attacking Columbus and had sent Gen. O. H. LaGrange through Opelika to West Point. There on 16 April, while the main body of Wilson's corps was attacking Columbus, LaGrange's forces crossed the bridges over the Chattahoochee, in spite of heavy Confederate fire, and assaulted the little fort which bore its commander's name. Gen. Robert C. Tyler, who had lost a leg at Missionary Ridge, hobbled around on his wooden leg and organized his 64 defenders inside the fort so well that LaGrange had great difficulty capturing it, even though he had Tyler outnumbered 10 to 1 (see this column, 18 June 1961). This was the last fort of the Confederacy to fall under Union attack.

Gen. R. H. G. Minty, with Long's division, was ordered to move toward Macon by way of Thomaston and the Flint River at Double Bridges. In the meantime LaGrange marched toward the Middle Georgia city by way of Barnesville and Forsyth. Gen. J. T. Croxton, it will be remembered, was also moving toward Macon to join the other forces of Wilson's corps there. Minty's advance guard reached Double Bridges, 50 miles from Columbus, ahead of Emory Upton's division which was guarding the rear and corps train. Upton's clerk, E. N. Gilpin, dated his diary at Double Bridges 19 April. It was there that he heard reports that the advance guard had captured Macon. An orderly brought dispatches from Gen. Wilson saying Gen. Cobb had surrendered. The report was a little premature, however, for Wilson himself says in his memoirs that the advance guard under Col. Frank White of the 17th Indiana had reached Mimms Creek at the crossing of Tobesofkee Creek, 15 miles from Macon, on the afternoon of 20 April.

About 300 Confederate defenders had taken their positions behind a mill house and a heavy barricade of fence rails. They set fire to the bridge to check the advancing Federals. But that did not stop them. They rushed through the flames, crossing the bridge on the "stringpieces" and charged the entrenchments. The Confederates broke and ran. A possible rallying point at Rock Creek was not utilized, and the pursuers rushed the bridge there before the retreating troops could destroy it. Soon after, Col. White met Gen. Robertson on the road bearing a flag of truce and a letter from Gen. Cobb. The letter related a message from Gen. Beauregard ordering Cobb to advise the Union officers that a truce had been entered into between Generals Sherman and Johnston. Col. White relayed it to Minty, his division commander. Minty sent it on to Gen. Wilson, at the same time ordering White to hold for five minutes. At the conclusion of the five minutes, White and Minty pushed on to enter the city before dark. Wilson was 19 miles from Macon when he received Cobb's communication at 6:00 that evening. The commanding general made no written reply, but sent an officer to halt the head column if he should overtake it. Wilson, himself, with his staff pushed on to Macon as fast as possible. By the time he arrived at 8:30, he found the city "safely in White's possession."

OUR BELEAGUERED CITY[2]

Two days after the capture of Columbus there was a skirmish at Pleasant Hill and another at Double Bridges on the Flint River. Excitement increased in Macon as the flying column, trained in the new cavalry tactics of fire and movement, penetrated farther into Georgia. One detachment of troops engaged in a skirmish at Barnesville on the 19th, but the main force rode down the Thomaston road and engaged in light skirmishes at Spring Hill and Montpelier Springs. The Union troops were only 13 miles from Macon on the morning of the 20th. By evening Wilson would enter the city to finish what Robert Bruce called the "longest and greatest single cavalry movement of the war." He had spared neither horses nor men. The distance from Columbus, 104 miles, had been covered in two days.

[2]This column, from today's installment to the concluding one, will, for the most part, consist of excerpts from my essay, "April in Macon," which appeared in *The Georgia Review*, Summer 1960. Permission to reproduce the selected passages has been granted by the *Review*'s editor, W. W. Davidson, for which I wish to express my sincere gratitude.

The poor little city on the Ocmulgee tried desperately to strengthen its defenses and hold off the enemy. Fanny Andrews, riding into Macon from Ft. Valley on the South-Western Railroad on 17 April, saw "some poor little fortifications thrown up along the line, with a handful of men guarding them." The *Macon Daily Telegraph and Confederate*, on 19 April, pleaded with the citizens to "strike one more effective blow." Macon had been saved on two former occasions by the "alacrity" and "courage" of its citizens, and the *Telegraph* was confident it could be done again. This, of course, was simply wishful thinking. "We are whipped, there is no doubt about it," Fanny Andrews admitted. The inadequacy of Gen. Cobb's forces was emphasized by his public appeal for all citizens able to bear arms "to unite at once with some military organization for the defense of the city." Col. Isaac W. Avery and Capt. Thaddeus Goode Holt had already attempted to organize a cavalry command. "The Yankee vandals cannot devastate our land and ravage our cities," they said, "if the freemen of Georgia will strike an honest, manly blow in her defense."

Capt. Thomas J. Key, charged with the responsibility of preparing the defenses around the city, complained that he had neither the tools nor the laborers to do the work. He asked the people to send to him, on the Columbus road, their Negroes and axes. The Macon paper suggested that cotton bales be used to barricade the streets. The editor thought such a barricade would hold off the blue-coated horsemen, and with "trusty sharpshooters" behind this barrier the enemy "might possibly be defeated." Hopes rose a little higher when Brig. Gen. Robert Toombs arrived with a few more Georgia troops. Some thought Macon could be defended if the Union forces did not number more than 8,000, but there were at least half again as many attackers.

Fanny and Metta, daughters of Judge Garnett Andrews, of Washington, Georgia, were on their way back home from Albany where they had been visiting relatives and friends in southwest Georgia far away from the sight of the Blue Coats. They reached Macon just a few days before the Federals came. Fred, their brother, met them when they arrived on the 17th, and put them on a train going over the Macon and Western line to Atlanta.

There they were to take the cars on the Georgia Railroad going to Augusta. Fred was stationed in Macon at the time, instructing new recruits. The train to Atlanta was carrying a large quantity of government specie. Macon ranked second only to Richmond as a depository of the Confederate Treasury. However, this train was carrying much more than money; it was carrying people, about 1,000 fleeing citizens.

Rumors that the road had been cut at Jonesboro or Barnesville made the train officials decide to run the train back to Macon. The southbound train came through, however, and brought the "tantalizing" news that it could have gone through anyway. The Andrews girls returned by way of Milledgeville and finally reached home safely.

The train to Milledgeville was extremely crowded, as were all outgoing ones, on 19 April. A young man, Sidney Lanier by name, "just up from a spell of typhoid fever," was there trying to get on one of the outgoing trains. Fred introduced him to his sisters, but the girls soon lost sight of him in the crowd. When the train backed up to load passengers there was a great rush to get aboard. Fanny saw one man knock a woman down and run over her. She hoped the Yankees would "ketch him" and give him his just desserts.

On 20 April, the day after the Andrews girls and many more had left Macon, Gen. Wilson's corps rode in. The garrison made a slight show of resistance, but the tired Georgia soldiers laid down their arms promptly at the summons of Col. Frank White. The Macon defenders were, for the most part, old men and boys too young to die.

The hour was 6:00 in the evening.

YANKEES TAKE MACON[3]

In the dusk of fading day, Col. White's victorious mounted troops began to invade the city. The first thing they seized on the outskirts was the nearly completed Confederate ammunition laboratory on the Macon and Western Railroad at Vineville. As the troops swept into the Tattnall Square section they crossed the South-Western Railroad and seized the armory. It was bounded by the railroad on the west and what are now Calhoun, Hazel, and Lamar streets on the other three sides. The armory's buildings covered 10 acres and the main building was 900 feet long. Small arms were made in this building which James H. Burton had built. Burton had a fine home at Tattnall Square which was later replaced by the president's home at Mercer University when the Baptist college, which was to move to Ma-

[3]The material here is taken from my "April in Macon," published in *The Georgia Review*, Summer 1960. Permission to use these excerpts is gratefully acknowledged.

con from Penfield in 1871, had expanded sufficiently to build its president a large brick residence. Lying between the armory and the river, at the location where the Farmer's Market now stands, was the big foundry which Robert Findlay had established some years before. No longer would it turn out "Napoleons" to hurl shot at the enemy, for it, too, was one of the places seized by the invading troops.

On the Indiana horsemen galloped, down the road we know now as Forsyth Street. They rode past a pistol and sidearm factory at the place where the Dudley-Hughes Vocational School now stands. At City Hall, which had been serving as a military hospital after the Battle of Chickamauga, it was said a picket was shot, probably in retaliation for the loss of a few Union cavalrymen who had toppled from their horses as they rode toward their coveted prize, the victims of snipers' bullets. Down Cotton Avenue they rode to Mulberry where a percussion cap factory stood.

To the west, at Cherry and Fourth (now Broadway), W. J. McElroy had turned his tinshop into a sword factory. From the vantage point of Concert Hall where Cotton Avenue enters Mulberry, they saw the C. T. Ward carriage depot just below the Lanier House, and farther down the street, the Southern Botanical Medical College. The jail was near Fifth Street, and nearby was another factory where women were making cartridges.

It was Gen. Wilson's intention to halt the advance on the outskirts of the city and see Gen. Cobb in order to satisfy himself "entirely in regard to every point" before consenting to acknowledge the armistice. Cobb had sent Col. Richard M. Cuyler to Wilson with copies of dispatches between Sherman and Beauregard concerning the armistice. "But," Wilson said, "before I could overtake the advance, Col. White had dashed into the city and received its surrender." Gen. Cobb protested the violation of the armistice, but Gen. Wilson held the view that his subordinates "could neither acknowledge Cobb as a channel of communication nor assume the responsibility of suspending their operations."

The commanding general entered Macon at 8:30 and found Col. White in possession of 350 commissioned officers, including

Generals Cobb and G. W. Smith and Brigadier Generals William W. Mackall, Hugh W. Mercer, and Felix H. Robertson. Col. White had herded 1,995 enlisted men into the stockade pen which had been built for Yankee prisoners. He had captured 60 pieces of artillery, small arms, arsenals, magazines, laboratories, "and other works of great value." Three large warehouses near the depot containing 20,000 sacks of corn were destroyed. That is, the buildings were destroyed; the corn was welcomed as food for the horses. Nor was this all. Off the record, but admitted in the Federal-controlled *Daily Evening News* of 26 April, is the fact that they took "horses and small articles of value, such as watches, money, silverware, and the like from the homes of the citizens in direct violation of orders. . . ."

Gen. Wilson sent a dispatch to Sherman informing him of the capture of Macon and advising him that the armistice order came too late to enable him to stop Col. White from capturing the city. He advised Sherman that he was holding Macon and all its garrisoned prisoners of war pending orders from the commanding general. At the same time Cobb was advising Beauregard that he had submitted to the unconditional surrender terms under protest. Sherman, in a communication to Wilson on the 21st, confirmed the fact that an armistice had been reached between himself and Gen. Johnston and told Wilson he wanted the armistice "religiously observed" and the captured generals released. But President Johnson did not approve the terms of the armistice, and Secretary Stanton ordered hostilities resumed. The truce was to expire on the 26th. On that very day, with his soldiers throwing down their guns and walking away, Johnston surrendered his army to Sherman at Durham Station, North Carolina.

April 25, 1965

YANKEE IMPRESSIONS

E. N. Gilpin, 3rd Iowa Cavalry, whose diary has been quoted in this column, thought Macon was "a great capture," with its military stores and "an immense amount of cotton." On 23 April he observed carloads of Confederate soldiers from Gen. Johnston's army coming in. As mentioned in this column last week, Johnston had surrendered to Sherman on the 26th. Much had happened between 9 April, the day of Lee's surrender, and this date. Lincoln had been assassinated, and though the news had not been confirmed in Macon either officially or in the press, Gilpin recorded in his diary on the 23rd, "The rumor has just reached us of the assassination of President Lincoln! We cannot believe it." (See this column, 12 May 1963, 2 June 1963). The next day Gilpin wrote, "News of Lincoln's murder confirmed. It comes like a stunning blow. The soldiers loved him, and grieved for him as though they had lost a father."

Though the news of Lincoln's death was confirmed, other news was merely rumor. News of peace was, for Gilpin and his fellows, "Unsatisfactory and doubtful." Nothing was really certain. Where was Jefferson Davis? Had Johnston really negotiated with Sherman for surrender? Prisoners from Andersonville were escaping now with regularity. Some of them who had been "living out in swamps for months" were coming into Macon "starved and naked."

Gilpin gives us a penned picture of Macon and her citizens during this time. Some of his observations made at the end of April 1865 are quoted below.

> *April 25. Saddled my horse and crossed the Ocmulgee on the pontoon bridge that General Cobb surrendered with the city. Visited the Macon arsenal and other government buildings, and rode about the city. The cars began running to-day. General Winslow came over to headquarters bringing his report and eleven battle flags taken from the enemy.*
>
> *April 27. Rode over the city and saw some beautiful houses, one of the most magnificent in the South, parks, lakes, statuary; outside of Temple's Vale, one would hardly expect to see anything more beautiful.*
>
> *April 28. Everything in chaos here, the most extravagant rumors prevailing among the citizens; no reliable news of any kind. The suspense is almost unendurable. We are reduced to about quarter rations, and no coffee, and nobody can "soldier" without coffee. Our clothing is worn out, and we nearly all wear Confederate uniforms. It is time the war was over.*
> . . .
> *April 29. The citizens seem friendly and most of the soldiers, though some of them are moody and cherish resentment. Pillaged property is to be turned over to the provost marshal. It consists of gold, silver, and all manner of trinkets. Fortune favors the brave! Rummaging in an old storehouse, I found a little bag of coffee, a sample lot it must be, bright yellow grains, inclosed in wicker, such as fancy baskets are made of. Lun was in an ecstacy while roasting and getting it ready to grind. "Let it simper slow," he insists, which, doubtless is the true method of making coffee. We keep it to ourselves, but as you can smell it a mile when the wind sits fair, we are likely to be besieged by the whole army.*
>
> *April 30. One trait is very noticeable in these Southern people, and it sets one a thinking. Certain families in each State hold themselves in a kind of superiority above the others. . . . I was talking about this with a nice looking old lady, who lives just across from our headquarters. She had returned my military salute with a stately courtesy, and so I stopped to chat with her. The kind old soul listened attentively while I stood at the gate and ran over the names of the Georgia boys that I used to know at "Old Hanover." They had come North to school, and brought a new charm to life with their handsome faces and chivalrous ways. There was*

*something captivating about their soft Southern accent. They taught us
how to swim and shoot and fence, and we taught them to skate and play
football. . . . When the war broke out, they all left for home, and I had
never heard of any of them since. I suppose, I said, most of them went
into the army. "The boys of the best families of the South," she answered,
"joined the army." This afternoon a servant came over, bearing a tray
with a round of Scuppernong wine. . . . I think I shall enlarge my visiting
list!*

*May 4. Lee's troops are going through here in all directions, a thou-
sand a day, for the past week, and Johnston's men are coming in, taking
the familiar paths to their homes after long years of absence, poorly clad,
some on crutches, some with empty sleeves, pale-faced from wounds or
sickness. . . . They have lost all. We must help them start, and keep them
from starving. . . . We are issuing provisions from our stores, and rations
of meat from captured Confederate beef-cattle; and that is as good as
Henry Ward Beecher's beautiful words "Forgiveness and Reconciliation."*

THE OCCUPIED CITY[4]

Those who had not fled before the advance of Wilson's raid now began to experience the life of a conquered people. Mulberry Street was no longer teeming with Confederate uniforms, prancing horses, and fashionable ladies riding by in their neat carriages. The gaiety was gone. Ragged foot soldiers lolled in front of the Lanier House, where Gen. Wilson had set up his headquarters, or across the street where, on the second floor, Col. J. G. Vail occupied Gen. Cobb's former office as commander of the post. Edgar Ross, walking with his sisters and their cousin, Viola Ross, came upon the Union flag hanging in front of post headquarters. They turned aside to avoid walking under "the old rag," as Viola termed it. For this demonstration of disloyalty, Ed was forced to march back and forth under the Stars and Stripes for 30 minutes. Also, making up a part of the street scene

[4]Permission to use the material below, which is from my "April in Macon," *The Georgia Review*, Summer 1960, is gratefully acknowleged.

were the Negroes, freed from slavery, following their liberators, expecting food. Most of them were men and boys, but some were women and children, looking woebegone, miserable, and completely helpless.

The *Telegraph* warned, "There is a great deal of whisky in Macon. Woe be to us and our property if it be not destroyed." The ladies begged the authorities to take "every possible step towards the complete destruction of all alcoholic drinks in our city." Fanny Andrews observed that all the intoxicating liquors that could be found had been seized and emptied on the ground. John Campbell Butler, the local historian, estimated that about 2,500 barrels of "corn whisky" were destroyed.

His estimate was likely an exaggeration, but, at least, it indicates that he remembered it as a bad situation. Miss Andrews said,

In some places the streets smelt like a distillery, and I saw men, boys, and Negroes down on their knees lapping it up from the gutter like dogs. Little children were staggering about in a state of beastly intoxication.

Colonel Vail, commanding the post, ordered all liquor not in the commissary and medical departments to be destroyed.

Besides the destruction of munitions, factories, and warehouses mentioned in official reports, Butler mentions incendiary acts: "Soldiers set fire to two blocks on Mulberry Street on the night of 22 April." Damaged were the Methodist Depository and the printing and publishing firm of Burke and Boykin. Had not Gen. Cobb surrendered the city without a fight Macon might have suffered the fate of Atlanta or Columbia.

Federal troops in Macon caused a disruption in the normal life of the citizens, but did not altogether stop social, religious, and cultural activity. Gen. Wilson said,

The people gradually resumed their usual avocations and, perceiving that we were not the barbarians they had been accustomed to call us, gradually softened in their behavior, and some even went so far as to speak to us as fellow countrymen.

Business, however, was practically at a standstill. The Lanier House, where Gen. Wilson had his headquarters, was not open to travelers. The manager, though he had not welcomed the

Union officers with any show of hospitality, had given the general and his staff the best rooms he had and, according to his unwelcomed host, "did all in his power" to make them comfortable. The inflationary condition and uncertainty of the currency prevented many business establishments from resuming their activity.

The *Daily Telegraph and Confederate* suspended publication after its issue of 20 April, and there was no resumption of it until 11 May. A two-page paper, under Federal control, was published in the interval under the name *Macon Daily Evening News*, and a sheet called the *Macon Daily Herald*, bearing the date 8 May, is preserved in the Washington Memorial Library in Macon. The stated purpose of the *News* was "to supply local news and publish orders of the General in command." The price of the paper, $2.00 in Confederate currency or five cents in specie, is indicative of the inflationary times.

Col. Vail, commander of the post, ordered all citizens off the streets at "Retreat," which was sounded each evening at 7:30, but he made an exception in the case of druggists, physicians, railroad men, those in public utilities, such as employees of the gas works, and members of the fraternal orders. All these could go to and from their business or meeting places. They would have to present passes issued by headquarters, of course. On the third night of the occupation, Ralston Hall, the theatre located at Cherry and Third, was reopened. Citizens wishing to see the performance of the Crisp family—a name that later became famous in politics—or to laugh with the comedian Sam Hubbard could procure passes when purchasing their tickets at the box office on the Cherry Street side of the theatre.

END OF CONFEDERACY

(The excerpts below are the concluding paragraphs of "April in Macon," which editor W. W. Davidson, of *The Georgia Review*, has kindly let me use to close the four-year chronology of the Civil War in Macon. This column will end next Sunday. As I approach the end of this series I wish to thank the many friends who have shared with me letters, diaries, and other materials which have augmented this column and enlivened its interest.)

The officers chose the best homes for themselves. Gen. Wilson, himself, occupied Overlook, the magnificent Greek Revival house which Elam Alexander had built for Jerry Cowles in the late thirties. It stands there now in all its grandeur at the top of Coleman Hill, overlooking the city, and is the present home of Stratford Academy. Brig. Gen. Edward M. McCook, who commanded the first division of Wilson's cavalry corps, occupied editor Joseph Clisby's large Georgian style home near the Vineville road. Union troops camped all around this 20-acre estate. This house, called Woodlawn, was built by an unknown architect from New England about the same time that Elam Alexander was building Overlook. It was the home of the late Thomas Edward Ryals.

At the time of Gen. McCook's stay, Joseph Clisby lived upstairs with his son and two daughters, by his first wife. The Union general and his staff occupied the entire first floor. Fortunately, Mrs. Clisby, the editor's second wife, was in New York at the time with their little children settling the estate of her father, who had died the year before. Mr. Clisby never let his daughters come down from their haven of safety on the second floor except when he attended them.

The girls, Louise and Emma, sat in their room, like birds in a cage, hearing strange sounds in the night and smelling unpleasant odors: the sound of Yankee soldiers feeding and bedding down their horses and telling lewd stories and cursing and laughing until these noises were transposed into a discordant chorus of snoring; the smell of unwashed men wearing sweat-stained uniforms, the odors of stale and rotting offal, the filthy camp smell of latrine and corral polluting the April air. How different from the fragrant flower odors that Lou Burge had smelled from her window at Wesleyan four years before. But poor Lou could smell nothing now. She had returned to her home in Covington ill with fever in the midst of the war and had died soon after at the age of nineteen.

The *Telegraph* resumed publication on 11 May, in time to report the capture of Jefferson Davis. After the surrender of the Confederacy, the president, his family, and a few members of his official family fled from Richmond and went to Washington, Georgia, protected by a force of about 2,000 soldiers. There, in the little town of Washington, the last official acts of the short-lived government were performed. A guarded wagon train carrying gold and silver coins wound its way over the rough country roads to bring each soldier his muster-out pay of $25.25. The men took this pittance and went home, leaving the president and his party protected by only a small guard.

The president of the fallen government attempted to escape from his pursuers. A price of $100,000 was on his head, and Gen. Wilson sent his cavalrymen in all directions seeking his whereabouts. Most of Wilson's chief lieutenants went searching for the Davis party: McCook went to Albany and Atlanta; Minty scouted the southeastern section of the state; and Gen. Croxton sent a detachment to the mountains of Alabama. The searchers literally combed the countryside looking for the beaten and sick man, fleeing with his family. They caught him in the gray dawn of 10 May in the vicinity of Dublin. The capture was made a mile and a half north of Irwinville by Lt. Col. Benjamin P. Pritchard, commanding the 4th Michigan Calvary. It was not hard to capture Davis, guarded as he was by about a dozen tired soldiers. He was wearing a woman's waterproof cloak and a shawl over his head when captured. His captors tormented the sick man, asking, "Was the woman's apparel for protection from the elements or from ourselves?"

They took him to Macon. Mrs. Davis and the children rode with the president into the city down the Houston road from Perry. They came in riding in an ambulance drawn by "four splendid mules." Little Maggie rode up front, according to an observer, where she could see the "vast throng of soldiers and citizens." Perhaps she, in her innocence, thought it was another procession honoring her distinguished father with such pageantry as Georgia could afford. The entourage moved through the crowd of curious and sad-faced people. The captors, with their prize, passed down the street now called Broadway, by the Brown Hotel, and moved up Mulberry Street to the Lanier House where Gen. Wilson's officer of the day sent the members of the Davis family to their rooms. A few hours later Gen. Wilson sent the ex-president of the Confederacy to Atlanta and, finally, to Fortress Monroe and prison.

Many years passed, and it was April again in Macon. The sun rose bright and clear on an Easter morning as hundreds of faithful Christians gathered on Coleman Hill around a large wooden cross for the traditional sunrise worship service. At the top of the hill stood Overlook, its huge columns rising majestically above the crowd. The worshipers sang hymns of praise and chanted, "He is risen!" Northerners, grandsons of Wilson's Raiders, stood shoulder-to-shoulder with Southerners in the act of worship. With heads bowed they gave thanks for peace in our land and petitioned the risen Lord to send us peace in our time.

And none remembered that one day in April 1865 when a conquering general stood in the shadow of the great columns of Overlook and gazed upon a prostrate little city that had become his prize of war. The therapy of time had done its work, and all nature was joyful.

• III •

A
SOLDIER'S
LIFE

THE "CHRISTIAN SOLDIERS"

The battle line was formed; the enemy was approaching in force. A strange, unexpected order rang out: "While we kill their bodies, may the good Lord have mercy on their sinful souls. . . . Fire!"

Thus spoke Brig. Gen. William N. Pendleton, of Virginia, an Episcopal minister who had taken up the sword. He had had soldier training early in life at West Point; therefore, it was only natural that he offer his services to the Confederacy when war broke out.

The ministers had waged a battle from their pulpits for states' rights before the war, and when war came some of them fought for their Southern faith on the battlefields. Gen. Pendleton, chief of artillery of the Army of Northern Virginia, was one of those. So was the militant bishop Leonidas Polk, another graduate of West Point. This corps commander gave his life at Pine Mountain in June 1864 and was carried to Atlanta for a big funeral at St. Luke's.

These were but two of many Christian soldiers of the Confederacy. Many became Christian during the war—generals such as Joseph E. Johnston, Hood, and Hardee, and many thousands in the ranks. Big revivals in the camps were not uncommon. Soldiers were able to hear the best of the preachers during the lull of battle. Many of the officers and men were of a religious bent. One of the best examples was the praying general, "Mighty Stonewall" Jackson. Bibles and religious tracts, many of them having run the blockade from England, were a source of inspiration and comfort to the soldiers.

On the home front women organized periodical prayer meetings, churches kept their doors open, and ministers led mass prayer services for the armies in the field. Henry Holcombe Tucker, the Baptist divine who would serve Mercer University as president from 1866 to 1871, started a movement for concerted prayer among the soldiers, sailors, and folks at home, urging them to all "fall on their knees every day at one o'clock and pray for Confederate victory."

However, religious fervor was not universal, as Capt. Robert A. Smith of the Macon Volunteers well knew. Writing from Virginia to Rev. John W. Burke in Macon, Capt. Smith suggested to the minister who was having difficulty keeping his Methodist publishing house going that he "look unto God both for guidance and support."

"I ought to feel pungent sorrow that religion is at so low an ebb as you mention in Macon," he wrote. "It is peculiarly a season when the church and every member thereof should give themselves to earnest prayer." He was anxious that "our friends at home not forsake the assembling of themselves together, but that rather let their hearts like those of Israel be 'knit together as the heart of one man' to pray for the success of our cause and the prosperity of Zion." Then he asked, "How can we who are in the field fight successfully unless our friends at home support us by their prayers?"

Many times during the long war worship had to be cut off while a battle raged. Drum or bugle would beat the assembly call bringing soldiers together at some lovely spot for divine worship on a beautiful Sunday morning. Singing, usually without an instrument to guide them, unless perhaps the bugle or drum that called them to worship, would be followed by prayer;

then the chaplain would commence his sermon. Sometimes the service would be concluded abruptly by a sudden order to form ranks. In minutes, companies of soldiers fully equipped would be marching into the face of fire—some to die with the last strains of a familiar hymn on their lips.

THE RELUCTANT CONSCRIPT

One of the most unique and interesting documents loaned to me since my call for Civil War items is a typed copy of William H. Parkins's reminiscences under the title, "Hiding Out." It is the property of Eugene Palmer Parkins, of Atlanta. It chronicles the experiences of a Northern-born man who loved the Union enough to undergo trials and tribulations for 18 months trying to keep out of Confederate prison and to avoid military service as a reluctant conscript in the Confederate army. It was the basis for a novel called *How I Escaped*, written by Archibald Gunter in 1889.

Parkins was born in New York State but had moved to Columbia, South Carolina, and was living happily there with his wife and child when his adopted state seceded. He was not at all sympathetic to the action that South Carolina took on 20 December 1861 and openly expressed his opposition to it. He held in ridicule the fantastic claims of divine approval by a lady who found a hen's egg with "Southern Confederacy" on it written

in blood; by a man who saw "South" written across the sky at
sunset one evening; by the parents of a baby who at birth opened
his mouth saying, "South, rejoice!" and expired. Parkins thought
if the babe had said such difficult words it surely would have
died of lockjaw; but he dismissed the whole business as a vain
attempt to justify disunion, which he knew in his heart was
wrong.

When the Confederacy began to gird itself for war, Parkins
prepared to escape through the lines to the land of his birth,
even though it meant leaving his wife and baby. Thus he began
a long and arduous journey through the Carolinas and into Virginia. He was aided along the way by Northern sympathizers
and Union men who worked up an organization with secret hand-
shake and secret signs. For instance, a house with a red, white,
and blue cord in the window was a sign of a friendly haven.
Being a member of the masonic order was also advantageous to
him. His wife bade him goodbye and agreed that she and the
baby would meet him in New York after she had learned of his
safe arrival there. But many months were to intervene before
she could start her journey northward—months of anxious waiting for her, months and miles of hiding and walking for him.
She sewed $60 into his coat collar, kissed him, and sent him on
his way.

Under an assumed name and using a false passport, the fugitive worked his way slowly northward. He was very close to
Federal lines when Confederate soldiers arrested him. They imprisoned him along with about 20 other fugitives and deserters
in Castle Thunder at Richmond.

Gen. John Winder, finding no evidence of his being a spy,
ordered him released and returned to Columbia. Soon after, however, the Confederate Congress passed a conscription law, and
he was drafted into the Rebel army.

Parkins was determined not to fight against the Union and
quickly escaped from his regiment. It should not be inferred that
such behavior was so uncommon as to be shockingly disgraceful.
Actually, it has been estimated that the Confederate army suffered one desertion to nine enlistments and that the record for

the Northern army was even worse, one to seven. [Ella Lonn, *Desertions During the Civil War*, 226].

Will Parkins's wife, though a Southerner, was strongly opposed to his being a soldier of the Confederacy. "She knew the intensity of my love and feelings towards the United States' flag," he said.

His service in the Confederate army lasted no longer than it took Parkins to perfect a plan of escape, which he did in short order. Then he began a journey of over 400 miles lasting many months, a journey that took him through western North Carolina along the French Broad River into Tennessee, a journey under cover of darkness much of the time.

As the fugitive walked his weary way through the mountainous terrain he was joined by others, some of them Confederate deserters from the Carolinas and Virginia, and one lieutenant, an officer of the Union army who had escaped from a Confederate prison. Finally, there were 11 "buffaloas," as they were called. They called themselves the Union Jacks of Blue Ridge. Occasionally the little band of dirty, ragged, and bearded fugitives would encounter pickets and run to cover under fire.

THE REBEL YELL IS GIVEN

Jubilation and optimism resulting from the Confederate victory at First Manassas continued to characterize the Southerners, both the men in uniform and the folks back home. The Rebel yell that was born in this battle reverberated throughout the South and became, according to Bell Wiley, as much a part of the Confederate soldier's equipment "as his musket."

Heard on the battlefields in hundreds of charges during the war, Wiley says it was "an unpremeditated, unrestrained, and utterly informal 'hollering' " with a mixture of "fright, pent-up nervousness, exhultation [sic], hatred, and a pinch of pure deviltry." E. M. Coulter quotes several contemporaries who describe the yell in various ways, such as a shout "more overpowering than the cannon's roar," or "a soul harrowing sound." Fitzgerald Ross, English soldier of fortune and officer in the Austrian Hussars who visited the Confederate cities and camps, thought they "learnt it from the Indians." Ross observed that by practice "many have arrived at a high perfection and can yell loud enough to be heard a mile off."

Col. Arthur Fremantle, another visiting British observer, noted that the Confederate troops, "when charging or to express their delight, always yell in a manner peculiar to themselves. The Yankee cheer is much like ours, but the Confederate officers declare that the rebel yell has a peculiar merit, and always produces a salutary and useful effect upon their adversaries." He observed that a corps was sometimes spoken of as "a good yelling regiment."

The yell was not meant to frighten the enemy when first used. Rather, "the primary function of the rousing yell was the relief of the shouter," Wiley says. However, the yell soon acquired such a reputation "as a demoralizing agent that men were encouraged by their officers to shout as they assaulted Yankee positions." The yells varied according to the origin of the individual. A Georgia Rebel's shout probably didn't echo as shrilly through the Virginia mountains as a North Carolinian's yell, but it gave him just as much relief; and a Confederate regiment charging down on Union troops, yelling in shrill unison, would often strike terror among Yankee troops, even after they had grown accustomed to hearing it.

Such was the confidence generated at Manassas where the famous yell originated. Optimism and confidence grew stronger as the fleeing Yankees disappeared toward Washington. In a spirit of fun a number of Georgia soldiers telegraphed messages home that indicated their jubilant humor. I am not sure that each signature was genuine, but editor Joseph Clisby printed each one just as it was received. I have strong doubts of the authenticity of the first one below, from L. Pope Walker, the Confederate secretary of war.

Richmond, Virginia
August 13

Mr. Nathan Wood, Macon, Georgia

   Furnish me 2,000 strong chains for prisoners of war, and send me your bill.

L. POPE WALKER

R. A. Smith may or may not have been Capt. Robert A. Smith, of the Macon Volunteers, but I am inclined to believe he was one and the same.

> *Sewell's Point, Virginia*
> *August 13*

To E. Saulsbury, Macon, Georgia

> *Great joy and lively demonstrations in camp. Sawyer gun seized and turned upon Fortress Monroe with killing effect. Butler gone crazy and taken to N. Y. Lunatic Asylum.*

> *R. A. SMITH*

Two of the telegrams mentioned handcuffs. An announcement concerning handcuffs was published in the *Macon Telegraph*. It makes clear the significance of these two telegrams, but it doesn't prove the truth of the handcuff story. It read:

> One of the Hessian Handcuffs for their Southern prisoners may be seen at Messrs. E. J. Johnson and Company's. We may state as fact that between seven and eight thousand of these bracelets were captured at Manassas, composing two entire wagon loads. . . . The design is said to have been to interpose a solid body of rebel prisoners to be captured at Manassas between the Federal ranks and their enemies when the former made their assault upon Richmond.

> *Richmond, Virginia*
> *August 13*

To Joseph Clisby:

> *Washington City in a blaze! Lincoln putting out!*
> *"Granny Scott" just arrived! Fitted to a pair of handcuffs, and serenaded by the Ethiopian Band with "Old Folks at Home," and "I've Left My Snow-Clad Hills."*
> *Reception tomorrow at 10 o'clock at the Penitentiary.*

> *PRITCHARD*

> *Richmond, Virginia,*
> *August 13*

To Col. Washington Poe:

> *Dear Wash—Handcuffs cheap! Ice scarce! Ely weeps! A good time geerally! Come on, my brave.*

> *E. A. NISBETT*

Sewell's Point, Virginia
August 13

To Mrs. Major Smith:

    Dear Grandma—I got drunk, and am mighty sick but am able to eat a little. Please send me a box.

                                           BEN J. SMITH

DEMOCRACY IN THE ARMY

The Civil War may have been fought, partially, to defend an aristocratic way of life, but the Johnny Rebs who fought Yankees were just as democratic in their military life as the Yanks against whom they fought, maybe more so. Many of the enlisted men in the Confederate army were from rural, even frontier, regions and had in their makeup an independent spirit and the self-reliance which is characteristic of such a background. Thus they were traditionally democratic, and though apparently fighting to maintain a caste system, they believed in and practiced an equalitarian philosophy—equality, that is, for whites only, for theirs was a white man's world.

Southern men were first citizens, then soldiers; military discipline was not natural to them. This may have been more true of a Yankee clerk, miner, or farmer who had never been to a military academy than it was of a Southerner. Southern boys, on the other hand, who had taken delight in their military schools and had enjoyed the pomp and color of militia drills had no liking for regimentation either. Even the militia musters were democratic—almost burlesque in their comical awkwardness, but thoroughly democratic.

Nowhere was democracy in the army better illustrated than in the fact that the enlisted men elected their officers. Sgt. W. J. Mosely wrote from Virginia to his parents in Georgia saying, "Thomas was elected the day before we left Petersburg. He got 26 votes to Lafayette's 12. . . . Lafayette went right off to the Hospital as soon as he got beat."

Only the highest-ranking field officers were appointed by the Richmond authorities. This system had grown up haphazardly in the militia during the antebellum period and was carried over into Confederate military organization. The militia had been more than a state organization throughout its history; indeed, it had all the attributes of a social club. It lost little of its social nature when carried over into the Confederate army. Generally, the person who organized a company was elected its captain. Such was the case in Georgetown, Georgia, when the Quitman Grays chose as their captain Theodore L. Guerry, who had organized the company [The *Macon Telegraph and News*, 30 April 1961]. Often the captain paid the expenses of outfitting his company. Though only men of property were able to outfit a company and though the gentlemen were usually able to win their offices by means of favors such as liquor and cigars, or simply by ability to demand respect, sometimes men of lower caste were elected. Popularity had much to do with the choice.

When the enlisted men were displeased with an officer, they could request his resignation. Kate Stone, of Brokenburn Plantation, Louisiana, tells in her journal of the resignation of a lieutenant whom she admired. "It was such a foolish thing to do," she said, "just because some of the men requested his resignation." She thought he should "have them put in the guardhouse" for such behavior. After all, he seemed "to be the only officer in the company who tries to do his duty, and of course he is unpopular," she concluded.

This kind of procedure was more conducive to disorganization than to organization and, therefore, affected adversely the military discipline. And, like the confiscation acts, lack of discipline hurt morale. However, the ordinary soldier was opposed to the exercise of strict discipline whether it was administered by his equal or by a gentleman. That was the democratic expression of his rugged individualism.

Sgt. Mosely related a story in a letter to his parents that shows the elective system in the army sometimes worked effectively. The captain of Mosely's company was court-martialed and reduced in rank for cheating his men in a raffle. The lottery was to determine who should get shoes. Most of the men were in need of shoes, but there were only three pairs to be raffled off. "Instead of giving them to the men that needed them the most," said Mosely, "he [the captain] must have them drawn for. He fixes up the tickets and puts them in a hat. Three of the tickets had the word 'Shoes' written on them. The others were blank." As Mosely relates it, the sly officer "slips the Ones with Shoes written on them under the lining of the hat and then let Several men draw and tells one of the men that he will give him a dollar for his draw and he draws himself and gets the Shoes. He bought two chances and got two pair of Shoes, for he knew where the tickets were. And then he Sells the Shoes to R. Wiggins and Crawford Smith for $15.00 per pair. . . . And he was Court-martialed and Cashiered. So he did not make much by the Operation."

The sergeant closed his letter with the philosophic conclusion: "I believe I had as Soon be dead as to be Cashiered for the Offence that he was."

MAJOR REDUCED IN RANK

"Bill Arp," already mentioned once or twice in this column, may or may not have created the story I am about to tell. I am certain he must have gotten many of his stories from camp talk during the Civil War in which he served—such as this one about a major in the Georgia militia who was "konscripted" into the Confederate army and reduced in rank to private. Charles H. Smith, who was endowed by his Irish father with a keen sense of satire and quick wit, began sending "Letters to Mr. Linkhorn" to the *Southern Confederacy* [Rome] in 1861. The story of the "Reduced Major," which was later included in a collection of his stories under the title *Bill Arp; So Called* [New York, 1866], was being read, laughed over, and copied in letters from home to camp during the war.

The late A. H. S. Weaver let me read such a letter which belonged to him. The family still keeps it, along with other treasured items of Mr. Weaver's kinsman, Alexander Hamilton Stephens. The letter was from Ann Maria Nickelson, of Greensboro, to her son-in-law, Capt. William Weaver. Dated 8 April 1864, it carried a little family news, but the remainder of the space related the story substantially as published in "Bill Arp's" collected stories.

Here is a condensed version of the story:

> Potash [he's been exempted from military service to make gun powder]: "What's the matter, John? Well, John we must all do our sher. You know I've been working for six months as hard as I could, makin' potash for the Konfederasy and that's to make powder for you boys to fite with."
>
> Rejuced: "Potash! Niter Buro! I'm told thar's about 12,000 of you fellers skulkin behind ash hoppers, pretending you are stewing down patriotism into powder. Blamed if I can't smell the lie on you. Don't you talk about potash to me, blamed if I'm in any humor now to put myself on a level with that everlastin Niter Buro."
>
> Potash: "Well, everybody must do their sher."
>
> Rejuced: "Do their sher? Blam'd if I cant do your sher and no body ever miss me from this Borough. I can find all sich as you any day without having to travel a hundred yards. Confound your Niter Buro and your potash, confound old Joe Brown and his durn staff, too— blanket, shotgun, Savannah, Borygard, the devil. Fact is, I've felt sorter like suckin eggs ever since I got on the durned old staff and maybe a little fittin will make me feel better."
>
> Rejuced [Ann Nickelson spelled it this way. The dialect was dropped later]: "Why nutin purpicular, only it's durned kurious. How in the dickens can Joe Brown rejuce a Major to a privet when he aint done nothin? What sort of a army regelashun do you call that? Joe Brown's new tacktics I spose. Double barrel shot gun, haversack, blanket, Borygard and all sort of nonsinse. I wasn't subjec no how. Its now the rise of forty two year since I lit into the cussed old world, but I thought the Konfederasy would be kallin 'em up to 45 afore long, so I took roundence and fudged on 'em and managed to get on one o' their dig'd ole staffs. I reckon I was about the last to get on. Durn the staff and Joe Brown too. They played smash amazinly writin 200 pages again Konscripshun. I thought from the way he pitched into Jeff Davis about trying to enroll his milishy officers that we wouldn't have to fite nuthin for the next 25 year. Now you see, he's konscripted the whole konsun hisself all at onst, in a pile, a rejuced 'em all to ranks. Blame his old hide. I'll bet he dont appear at Savannah, not him. Durned if I dont go any whar he'll risk his old karkas. He turns us all over to old Bory and old Bory'll fite, gog'd if he wont. He'll put just such fellers as me into the front ranks whar David put Uriah and suf of them whislin bullets or singing bumbs will take my old gizzard out."

Potash: "Well, but John, he aint agwyne to keep you but a little while."

Rejuced: "Little while! Little while, you say! Bet my ears if old Bory onst gits his French claws on a milishy officer he'll hold him durin the war and fite him sum afterwards, and just fur the fun of it. Farewell, vain world. When they aint fitin they'll be diggin and when they ain diggin they'll be fitin. Little while! One day wont be while enuf for my day lights to be shelled out. I tell you what, when them Yanks git to throwing their blasted hot shot at Savannah they'll throw 'em thicker and faster than hail ever fell in a kotten patch. Sumbody's gwine to git hurt shore. Durn old Brown, he's as big a fool on a Proklymashun as old Abe Linkhorn. I went down to see the General; that he mout resist or sumthin, but, ding it all, I found him in a store buyin a haversack, fixing to go up. Well, I tried to laff it off, but it wouldn't laff. Blam'd if every gigle I tried to make didn't fizzle out half way into a regular whine. Blast Joe Brown! I got skeered too soon. Thot onst I would put in a substitute but durn the luck I dont see anything about substitute in this order. It don't give a man time to know what to do, but just says kum along, be in a hurry, right away, cars waitin on you, last whistle blowed, bring shotgun and blanket, don't look back, old Borygard's callin you, enrollin officer's after you, court martial will get you, run, run, like the devil to Savannah."

PROFESSORS STUDY WAR

When war came to the little Baptist college called Mercer University at Penfield, in Greene County, the professors and students were not found wanting in patriotism and willingness to serve the Southern Confederacy, however lacking they might have been in military preparedness. Many Southern boys were in military schools when the war began, but not the Mercer boys. They, along with their professors, were devoting all their school hours to classical languages, moral philosophy, arts, and sciences other than military science.

We know that professors Shelton P. Sanford and J. E. Willet were willing to serve to the best of their ability and were anxious to learn the art of war. Documentary proof of this is in a letter, which is deposited in the State Department of Archives in Atlanta. Sanford was professor of mathematics and Willet was "Professor of Natural Philosophy and Chemistry." They wrote jointly to Gov. Brown on 10 October 1861 seeking clarification concerning the proper dress for themselves as officers of the militia of their district. Sanford had been elected captain, and Willet had been made lieutenant of that militia, and they were perturbed about the authorized color of their frock coats.

Another question that bothered the professors was the relation of the "Mercer Cadets" to the militia. Sanford had been drilling the Mercer boys under his authority as their captain, and he and Lt. Willet wanted to know whether or not the Mercer company was to be included with the 148th District Militia. Another document also in the valuable depository in Atlanta is in the form of a requisition to Gov. Brown for 80 muskets and the receipt for them. Both the requisition and the receipt appear on the same form and are signed by Capt. Shelton P. Sanford. They were signed on 27 March 1861. Bearing the same date along with that form is a bond for $1,600 promising payment on receipt of the shipment. It was signed by members of the Mercer faculty. The professors signing the bond were Sanford, Henry H. Tucker, U. W. Wise, S. G. Hillyer, William G. Woodfin, and Willet.

The next day Sanford forwarded the bond to Adj. Gen. Henry C. Wayne in Milledgeville. We can only surmise when or if the weapons reached Penfield.

These interesting documents throw some light on the part that the little college at Penfield played in the Civil War. I am indebted to Mrs. Mary G. Bryan, director of the Department of Archives and History, for photostatic copies of these documents. I have placed them in the library of Mercer University, here in Macon where the institution has been since 1871.

The letter from professors Sanford and Willet is quoted in full below. Before you read it, however, let me tell you professor Willet rendered a valuable service to the Confederacy in laboratory work in Atlanta in the production of munitions. Professor Sanford? He helped keep the college alive throughout the war, teaching mathematics to a few students too old, too young, or too severely wounded to perform further military service.

Penfield
October 10, 1861

Governor Brown
Dear Sir

In conformity with your requisition, the military Authorities of this region are endeavoring to organize the Militia of the Several districts. Prof. Willet and Myself have been elected respectively first Lieutenant, and Captain of the 148th district, which embraces the town of Penfield within its limits. As good citizens, we desire to "obey the powers that be," but on some few points, we need information as to our duties. In the first place, we wish to know what is required of us in the way of uniforms. In consulting "Cobb's Digest," the Law seems to require that Commissioned officers should be provided with a blue frock coat, yet others who profess to know, assert that gray is now the established color of the Southern Confederacy. You would materially aid us in discharging our duty, by stating, whether any uniform is required of officers of the Militia in the present conjuncture of affairs; if so, what uniform is requested. Another point upon which we desire information is this. For the last dozen years, the students of our college have not been called upon to perform militia duty. Is it expected that they will now be regularly enrolled, and drill with the rest of the district?

Excuse us, for thus trespassing upon your time, for we are well aware that graver and more important questions fully occupy your attention.

With great respect, we remain

S. P. SANFORD
J. E. WILLET

TIME OF DISCOURAGEMENT

The month of October 1861 found the Confederates under Gen. Robert E. Lee in western Virginia very much discouraged. The spirit in Virginia and the South was vastly different from the jubilation of the weeks following First Manassas. In September Lee had failed in his efforts to get control of the pro-Union Virginia mountain region. Bad weather conditions had something to do with the failure of Lee's first campaign of the war, but a crucial point was Col. Albert Rust's bungling the attack at Cheat Mountain in the middle of September. The Confederate occupation of Bowling Green, Kentucky, on the 18th was not enough to dispel the atmosphere of gloom.

Added to Lee's disappointment because of failure, and partly contributory to it, was the lack of coordination and, seemingly, a lack of desire to cooperate between Generals Floyd and Wise. Gen. Henry A. Wise, former Virginia governor, was at Sewell Mountain, but Gen. B. Floyd, former United States secretary of

war, objected to Wise's choice of location and had occupied a
position at Meadow Bluff, about 12 miles from Wise.

Theodorick W. Montfort, from Oglethorpe, Georgia, wrote
home from Salem on 26 September, saying, "General Wise has
been compelled to retreat from Rosencrantz, the Yankee General. The enemy [Yankees] are now within 12 miles of Lewis-
burgh, our camp, so you may expect to hear of our being engaged
in a fight in 8 or 10 days. I hope it will not take place until all
of our Regt arrives and I get there with them." Floyd's camp
was 90 miles from Salem. On 8 October, Montfort wrote home
saying he thought he would have to remain at Salem for about
a week or longer until Col. B. A. Thornton arrived, "as it is my
duty to furnish them with transportation and provisions from
this point to Gen. Floyd's Camp." He was anxious to leave, "as
I wish to join the boys under Floyd." Wise, he said, had been
"recalled, or removed for the present."

In his letter of 26 September, Montfort reflects some of the
discouragement that ran through the camps from Gen. Lee to
the lowest private. He said,

> I am beginning to realize some of the Calamities of War and I wish
> to God some of the luke warm people of Ga were here to witness the scenes
> of distress that follows an invading army of Yankee enemies—women
> and children flying with such of their property as they could gather up
> in the hurry of the moment. The scenes are distressing. It would move
> the hardest heart to tears to witness it and hear their accounts of hardship
> and out rages that has been committed upon their persons and property.
> Unless we get assistance in this section of the state, I have fears that we
> shall be driven still further back.

Nevertheless, Montfort was determined and confident, and
found his comrades of like mind.

> Yet I have an abiding confidence in our Cause and Men. We are
> determined to fight with a reckless and desperate determination of men
> that have everything at stake and every wrong to avenge. The distress we
> daily witness added to the universal kindness and hospitality of the people
> and especially the ladies, moves every man with a feeling of determination
> to conquer or die.

Montfort's complaint about the "luke warm people of Ga"
may have been justified, but the boys from Middle Georgia farms

continued to join up. A neighbor of Montfort's not far away in Bibb County by the name of William J. Mosely was one of those boys to go into Confederate service about this time. Mosely's first of many letters that cover the entire war period is dated 27 October 1861. It was written from Camp Harrison, in Appling County. He had just reached camp when this letter was written. After being mustered in he was sent to Savannah, and later to Virginia. He much preferred Brunswick to Savannah for training, as Savannah didn't appeal to him for some reason.

He reported that 5,000 or 6,000 men were at Camp Harrison. So, we can conclude that a number of Georgia men were not "luke warm." In describing the provisions that were issued to the men, Mosely said, "We got beef, rice, flour, meal, sugar, soup and rye to make coffee when we have not enough coffee."

"I walked up the railroad," he said, "to a pond of water where the boys were washing themselves and if I ever told the truth in my life I think there was grease enough on the water to make a pot of soap."

A Visit to Andersonville

Earlier this month I found myself at Andersonville, the national cemetery where 12,912 Federal prisoners died in the adjoining stockade at the close of the greatest and most costly of all American wars, as reckoned in mortality statistics.

We were 200 strong in the motorcade from Americus which visited the prison grounds and cemetery. We were delegates attending the state conference of the Junior College Association at Georgia Southwestern College. Our guide was Dr. Robert Pendergrass, widely know radiologist, who has spent, as a hobby, as many years in research on Andersonville as McKinley Kantor spent in collecting material for his novel, and with closer scrutiny, geographically speaking.

Dr. Pendergrass confirmed many ideas of mine concerning the story of Andersonville and gave us much new and fresh information. He was particularly interested, of course, in the causes of death at the prison. More than a score of deaths was a normal daily mortality rate. Louis Manigault, on an inspection tour with Maj. Joseph Jones in 1864, reported 130 deaths one hot August day. The bodies were laid in long trenches with only the men's blankets to cover the bodies from the dirt that filled their long and shallow graves.

Our guide told how Gen. John H. Winder's nephew went to Blue [Radium] Springs to pick a location for the Confederate prison. He was ordered to locate it outside the war area. The people of Albany talked him out of choosing that place and he determined upon Andersonville, a village about ten miles north of Americus on the Southwestern Railroad. The location chosen showed his lack of sanitary engineering skill. Only a little sluggish stream flowed through the stockade, insufficient in force to carry off the waste of the prison. Filth was one of the major causes of death.

In addition to poor sanitary engineering was the fact that over 40,000 men finally were crowded into a stockade that was built to accommodate 10,000. Deep holes still seen near the line that had been the inner wall of pine poles around the prison are mute reminders of how the prisoners tried desperately to escape.

Lack of proper diet was another major reason for sickness and death. Louis Manigault said "scanty diet, with no variety, [caused] many of them [to] succumb to Hunger, not being accustomed to our Corn Harmony, and the Confederate government not having it in their power to furnish them wheat." Dr. Pendergrass gave me a letter which an Americus woman, Mrs. Florence Hollis, had dictated to her daughter in 1929. In it she said,

> Although this strain of getting food to eat and clothes to wear was hard, we never lost sight of our Soldiers, and when the prisoners and our own Soldiers were brought to Andersonville, the ladies formed a Society—The Ladies Aid Society, it was called—and every day so many were appointed to go to Andersonville to take food . . .

Our doctor guide gave statistics on the deaths. I do not recall the specific count, but more, I believe, died of dysentery and scurvy, dietary diseases, than of other causes. Some died of pneumonia and others of gangrene, and so on. He had exact figures for all, as the records were carefully kept and are now on file at the superintendent's office on the grounds. Uniform white stones, standing inches apart, mark the nearly 13,000 graves. Willie Collins and his five bad companions are set apart behind great magnolia trees. They died, as readers of Kantor's book well know, by hanging. Capt. Henry Wirz, prison keeper—the only "war criminal" to be executed in that war—gave the prisoners permission to organize their own Kangaroo Court. The six were found guilty as charged and were hanged on a gallows constructed in the prison yard. The most pathetic casualty in the records was the one lone soldier who died of "nostalgia."

I was standing with Allan Nevins one day as he reflected on the meaning of the row on row of white headstones at Andersonville. "The great tragedy of it is the unborn children of those who lie here," he said. "And," I replied, "what an inestimable loss for both sides in potential usefulness and goodness."

MEMORY OF CAPT. WIRZ

Last Sunday I wrote on Andersonville Prison. Today I want to write about Capt. Henry Wirz, the keeper of the prison.

The beautifully kept cemetery and the well-marked boundaries of the stockade, all part of an attractive national park, draw visitors by the thousands year in and year out. The crowds have grown larger since MacKinlay Kantor's Pulitzer prize-winning novel appeared.

Few people can resist the desire to turn in at the entrance to the stockade, drive around the ground viewing the deep holes near the borders where desperate Yankees tried to dig to freedom, get out of their cars and walk about the deep entrenchments that mark the fortification points, view with mystical awe the Providence Spring or drink the pure water with skeptical indifference. Fewer still, after an introduction to the stockade, can resist the urge to visit the nearly 13,000 headstones, row on row, that mark the graves of the human cordwood that rotted long ago underneath the green sod, admire the handsome monuments erected by the Northern states in grateful remembrance of those dead soldiers. But very few tourists drive 50 yards down the road running west of state highway 49 to the little village of Andersonville. It is just as well.

My grandfather was a civilian with Capt. Henry Wirz at Andersonville. His civilian status came about in this wise: the fingers of his right hand were stiff from the bite of a squirrel in his youth which prevented him from doing military duty. He was doing what he could in preparing drugs for the aid of the sick and wounded. This duty consisted chiefly of gathering roots and herbs around the countryside near Andersonville and Americus. Never let it be said Southerners were not trying to save lives. Yet, few lives were saved. Urgent requests were made of the Union to supply more medicines, and the Confederacy was begging for exchange of prisoners, all in vain. But that is another story.

After the war, many years later, my grandfather was in Chattanooga attending a joint reunion of the veterans of the Blue and the Gray. Finding himself in a group of Yankee veterans who embarrassed him by their boasting, he could not refrain, when asked by one of them what he did in the war, from saying, "Well boys, I helped administer drugs at Andersonville. Of the 13,000 Union soldiers who died there, surely you can credit me with a sizable number of them!"

But neither my grandfather nor Capt. Wirz can be held responsible for all that happened there. Not even Kantor blames Wirz. The villain in the story of Andersonville was Winder, he says. But Wirz was sentenced by a military court and put to death as a war criminal.

Just a few yards west of the highway that runs by the beautiful national cemetery and park, and at the intersection of the roads that cross to make the business corner of the little town of Andersonville, is a granite monument to Capt. Wirz, covered with the red dust of the roadway, ill-kept, and unattractive in its setting.

Many people feel that Capt. Wirz did not deserve the shame of being the only war criminal of that terrible bloodletting that did so little to drain off the poison of hate from the national body we call America. But the deed was done. It cannot be undone.

Wirz is just as surely dust now as the Yankee prisoners he kept confined in that crude stockade made of upright pine poles. But his monument deserves better treatment than it is getting. It is an embarrassment to Georgia to have travelers from distant states and foreign lands see the unsightly and dusty monument to one who paid a penalty for sins not his own.

An Americus lady who died at the age of 102 several years ago tells in her reminiscences of how she and a young girl went with Capt. Wirz to look at the prisoners from the top of the stockade wall. The "beautiful" but ill-advised young girl "was disposed to say ugly things to them, and glory in their being captured, and they in return would answer her . . ."

Today, young ladies have put away harsh words for the Yankee prisoners of Andersonville and are glad our national government keeps the park so clean and attractive. But could not our ladies find a way to relieve us of the embarrassment of an ugly monument? Could they not do something for a little pathetic German prison keeper who once let their grandmothers walk around the top of the prison wall to view the ragged mass of bluecoats within the stockade?

LETTER FROM A FATHER

There was a lull in battle activity in the late fall of 1861. In this period of comparative quiet, we have the opportunity to examine the life of the soldier in camp through letters to the folks back home. I have chosen one of Theodorick W. Montfort's letters to start this series of letters from camp. Montfort had joined the Wise Guards [Co. K, 25th Georgia Infantry] at his hometown of Oglethorpe. The letter follows.

Camp Meadow Bluff Va.
Nov. 3d 1861

My Dear Children

    David, Molley and Tebo

    Your father is here in the mountains of North Western Virginia, some eight or nine hundred miles from you, encamped with Several thousand Soldiers in a low wet marsh at the foot of the Mountains, doing his duty as a Soldier, in serving his Country.

I was gratified to learn from the letter of David and from your dear mother that you were all getting well. I hope that by this time you are all entirely recovered and able to attend to your mother.

I have requested your mother to write me if any of you fail to obey and attend to her kindly. I have no fear but what you will all do your duty and be kind and dutiful to her. It would distress me very much to know or hear that either one did not do it. I do not believe however that you will ever act amiss.

I have been quite sick since I left home. So sick that I had to be carried from the carrs to the Hotel; and I once feared I should never see you all again, but I am glad to say that my health has improved and my health is now good with the exception of a bad cold and cough—that everybody in the Camp has, oweing to the wet muddy place we are encampted at.

I have plenty to eat. Yet the life of a soldier is a hard one. The weather is now and has been for ten days very cold. The ice here is several inches thick and has not melted for ten days—and it raines about every other day.

On day before yesterday, I had to take thirty men and stand picket Guard some three miles from Camp for twenty four hours a day and night without fire and it raining and sleeting all the time.

These are hardships that all soldiers have to under go, and when we are relieved from duty, we have no comfortable room with a fire place to go to and dry or put on dry clothes, but have either to go to our tent that is damp and wet and go to sleep in this fix or stand around a fire out doors in the cold and rain.

So while you are all at home where you can keep dry with a good room fire and bed to sleep in you should feel grateful and take care of everything as your father is undergoing these hardships and dangers that you might remain at home and be comfortable as you are.

You should never do wrong or any thing against your mothers wishes. I shall know from time to time which of you do the best and I intend to give that one a hansome present of some kind. I wish I had something to send you all but I am here in the mountains away from Towns and Rail Roads and can get nothing to send you. I sent you chesnuts by Mr. Burnes which I hope you all recd.

We are expecting in a few days to be moved from this place to some other, to go into winter quarters where I hope to be more comfortably situated and where also I hope to be able to get something to send you.

I hope to be able, my Children, to Come home once at least to see you before my term of service is out, but Cannot tell that I shall be able to do so. But when I do come I want to find that you have done every thing right and have improved in every respect.

Molley must study hard and learn to write so as to write me, before my time is out and David must be particular in his spelling. He must

Superintend and see to evry thing on the place as no one else is there to do it, see to the feeding of the horses, hogs and cows and locking up the corn house and evry thing else that needs and requires attention.

There are a great many cases of measels in camp. Some 1800 are at the Hospital from sickness mostly measels. Out of our Company of 80 or 90 men only 20 are able to do duty and they have bad colds and coughs. I have yet got to have the measels.

I dread to be sick in Camp with none of you or your mother to wait on me, with no house or bed to ly on and no fire. I hope I may escape this army scourge. If, however, I should not, I must submit to it as it is a soldier's lot.

Tell your mother to send me with my other things that I have written home for, several pair of good new woolen socks, as I am nearly out of socks. Can't Mollie nett me a pr. How glad I would be to have a pr nett by her. Can't she and Floyd and some of the other little girls make with their own hands one of the Comforts I have written home for.

You must also attend to evry thing but especially your mother, as I should be deeply mortified for her to write me that either one of you was not dutiful and kind. I do not think she will ever have to do it.

I wish I was there with you all if it was only to remain one hour, yes if it was only long enough to kiss you all. David and Molly must not loose a day from school, so go ahead, study hard and do right.

I have written now untill I am nearly frozen and must close this letter to go to the fire. Each one of you kiss your mother for me and tell her to kiss you all for me. I hope some day to get back home to kiss you all whom I dearly love.

Your Father
T. W. Montfort

LETTER FROM SKIDAWAY

Last Sunday this column carried a letter from the western part of Virginia written by Theodorick W. Montfort of Oglethorpe, Georgia. Today's letter in the series of soldiers' letters from the camps was written from Camp Adams on Skidaway Island, near Savannah. Many boys were experiencing their first taste of army life in Georgia camps before being sent to Virginia and elsewhere. William W. Head, from Milner, Georgia, was in Co. D, 31st Georgia Infantry, popularly known as the "Monroe Crowders." He remained in and around Savannah until the summer of 1862 before going to Virginia. The original of this letter is in the possesson of Mrs. Ted R. English of Macon. Her permission to use it is gratefully acknowledged.

Camp Adams Skidaway Island
Nov. 3rd, 1861

Dear Fannie,

I received your letter of the 30th, ultimo a few minutes since and hasten to reply. It affords me indescribable pleasure in my island home, to hear from you. Fannie, to tell you how I am getting along in every respect is difficult indeed. The incidents of every day's occurrence, would fill a little book. And we are near thirty miles from any post office, entirely dependant upon the wagoner, who brings in our daily supply of beef, to send letters to Savannah or to receive them when sent to us. Again we cannot pay postage on our letters, though they must be paid to us.

Since I wrote to you and the children, I have had a regular spell of camp dysentery, though my health is now first rate. Indeed my health was never better. James Smith has been at the very door of death, but is now considered out of danger, for 24 hours I sat by him nearly all the time expecting every hour to be his last. Mark Weldon died in camp day before yesterday. His remains were sent to Griffin for interment. On last Thursday our company, "Monroe Crowders," were ordered to the extreme Southern portion of this island, where we are now, on picket duty.

We brought 8 of our tents, 29 Enfield rifles, 35 double barrel shot guns, 63 men, knapsacks etc. and are here in fine health and spirits. We left 8 men at Camp Skidaway in charge of our property and tents left behind. We sought and obtained the post of honor. Our provisions are plentiful though plain, consisting of sea bread, corn meal, rice, coffee, sugar, bacon, fresh beef, etc. Fish and oysters too plentiful to be good. I have not eaten any of either yet. I can stand up and see the waves of the ocean as they chaise each other to shore and back to sea again. Vessels of various kinds are passing regularly all of which are hailed by our sentinels and friendly signals exchanged. We heard the canonading of a little fight on Warsaw Island 4 or 5 miles from us on Wednesday evening last. Nobody hurt on our side. Like Robinson Cruso we are monarchs of all we survey. Seldom seeing any landsmen except our own men. I have not seen a white woman since leaving Savannah.

Fannie, I get up at day break, attend roll call and prayer, have breakfast about 7 o'clock, go on duty until about 10 o'clock, have dinner at noon, work from 2 to 5 p.m. Sup at 6, prayer at 8, go to bed at 8 1/2 p.m. Thus the time passes from day to day. I enjoy myself saving your absence and my concern about home. We have a system of signals, so arranged, that should any one point be attacked a large force can be concentrated in a short time.

On yesterday I received a long, and very welcome letter from Bro. Lawson which I will answer at my first opportunity. Also one from little Billie Ogletree.

Fannie, send William, Smith & Lucinda word about Jimmie's sickness and that he will be sent home as soon as he is able to travel. He receives all the attention that kindness can bestow, though I cannot now visit him, I hear from him regularly. Every man in our company is well excepting slight colds. Nearly all the boys have had the dreaded dysentery and passed through safely. Tell Ola if she has the mumps when Pa comes, he will give her forty six, well laid on. Tell Johnny Jimmie and Sis I shall bring them something nice when I come home, which I shall do sometime before or by Christmas if possible. I forgot to tell you that Capt. Crowder, Lieut. Settle, myself and eight others were quartered in one tent now, though regularly the Capt. & I have a tent to ourselves.

I want you dear Fannie in your next to tell me how much corn you put up, how much peas you gathered, how much you collected or recd from the churches and all about the business. When you get done sowing wheat, sow oats & rye if you can get seed.

I have many things to tell you when I see you. Till which time good bye & may God bless you all.

Wm. W. Head

As a Colonel Sees War

Lt. Col. James M. Newton of the 5th Georgia wrote his Butts County neighbor, Charles Hammond, from Yorktown, Virginia, on 18 July 1861. Newton went into service with the Butts County Volunteers as their captain, but was immediately elected lieutenant colonel of the regiment. He was killed on the bloodiest day of the war at Antietam, 17 September 1862. His letter written at the beginning of the war is so full of meaning that I quote it here almost in its entirety. The original is in the possession of Mrs. Paul E. Middlebrooks, of Macon, to whom I am indebted for its use.

York Town Va.
July 18, 1861

Friend Hammond,

I thought when I left Georgia that I left behind a number of warm friends, but if I judge their friendship by the number and length of their correspondence they prove to be few and far between. Is it so? Have you all forgotten me? Or do you think I need no word of encouragement? Where are those warm friends of mine that contended so strongly, and fought so bravely for immediate Secessun?

Have they made any great sacrifice to aid in establishing our independence? Are they sustained those men that have sacrificed their lives to sustain Southern independence? For myself I ask nothing only to be gratefully remembered by my friends at home. . . .

Encamped as we are upon the very ground that witnessed the closing scenes of the American revolution, I sometimes think that it is but a continuation of the same. For it is but a revolution, that same principle of self-government that our fathers contended for is the very principle that we are contending for to day. And we pledge ourselves as men and patriots never to lay down our arms nor return peaceably to our homes until that inestimable right so dear to every patriot's heart is firmly established in the South. To do this from present indication may require time and money. So prepare the Southern mind for heavy taxes or liberal contributions in the way of Subscriptions. Our men must be sustained either by voluntary or involuntary contributions. But our drums are beating for Battalion and I must take charge of my wing.

Our drill is over and I will fill up my letter. It is impossible in the short space of a letter to give you even a faint idea of the many little incidents that have occurred since our arrival at this place. We have been busily employed all the time in throwing up fortifications and drilling our men. We have marched over and explored the whole country between York & James river. A portion of our regiment went under and within range of the enemies' guns, at Hampton & Newport News drove in their pickets. We had only 3000 men, the enemy 6000 but we could not draw them out. We remained a week, sleeping in the woods and swamps with but a single blanket for covering to each man. Our boys stood it like heroes.

The only complaint was that we could not meet the enemy. We have been anticipating an attack on this place for some time. But I begin to think that they are afraid of us since the decent thrashing we gave them at Bethel, and fear that we will remain here sometime without having the pleasure of a fight with them.

We have many privations to undergo, but notwithstanding I enjoy camp life finely, much better than I expected. A man with a sword by his side and feather in his hat, it matters not what may have been his standing at home, is looked upon as some "pumpkin." But poor privates! What shall I say of them? They have all the work and in many regiments are hardly treated with common respect. I am proud to say we have the cleverest, most honorable set of men for privates of any Reg. in the service. I visit them in their afflictions, converse with them. Generally, the con-

sequence is *I know them well and have formed strong attachments for them.*

My paper is full. If you can make out anything from this disconnected letter it is more than I can do.

Your friend

J. M. Newton

LIFE AMONG THE SOLDIERS

Some Christmas cards in this year's lot were as beautiful as any I have ever received, some were traditional—and I love the ones that follow the central theme of the season, that is, the birth of Christ—some were ultramodern, and some were amusing. The most amusing one this year was a "Johnny Reb" card from Bell Wiley and his publisher Seale Johnson. It was expected, for they have been sending this type of card at Christmas for some years. I look forward to it each Christmas because it not only is amusing but because it always points out some interesting phase of the life of the common soldiers during the Civil War.

The card contains a print of a fraternizing scene between Union and Confederate soldiers. They are bantering one another and swimming in the Chattahoochee river. The sketch was drawn by Wilbur Kurtz, long recognized for his ability as an artist and his knowledge of Atlanta during the war period. The text is in the form of a letter, which results from Bell Wiley's reading of thousands of letters from the common soldiers on both sides of the conflict.

One of the most peculiar things about this strange war was the informal mixing of the common soldiers of the armies of both the North and the South. They would meet quite often on neutral ground between the lines to confab, trade, pick berries, and even bury their dead, as Wiley points out in his *Life of Billy Yank*.

Often the Confederates would trade or barter tobacco, which they usually had, for coffee, which they could get more often from the enemy than from their own commissary. Newspapers made another item of barter for the Rebels. These could be traded for Yankee articles such as canteens, pocketknives, or soap— one of the scarcest articles in the Confederate army, and least used, Billy Yank might say. In one of William Mosely's letters, I recall, he implored his mother to send soap: "We get plenty of everything except Soap. If you ever Send me anything I want it to be a piece of Soap."

Gambling with the Yankees sometimes was more exciting than with one's own comrades, and sometimes more lucrative— when Johnny Reb won the stakes. Swimming together seems to have been a not unusual practice, according to Wiley. This, of course, was unofficial and against orders. On the other hand, sometimes a formal burial service might take place at which time chaplains of each army would perform the rites for their respective dead on the same burial ground. One time, Wiley says, the "Rebs borrowed shovels from the Yankees to dig graves for their dead."

I have only space left for Bell Wiley's and Seale Johnson's "Krismus" letter. Here it is in full.

Banks of the forky dear
Jaxsun, Tinysea, Krismus 186-

Deer frens

 The kalender sais hits krismus agen tho we'd knot have node hit ef'n the ofisers hadnt got tanked up on How Cum You So and frolicked til well nigh dalite. We privets kaint affoard to by the stuff eny moar and hits giting nigh onto imposable to steel hit from the commasary. Our krismus dinner konsisted of sow belly so fresh that the tits was still on it and korn poan that was so full of wurms and weavils thet it was mor on the order of meet than bred. We ar hoping Ole Forris wll taik us on a rade sune so we wont have to bea so hongry, thursty and ragid. Hits onley rite thet the hi and mity Yanks shuld sheer thear plinty.

When we wuz down in Gawga last suma and was bathing our karakases in the Chatyhoochy [ef'n you kaint pro nouns hit jist sneaze and you'll cum purty clost] sum blue bellys cum up and wanted to jine us in the swim. We toald 'em they'd have to wate til we got threw on account of we didn't want to be poluted with thair kind of dirt. After we'd shed all our grabacks we cleered out and bid em take a dip. Thair blud will probly pizen our diskarded lise but 'twil serve both partys rite. The pichur of this scean was drawed by Wilber kirts a fren we met in atlantuh. He sed we cood send you a kopy. Best wishes uf the seeson

Ever yoarn with bes respecks

Seale Johnson
Bell Wiley

THE NONBATTLE DEATHS

Among the great tragedies of the Civil War is not simply the fact that more than 600,000 died on both sides, but that the majority of these died of causes other than battle deaths. Many of the wounded, moreover, died because of a lack of germ-killing drugs—one might say they were the victims of germ warfare, in a passive sort of way. The statistics bear this out. Union forces lost only 110,000 in battle deaths while losing more than 250,000 from other causes; the Confederates lost 94,000 in battle deaths while losing 164,000 from other causes.

Of course, one cannot say the nonbattle deaths were useless— in a sense all the war dead, pragmatically speaking, would have served a greater cause had they lived—but present-day drugs and care would have saved most of these. One of the very few benefits gained from this or any other war is the forward progress in the field of medicine, which is born out of necessity.

A case study of the question of how the soldiers died has come to my attention recently in the form of a roll call of the 29 Mercer

University students who gave their lives for Southern independence. This book of the dead was prepared by the hand of
Prof. Joseph E. Willet, who was teaching chemistry at the Penfield institution [Mercer was then at Penfield, in Greene County]
when the war broke out and who volunteered his services as a
chemist in Confederate laboratories for the duration of the war.
Prof. Willet recorded the names of those who died, along with
pertinent information including cause of death and other notes,
with what seems to have been loving care. He has, in effect,
created a memorial volume from this data.

I have taken this very human and tender document and reduced it to cold statistics. In my analysis I find only 9 of the 29
were known by Prof. Willet to have died on the battlefield; 11
died of diseases, 4 died of wounds after being removed from the
field of battle, and 5 were listed without any information as to
cause of death.

The 9 killed in battle were as follows: Pvt. Pleasant Stovall
Bonner, of Morgan County, was killed at the Crater, near Pe-
tersburg, Virginia. James Alexander Simmons, a first lieutenant
from Alabama, was killed at the Battle of Yellow Bayou on 18
May 1864. Second Lt. Frederic Ezekiel Wimberly, of Twiggs
County, was killed at Sharpsburg [Antietam]—that bloodiest
day of the war—27 Sept. 1862. Sgt. William C. Chapman, of
Crawfordville, was killed at Second Manassas "while trying to
carry off a wounded comrade" in retreat of his regiment. Pvt.
Leonidas Walter Howell, another Alabama boy, was killed at
Chickamauga—shot in the head. Pvt. Charles Baldwin Harris,
of Greene County, was killed in the battle of Spotsylvania Court
House. Sgt. William Thomas Head, of Monroe County, was killed
at Seven Pines, his body "pierced through by minnie balls." Lt.
F. Lorraine Hillyer, from Baldwin County, fell mortally wounded
defending a position near Manassas Gap on the retreat from
Gettysburg. He had earlier been wounded near this very place
in the Second Battle of Manassas. Sgt. Richard Montgomery
Preston, from Walton County, was hit in the head by shrapnel
and died on 23 Aug. 1862 at Rappahannock Station on the Manassas railroad.

Lt. Judson C. Sapp, from Burke County, died at Martinsburg, Virginia, on 19 October 1863, from wounds he received in the second day's fighting at Gettysburg. His arm had been amputated in an effort to save his life, but all in vain. Sgt. Thomas Jefferson Dyson, of Monroe County, was mortally wounded at the Battle of Bakers Creek, Mississippi, on 16 June 1863, and died three days later. He lived long enough to write his father: "I have done all I can, I die for my country." George Tilly Burch, a Crawfordville boy 19 years of age and captain of his company [Co. I, 29th Georgia], was wounded at Kennesaw Mountain on 15 June 1864 and carried to Atlanta where he died. Lt. Robert Henry Cadenhead, from Alabama, another 19-year-old boy, was wounded [the battle is not recorded] on 14 May 1863 and died two days later.

MERCER'S ROLL OF HONOR

In the previous installment it was pointed out that more soldiers in the Civil War died of wounds and diseases than were killed outright on the battlefield. This was true also, as we have seen, of the 29 Mercer University students who gave their lives.

Prof. Joseph E. Willet, Mercer chemist who served the Confederacy in the production of explosives and who kept the record of the Mercer dead, was not as thorough in recording types of diseases as he was in describing the details of battle deaths. In one instance he says one of the boys died of "fever," in two others he speaks of "camp fever," and in another he simply names "disease" as the cause of death.

Adj. Francis Callaway Shropshire, of Oglethorpe County, died of "typhoid fever" on 4 July 1862 in a Richmond hospital. Lt. Thomas Joel Pinson, of Coweta County, died of "typhoid fever" on 3 Aug. 1861 at Culpepper Court House, Virginia. Just a little while before, he had been under fire at Manassas. When his gun failed him, he seized one from the hands of a wounded comrade and continued firing.

Thomas William Davis, of Newton County, died of "typhoid dysentery" on 19 July 1863 at Vicksburg. For acts of bravery in defending the city, he had been promoted to the rank of captain of Company G, 42nd Georgia. Pvt. William L. McElmurray had enlisted in the Burke [County] Sharp Shooters [Co. D, 2nd Georgia] on 19 April 1861. He died of typhoid on 3 Oct. 1862 at Manassas. A Mrs. Wheeler, who lived on the Manassas battlefield, nursed him in his last hours.

George Welch Kimberly, of Twiggs County, was made captain of his company [Co. K, 11th Georgia] at the time of its organization. He died of "disease" in Richmond on 21 June 1862. Sgt. Robert R. F. Prior, of Morgan County, a member of the Pamola Guards, Cobb's Legion, died of typhoid at Richmond. His mother visited him before he died and brought his remains home to lie in the old family cemetery. Pvt. Joel Hogg, of Greene County, died of typhoid fever in Petersburg, Virginia, on 10 July 1862. Lt. Albert Thomas Johnson, also of Greene County, died of "camp fever" on 7 Aug. 1862 at Drury's Bluff, Virginia. John D. McFarland, of LaGrange, enlisted at Savannah in May 1862. He was in Company B, 60th Georgia, Gordon's Brigade, Jackson's Corps. He died of "camp fever" on 24 Aug. 1862 at LaGrange, after having been sent home from Richmond. Pvt. William Marshall Walker, of Columbus, died of "fever" on 30 July 1863 in a hospital at Mt. Jackson, Virginia. The stepmother of this boy, just turned 18, was with him when he died.

Three illustrations of heroism will suffice to show the spirit in which 29 Mercer men, 258,000 Confederates, and 360,222 Federals died. The first reveals cowardice on the part of a major but bravery on the part of his subordinate. Capt. George Burch had an opportunity to show the stuff he was made of when the major of his regiment lacked the courage to attack the enemy, strongly entrenched in a certain sector. Burch took command and led an attack at Kennesaw Mountain until he fell wounded. He died soon after in Atlanta.

Sgt. William Chapman was killed while trying to carry a wounded comrade off the battlefield. He had participated in several battles, including the Seven Days' fight around Richmond. He had been slightly wounded at Malvern Hill and severely wounded at Second Manassas. He saw action at Fredericksburg, Chancellorsville, and Gettysburg. It was in retreat from Gettysburg that he was mortally wounded. His regiment was ordered to cover the retreat of the army at Manassas Gap. His comrade, Lorraine Hillyer, was dying of wounds and asked to be carried back with the retreating army. It was while assisting in this service to his friend that Chapman was killed.

According to Prof. Willet, Adj. Thomas Dyson was a "quiet unassuming, kind, generous" lad, "brave to a fault." He had dismounted—"it's pretty high up here"—and was "holding his sword high with his right hand and waving his hat with his left and urging his men on" when he was hit at Bakers Creek, Mississippi, 16 June 1863.

THE LITTLE BLACK BOOK

I love a mystery. This one I especially like because it has a real challenge and seems impossible to solve. But I believe I will end up with a probable answer—at least it will be logical. The mystery concerns the day-by-day account of one of the "Baldwin Blues" from 1 November 1861 to 28 April 1864, which is contained in a little black book loaned to me by Miss Elise Denton, of this city.

The little book, with its leather binding, pocket size and a half inch thick has been in the Denton family ever since Miss Elise's father got home from his two-year imprisonment at Ft. Delaware, having been released in June 1865.

My first theory was that the unsigned diary was that of Pvt. James Washington Denton, Miss Elise's father. But this was proved impossible by a quick check on his military record, which showed that he was captured at Gettysburg on 3 July 1863 and imprisoned at Ft. Delaware, where he was confined until his release after Appomattox.

Since the diary covers in detail the movements of the writer from 1 November 1861 to 3 July 1863—the Battle of Gettysburg—and battle and camp experiences on beyond to 28 April 1864, it would have been impossible for James Denton, in prison most of this time, to have been the author of the diary.

Then who was the author? My second assumption is more plausible, but not proved. It is that Elisha D. Holcombe was the author. He was originally from the vicinity of Asheville, North Carolina, if certain evidence in the book is correctly interpreted. Near the front of the book, in what appears to be the same handwriting as the diary, is a notation dated 10 March 1861, which reads, "My notes in care of James Sawyer of Buncombe Co., N. Carolina." Another entry dated 22 Nov. 1859, shows the same person bought "one over coat for $7.00 from Lindsey, Holcombe & Co." And again one reads, "Wm Carter Started to Georgia Nov. the 18th, 1858." It is a fact that Elisha Holcombe enlisted in the "Baldwin Blues" at Milledgeville on 26 April 1861. Pasted into the little black mystery book is a 30-day furlough issued on 30 April 1864 to Pvt. Elisha D. Holcombe, Co. H, 4th Georgia Volunteers. This was the "Baldwin Blues." Pvt. James Denton was also a member of this same company. Since Denton could not have kept the diary and since this much evidence favoring Holcombe is contained in the book, I believe Holcombe kept the diary. But how did it find its way back to Denton? Next week I shall give the clue that seems to unlock this secret. In the meanwhile, if any reader of this column has any guesses I shall be happy to hear them. It is entirely possible that someone in Baldwin County may come up with a solution.

A roster of the company appears in the book. Four of the captains who served are named. They are J. W. Caraker, E. A. Hawkins, J. W. Green, and J. W. Butts. In checking the records I find that George Doles was its first captain. Doles rose to the rank of brigadier general and was killed at Bethesda Church on 2 June 1864. Samuel McComb was also captain for awhile, but was killed, as was Eugene Hawkins. James Wallace Butts was elected captain of this company on 6 Feb. 1863. He was wounded once in the hand and lost it, and later was wounded in the leg, and it, too, was amputated.

I have established the fact that the diary did not record the events in the life of James Denton, but there are two scraps of paper in the book that apparently did belong to Denton. One is an unsigned letter presumably from Denton to a Miss Pedrick, of Baltimore. The other is one from that lady to "My Dear Friend." The soldier's letter is positively in a different handwriting from that of the diary. Miss Pedrick had already written to prisoner Denton when he penned the following:

Fort Deleware March 31st 1865

Miss Pedrick

Yours of the 25th has been received with contents for which I have not words to express my thanks. The favor will ever be remembered by me having no reward to promise to you for your kindness of only the reward from him who rules all things both in heaven and earth it looks like I with many others are doomed to live and die upon this Island though I hope God will be with us, and guide and direct our rulers in the right and maybe Speed the time when we can return to our home and friends in peace, from your true friend I have been blessed with health Since my imprisonment except a Severe case of Small Pox [.]

Then Miss Pedrick replied:

Baltimore April 11th 1865

My Dear Friend

I can scarce hope my letters will be of interest to you, and only regret my inability to give you such comfort as your situation demands. But dear friend, your time of imprisonment I think now will soon expire and you can return to your long absent home. You have never told me what part of Georgia you lived and tell me what relations you have. I ask not for idle curiosity, but for the feeling of interest as an older sister for a younger brother. So you see I imagine you quite young. Now tell me if I have guessed rightly! Do you know any one residing at Fort Gaines or any one by the name of Williams? Can you tell me if there are among the prisoners any Masons? With best wishes I remain truly your friend

A. F. Pedrick

This correspondence led to no romance, however. Denton returned home to marry Mary Powers, and Miss Pedrick became simply a name in a little black book brought home from the war.

DIARY ON BALDWIN BLUES

In this column last week I introduced the mystery diary and showed how Pvt. James Denton could not possibly have written it. I also quoted from correspondence that appears to have been carried on between Denton and a Baltimore lady who was interested in his imprisonment at Ft. Delaware. Now, let us follow Pvt. Elisha Holcombe, or if not him, then some unknown soldier who recorded his day-to-day experiences in the little black book.

Holcombe, who in all probability kept the diary from which the excerpts below are taken, made no more entries in his diary after 28 April 1864. About two weeks later [10 May], he was captured during the Battle of Spotsylvania Court House. He died of pneumonia at Ft. Delaware on 19 Jan. 1865.

And here we have the clue promised last week—the clue that solves the riddle of how the diary fell into the hands of James Denton. The answer is now clear. Has it already been guessed? Obviously, Denton brought his dead comrade's diary home with him when he was released.

The diary is a good record of the activity of the Baldwin Blues during the period that it covers. I shall quote a portion of it below, as space allows, and from time to time I shall return to this very interesting diary to follow the Blues through important days in Virginia, Maryland, and Pennsylvania. The Blues were in the thick of it, in and around Petersburg, Richmond, and the Shenandoah Valley. They saw action at Drewry's Bluff, Malvern Hill, Orange Court House, Antietam, Fredericksburg, and Gettysburg, to mention a few of the major battles covered by the diary.

Now that the mystery has been cleared up, as indeed I believe it has, let's accept the theory that the diary was that of Elisha Holcombe, at least until and unless someone proves otherwise.

Holcombe was apparently a sentimental man, for pasted into the book is a sheet of paper containing a poem, penned in the same handwriting as the diary. It is called the "Sunny South." It is too dim to enable one to read all the verses easily, but the fourth and fifth verses are as follows:

I left a pretty girl my heart's gallant Star
More beautiful than others more precious by far
Though she weeped when I started she asked me not to stay
And I gave her my hand as I hastened away.

Oh Mother, dear Mother, for me do [not] weep
Your kind advice I forever shall keep
You taught me to be brave from my boyhood to a man
And I am going in defense of my own native land.

The diary for the month of February 1862, includes the following:

Camp Jackson
Februrary 1862
   1/ [Saturday] Rained all knight & east winds I slept half the day Burnsides fleet at Hateras.
   2/ Cool 10 O. C. Company Inspection 4 O. C. dress parade I stayed all knight with Wm. Butler.
   3/ 7 O. C. Snowing fast 12 O. C. turned rained all the eavening.
   4/ The forenoon raining 4 O. C. dress parade T Nappin & Mahler arrives letter from Mrs. J. R. J. & one from Miss M. J.

5/ fair morning Payne & me out in the Country 10 O. C. [Battalion] drill 4 O. C. dress parade strong appeal to the twelve months [Volunteers] to re-enlist.

6/ 7 O. C. raining 12 O. C. raining 2 O. C. rain ceased. The Merrimac men sent after.

7/ fair and warm Books open for re-enlisting Brand Gellespie & me on Picket No. 4 on other side.

8/ Reamy leaves for home on furlough Raining all day.

9/ no inspection fight on Roanoke.

10/ grate excitement Elizabeth City Burned.

11/ 10 O. C. Batalion drill Payne & me takes a trip in the Country plenty of fun.

12/ Commenced Picketing the beach 10 O. C. B. D. 1 1/2 O. C. B. D. 4 O. C. D. P. letter from Miss N. S. R.

13/ Warm 10 O. C. B. D. 4 O. C. D. P.

14/ Payne & me in the Country 10 O. C. B. D. Mappin Gellespie & me on Picket Post No. 3 on other side.

15/ writing all day cold and sleeting.

16/ Cold no inspection 4 O. C. D. P.

17/ rained all day recd a letter from Miss E. R. H.

18/ grate excitement fighting at fort Donaldson 4 O. C. D. P.

19/ rain bad news from Donaldson.

20/ fair and warm 10 O. C. B. D. 4 O. C. D. P. Paid off Mappin Green & me on picket No. 1 on this side.

21/ fair 10 O. C. B. D. 4 O. C. D. P.

22/ lazy fogg Vice President Hamlin visit for Monroe and Newport Neuse.

23/ Delanney & George Caraer leaves for Geo.

DEAF EAR TO DUTY'S CALL

It can be said to the credit of both the Rebels in Gray and the Yankee Blue Coats that most of them took whatever suffering or even death that fate had in store for them, endured it with courage and fortitude. Fear and uncertainty drove comparatively few of them to desert or find other ways to avoid battle, but desertions were not uncommon, and the officers had difficulty keeping some men in line of duty.

A number of men were clever enough to avoid service altogether. I am reminded of a story of one such young Southerner who never hid from the guard sent out to find him. He merely sat on his front porch in a rocking chair, dressed as a woman, and when the soldiers appeared he would send them off on a wild goose chase by giving false directions in a high, squeaky voice.

Bounties as high as $50 were offered volunteers. I have heard of men who worked their way through the war without ever fighting in a battle or firing a single shot. The bounty jumper would volunteer at one place, collect his bounty, then desert and volunteer at another place, collect his bounty, desert again, and so on until the war ended.

Officers were often annoyed by desertions from camp, especially on the eve of an important campaign. On the other hand, the officers were sometimes so terribly irritated by recalcitrant privates that they wished they would desert. This brings to mind a complaint of a Capt. Hoge.

Pvt. William Kendall had been sent to the hospital the previous November and had skipped out. According to the records he was heard from no more. Capt. Hoge hoped Dell Mann would do the same, for he was "so mean." Here is the way Capt. Hoge described it to Miss Gene:

> Dell Mann the vilest rascal on the face of the earth has at last managed to get to the Hospital at Richmond. I sinerely hope he will desert from the Hospital as Kendall did, it would be a very great relief to the Company. Mann is such a thief and in every way so mean that none of the boys will allow him to stay with them and for the last two weeks that he was with us I let him board out of camp because the boys were all unwilling to associate with him.

A check of the records shows Dell did get a discharge from the hospital because of "disability." This must have been quite a relief for his captain, and from Hoge's remarks neither did the men of his company shed tears for him.

The rate of desertions increased as the war dragged on, and in the closing months many Rebels were lured away from duty by promises of reward by Union troops. W. J. Moseley writing to his mother a few weeks before the end of the hostilities described conditions in his regiment, which was stationed near Petersburg.

> I was in pretty good heart until I returned to the command and found this army in such low spirits, just between me and you, we are in a bad fix and must have help soon or we are Surely gone by the board [.] I would not talk this where it would have any influence towards injuring our cause if it can be injured. Ma I think all that lives to See the 25th day of next December, will See peace on Some terms, for if we put the Negroes in we have got to make a quick fight of it, for we cannot feed them long, and I do not believe they will be any advantage to us nohow. I will tell you how we have to do our men on Picket, when one goes after

wood [the wood being between the lines] we have to Send with them a
guard with loaded guns under an officer to keep them from deserting
and going to the Yankees. And then there is from five to ten leaves our
Brig. every week [.] The reason they desert worse now than before [is]
the yankees have Sent around some handbills to induce them to come
over[.] They offer to give them $150.00 in green backs for every gun and
accroutrements they bring, and give them 10 days rations and Send them
free of charge to any part of the world that they [the Yankees] have
correspondence with or give them employment in the government Shops
north. Well I never have Seen Such a gloomy time before[.] We are a
whipped People if we can't Stop So much desertion.

The quotation above is from Sgt. William Mosely's letter of
19 February 1865. Readers of this column are now familiar with
Sgt. Mosely. The desertion rate as determined by Ella Lonn,
mentioned previously, was one out of nine in the Confederate
army, one out of seven in the Union army [*Telegraph-News*, 13
Aug. 1961].

CALLING MORE VOLUNTEERS

With the spring campaign in Virginia opening up and the moving of Union gunboats down the Atlantic coast toward Savannah, there was renewed effort to enlist more volunteers for defense of the Southland and especially for the Georgia coast. Macon had been getting ready for some time to welcome the two local companies, the Floyd Rifles and Macon Volunteers, which were with the Second Georgia Battalion at Norfolk. But as late as 28 March, the town was still looking for them in vain. Through the *Telegraph*, the local citizens were advised that the planned "Basket dinner is postponed." W. H. Ellison had left Macon for Norfolk the first Monday of the month and had announced through the newspaper that he would "cheerfully take letters and small Packages for the Floyd Rifles and Macon Volunteers."

Where were the men most urgently needed, in Virginia or on the Georgia coast? That was the question, and President Davis and Gov. Brown were having difficulty in agreeing upon the answer. Some men were shifted to Savannah and some were transferred from Savannah to Virginia. Capt. Hoge wrote saying that 16 men stationed in Savannah had applied for a transfer to his company in Virginia. He thought there would have been as many as 40 had it not been for the fact that "Joe Wardlaw had been to Skidaway and had told such awful tales concerning the condition of our company that many were afraid to make the transfer."

The Macon paper made a strong appeal for volunteers: "Come up at once and join the Volunteers—learn the training and discipline of the soldier—and go forth to do battle for your country's honor! Arouse! Awake! or we are forever fallen." A parade was held to raise the Bibb County quota. One hundred and forty-six volunteered, which was 17 above the quota. An observer said it was

> a frightful sight to see the number of gray and bald headed men in the ranks, who refused to confess to overage . . . we . . . admired their spunk, but still men between sixty and eighty should be more careful of themselves.

Even the politicans felt the call of duty on the battlefield. When Gov. Brown advised Robert Toombs that the Georgia legislature had elected him to the Senate of the Confederate Congress, Toombs replied, "I have determined that I can now better serve my State and Country in the Army than in the Senate." The response statewide to the appeal for volunteers was gratifying. With a quota of only 12,000, Georgia raised 22,000 before the month ended.

But there were obstructionists. And they bothered Capt. M. R. Rogers of the Gresham Rifles. He sounded off about it in a letter to the editor of the *Macon Daily Telegraph*.

> I suppose every community is cursed, like this one, with a class of persons presenting every obstacle possible to retard and prevent our success as a nation. Their modes are various; they will not volunteer to fight our battles or help the families of those that do, only when it is forced upon them—always predicting misfortune to our cause, and where volunteers are called for, by false reports and base insinuations do everything they can to keep men from volunteering. Some of this class for the last few days have made themselves busy about the Gresham Rifles being disbanded, and not having efficient officers, and various objections which they have to the organization. The same difficulty

has been presented to every company formed in the city by these blights
that infect every Southern community.

E. M. Coulter, in *The Confederate States of America*, quotes
a patriotic Georgian as saying he hoped "history may not per-
petuate the damning disgrace that ten millions of freemen, for
the love of money, let themselves be subjected by twenty millions
whom they pronounced cowards." The Peninsula Campaign,
which opened up a Union drive on Richmond in the spring, made
such heavy demands upon the men of the South that in spite of
the fact that the states were exceeding their quotas, more men
were needed. President Davis recommended conscription to the
Confederate Congress on 28 March, and Congress enacted it into
law on 16 April. There was a great deal of opposition expressed
in Southern papers to compulsory military service. A lengthy
and forceful protest had appeared in the Macon paper on 9 April.
A conflict between Davis and Brown over the question of conscription into the Confederate armies became as hot a fight as
some of the battles between the Blue and the Gray, and many
Georgians joined Gov. Brown in contending that Georgia boys
should not be used to fight for Virginia but for Georgia.

Some Weapons of War

Many fantastic ideas and wild dreams during the Civil War brought forth a number of crazy, impractical weapons that were conceived and manufactured on both sides of the Potomac. However, some of them developed into very effective instruments of war in later times.

I had promised the readers of this column an essay on unusual ways of killing one another during the only American war in which brother killed brother in their common country. This was a long while ago, and I had nearly forgotten about it until the other night when I spoke to the History Club of the Lanier High School. I thought the subject would appeal to the young men of that club, and it did. Here is what I told them.

The submarine is an example of a weapon that began under less than auspicious circumstances and with very little success—none for the Union—but which finally developed into a most effective weapon for attack. The sub was invented by David Bushnell, of Connecticut, and was developed by Robert Fulton—

but not very highly. It was the Confederates who first put it to use. The Confederates used the subs in an attempt to break the blockade at Norfolk and also at Charleston. The *David* was steam-propelled, cylindrical in form with conical ends. It was semisubmersible and armed with a spar torpedo carrying a charge of 24 to 132 pounds. The *David* damaged the *Ironsides* at Charleston on 5 Oct. 1863; and the *Hunley*, which was hand-propelled, sank the *Housatonic* on 17 Feb. 1864. Both of these subs were lost in these operations, however, and the invention had a long way to go before it could roam under the seas with nothing but a periscope above the surface to pick up an enemy ship.

The Union had no luck at all with the sub during the Civil War. One was built, called the *Alligator*, but it was sunk under tow off Cape Hatteras in April 1863.

Now, today, we have one of our most potent weapons in a stealthy and hidden submarine that carries a nuclear-armed missile. This is called the ballistic-missile submarine: the Polaris. History was made on 10 May 1960 when the U.S.S. *Triton* surfaced after traveling underseas by nuclear power all the way around the world. Then the Polaris *George Washington* set out from Charleston Navy Yard in November 1960 on history's first underwater missile patrol. But back to the screwballs.

A very unusual weapon made in the South, principally for defensive purposes, was the pike. This was manufactured all the way from Baltimore to the Deep South, but so many were made in Georgia that numerous people down this way have seen some of them in collectors' homes or in museums. Those made in this state were known as "Joe Brown Pikes" because Gov. Brown authorized them and called upon every mechanic in the state to turn out as many as possible. The pike was an eighteen-inch, two-edged blade fastented on the end of a six-foot staff. It weighed about three pounds.

Gov. Brown began to feel the need for such a weapon in the spring of 1862 when Ft. Pulaski was threatened by the Yankee gunboats and the Union batteries, which had been placed on Tybee Island during the preceding winter. He agreed to a plan to raise a battalion armed with such weapons to defend Savannah, but this was not done. We have the governor's own word for it, however, that "one brave company was raised." They were armed with pikes and went from the mountains to defend the coast. They were "the favorites of the gallant [W. H. T.] Walker," in whose brigade they were placed.

In answer to Gov. Brown's call, the machine shops turned out over 12,000 pikes in the short period when they were being made. I have seen one at the museum at Kennesaw Mountain and one at the State Archives in Atlanta, in addition to one or two in private collections. Most of those that I have seen bear the mark of S. Griswold.

Samuel Griswold was turning out pikes until June 1862, after which he turned to making revolvers. Griswold and his associates [Daniel Pratt was an early one who went on to Alabama] at Griswoldville, in Jones County, operated the largest gin and saw factory in the country. With 24 workmen—22 of them being slaves—they turned out more than 3,600 revolvers of the Navy Colt model, more than all the other Confederate revolver makers put together. These were six-shooters, .36 caliber. The early models had round barrel housing, the later models part octagon barrel frame. Production continued until November 1864 when Sherman's army burned the shop.

More Unusual Weapons

The search for a gun that would deliver greater fire power with striking force strong enough to break through the thick walls of a fort at a mile's distance or pierce the armor of the new ironclads that were beginning to make their appearance after the *Monitor* and *Merrimac* made wooden ships obsolete, that was the big problem of ordnance during the Civil War. Here, too, as stated last week in this column, the development of more effective weapons went through a stage of wild imagination and impractical dreams. Nevertheless, the fantastic inventions, in both North and South, began to be modified into workable instruments of destruction. The Northern manufacturers won out in the race to perfect a big gun with great striking power, as we shall see. But first, let us observe the most fantastic idea to come out of the South. It was the double-barreled cannon.

This strange and useless gun with two heads, or eyes, I should say, was invented by John Gilleland, and was manufactured in the Athens Foundry. The idea in the mind of the inventor was to have the two barrels fire simultaneously, throwing out two balls between which was attached a long chain. When fired, the balls were supposed to spread and the chain was to mow down the enemy. When it was tested, however, those who operated it unfortunately failed to synchronize the firing of the two barrels. Observers say the chain broke and one ball destroyed a Negro cabin; the other plowed up the ground and killed a calf in a nearby field. No other attempt to use this gun was ever made, and it stands in Athens today in front of the City Hall, a two-eyed monster on two wheels, a mute reminder of the desperate efforts of Confederate Rebels to defend their homeland from Yankees, who were beginning to produce more and stronger guns than they. But the Union inventors also went through their adolescent stage in the matter of ordnance.

The Northern gun makers were trying very hard to perfect a multiple-barrel gun that would work satisfactorily. Where a Southern inventor tried a double-barreled cannon and failed, the Yankees perfected a gun that would fire many cartridges. Thus it was fed from a hopper by the turning of a hand crank. It was known as the "Coffee Grinder." Earlier efforts to produce a multiple-barrel gun go back to the early days of muzzle-loading weapons when the ignition was by a slow-burning match or fuse. Some of these guns had as many as 40 or more barrels. The chief trouble with the single-barrel "Coffee Grinder" was that the barrel heated rapidly. This problem was finally solved, and before the war was over crude breech-loading Gatling guns had begun to appear. C. E. Fuller, *The Rifled Musket* [1958], describes the "Coffee Grinder" in detail and carries a good picture of the Billinghurst & Requa multiple-barrel rifle [p. 263]. Adm. John A. Dahlgren, who is credited with the invention of the rifled cannon, was pleased with the "Coffee Grinder" and agreed to order some, but Lincoln was skeptical of them.

One of the most unique among the big guns developed by Union inventors was the Winans Steam Gun. This gun, which operated with steam power and looked somewhat like a steam locomotive as it moved along on its four wheels, was invented by Charles S. Dickinson. It was his hope that it would have sufficient firepower to do the work previously assigned to the mortars and cannon using explosive powder. The big gun took its name from the manufacturer, Ross Winans, a locomotive builder of wealth and prominence in Baltimore. Fuller quotes a description of the gun as given in the *New York Tribune* of 4 May 1861.

> It is on four wheels, the boiler is like that of an ordinary steam fire-engine, the cylinder being upright. There is but one barrel, which is of steel, on a pivot, and otherwise is like an ordinary musket-barrel. It is fed or loaded through a hopper entering the barrel directly over the pivot. The barrel has a rotary motion, and performs the circumference, by machinery attached, at the rate of about sixteen hundred times a minute. The balls are let into the barrel through a valve at will, and every time the barrel comes round to a certain point, another valve, self-operated, lets out a ball, which is propelled solely by the velocity of the barrel in revolving. It will discharge a two-ounce ball three hundred times a minute.

This big gun weighing 6,700 pounds not only looked like a locomotive, but was about the size of one. Would it work? That we shall never know because the gun, the inventor, and the manufacturer were all captured by the Confederates in May 1861, before the gun could be tested against the enemy.

Conscription Opposition

Enlistments were slacking off in the spring and summer of the second year of the Confederacy's war for independence. To meet this situation President Davis had asked Congress to pass a compulsory military service act. This the Confederate Congress did on 16 April 1862. This act required men between the ages of 18 and 35 years of age to be enrolled for three years' service, or until the war ended. It placed requisitions on the states; and there was a strong voice of protest raised against it, especially in Georgia and the Carolinas where the Federal forces were already occupying coastal towns and forts. The common people resented the system because of the long list of exemptions granted to the privileged class and because the law allowed the wealthy to hire substitutes. It was also attacked on constitutional grounds.

An unidentified writer in the *Macon Daily Telegraph* [4 April] who signed his name "Georgia" said the Conscription Act was "a tremendous engine of military despotism." In his opinion it was "in truth the devil's own invention for the subjugation of liberty." Editor Joseph Clisby published "Georgia's" long letter of protest, but he also ran in the same issue a contrary view quoted from the *Richmond Dispatch*. His readers could choose between the two. " 'Georgia' takes a legal and constitutional view of the question," he said, "and the *Dispatch* urges a necessity which knows no law. Let the reader judge." Another, who signed his letter of 9 April "Old Fogy," agreed with "Georgia" saying, "I am certain that 'Georgia' is not alone by many thousands in opposition to a measure that is admitted, even by its friends, as an infringement of State rights and a step toward arbitrary and despotic power." "Old Fogy" closed his letter by saying, "The measure proposed by our President will and ought to be condemned by the people."

Gov. Brown assured President Davis that he was willing to furnish all the men Georgia could spare for the Confederate forces, but he kept an eye on his state's needs, and he was very upset over the conscription law. This was only one of many controversies between the Georgia governor and the president of the Confederacy, but no controversy was more violently fought over than this. In a letter to the president on 22 April, Brown said,

> The plea of necessity, so far at least as this State is concerned, cannot be set up in defense of the conscription act. When the Government of the United States disregarded and attempted to trample upon the rights of the States, Georgia set its power at defiance, and seceded from the union rather than to submit to the consolidation of all power in the hands of the Central or Federal Government. The conscription act not only put it in the power of the Executive of the Confederacy to disorganize her troops, which she was compelled to call into the field for her own defense in addition to her just quota because of the neglect of the Confederacy to place sufficient troops upon her coast for her defense, which would have required less than half the number she has sent to the field, but also places it in his power to destroy her State Government by disbanding her law-making power.

The first Conscription Act was obnoxious enough, but when the second was enacted on 27 Sept. 1862, increasing the age limit to 45, the Georgia governor would not permit its enforcement in his state until his legislature determined what the people wished to do about it. Friends of the Davis administration in the Georgia legislature proved stronger than the governor had thought, and the state supreme court unanimously upheld the law. There was nothing to do but submit. However, Brown showed a very obstinate attitude by using the exemption clauses in declaring 15,000 persons "indispensible state officers" not subject to the Confederate draft.

Toward the end of the following year, up in Virginia, William Mosely wrote his father in Bibb County saying he hoped that if his father, a middle-aged man, was drafted that he would serve his state rather than the Confederacy. He said,

> *I was sorry to hear that there was a probability of the men being ordered out from 16 to 60 but if it is done I think the war will come to a Speedy Close . . . Pa, if you do have to go into Service my advice to you would be to go in the State Service if possible. . . . You will be nearer home, and if they do order them out to 60 it will be for a Short turn . . . I know I want you with me as bad as anybody but when there is a prospect for you to get to Stay at home by not coming, I don't want you to come.*

The Confederate law did finally expand the age limits from 17 to 50 [17 Feb. 1864], but those under 18 and over 45 were put in reserve for defense of their state.

THE BALM OF MUSIC

Celestine Sibley, well-known Atlanta columnist, quoted someone recently—the name slips me—as saying, "If war cut a gash across the South, music healed the wound." Music helped the soldiers on both sides of battle lines in our war of 100 years ago; it helped the South endure the pain of slow healing during Reconstruction, and it now helps the nation remember that war with a feeling of tenderness.

Richard B. Harwell, in his *Confederate Music* [Chapel Hill, The University of North Carolina Press, 1959], turns to William Gilmore Simms to emphasize the importance of music as a factor in interpreting the history of a people. "The mere facts in history do not always, or often, indicate the true animus of the action" is the opinion of the Charleston writer. And he goes on to say, "In poetry and song, the emotional nature is apt to declare itself without reserve." Harwell disputes the *New York Herald* violently when that paper states that Southerners "have no music in their souls." And we know he is justified in positively denying the *Herald* when it uses Shakespeare's words to condemn the South as, therefore, "only fit for treason, rebellion, stratagems, masked batteries, spoils and knaveries." But I am not trying to fan the flame of war again; my intention is to take a look at the music of the period, especially the music of the South.

The Johnny Rebs could not have endured the rigors of war and the tediousness of camp life without their songs. They sang patriotic songs like "Dixie," "Maryland, My Maryland," and "The Bonnie Blue Flag" which stirred them to a high pitch of patriotic fervor. For romantic and sentimental moods in the evenings around the camp fire, such songs as "Lorena," "Sweet Evelina," "Juanita," "Annie Laurie," and "Annie of the Vale" would release pent up emotions. And when they were in a severe state of homesickness they would sing "Her Bright Smile Haunts Me Still," "Just Before the Battle, Mother," and "Home, Sweet Home." William Mosely, writing to his mother back in Bibb County from a camp near Savannah, told her how singing helped him pass away the time. He assured his mother that his time was not spent in evil ways, as some were doing.

> *I expect some of the boys gambol off all their wages when they get it, but I am like I was when I went off. I don't know one card from another, nor I don't intend to, but I know one note from another so I tried a game of that tonight. We can have some good singing here when we try.*

A while ago I was pleasantly surprised by a visit from Fred Frank, of the Mercury Record Corporation. He brought me a record album of Civil War songs. It contained more than Union and Confederate songs; it had authentic sounds of the battles, complete with the Rebel Yell. It also had the camp, garrison, and field calls for fifes and drums, and cavalry bugle signals. The "Sounds of Conflict: Fort Sumter to Gettysburg" is narrated by Martin Gabel and fills the entire side 4 of the two-record album. Mr. Frank told me it took his company four years to produce this album. The band music of the Union troops [side 1] consists of "Hail to the Chief," "Listen to the Mocking Bird," "Palmyra Schottische," "Hail Columbia," "Freischutz Quick-step," "Parade," "Port Royal Galop," "Nightingale Waltz," and "La Marseillaise."

The band music of the Confederate troops [side 2] consists of "Dixie," "Bonnie Blue Flag," "Cheer Boys Cheer," "Luto Quickstep," "Old North State," "Easter Galop," "Come Dearest, the Daylight is Gone," "Maryland, My Maryland," "Waltz No. 19," and "Old Hundredth." I was disappointed not to find my favorite "Lorena," included, and if Mercury does not include "Lorena" in its next album, which I understand is being planned, the company will have to give it to me, for I refuse to buy it if "Lorena" is not included.

MUSIC OF CONFEDERACY

Last week I expressed disappointment in not finding the song "Lorena" included in the album that Mercury Records gave me. Now, since writing that, my sister and her husband, Luther C. Davis, of Thomaston, have given me a recording with "Lorena" included in a collection of Union and Confederate songs sung by the Smith Brothers. This has made me very happy, or rather did make me happy until the Smith Brothers strummed and twanged my wife out of the house. She has now gone on an extended visit, leaving me to my recorded music and TV dinners. If one of my male readers who can broil a good steak would like to hear "Lorena" on my automatic repeating phonograph, he is invited over. Please bring the steak! The reason why masculine visitors only are invited is not because I have reached an age considered "safe" by my wife—heaven forbid! It is simply because "Lorena" can't cook.

Some of the Confederate songs included in this record, in addition to "Lorena," are "Dixie," "Eating Goober Peas," "The Yellow Rose of Texas," and "The Bonnie Blue Flag." Among my

favorites on the "flip" side are "When This Cruel War is Over,"
"When Johnny Comes Marching Home," and "All Quiet Along
the Potomac Tonight."

Then, there is also one about "an old soldier who had a wooden
leg. He had not tobacco, but tobacco he could beg." Another old
soldier was "as sly as a fox; he always had tobacco in his old
tobacco box." When the first old soldier tried to beg a "chew" off
the second and was refused, it left the old soldier "feeling mightly
bad." He said, "I'll get even, I will by gad." He went to the corner
and "took a rifle from the peg." But the other soldier stabbed
him "with a splinter from his leg." If you wish to sing it, the
tune is "Turkey in the Straw."

But let us get back to "Lorena." This was, according to Richard Harwell [*Confederate Music*], the most popular of the sentimental songs of the war period. It was written by a preacher,
H. D. L. Webster, and set to music by J. P. Webster. It was first
published in Chicago in 1857. The Schreiners put it out in three
editions. These two Websters, not related, also wrote and composed "Paul Vane; or, Lorena's Reply," which was published by
Blackmar in Augusta and by Schreiner in the collection of "Parlor Gems," published in Macon.

The way it comes out through my speaker is something like
this:

> *The years creep slowly by, Lorena;*
> *The snow is on the grass again.*
> *The sun low down the sky, Lorena;*
> *The frost gleams where the flowers have been.*
>
> *But the heart throbs on as warmly now*
> *As when the summer days were nigh.*
> *Oh the sun can never dip so low,*
> *Or down affections cloudless sky.*
>
> *The story of the past, Lorena,*
> *At last I dare not to repeat.*
> *The hopes that could not last, Lorena;*
> *They live, but only live to cheat.*

There are many more verses, but I reluctantly leave "Lorena"
to write about a few more.

"Goober Peas" did not impress Harwell enough to get recognition in his *Confederate Music*, but it has a catchy tune with a rhythm suitable for marching. It begins like this:

Settin' by the roadside
On a summer day;
Chatting with my messmate,
Passing time away.

Lyin' in the shadow
Underneath the trees.
Goodness, how delicious,
Eating goober peas.

After many more verses:

Just before the battle
The General hears a row
He says, "the Yanks are comin;
I hear their rifles now."

He turns around in wonder
And what do you think he sees?
The Georgia Militia—
Eating goober peas.

The "Yellow Rose of Texas" was first published in 1858 at New York. The author signed his initials only "J. K.," but the New York Public Library records indicate that the name was Knight. J. C. Schreiner and Son, with locations in Macon and Savannah, was among the publishers promoting this popular song. Harry B. Macarthy, "the Arkansas comedian," introduced "The Bonnie Blue Flag" in New Orleans in 1861 to a large group of soldiers on their way to Virginia. It was immediately popular. Blackmar published six different editions of it between 1861 and 1864.

Lack of space prevents further quotes and notes on Yankee songs, but if you (masculine) readers wish to hear the Smith Brothers sing and strum and twang my Confederate and Union favorites, come over—and don't forget to bring the steaks.

FROM A YANKEE FRIEND

One day a Confederate Rebel languishing in a Northern prison got a letter from a New York man whom he did not know. More than that, he got some clothes and reading material. The Confederate prisoner was John Summerfield Wimbish from Edgefield, South Carolina, and the Yankee was W. R. Sprague of Albany, New York. John had been captured and sent to Rock Island Prison in Illinois. Imagine his surprise when a box of clothing and reading matter arrived at the prison addressed to him. The explanation that I have been able to piece out from information given me by descendants of John Wimbish, now living in Macon, makes an interesting story. A cousin of John Wimbish lived in Macon. He was a well-known Georgian, the Rev. George C. Smith, author of *The Story of Georgia* and *Georgia People*. Many citizens of Macon remember him and some, including myself, knew his daughter, Mary Bond Smith. Their home still stands at the corner of Vineville and Rogers, across the street from Clisby School.

The Rev. Smith, unable to help his cousin directly, wrote to his friend in New York requesting him to encourage and help John in any way he could. Mr. Sprague proved his friendship by sending a box of clothing to Rock Island Prison addressed to "John Wimbish, Prisoner-Of-War." A friendly correspondence resulted. The following letter eventually found its way to Macon.

Albany, Feb. 13, 1865

My Dear Sir:

I rejoice to hear that the bundle of clothes has reached you safely and especially that the different articles fit you so well. I wrote immediately after the date of my last letter to you, to your cousin, the Rev. George G. Smith, Jr., and sent the letter open by way of Fortress Monroe according to directions but whether he has received it is, I suppose, a somewhat doubtful matter. I sent your message to your wife in your own language but I have some fear that the Rebels will "smell a rat," and will not suffer it to pass.

I sympathize with you most sincerely in your present trying condition, especially in the separation from your family to which you are subjected. But I trust that a gracious providence will watch over them, and will restore you and them to each other and end the temporary separation, subservient to your highest ultimate good.

I rejoice to know that you have no sympathy with the demoralizing influences that surround you and that you are no stranger to the richest of all enjoyment that comes from a trust in God's providences even in the deepest hour. He is indeed leading you in a way that you know not but it is a blessed relief to reflect that it is his wisdom that is ordering your lot and that he has promised to the Christian that his afflictions shall have their issue in the [?] and eternal sight of glory.

I was deeply interested in the account your last letter contains of your refugee brother. I hope he has reached comfortable quarters and that his health will not prove to be seriously affected. I cannot believe that the war will last much longer though it is evidently to be concluded not by negotiating but by fighting. The newspapers would make us believe that the Southern heart is wrought to desperation but I am inclined to think that it is the heart of the leaders rather than of the people.

Do you know how your cousin, my friend & correspondent feels in retrospect to the great question of "issue"? From a letter that he wrote me about the time of Lincoln's first election I inferred that he had a very unsavory impression in respect to the feelings of the North toward the

South. As to books, I could gladly send you all you could desire if I had
an opportunity. As it is I will send you some pamphlets.

> *Very sincerely*
> *Yr. friend,*
> *W. R. Sprague*

Conditions at the Rock Island Prison were so bad that rations had to be cut to about a third of normal. A large number of prisoners died of disease and lack of proper diet. In order to relieve the situation at the prison those inmates who desired to do so were permitted to go west to fight the Indians. Prisoner Wimbish was among those who volunteered to go. It is said he walked with bruised and bleeding feet from his prison in Illinois to New Mexico. Many who went died from the hardships of the journey, but John Wimbish lived to return to his home in Edgefield—carrying this precious letter from his Yankee friend all the way with him. It was handed down from father to son, and finally found its way to our city when the family moved to Macon.

Hardship, Endurance

"We get plenty to eat and plenty of everything except Soap," wrote Sgt. William Mosely to his Bibb County parents from Virginia in the winter of 1863. Sgt. Mosely was more blessed than many of the soldiers, for the winter of the year that marked the midpoint of the Civil War was a hard one and there was much suffering and want in camp and on the home front. During this period of comparative calm between the great battles, when soldiers were more active in fighting to keep alive in the face of hunger and cold than they were dodging bullets, endurance was the objective both at home and in camp.

From time to time this column has stated that endurance is one of the great lessons the South learned from a war that left this region little else but a few lessons. February and March seem to be appropriate months to look back on the camp and home conditions of the Confederates one hundred years ago. I shall devote this space, for a few weeks at least, to the subject of shortages and substitutes in wartime.

Mary Elizabeth Massey, in her interesting and scholarly study of this subject published by the University of South Carolina under the title *Ersatz in the Confederacy* [1952], says "the Southern people surprised themselves with their resourcefulness" in finding substitutes for many items that were used up or unattainable; but she points out that even though they stretched ingenuity to the limit in an effort to overcome the obstacles, circumstances continued to make their lot harder and sometimes to thwart them altogether.

She shows the cause for the South's difficulty in overcoming the handicap of shortages to have been the failure of the region to develop a diversified economy before the war began. And after the war had started it was impossible for the Southern people to produce the necessitites and fight at the same time. She lays much blame also on the Union blockade of the Southern ports, and rightly so.

Another problem was the "inadequate transportation system of the Confederacy." The problem was aggravated by speculation and hoarding. These, along with a large number of minor and related causes, created a situation that, when understood, explains the plight of the Confederacy's trying to win a war, or at least trying to defend itself against invading armies.

The Richmond government, and the individual states as well, gave the soldiers preemption; and where there was not enough in the way of clothing, food, medicines, and supplies the soldier was taken care of first. Most of the civilians acceded to this, but some found the policy to have been very burdensome and annoying.

An illustration of this situation is seen in a petition signed by Floyd County people begging Gen. Bragg to order Gen. Cobb to stop allowing his officers the privilege of taking corn and other supplies for the use of the Georgia troops in the northwestern part of the state. An impressment law permitted the military to take what was needed within certain limits and under certain conditions. However, in the case of the mountain folk around Rome, the shortage had become so acute that the people cried out for relief from their distress.

Mosely, the Bibb County sergeant quoted above, kept trying to console his mother, who was worried about his lack of conveniences.

He wrote her from his camp near Fredericksburg on 24 January 1863: " . . . Ma you Seem to think that I sleep Cold. You are badly mistaken about that[.] We are Stationed on a high, dry place and we have a good chimney to our tent."

But he was beginning to realize the full implications of the law of supply and demand.

> I will give you an idea of the price of things. Butter $2.00 per pound, eggs $1.50 per lb. Soap $1.50 per lb. Turkeys $7.00 a piece and whiskey— if I just had a gallon I would be rich. A man sold out a gallon by the drink for one hundred and six dollars. . . . A man told me the other day that I could get $10 for my pocket nife but I said I did not want to Sell it at any price but I believe I Shall Sell my Watch. I can get $50 for it and I have got very little use for it now. . . .

Hardship was the lot of plain people and of the aristocrats as well; it was no respecter of classes. In fact, the aristocratic planters and townspeople probably suffered more acutely because they had been accustomed to whatever luxuries could be had in peacetime, while the farmers had habitually hammered out a frugal existence from earliest days. Their ingenuity had already been tested and proven. But the upper class learned the lesson of frugality too, as we shall see in subsequent installments.

SHORTAGES IN MEDICINE

Someone has said the Southern woodlands had become "the apothecary shops of the Confederacy" before the Civil War ended. The Union blockade caused shortages and suffering to soldiers and civilians throughout the South, but nowhere did it have a more serious effect than in shortages of medicines. Southern people, especially the women, scoured the woods for herbs and plants that might provide substitutes for medicines then no longer available. Nearly all medicines except local remedies had been obtained from the North or from abroad before the war, and with the normal supply cut off, the people were driven to desperate ways of relieving pain and curing diseases.

One of the most prevalent diseases in the South was malaria. Thus when the supply of quinine was exhausted, every effort was made to find substitutes for it. The most effective of these was a remedy made from the dogwood berry, which was boiled to a paste to produce something approaching the alkaloid properties of the Peruvian bark. Dogwood was plentiful in the South, and many a berry was boiled to relieve the folks at home and the men in camp from this very common malady. Other substitutes for quinine came from the bark of chestnut, cherry, willow, and the Spanish oak.

Turpentine, which Southern pines yielded most generously, served many medicinal purposes, such as the treatment of common colds, sore throats, and other respiratory ailments, as well as cuts, bruises, and sprains. The mixture of turpentine with a syrup made from the bark of the wild cherry tree or the leaves and roots of the mullein plant made a very satisfactory medicine for coughs.

One of the big unsolved problems for the surgeons in the crowded hospitals in the cities and the improvised hospitals near the battlefields was the absence of anesthetics. When the morphine was used up, about all a surgeon could do to help a poor soldier through the ordeal of having his leg removed to save his life was to give him a shot of whisky and a lead bullet to clamp his teeth on. This didn't relieve the pain particularly, but it numbed his senses a little and made him reckless enough to give his doctor the "ready-go" sign.

Next to malaria, and perhaps an even greater malady plaguing the soldiers, was dysentery, an internal disorder due principally to the unsanitary conditions, which were the soldiers' lot. A soothing cordial made from the root of the blackberry vine was used to combat this and similar disorders. Sometimes the drink was made from persimmons, or even tomatoes.

High on the list of fears of the soldiers was the fear of bleeding to death. Gen. Albert Sidney Johnston did this very thing at Shiloh. Bleeding was checked, but not very effectively by the juice of berries or an extract from black-haw roots. Calomel, a familiar medicine before and after the war, was replaced by dandelions, or pleurisy root, or even butterfly-weed. Sassafras was thought to be effective as a blood tonic; and snakeroot and peach leaves were used in treating dyspepsia.

The soldiers, often sleeping on the wet ground, were plagued by rheumatism and pneumonia. Remedies for neuralgia and rheumatism were found in sumac, sassafras, alder, prickly-ash, poke roots, and certain berries. For pleurisy and pneumonia, plasters made from mustard seeds or hickory leaves and pepper were used.

My grandfather dispensed what drugs could be gathered from berries, roots, leaves, and barks in the neighborhood of Andersonville Prison, but these were of very little benefit in combating diseases and death, and nearly 13,000 Union prisoners died there within a comparatively short time. The North was very critical of the authorities at Andersonville because of the high mortality rate at the prison, and executed Capt. Henry Wirz, the prison keeper, as a war criminal.

But the South had a valid defense: the Union had put medicine on the contraband list and would not change its policy. A motion was made at the American Medical Association meeting in New York in 1863 to get medicine lifted from the contraband list, "in the name of humanity," as Mary Elizabeth Massey [*Ersatz in the Confederacy*] puts it; but it was tabled "indefinitely." The following poem, which circulated in Northern newspapers is quoted by Miss Massey. It indicates the strong animosity existing at that time.

> *No more quinine—let 'em shake*
> *No more Spaldings pills—let their heads ache;*
> *No morphine—let 'em lie awake:*
> *No mercury for the rebels take*
> *Though fever all their vitals bake;*
> *No nitre drops, their heat to slake;*
> *No splinters though their necks they break,*
> *And, above all, no Southern rake*
> *Shall have his "wine for stomacks sake,"*
> *Till full apology they make.*

SENSE OF HUMOR HELPS

Many stories coming out of "The War" remind us that it was not all on the tragic side, and even the hardships suffered by soldiers and civilians were sometimes humorous. Often that humor was burlesque. Both Northerners and Southerners could see the humorous side of situations which might otherwise have been tragic. Each side took its turn in making a difficult situation produce a laugh, though often a coarse and sometimes a hollow laugh.

Johnny Reb could describe his plight in such a way as to convince you he had enough of a sense of humor to carry him through the rough life of camp and into battle. Bell Wiley, putting together words from thousands of Confederate letters he has read, expressed Johnny's feelings this way:

> Seems like yankeys is getting thicker than lise on a hen down here in Dixie and sum of them is a dam site ornraier and the wust part of it is that sum of our folks is acting mor like Yankeys evry day Coffy aint to be had fur eny price and a helthy swig of how-cum-you-so costs a hole

munths pay Speculators seem to be taken the cuntry and offisers gits
sorraier all the time.

Something illustrative of the way Johnny Rebs could make
light of food shortages is seen in a menu found in camp at Vicksburg in July 1863. The *Chicago Tribune* published it as "a mel-
oncholy burlesque," but *Southern Punch*, according to Richard
Harwell [*The Confederate Reader*, 1957, p. 210], thought the only
thing melancholy about it "is the reflection which it must suggest to a thoughtful Yankee—if there be such an animal—on
the prospect of conquering the men who can live and jest on such
fare."

A few items from the bill of fare will illustrate: Mule Tail
Soup, Boiled Mule Bacon with Poke Greens, Mule Rump Stuffed
with Rice. Entrees: Mule Head Stuffed a-la-Mode, Mule Ears
Fricassed a-la-Gotch, Mule Beef Jerked a-la-Mexicana. Side
dishes: Mule Salad and Mule Tongue Cold a-la-Bray. Mule Foot
Jelly, China Berry Tart, and White Oak Acorns provided some
of the sweet dishes, and the beverage was a choice between
Blackberry Leaf Tea and Genuine Confederate Coffee. The last
named was something Southern farmers had learned to make
even before the war. Poor whites in the hill country had long
before learned to make a substitute for coffee by roasting to a
dark brown the ripe seeds of okra.

The informality of dress and uniform in and out of camp was
due as much to shortages as to carelessness on the part of the
dresser, but carelessness was typical of some men and officers.
Charles Adams, of Fort Valley, tells the following story in his
History of the Twelfth Georgia [which I hope will be published
in the near future]. The story, as he tells it, goes like this: Gen.
Henry Rootes Jackson, dressed for comfort with no insignia visible, encountered a sentry sitting on a boulder with his musket
dismantled, the various parts lying all around him.

"Who are you?"

"I'm a sort of sentinel, and who are you?"

"I am a sort of general."

"Well, general," came the unabashed reply, "if you'll wait till
I get my old gun together I'll give you a sort of salute."

This reminds me of a story told by Burke Davis in his biography of Lee, *Gray Fox* [1956]. As the general rode over the field littered with the dead after Second Manassas, he met a sergeant sauntering about. The sergeant failed to recognize Lee, and when the general called him a straggler, he shouted,

> It's a damned lie. I only left my regiment a few minutes ago to hunt me a pair of shoes. I went through all the fight yesterday, and that's more than you can say . . . You were lying back in the pine thickets . . . but today you come out and charge other men with straggling, damn you!

As Lee laughed and rode off, a fellow officer informed the sergeant that it was Gen. Lee whom he had cursed. Burke Davis quotes the sergeant as saying, "Scissors to grind, I'm a goner," as he ran "out of sight down the muddy road."

The story of how Lee "accidentally" surrendered to Grant is rather well known. It seems that Lee, tired of chasing Grant, stopped to rest at Appomattox. When Grant came to surrender he was so slovenly dressed that Lee thought he was an orderly and gave him his sword to polish. Grant, surprised, took it and thanked him, thinking Lee had surrendered it to him. Lee was too much of a gentleman to take it back! And that's how the Union won the war.

The actual truth of the matter is that Lee never gave Grant his sword. According to J. William Jones, chaplain of the Army of Northern Virginia, Gen. Lee, when asked if Gen. Grant returned his sword, replied, "No, sir, he did not. He had no opportunity to do so. I was determined my officers should be exempt by the terms of the surrender [which permitted the officers to keep their side arms], and of course I did not offer mine."

JAMES M. GREEN, M.D.

"We can assure those who may have friends or relatives in the hospitals of Macon, that they are as well cared for, and as attentively nursed, as could be desired," according to a contemporary newspaper account describing the four hospitals in Macon during the Civil War. The general good condition of the hospitals in Georgia as a whole was due to the supervision of Samuel Hollingsworth Stout of Tennessee, according to Horace H. Cunningham [*Doctors in Gray*, Baton Rouge, 1958], and in the opinion of this same authority, the reason for the high standing of the Macon hospitals was due to the abilities of James Mercer Green who supervised them.

Dr. Green, according to his granddaughter, Willie Norman Poe, was born in Athens on 15 Nov. 1815, but the family moved to Macon in 1831. After graduating from Jefferson Medical College in Philadelphia in 1837, he returned to Macon where he married Sara Virginia Prince on 5 May 1846. They were married at the home of Washington Poe by the Rev. S. G. Bragg. In 1858 the Greens bought a house on Poplar Street which was built by Ambrose Chapman in 1840 and had been the home, successively, of Henry G. Lamar and Judge Abner P. Powers. The house still stands as one of Macon's historic landmarks.

Miss Poe says her grandfather was one of three brothers, all of whom were doctors, and their father, William Montgomery Green, who came to Georgia from Dublin, Ireland, was also a physician. One brother, Dr. Thomas Fitzgerald Green, was connected with the early history of the mental hospital at Milledgeville; another brother, Dr. H. Kolleck Green, practiced medicine in Macon. James Mercer Green, the youngest of the three brothers, was one of the leading spirits in the founding of the Academy for the Blind here.

Dr. Greene was appointed surgeon in the medical department on 5 Feb. 1862 and sent to Richmond before the year had ended, but on 17 Jan. 1863 he was appointed surgeon in charge of the hospitals in Macon, under the command of surgeon Stout. Stout's Georgia hospitals in the fall of 1863 numbered 50—a greater number of general hospitals than any other state in the Confederacy had at that time except Virginia. The success of Stout in this heavy responsibility was due to sincere, hard-working physicians, among whom was Dr. Green in Macon. An observer reported glowingly of the cleanliness of the four Macon hospitals.

> What most attracted our attention and approbation was the perfect cleanliness of each and every part of the establishment. The kitchens were as free from dirt or disorder as the offices of the surgeons in charge, and we confidently assert that no gentleman's residence in the whole South is cleaner or more tidy than the Macon hospitals.

Miss Poe tells how her grandfather brought home from Virginia some pottery which he had acquired from Indians living in a village near Richmond while he was stationed there. She says all that she has left of that collection of pottery is a quaint old teapot. Her grandfather loved children and animals. But he died in 1881, too early for Miss Poe to have known him. However, she remembers her mother telling about his tenderness and consideration for pets and children. She says her mother often told her that "he always had either a kitten or a puppy in his dressing gown pocket."

But during the hard days of war, with thousands of wounded soldiers being brought to the Macon hospitals, Dr. Green's tenderness gave way sometimes to impatience and harsh words. The need for adequate space for the wounded caused the government to requisition public, and even private buildings. Dr. Green was sued after the war for impressing a private residence. Prevented by court action from taking possession of the Planter's Hotel for hospital purposes, the Macon hospital superintendent, according to Cunningham, let out a blast in his report to surgeon Stout saying,

> I want these people to have some little of the war as well as all of its profits. It is disgusting to see the contemptuous indifference and even hatred that many of these wealthy foreigners & Yankees & some disloyal men of Southern birth have to everything concerning the soldiers, hospitals, etc. I desire most sincerely to learn some of these men their duties to the Govt. that protects them.

He was concerned in his report that "the judge went out of his way to say that we could not take the Female College [Wesleyan]."

Something of the resourcefulness of the Southern people in enduring the hardships of war is seen in an old knitting needle which Miss Poe showed me. Dr. Green had made it for his wife Sara from a tooth brush handle. It is one of the very few possessions left to an honorable old Macon family which once lived happily in the two-story brick house still standing on Poplar Street, with its four fluted columns and its delicate lace-like ironwork gracing its facade like a beautiful lady wearing a black veil.

GEORGIA BOY IN VIRGINIA

Sgt. Maj. William J. Mosely, a Bibb County boy with Lee's Army of Northern Virginia, wrote frequently to his parents. Mosely's letters, which his son, the late T. H. Mosely of Macon, loaned to me, describe vividly the life of a typical Georgia farm boy in camp and on the battle lines of Virginia. We shall follow the young soldier's experiences through his letters in a series of four installments.

The military camps in the Confederacy were quickly built and were crude and uncomfortable, but this did not prevent the boys from sometimes writing cheerful letters to their home folks. Occasionally, the men were on short rations due to transportation difficulties, but there was no shortage of food in the early stages of the war. There were, however, shortages other than food, and the soldiers had to practice strictest economy from the very beginning of the war. Letters often told of sickness and suffering; they were not always cheerful. On Christmas Eve in 1861 we find Mosely in camp near Savannah, a very homesick boy. He was in the 10th Georgia Regiment, Co. D. Ultimately, the regiment would find itself in Hood's Division of the Army of Northern Virginia, but at Christmas in the first year of the war it was stationed at Camp Jasper, near Savannah. Mosely wrote his parents:

> We have just opened our box which was very acceptable as Christmas is close at hand. The captain says he is going to give us all an eggnog so cake and eggnog go well together but it will not be as much of a Christmas here with both as it would be with eggnog by itself made of the eggs that Georgia [his sister] is saving for me.

Writing about two weeks later from the same place, Mosely indicated his love of singing, but affirmed his scruples against card playing, at least when gambling was involved:

> I expect Some of the boys gambol off all their wages when they get it, but I am like I was when I went off, I don't know one card from another, nor I don't intend to, but I know one note from another, for I tried a game of that. We can have some good singing here when we try.

Later the Georgia boy was briefly at Camp Oglethorpe, near Macon, en route to Virginia. He didn't get to visit his parents, who lived not very far away, but he did write a letter saying some of the boys were skipping out. "It takes about half of the company to keep the other half at camp," he wrote. Capt. Jones "sent out 24 men yesterday to bring in deserters. They keep the guard house full all the time. I am thinking I have got in rather bad company."

It took Mosely's company about a year to get to Virginia, but finally the Georgia Rebel reached Richmond on 4 January 1863. About a week after arriving there he wrote,

> We get plenty to eat as beaf & sow bacon & pickled pork and a plenty of the best flour you ever saw, we get plenty to eat and plenty of everything except Soap, if you ever Send me anything I want it to be a piece of Soap.

January 29th was his birthday and he had a good time, in a rough soldier's way. He was in camp near Fredericksburg where a major battle had taken place the month before, resulting in a major Confederate victory. But he was engaged in another kind of battle on his birthday. He wrote his parents about it.

The Snow is about a foot deep, and we have had a fine time today. We had several Battles today, though we fought with Snow balls. First a Texas Brigade attacked ours, and we got the best of the fight, and then a South Carolina Brigade attacked us then our Brigade and the Texas combined and fanned them out, drove them through their Camps. . . . I tell you it is amusing to See two or three thousand men get to throwing Snow balls at each other.

A month later the snow was still heavy. Mosely's regiment was stationed about a mile or two below Richmond. "I have no idea how long we will Stay here," he wrote. "We are doing fine here without any tents and the Snow knee deep, but we make our tents of pine brush and Sleep the best you ever Saw, and all I want to eat is raw bacon and crackers I used to think I could not eat raw meat but I Can eat it Just as well as if it was done. I sit by the fire and eat it raw."

There was a temporary shortage of food when Mosely wrote from camp near Petersburg on 3 March.

It Seems that rations are getting rather Scarce we only got half rations yesterday and have had none today yet but we are looking for them every minute . . . and I tell you they complain very much and if they were to miss their rations today I will warrant not less than 2000 men would desert this army tonight for they Swear they will go home if the government does not feed them and I dont blame them for they cant live without eating.

A CAPTAIN IS CASHIERED

The soldiers elected their own captains, but sometimes those officers lost favor with their men and for one reason or another they were removed from command. Such was the case with Mosely's captain. The sergeant wrote home about it, describing it as follows:

> *Company D is without a Captain. W L Jones has been Cashiered. And if I was in his place I believe I had as Soon be dead as be Cashiered for the Offence that he was, I don't [know] whether you know how he did about the Shoes that were drawn for the Company. There was only three pair and instead of giving them to the men that needed them the worst as they [him and Bushy] ought to they must have them drawn for. So Jones fixes up the tickets and puts them in a hat, with three of them written Shoes. . . . Jones slips the Ones with Shoes written on them under the lining of the hat and then let Several men draw and tells one of the men that he will give him a dollar for his draw and he draws himself, and gets the Shoes, for he knew where the tickets were that Called for them. And then he Sells the Shoes to R Wiggins and Crawford Smith for $15.00 per pair when they only cost him Six. And he was Court-marshaled and Cashiered. So he did not make much by the Operation.*

Mosely's letters do not indicate that he was blessed among the more literate, but they were better than the letters of some of his comrades. He and his fellows had an opportunity to improve their education in camp thanks to Maj. Rylander, whose home was in Americus. The major was killed later by a stray bullet, but until his accidental death he gave generously of his time to improve the minds of the soldiers in his battalion. Mosely described it to his folks in a letter of 31 March 1863.

> We have a military School in our Battalion, Major Rylander the teacher, he has a Class of about ten with myself and we recite a lesson every day at eleven o'clock [He said] he would teach a Class if they would study, and don't charge any thing at all. So I pitched in and expect to hang on as long as any of them does.

The first mention this Georgia soldier makes of any real danger from enemy fire is in a letter written from Ft. Powhattan on 7 May.

> I taken off my Haversack and blanket and made out my report and Started to Carry it to the General's Quarters, when the command Attention was given. The pickets had Commenced firing about a mile ahead. And I never Saw men get about as fast in my life as they did getting to their guns. Some nearly Scared out of their Countenance. I don't know how I looked but the rest looked very pale.

Troops were kept constantly on the move, never staying very long at any one place. Mosely didn't mind when the march took him through Petersburg. His letter of 31 July 1863 tells the reason why.

> . . . they just keep us a moving from one side of town to the other. We have moved five times and pitched our tents in the same place three times. I think they just do it to See us march through Petersburg. I don't mind though for there is Some of the prettiest women in Petersburg I ever saw and the ugliest in Richmond.

We see his interest in girls again in a letter written on 10 August.

> I went to church yesterday in Petersburg and heard a very good Sermon and the best Singing I ever heard and I saw Some of the prettiest kind of ladies. Petersburg is the greatest place for conscripts and pretty women I ever saw.

The Georgia Rebel began to get homesick and weary of camp, the marching back and forth, and the eating raw bacon, in spite of the pretty girls in Petersburg. Writing home from Franklin Depot, Virginia, on 17 March, he said,

> . . . we are getting furloughs very fast now I think if nothing happens it will come around my time before long Well Ma, that waxed String you Sent me is the very Idea I can cut off as much as I want and wrap it around Something and it gives a Splendid light I am writing by it now.

The soldier from a Georgia farm was not fortunate enough to get his furlough soon; many experiences would be his before persistent efforts would bring final permission to visit his folks. Most of those experiences were of a light and humorous nature. Actually, this soldier saw much less fighting than most of the Johnny Rebs. To get at battle experiences one would have to read other letters, but for interesting happenings, some humorous, some pathetic, I know of no better collection of letters than those of Sgt. Mosely from Bibb County, Georgia.

WON'T MARRY VIRGINIAN

For Sgt. Mosely, the Georgia farm boy in Virginia, soldiering was secondary to social life, that is, what social life he could manage to get in between marching to and fro and camp duty. He wrote again from Franklin Depot on 27 March, as follows:

I and Lieut. Amason went over the river and had a few rounds with Some very nice ladies, and while we were over there we heard of a wedding, which came off that morning and they were going to have a frolic that night So we came back and got Sgt. Parker and here we went through the Snow about a mile and a half and we arrived at the place [Mr. Daughtry's] and the house was crowded with young ladies, but I never saw as ugly a Set in my life, they are so ugly the flies will not light on them, and I never heard Such Singing in my life, I have heard Something Similar, though better, in our negro kitchens down South, though we passed off the time very well, we made them believe that we had never Seen anything like it, and Shur enough we never. If nothing hapens I will go to a party tomorrow night where there is Some pretty girls and a little more like they are in Georgia, but none of them Suit me near So well as the Georgia girls. Some of the boys Say if they get to go back to

Georgia, they are going to carry a wife with them from Virginia, but if the war was to last 20 years, and I had to stay in Virginia all the time, I would never marry a Virginia lady, unless I could find one that Suited me much better than any I have ever come across yet, and I think I have Seen about as good as the State affords.

But a soldier's life did not always consist of girls and parties, sometimes there was more serious work to do.

Our Scouts came in from the other side of Black water this morning and brought in two deserters from our army one deserted twelve months ago when Gen. Longstreet was at Suffolk, the Scouts Shot at him twice before they could Stop him and he was Shot at three times last week by the Zouaves who are Stationed at South Quay. I think he had better be in service, he would be in less danger.

Sometimes Mosely himself was in danger of being shot; but, if shot, it would be by the enemy, never as a deserter shot by his own men. The Battle of the Wilderness took place 5-6 May 1864; fighting at Spotsylvania Courthouse followed immediately. The Georgia soldier wrote as follows from a camp near Spotsylvania Court House on 13 May:

I don't think that our army has had many men killed considering the number engaged, the reason is that we have breast works to fight behind. Genl. Lee is fighting on the defensive, we can throw up very good fortifications in a few hours with nothing to work with except bayonets and tin plates . . . the fight has been going on now 10 days I thought it was only 9 but they Skirmished a little on Wednesday before last and has been fighting every day Since and is Some firing on the lines this morning. I hope you will not give yourself any uneasiness about me for I put my trust in one that rules all things.

Mosely was very religious, as we see by his letters. In fact, his father, though a poor Georgia farmer, must have preached occasionally. In one of Sgt. Mosely's letters he speaks of having dreamed about hearing his father preach a sermon. The family was of the Primitive Baptist faith, and it was not at all uncommon in those rural areas of Middle Georgia for a farmer to preach or a minister to farm.

In June Mosely wrote home from Cold Harbor. His letter was marked "In line of battle." Here we see a bit of the human side of that inhuman thing, war, as we note the men fraternizing

with one another and stopping the fight so that the dead could
be buried.

Well we have had a little rest Since the commencement of this camp-
gaign, Genl. Grant Sent over a flag of truce the evening of the 7th inst.
to bury his dead, and there was a cessation of hostilities from about 4
oclk. P.M. to 8 and there was very little firing during the night and Grant
did not get a reply from Genl. Lee in time to accomplish his object that
evening. So he Sent in another the next morning which lasted until about
10 A.M. and we all felt like I imagine a bird feels when let out of a cage,
ours and the enemy's lines were about 150 yards apart, and we would
meet the Yankees on the half way ground, and exchange papers and talk
with them, like we had always been friends, we draw tobacco now and
we can get anything we want from them with it, one of our men got a
fine knife from them [for] a plug and a half.

THE WEARINESS OF WAR

The war was cruel; it was brutal. Men who were killed out-right suffered least; those who were wounded and had to die slowly, victims of germs more than of bullets, suffered most—and those were the greater number. But men, like Mosely, who were never wounded also found the war cruel and hard to endure. War weariness came over them. Some, many more toward the end, deserted and found their truant way home to try to pick up the work on the farm where they had left off—if there was anything left to pick up. The land was there, but little else remained.

Back in May of the last full year of war, when Mosely was living through the hell of the Wilderness, he had written:

> *Well, my dear parents, I think the hardest of this fight is over, there has not been any fighting of any consequence Since last Saturday evening when we were engaged. I want it to close So I can put on Some clean clothes. I don't believe I have put off my shoes or any of my clothes since the 3rd or 4th of this [month] and we have been on the front lines nearly all the time.*

This was written on 17 May, which means the war-weary Rebel had not had his clothes off for two weeks. Try wearing your shoes day and night for two weeks!

One thing that made Sgt. Mosely more impatient with the war in Virginia was the fact that his father was in poor health. He was very uneasy about his father and about conditions at home. Writing from the battle lines near Petersburg on 24 July 1864, he told how he had made a request for a furlough and hoped to get home and "find Pa up . . . " Again, on 29 October, he "was very Sorry that Pa was no better." He went on to say, "Pa I dream about you every night last night I dreamed of hearing you preach a Sermon, night before last I dreamed you was very low. . . . " By 31 October he had heard that his father was in serious condition, and he wrote as follows:

> *In reply to Such Sad news as I have just recd. What can I write, words cannot express the grief which it has caused. I am going to write out an application for Furlough this evening. Captt. Greer [the comdr. of the batt.] Says he will do all he can for me, and I am going to get Adj. Carter to write out the application, he being a good hand and I think under the circumstances it will be approved . . . the Adjt. Seems to think the Drs. certificate will be advantageous, and I shall Send it up with the application. But Alex! [alack] I am afraid it will be too late from what you write.*

The next day the homesick son wrote:

> *Well Ma, I wrote to you yesterday and Stated that I was going to Send up a furlough which I did this morning, I applied for Thirty days, and Capt. Greer put quite a favorable endorsement on it. . . . I do not know what I Should do if it was to come back Disapproved.*

But it did come back disapproved. The heartbroken boy wrote on the 9th:

> *I am Sorry to inform you that my furlough came back [last night] dissaproved . . . [It] was Approved all the way up to Genl. A. P. Hill, who disaproved it, then Genl. Lee Said he could not grant it unless Genl. Hill thought I could be Spared from the command. . . .*

This must have been one of the more difficult things for the kind-hearted Lee to bear. To deny a war-worn and homesick soldier boy the right to go home to see his dying father would add more white hairs to the general's graying head. His tender heart was touched by men dying in agony, shot to pieces on the field of battle; his mind was burdened by the knowledge of the inevitability of final and complete defeat; and his soul was torn by the thought of his own separation from home and family where there had once been contentment. But with all his burdens and greater sorrows, Lee could suffer with a poor Georgia boy who wanted to go home to see his dying father.

Finally, after continuous effort, Mosely did get his furlough approved. With permission to do so, and not as a deserter, as some of his comrades had been, the Georgia Rebel made the long, slow journey from Virginia to his Georgia home. But when he finally arrived, he found that his father had already been two weeks in his grave.

A. O. Bacon's Journal

Augustus Octavius Bacon, a Georgian who later became one of the leading figures in the United States Senate, was adjutant of the 9th Georgia Regiment in August 1861 when he began to record his thoughts and experiences in his wartime journal. The journal covers the summer and fall months of that year. It tells of Bacon's trip from Georgia to Richmond, of his life in the army in the vicinity of Winchester. It recounts the battles and movements of the army in northern Virginia during that early period when both Union and Confederate armies were learning a great deal more about war than they knew before First Manassas.

Up to this point this column has stuck to chronology, but during the "lull" of the next few months while we wait for Sherman's breakthrough at Chattanooga and his Atlanta campaign, I believe readers of this column will get from Bacon's journal something of the true heartbeat of the Georgia soldier on the Virginia front. Except for certain changes in paragraphing, some deletions, and punctuation changes for clarity, the journal is just as it was originally written.

I have now been in the service a little over two months and during this time I have been through a great deal and seen much which I wish to remember and much of which will be in the history of the country. While these incidents are fresh in my memory I will endeavor to give an outline of my experiences since I left Georgia.

On my journey to Richmond I don't think that anything of interest occurred aside from that usually connected with the route, except the evidences everywhere given that the nation was preparing for the great struggle which awaited it. At every depot the express train which I was on passed a number of other slow moving trains loaded down even to the very roofs of the cars with troops pressing on to the seat of war. Their enthusiasm was most unbounded and as we passed each train cheer after cheer would greet our regiment which was responded to in no feeble tones. Nor was this enthusiasm confined to the soldiers. Everybody down even to the little darkies seemed to vie with each other in seeing who could give the soldiers the warmest reception. This was not so remarkable in Tennessee, especially the South Eastern portion where I am afraid the inhabitants are not very loyal to our new government. In fact the day we passed through Greenville traitors of the Johnson and Brownlow stripe were there plotting treason. . . . As we neared the Virginia line however the change of sentiment was distinctly visible.

When at last we crossed the Virginia and Tennessee line and were fairly upon the soil of the "Old Dominion," the enthusiastic reception given them by the inhabitants of every grade, sex and condition and the reflection that they had reached the land they had come to defend against the invader seemed to render our soldiers perfectly intoxicated and until night closed the scene they shouted and yelled like madmen. It was certainly a sight sufficient to excite any one in their situation. From every house top there waved the Confederate flag. Every person whom we passed stopped his or her occupation and shouted and waved a hat or handkerchief for some encouragement.

Not the least inspiring part of the performance was the part taken by the young ladies. And I here record the deliberate opinion founded upon two months observation that Virginia can boast of more pretty girls than the whole of the remaining Confederate States. Not only are the large majority of their girls pretty but there are so many of them. It seems to me that the proportion between the male and female sex among the rising generation in this state must be very much in favor of the latter. What glorious times the Virginia boys must have with so many pretty girls; and after the war when the proportion will of course be still greater it will be an Earthly Paradise. Every house which the railroad passed was sure to have its delegation of from three to five pretty girls stationed near

the road to wave their handkerchiefs and flags at us as we passed. These
were always in high glee and seemed to think it high fun to see so many
"gay Soldier boys" sailing by in their new uniforms. Some of the older
ladies however who occasionally matronized the groups looked upon the
matter in a more serious light. Most of them looked at us very sadly and
some who waved their handkerchiefs, wept while they waved. At every
depot great crowds would be collected the pretty girls always occupying
the front rank loaded down with boquets and wreaths which they would
shower upon us . . .

The prettiest girl whom I have seen since I left Georgia was an un-
sophisticated country lass whom we passed when the train was fortunately moving very slowly. She was dressed in what I took to be white
homespun "sine crinoline," so that there was nothing artificial in her
beauty. I shall not attempt to describe her but simply notice her hair and
complexion neither of which in my opinion could be improved. The latter
was coal black and hung loosely on her shoulders. I said I would not
attempt to describe her. I don't know that I could as I had not time to
note her different features. I only know that the sight of her had a most
magical effect upon the soldiers as was evidenced by the tremendous
shout with which they greeted her. She stood and kissed her hand at
them in the most earnest manner imaginable, not the least particle of
coyness or coquetry to be seen in it. I verily believe from her manner that
if the train had stopped she would have kissed as many of the boys as
time would have permitted and considered that she was doing a patriotic
duty. If my surmise is correct I am sorry she did not have an opportunity
of fully manifesting her patriotism.

RICHMOND IN WARTIME

We arrived in Richmond on the 20th of June and camped on the Eastern side of the city. The whole town was crowded with soldiers. All the suburbs of the city were taken up with their tents and in walking the streets one passed very few who were not in uniform. Very few ladies were to be seen upon the streets, the multitude of soldiers present causing them to keep within doors . . . During my stay in the city I met an acquaintance, Mr. James Thomas, who invited me to tea telling me at the same time to bring some of my friends with me. As there were three young ladies at the house (his daughters whom I met last summer at the Virginia Springs), I carried two others with me, Captain Hillyer and Lieut. Tennille. The girls are very pretty and entertaining and, of course, we enjoyed the evening hugely. In the course of the evening the subject of Bibles having been in some way introduced Capt. Hillyer and myself each mentioned the fact that in the hurry of leaving home we had accidentally left ours. They were perfectly horrified at the idea of our going to the war without our Bibles and said that they intended to send us each one. They did so several days later and I now have a very handsomely bound one, a present from Miss Alice C. Thomas . . .

On the 25th of June my regiment was ordered to Winchester having been assigned to Genl. Johnstons army. The road as far as Manassas

Junction was not new to me as I had been over it several times before. From this point to Strasburg the Manassas Gap Rail Road runs through a beautiful country, the greater part of the distance being among mountains, the road at one place crossing the Blue Ridge.

From Strasburg the regiment marched to Winchester. At the former place I bought my horse and consequently made the journey much easier than most of my comrades. The distance was eighteen miles which was accomplished by us without much difficulty some few lagging on account of sore feet, etc. On the 29th of June we arrived at Winchester and were assigned by Gen. Johnston to the 2nd Brigade of his army then under the command of Col. Bartow. At the time the Brigade consisted of the 7th Ga. Regt., Col Cartrell, the 8th Georgia Regt., Col Bartow, and a Kentucky Battalion. After our regiment had joined the Brigade it therefore consisted of three regiments and a battalion. We were hardly allowed a breathing time, however, for on [the] afternoon of the 2nd of July Gen. Johnston issued an order for the whole of his army to start on a forced march to met Gen. Patterson's army which had crossed the Potomac at Williamsport and was advancing in our direction. It was expected that the armies would met at Martinsburg. We left Winchester about sunset and on account of some intelligence which met us on the way halted for the night four miles from town. This night was our first experience in bivouacking. On a forced march neither tents nor cooking utensils nor anything else are carried except such as are upon the persons of the soldiers, and as a forced march is generally made in long stages the men must be loaded very lightly. On this night therefore we slept in the open air. I had no other covering than my shawl and before morning it turned not only cool but cold and large fires were in considerable demand.

Early in the morning we were again upon the march and soon met messengers who reported a fight on the other side of of Martinsburg on the day previous, between a portion of Jackson's Brigade and the advance of Patterson's army. It was nothing more than a skirmish but was very creditable to our troops, some three or four hundred were surprised and attacked by fifteen hundred Yankees. Our men resisted the attack gallantly, killed many of the enemy and took forty odd prisoners. Reinforcements coming up to the assistance of the enemy, our men were obliged to retire, leaving two or three dead upon the field but bringing the prisoners off with them. The Yankees certainly did bad shooting upon this occasion, especially their artillery, as not a single one of our men was killed by a cannon shot. Our artillery, on the contrary, under command of Capt. Pendleton, a preaching, did most effective service, having at the first fire struck a cavalry squadron which had begun to charge them, full in the front, producing such a slaughter that they fled from the field and did not afterwards return to the attack.

October 27, 1963

AWAITING ENEMY ATTACK

Later in the day we met the prisoners who under an escort were being carried to Richmond. They were sitting by the road to let the army pass and I stopped and held a short conversation with them. They were the first "hostile" Yankees whom I had seen and were certainly a hard looking set. I have seen a great many Yankee prisoners since then but none who were as inferior in looks except some who were taken from Patterson's army on this expedition and belonged to the same class.

In one thing however they agreed with nearly all the others whom I have since seen. This that they disclaimed any intention of invading the South when they enlisted most of them saying that the defense of the Capitol was their only object. I have heard this tale so often that I am perfectly sick of it.

About 12 o'clock we halted a mile this side of a little village, called by some Darksville and by others Bucklestown, to rest and distribute ammunition to the army, it being the general impression that we were about to have a battle. After an hours rest we again started and again halted in Darksville. My regiment was near the rear of the army.

Darksville is on a high hill and half a mile beyond there is another hill of open country plainly to be seen from town. When my regiment reached the town most of the army had already reached the hill beyond which would, more properly from its size, be called table land. On this, from our position we could see the army extending itself on each side of the road for a mile arranging itself in line of battle.

I should have mentioned that where we halted our scouts brought in word that the enemy had reached Martinsburg which was only five miles distant and that they were still advancing. When therefore we saw our army forming itself in line of battle we all very naturally concluded that we had met the enemy and that the fight was about to begin. Soon the report was in circulation that the enemy was in the valley beyond the hill. We all believed it and when we were ordered to march started off under the impression that we were marching into battle. When we arrived on the ground we found that information had been received that [the] enemies force was much larger than ours and that they were fortifying Martinsburg, a place already strong from its natural position.

Our army numbered about 8,000 strong with 14 pieces of flying artillery. The best information we could obtain estimated the enemy at 15,000 with 20 odd pieces of artillery. With these odds against us it would have been, to say the least, imprudent to have attacked them in a position chosen by themselves which we knew to be strong. Still we were willing to give them battle if we could do so on anything like equal terms.

Our line was accordingly, as above stated, drawn up in battle order to wait the attack which we were confident would be made upon us.

At night a general order was issued for the men to sleep in battle order upon their arms. To sleep upon arms means simply to sleep within reach of the arms so that they can be caught up at a moment's notice. Our men, however, being unuse to military terms construed it literally and as I passed along the line at night there they were lying down with their muskets hugged tightly in their arms. As this was erring on the safe side we did not disturb them.

The next morning the men were roused up very early and told to stand in readiness, the commanders stating that they had every reason to anticipate an attack some time before 9 o'clock. In this, however, we were again disappointed, and such instances became so frequent that although the enemy were only four miles distant the men began to place no reliance in them and said that they wouldn't believe the fight was going to commence until the guns commenced firing.

This was the 4th of July and from our camp the enemy could be plainly heard firing guns in honor of the day. This seemed strange to me while I listened to the dull heavy sound of their cannon. The day was certainly as much ours as theirs and now certainly more so, for while we were in arms to defend the very principle announced on that great day they had hoisted the banner of oppression. Yet they were celebrating the day while we were silent. I am one of those decidedly opposed to *surrendering our national anniversaries and national songs unless it is Yankee Doodle which I always did despise.*

A READINESS TO FIGHT

Lt. A. O. Bacon's journal has filled this column since 13 Oct. and will continue for several weeks, until its conclusion. For those readers who did not see the first installment I wish to remind them that Lt. Bacon was the adjutant of the 9th Georgia Regiment. His journal covers the time of First Manassas, the first major battle of the war. The year is 1861, the month July.

> *In this way we waited over on the watch although our faith in the alarms had almost vanished, for although we all believed we would fight before we left Darksville still we would, as each alarm was given, think that each particular one was a sham. At last on the afternoon of Saturday the 6th an alarm was given which roused us all up and made us think the fight had come now to a certainty. Firing of muskets was heard in the direction of the enemy, the cavalry came dashing in saying that our Pickets had been attacked and driven in, and that the enemy were advancing with their whole force to the attack.*
>
> *Instantly the drums were beat & the men were formed in battle line having on their battle badges which had been ordered and was a strip of white cloth around each man's hat. The artillery (one battery) charged*

off towards our left where the attack was threatened and we all listened
expecting every instant to hear them announce the opening of the battle.

Unwilling to be a mere spectator of the fight I gave my sword to a
servant to keep for me and took a musket determining if there was any
shooting done to have a hand in it. At last the artillery came back with
the news that the enemy had only advanced a short distance when they
returned to Martinsburg. I won't say anything for myself as I have always
been on the Peace list but I know that to the large majority of the army
this was a sore disappointment. They had most of them been marching
and counter marching over the country between Harpers Ferry and Win-
chester for several weeks and they wanted something more practical in
its results. When the line was formed and as long as the prospect of the
fight remained good they whooped and yelled like demons, but after they
were told that there would be no fight there countenances fell and they
vented their anger in loud abuse of "the cowardly hounds" as they called
them. Before they were dismissed from the ranks Genl. Johnston reviewed
the whole army riding with his Staff in front of each regiment, the boys
cheering vociferously as he passed. This affair was what produced the
"authentic" account of a great battle between Johnston and Patterson
which went the rounds of all the papers in the South about this time.

While things were still at the most threatening stage and a battle
seemed certain beyond a doubt, the coach left Darksville for Winchester;
the passengers who at first contented themselves with stating to those
whom they passed that the battle was about to begin, next said the fight
was in full progress and by the time they reached Winchester reported a
brilliant victory won by our army. This was telegraphed to Richmond
and then away it went all over the country. We had now been here four
days enduring uncommon hardships even for soldiers. We were without
tents and with very little covering. Although it was the middle of summer
the nights were really cold and if one would lie awake at night he would
hear the teeth of the men who were asleep striking together in a manner
which threatened to knock out their grinders. The whole army chattered
nights at a time as if a regular built ague had taken possession of it. I
suffered very much; so much so that I slept very little at night generally
making up for it in the day if I could get a shade. Although the nights
were so cold the days were very warm and we were out in the open fields
with no protection from the sun except a few little trees which were always
patronized.

In addition to this we nearly starved. We had brought no cooking
utensils and our meals consisted of flour and water without salt baked
on rocks and beef cooked in somewhat the same manner. The bread when
presented for us to eat was two crusts baked as hard as the rocks on
which they were cooked containing between them a mass of tough dough
which would be hardly dried. The consequence was that this exposure

and such food were making all of our men sick. In addition to this the measles were appearing very rapidly among them. My servant, Richmond, took them and I had to send him back to Winchester in a wagon.

Gen. Johnston issued an order to the army saying that for four days we had challenged the enemy to open fight with the advantage of numbers in his favor and that he had steadily declined it and there was no prospect then of his accepting it. He therefore ordered that the army return to Winchester where they could be comfortably provided for, and there await the advance of the enemy. The soldiers however could not look on the matter in this light, but thought it had too much the appearance of a back down on our part. Their faces as they fell into ranks to take up the line of march were exceedingly grim, and they took no care to conceal their disapprobation of the movement either by word or look. As the army marched past Gen. Johnston's headquarters only one regiment cheered him. He had evidently gotten into the bad graces of most of them. The news had reached us that the enemy had been largely reinforced on the day previous and that the soldiers were of the opinion that this fact as well as the scarcity of food influenced the general in making this order, they were accordingly very much discontented and expressed their readiness to fight the Yankees at any odds.

I don't think that Gen. Johnston wished to bring on a battle during this expedition. In my opinion (lately formed) he had the ultimate junction of his army with Beauregard's constantly in view, and that in all of these marchings and maneuverings his object was to hold the enemy in check and at the same time avoid a battle. If he had while in the Shenandoah Valley suffered a defeat at the hands of the Federal army under Gen. Patterson, or even won a victory which would have placed his army in the prostrated condition which always succeeds a severe battle there can be no doubt but that McDowell would have been victorious in the battle of the 21st and over Richmond the Federal flag would now be waving in triumph. Gen. Johnston is certainly a master strategist.

A SORROWFUL RETREAT

*On Sunday morning the 7th of July (1861) . . . as soon as every thing
could be placed in readiness the army started on its march to Winchester.
This was one of the hottest days I ever experienced and the soldiers
suffered awfully from heat, dust and thirst. When an army is marching
it is the custom if there is nothing to prevent it for the different regiments
to march a considerable distance behind one another so that the dust
raised by one will not inconvenience the other and also because small
detachments can more easily procure water, an article very essential to
soldiers on a march.*

*Under circumstances like those by which we were then surrounded
however this cannot be done as the neighborhood of the enemy makes it
necessary for the army to keep close together so as to be able to resist an
attack if one should be made. Marching then closely together those of us
whose regiments were in the rear of the army were during the whole of
the day nearly suffocated with dust.*

*In addition to this the heat was intense and it was almost impossible
to get any water. Whenever we reached a stream or spring or well we
would find that it was so muddied by troops who had gone on that it
was totally unfit even for hogs to drink: nevertheless the soldiers would
rush to it and drink it most greedily, and where it was a spring or well*

and consequently but few of them could be accommodated at a time they would struggle and fight over it as desperately as if their lives depended on getting to the filthy water. Some places in their struggles they would fall down and get piled up over a spring struggling and yelling frantically, each one being pushed on by those in his rear who were equally as anxious to get to the water.

At last late in the evening we arrived in Winchester, the troops hungry, footsore and broken down and dispirited. Col. Bartow was awfully mortified by the result of the expedition. We had to pass through Winchester to get to our camps but he would not let us pass through the principal street but made us take a back street. He told me that although he was not in Gen. Johnston's councils and consequently not at all responsible for the retreat, yet the movement had actually cost him some of his self-respect.

On our arrival in camp I found all of my goods safe but my servant Richmond very sick. I took him in my tent and in a few days had him well again. I don't know that anything outside of the regular routine of camp life occurred until the evening of Monday the 15th of July when we were ordered over to the other side of Winchester as every body said to meet the enemy "who were advancing upon us" again.

That they were advancing was certainly true, as our advanced pickets (Col. Stuart's regiment of cavalry) which always kept in sight of the enemy, and which did not return to Winchester with the rest of the army but had remained at their post between Darksville and Martinsburg, had been compelled by their advance to retire within eight miles of Winchester.

The week which followed our retreat to Winchester had not been unimproved and at this time we had a very handsome redoubt and two or three small breast works upon which were mounted some of five cannon one or two of them being of considerable calibre, at least in comparison with common field artillery. The redoubt for our line of battle with a breast work on either hand or side rather distant about a quarter of a mile.

My regiment was stationed on the right of the redoubt next to and on the left of the right hand breast work. I did not see the breast work on the left of the redoubt but understood that it was similar to the one near which we were stationed. This one was mounted with a thirty two pounder and was about large enough to protect one regiment. The redoubt was mounted with three pieces and was large enough to protect another regiment. So that if the other breast work was the same size the large majority of the army would have had to fight without cover. The object of the earthworks however was not to shield the men particularly but to give position to the heavy artillery. With these supported by our flying artillery, infantry and cavalry I am confident we would have gained a glorious victory.

I don't know what might have happened if the battle had been fought at Darksville, but if we had been attacked here with the advantage of this heavy artillery and the choice of position in our favor I haven't a doubt of what would have been the result. Our troops were all confident of victory also and that is always invaluable to an army provided this confidence is based upon a desperate determination on their part.

THE FENCES GO DOWN

On Tuesday morning I heard the first cannon ball whistle which I heard during the war. It was a friendly one however and consequently not very alarming to us, although I have no doubt but that its sound made many hearts beat quicker when anticipating that before sunset they would be whistling around in a much more disagreeable proximity. The ball referred to was fired from the battery on our right, the gunners testing the range.

The whirring whistle which it makes would be very pretty were it not so indissolubly connected with the idea of tearing things to pieces wherever it was opposed. The small space of time which it took to tear up the ground on a hillside two miles distant was almost incredible and not at all calculated to quiet unsteady nerves. And here we remained all day Tuesday drawn up in a line of battle in an open field exposed to the boiling Sun of a July day. Remaining in this position even without the addition of the Sun is not pleasant. The mind is kept on a stretch of excited expectation which after a while becomes extremely wearying and even painful. At first there is an enthusiastic thrill running over the body which is pleasant and makes one feel strong enough to conquer a dozen. After an hour or so this dies out and a feeling of uneasy relaxation comes over one which if long continued becomes almost insupportable. It requires much less nerve and courage to march to an attack than to wait for hours expecting one. The want of occupation is an important item.

The Yankees did not come however but contended themselves with an exploit which was heralded by the Northern press as a brilliant victory. This consisted in Gen. Patterson's sending out a battery of artillery supported by two or three regiments of infantry who stood off two miles and fired at Stuarts Cavalry which was of course obliged to retire and take a position out of range of the guns. They were not stationed there for the purpose of engaging in a regular fight but to watch the enemy and give us notice of his movements. One man was wounded in this "brilliant" victory and was brought into Winchester, having been struck in the side by a piece of bombshell.

That night the army bivouacked in their places and arose next morning again expecting an attack. The morning wore away however without any event of particular interest: at least except such as was usual for there is always in camp something interesting to be seen by one who keeps his eyes open and looks for it. Early in the afternoon Col. Bartow ordered the different Regiments to form and make ready to march with nothing but arms. We were marched off in a direction east of that by which we had been anticipating an attack. We did not know where we were going nor for what purpose but by this time we had begun to learn what all soldiers have eventually to learn, to obey all orders without even expecting to know their purpose or cause. When we reached a point about one mile east of Winchester the regiments were halted and ordered to stack arms in the road.

Col. Bartow then ordered the men to their infinite surprise to go to work and throw down the fences. As soon as the boys were made to understand that he really meant them to do so they began tearing down long lines of fence in an almost incredible time. A fence would literally seem to melt before them. Twenty five hundred men formed a considerable crowd and would tear down a piece of fence four hundred yards long in three minutes. The exercise excited them and when one fence was demolished they would run whooping and shouting to the attack of another.

Some not very active soldiers whom I saw could not catch up at all with a fence as each one would be down before he could reach it. Working in this way a piece of country some two miles square consisting mostly of open fields was cleared up and the brigade returned to their position, their spirits very much elevated by what was to them high fun. The owners of the fields doubtless considered it serious fun.

Fortunately most of them were wheat fields on which the crop had already been gathered. There were only two or three fields of growing crops. This was a queer proceeding and one which we were at a loss to understand. I afterwards learned what was the cause. Gen. Johnston learned that Patterson's army had moved South Easterly and thinking that probably it was intended to advance against Winchester by the Eastern road, he had ordered Col. Bartow to take our brigade and go out and throw down the fences so that we might have an open field to fight in. The result proved that it was useless labor for Patterson instead of attacking us simply marched towards the Potomac in the neighborhood of Charleston where he remained until Johnston marched to the assistance of Beauregard and decided the fortunes of the 21st of July 1861.

The Northern people were perfectly justifiable in the indignation which they entertained and expressed for Gen. Patterson's course at this time. There can be no doubt but that without the assistance of Johnston's army, Beauregard would have been overcome by McDowells overwhelming superior numbers and Patterson could by an attack at the right time have certainly prevented that assistance even though he had been completely defeated in so doing. If Johnstons army had fought a battle on the 17th of July, it never could have reached Manassas in anything like its proper strength and efficiency by the 21st never mind if it had been a complete victory in its favor. A battle which is at all severly contested unfits an army for immediate operations of an active nature.

LONG, STRANGE MARCH

On the 17th [July 1861] Patterson's army was within eight miles of Johnston's army and by two hours brisk marching the former could have engaged the latter in battle. He chose another course however and the world knows what was the result. I have read several speeches which Patterson made after he had been very properly removed from his command in which he attempted to justify his action alleging that Johnston's force was greatly superior to his &c &c. This was decidedly an incorrect statement of facts, but even if this had been so, in my mind there can be no excuse for him. He certainly knew of intended invasion of the "Grand Army of the Union" at this time and with his military experience he might have known that unless prevented Johnston would attempt to effect a junction of his forces with Beauregards and under such circumstances he ought to have engaged Johnston even though the certainty of defeat had stared him in the face, and as he failed to do so I think that it was a fit case for the judgment of a Court Martial. It seems rather strange for a young man of twenty two and by profession a civilian to be censuring in such unmeasured terms one who was a major general in the Mexican war. Nevertheless I am so well satisfied that this criticism is just that I am willing to submit it to the decision of any one versed in military affairs. For his conduct both the Confederate and Federal States are under great obligations to Genl. Patterson, though of rather different natures.

This ended the campaign in the valley of the Shanandoah in which to all effects and purposes Gen. Johnston gained a complete victory over the Federal army without firing a gun. Without the loss of a single man he cleared the valley of the enemy and reached Manasssas in time to achieve a great and inestimable victory. To him be all honor for his consummate Generalship as Commander of "The army of the Shanandoah." For this he deserves more real praise than for his conduct on the glorious 21st than which nothing could have been more gallant.

The tearing down of the fences already spoken of took place on Wednesday afternoon July 17th. On the next morning the regiment received orders to pack up all of its tents and baggage and pile it up on the ground where our camp then was. This done we all sat down waiting patiently for what might come next, each expecting orders of importance, but as little dreaming what they really would be as did the people in Georgia.

I was just prepared to commence my dinner when in a hurry the couriers dashed in to camp with orders for immediate marching. That meal however could neither be lost nor delayed, and as there could be no delay we mounted our horses, dinner in hand, and began this memorable march, dinner in hand. It was well that we did so for in the next twenty four hours we went through by far the most fatiguing march which has been taken by any troops in this army during the war.

The army did not know where, or for what purpose they were going. The higher officer, only, had the information. The commander of our regiment was the only man in it who knew anything about it. Just after we started he told me what was the intention of the movement. We went through Winchester, the men marching along very cheerfully thinking that probably there were some more fences to tear down or something else to do of about equal importance. When out of town the army took the road to Piedmont by direction of the Officers in command.

After we had gotten well started on the road, Col. Bartow rode along his brigade and as he reached the head of each regiment, waved his hat and shouted to them say[ing] in an excited manner that now they would be put to the test and their manhood proved for that they were marching to the assistance of Beauregard who that morning had been attacked by the enemy in overwhelming number. What a shout greeted the announcement! Their eyes brightened, their cheeks flushed and with a tighter grasp upon their guns the brave fellows quickened their steps as they trod on the succour of their comrades.

To some extent it was a march to glorious victory, but a march to the grave for many of that noble band.

It was about one o'clock when we started and through the whole of that long July afternoon until 10 o'clock that night the army marched steadily along making in that time but three regular halts for the purpose of resting.

I wish I had both the ability and the time to give a proper description of that march that those who may read this short account might have some conception of what I saw. The day was excessively warm and our position was again in the rear of another brigade where we marched on blinded and suffocated by the clouds of white dust. The road seemed to be along ridges where no water could be found and the sufferings of the men from thirst were intense.

ON TOWARD MANASSAS

The orders issued to the army were, that in marching every man should keep steadily in his place and under no circumstances to break the ranks. This order was at first enjoined by the officers and obeyed by the men. But at last when thirst had become intolerable they would rush frantically to a spot which seemed to have a spring or stream near by, and the officers would march on refusing to notice except by gentle remonstrance an insubordination which there was so much to excuse. The painful scenes which I had witnessed on the retreat from Darksville to Winchester were still more painfully reenacted: still the men toiled on as best they could, but the increasing number of stragglers whom we passed on the roadside where they had fallen in their exhaustion, began to considerably thin our ranks. When we halted to rest however (which we did three times before 10 o'clock that night, for about half an hour at a time) these stragglers would generally catch up with us and somewhat refreshed by their short rest, push on with their comrades.

But this, hot, dusty and wearisome march was not altogether cheerless, for all along the stone walls and hedges which lined the road there were groups of the inhabitants who had come from the surrounding country to see the army pass. Among these were a great many pretty girls who had other encouragement to offer besides that given by their smiling faces.

Knowing how thirsty we would all be they had troops of servants with their water buckets which they would refill as soon as emptied by the thirsty crowd which was passing by.

Marching in this way we reached the Shanandoah river about ten o'clock that night. As some time was occupied in getting across, the troops in the rear had an opportunity for resting. When troops have marched a considerable distance it is really remarkable how quickly they will go to sleep. I really do not think that after half a days march when a halt is ordered more than three minutes elapse before four fifths of the army is asleep. This is especially so if as in this case it is at night. When in about an hour and a half our turn for crossing came and we tried to rouse our men it seemed almost as if they slept the sleep of death. There they lay in the road and in the ditches and fence corners in all conceivable positions and each man seemed to require a most particular and vehement shaking before he could be waked. This nap had very much refreshed them and they were some what reconciled to being waked up when they were told that crossing the river was all that would be required of them that night. That was the general opinion as we never dreamed that after marching for half of the day previous that we would still be required to march most of the night on that weary road which seemed to have no end.

During this time while they were resting I had never once gotten off my horse but had been occupied in carrying some of my friends across the river. I did this by taking them one at a time behind me on my horse, crossing him over and coming back for another. In this way I crossed the Shanandoah eleven times that night.

As they (my boots) were water proof and I did not take them off until the next day, I had my feet in water for about twelve hours.

The crossing of the troops that night was a sight to be remembered. The men of each regiment as they reached the waters edge, stripped all clothing except shirts and with the garments which had been removed hanging upon their bayonet points, they struck for the other side of the river, the first step into the cold mountain stream generally forcing a shout from each man which he would keep up until he reached the Eastern shore.

Ah there were many there, some of whom too I knew well, whose voices were that night heard merrily pealing forth in song and laughter, who in less than three days from that time lay stark and still in death upon the bloody field of Manassas.

THE AGONY OF A MARCH

When the troops reached the other side of the river the order to continue the march seemed as if it would almost stir up rebellion. It did seem cruel to require it of them. They had been on the march twelve hours. For hours they had been hungry and tired and at last there had been added to these sufferings an almost overpowering want of sleep. They had just forded a wide, deep, cold river and yet they were told that the tall Blue Ridge Mountains which loomed up before them must be climbed before they could be allowed to rest. Murmurs were heard on every side but still they marched on. Soon after we began the ascent of the mountains stragglers began to be seen by the roadside. The farther we went the more numerous these became.

At first only one man at a time as he became exhausted would stop by the wayside. As the night wore on two or three would stop together, and at length, weary, hungry, footsore and so sleepy as almost to be deprived reason, whole detachments and companies would desert a regiment at once and falling by the roadside refuse to go any further, alleging there for the best reason in the world; viz—that they couldn't.

It was now three o'clock at night and some regiments which had crossed the river with seven hundred men did not now have 75 men in their ranks. The others were scattered on the road for miles, where they had fallen perfectly worn out.

As for myself I was never so nearly worn out and broken down in my life. For 14 hours I had not been out of my saddle except when occasionally, I would let some tired friend ride while I walked. During this time therefore I had not closed my eyes to sleep or rested for ten minutes. I was perfectly exhausted and so sleepy that I came very near sleeping on my horse. Some men have assured me that they slept that night as they walked along. There is nothing so overpowering and perfectly irresistible as drowsiness after long continued exercise and loss of sleep. Hunger, thirst and fatigue are trifles compared with this. A man feels as if he must sleep or he will die.

I had almost arrived at this stage when the ambulance belonging to our regiment caught up with me. It was filled with wornout and brokendown members of our regiment whom it had picked up by the side of the road. Hailing it I found that it contained among others Mr. Waddy of the Wilkes Co. Company. I asked him to exchange places with me telling him that I was very tired. He kindly consented to my proposition and giving him my horse I took his place in the ambulance feeling almost as much dead as alive.

It is a mistaken idea that the footsoldier has so much harder time than one on horseback. It is true there is a difference but not as much as is generally supposed. The reason is that the footsoldier has opportunities for resting at every little halt, many of which necessarily occur in every march. Halting however does not rest the horseman unless he dismounts.

There was not room in the ambulance for me to lie down but by hanging my legs outside I succeeded in getting into somewhat of a reclining posture and although the road was of the roughest character I think I was asleep within three minutes from the time I left my horse.

I woke about two hours after which was about daylight and found that we were halted at a little town named Paris on the Eastern side of the Blue Ridge Mountains. When I woke we had already been there about an hour and we remained there about an hour longer which time most of the stragglers who had dropped behind caught up with their various regiments. The march was then continued.

The morning was beautiful and pleasant but it was really distressing to look at the men. They were hungry, tired, sleepy and footsore and dragged themselves along without life or energy in either action or countenance. At every stream the poor fellows could be seen sitting down and washing their blistered feet trying in this way by the application of cool water to alleviate their pain. Some of them actually had upon their feet raw places as large as a quarter of a dollar. But the brave fellows would put on their shoes and march on although every step must have given them excruciating pain. At the time I freely confessed to myself that their fortitude was far greater than mine.

At 10 o'clock A.M. we reached a little village on the Manassas Gap R.R. called Piedmont where the troops were to take the cars for Manassas which was 25 miles distant. This was indeed a most terrible march.

The distance marched was about 30 miles in which as I said the Shanandoah river and the Blue Ridge Mountains were crosses. For 20 hours mind and body had been on a constant strain almost entirely unrefreshed by sleep or food.

Marching 30 miles may seem to be a small affair to many who have walked considerably over that distance in one day. But the difference between walking a certain distance under one's own command and marching it in the ranks is so great that it can never be appreciated except by one who has tried both. There is many a man who could walk 25 miles a day on a squirrel hunt with very little fatigue who would be utterly broken down by a ten-mile march with the army.

There were only enough cars at Piedmont to carry two or three regiments at a time so that many would be delayed for some time. We accordingly bivouacked in the neighborhood of the depot and awaited our turn to be taken on the cars which would be according to the number of our Brigade.

Jackson's Brigade which was the first went off during that day. In the afternoon the trains returned for our Brigade which was the second. There were at this time five regiments in our Brigade. The 7th, 8th, 9th and 11th Ga. and the 1st Ky. The trains could only take two of our regiments at once, which were the 7th and 8th.

Col. Bartow went off with the 8th and the last time I ever saw him he was sitting on the tender of the engine as it sailed off.

WAITING FOR A TRAIN

When the trains returned that night it was by rights our turn to go next but our Brigade commander, Col. Bartow having left, we had no one of sufficient authority to represent us and the other Brigadiers pushed us aside and carried their Brigades on ahead of us. If Col. Bartow had stayed and seen his Brigade off as the other Brigadiers did this would not have happened. As it was we were thrown "to the heel of the Docket." This was Friday evening the 19th of July 1861.

At Piedmont we learned the particulars of the fight which had taken place at Manassas the day before. It was considerable of a fight but coming as it did so near to the great battle of Manassas on the Sunday following, it has never received the attention from the public which would otherwise have been given it. It was fought on the part of the Yankees by their advanced or reconnoitering body of troops under Genl. Tyler, and on our side principally by the troops under Genl. Longstreet. This is called the Battle of Bull Run as the opposing forces were situated on opposite sides of this stream.

The enemy were repulsed with considerable loss. At first it was re-ported that they had lost over 600 men but this is not at all probable. I think Beauregard states in his official report that some sixty odd bodies of the enemy were counted on one part of the field, so that I suppose there were about one hundred killed and the ususal proportion wounded. Our loss was about 65 killed and wounded. It would have been much greater doubtless but for the fact that most of our troops were entrenched.

By this fight the enemy found out the situation of our position and on the Sunday following so directed their forces as to completely avoid our trenches. Hearing accounts of this fight inspired our troops at Piedmont with great enthusiasm and they all waited impatiently to be carried to Manassas where they were told the great decisive battle was daily expected. The trains, however, seemed to carry off the troops very slowly.

In the meantime although in an anxious state of mind we passed some very pleasant hours in Piedmont and its vicinity. The people from the whole country round brought their families to see the soldiers. As usual in Virginia the girls were quite abundant. They were not ceremonious and did not require introductions but conversed freely with all soldiers who approached them.

I formed in this way some very pleasant acquaintances. Two of them I particularly remember for their kindness to me, Miss Lizzie Archer and Miss Edmonds, who both of them carried me home to tea with them during my brief stay in Piedmont.

On Sunday the day of the fight, the distant booming of cannon could be heard by which we knew that fighting was going on but whether it was the big fight which was expected or whether it was another preliminary fight similar to the one on the 18th we could not tell. It rendered us very uneasy nevertheless for we knew that if the decisive battle was going on and our army should be defeated those of us at Piedmont would be doomed and would certainly be captured as in that case we would be completely surrounded and cut off from support.

Without artillery or cavalry 5,000 of us would have been opposed by 5,000 men under Genl. McDowell in our front and 3,000 under Patterson in our rear. This was not a pleasant prospect and we waited impatiently for news from the fight. Our anxiety increased very much as the afternoon approached and the train which should have returned by 10 o'clock in the morning did not arrive. This could not be accounted for in any other way than that our army had been defeated and the railroad taken possession of by the enemy. The afternoon wore away and still no train arrived.

At length about dark there was heard in the distance the welcome sound of the steam whistle. Upon its arrival we heard the first news of the battle. This was such as did not very much quiet our apprehensions.

The men belonging to the train reported that the battle had been raging fiercely all day; that in the morning our troops had been badly beaten and driven from their position; and that when the train had left the battle was at its height and they had no idea which side had gained the victory. This news produced a most tremendous excitement among the troops and all were impatient for the cars to start back.

For some unknown cause, however, they stayed and stayed, notwithstanding all our fretting and fuming and it was not until after midnight
that the cars at length moved off with the troops. The people along the
railroad had heard the cannonading on the day before and they were all
out that night with torches trying to find out the result of the fight. The
soldiers could tell them nothing and they could tell the soldiers nothing.

At length we reached a station called Gainesville where we heard the
first reliable news of the result of the battle. Here we heard from men
who had participated in the battle, of the desperate fighting, of the great
slaughter on both sides, of the fall of Bartow, Bee and others, and of the
final repulse of the enemy after a fight of seven or eight hours.

These men however did not know how badly the enemy had been
defeated but were of opinion that the fight would be renewed that day.
This place is seven or eight miles from Manasssas and three miles from
the battle field.

Our train started off again and soon we began to meet swarms of
soldiers, some with their arms going in search of the fugitives, other with
spades and shovels going to bury the dead and many with no other object
than to look at the horrid scenes which I saw later in the day and to
gather trophies of the fight.

What cheers, what shouts did they send forth. On every countenance
there was the triumphant expression of a wild, fierce joy which was totally
unlike and I had ever before seen in human face.

DEATH AND SUFFERING

As we came nearer Manassas Junction these crowds and this enthusiasm increased. At last our train ran up and stopped in the midst of a scene so horrible that my brain seem to reel as I looked. Spread around were many of the dead and the wounded who had been brought in from the battle field. Immediately by us there was a train full of men wounded in every way imaginable who were to be carried down the railroad to the different hospitals. How piteously many of them groaned in their agony. The hardest heart must have melted at such sounds.

Scattered around some on boxes, some on barrels and some on the ground lay the wounded and dead, the former going to be carried to hospitals, the latter in charge of friends who were taking them home to be buried. There was no cheering, no shouting, no laughing here. All were grave and solemn for here was death in his most terrible form and here was human anguish such as few of us had ever seen or realized. Very few sounds were heard save the groans of the wounded and the low tones of those who sought to relieve their pain.

The hospital which stood with in twenty yards of the railroad was sickening to look into. On the outside, although the rain had been falling for several hours, the blood stood in clots and pools and actually ran in little streams. . . . Inside were the men from whom some of this blood

had flown. Some had had their legs amputated, others their arms, and
these limbs had not yet been removed but lay there white and livid since
no blood was left in them. Some of the wounded were still under the
influence of chloroform and had not yet waked to the consciousness of
the fact that they were crippled for life.

On some barrels near the railroad I saw Lieut. Col. Johnston of
Hamptons Legion lying dead. He must have been killed instantly as there
was a horrid wound which had mangled his head awfully. These scenes
which I saw at the Junction were by far more painful to me than any
thing which I saw afterwards although they were as nothing to what I
saw after I arrived on the battle field. This may be accounted for in
several ways. One reason manifestly was that they were the first I saw
and prepared me for what I afterwards saw. The principal reason however, was, I think, this.

At the Junction I saw death, and inconceivable suffering in the abstract and almost entirely unaccompanied by the thoughts of glory of the
occasion. On the battlefield itself however, although the dead and
wounded lay on every side and the groans of the latter were constantly
in my ears, yet from all this I could not separate the idea of the great
scene which had been so lately enacted where I then stood, the great
victory which had been achieved by our arms and the bright promise
which it seemed to hold out of a speedy determination of the war.

Soon after my arrival at the Junction I met several of my friends
whom I was glad to find safe. Four members of the Oglethorpe Light
Infantry whom I had carried across the Shenandoah on my horse were
among the number. Winder Johnston and my three cousins Ed Law and
the two Holcombes. Although all of them I believe had their clothing
more or less cut by bullets yet none of them were hurt except Ed Law who
was limping from a bruise received on his shin by the fragment of a shell.

These however like most of the others who had been actively engaged
on the day before were very dirty. On the night before they had I suppose
been too tired to think or care about cleanliness and when I saw them
they had not performed their morning ablutions. I was pained however
to find many of my friends and acquaintances killed and wounded.
Among others James George from Atlanta a classmate of mine at the
Law School was mortally wounded and died that day. Adjutant Branch,
Capt. Howard, Wiley Crane and others of the 8th Ga. with whom I was
acquainted, killed. Bob Baker, Johnny Fleming, two Hammonds of the
8th wounded. There were many others with whom I was more or less
acquainted included among the killed and wounded.

At the Junction I also saw the prisoners who had been taken. There
was a passenger car filled with officers and outside surrounded by a
guard, about nine hundred men. Among them was U. S. Congressman
Ely of New York who looked decidedly cast down, and doubtless thought

he had seen a little more of the battle than he had bargained for when he left Washington City. The prisoners were eleganty equipped and clothed and in this presented quite a contrast to the prisoners whom I had seen from Pattersons army while in the Valley.

From the Junction our regiment marched to the battlefield four miles distant where we camped by order of Genl. Johnston. After the regiment was located I went over the portion of the field where there had been the hardest fighting. It was truly a horrible scene and one calculated to induce solemn thoughts. At this time few of the dead had been buried and many of the wounded still lay upon the field in the rain. Everything around bore painful testimony of the fierceness of the fight. Men lay upon the ground dead and wounded as far as I could see. Artillery horses lay in heaps where they had been shot while harnessed together . . .

DEAD OF BATTLEFIELD
DON'T LIE IN "HEAPS"

Dead men upon a battlefield do not lie so thickly together as is generally supposed. Where a battery of artillery is taken there lie thickest the dead men generally being artillerists. Artillery men do not generally suffer much in a fight unless their guns are taken and then if they fight well there are always a great many of them killed. But as a general thing the usual account of the "dead lying in heaps" is all humbug for it is very seldom even that they lie in groups unless they have been fighting over a particular object as a gun or something of the kind. In this I refer to a field fight as this was. In the storming of a fortification I suppose the case is different. Although how ever they did not lie as thickly as I had expected to see them yet the sight of the dead, even of the enemy was very sad. Friend and foe lay mingled together and the feeling with which I regarded the bodies of each were more alike than I had anticipated. It is true the one fell in my defence and the other in an attempt to deprive me of my rights but still I could not help feeling sorrow for both. For the wounded of the enemy I felt very sorry. For our own wounded everything was being done that could be, but for them of course nothing could be done until our own had been attended to.

Most of the dead had been killed with bullets and grape shot and very few by cannon balls or shells. In one or two places it was evident that several of the dead had been killed by the same shell. The expression on most of the countenances of the dead was one of pain. A man has to be killed instantaneously for the fierce expression which he wears in battle to be stamped upon his countenance. I saw some few instances of this character. Where a man was killed by the cannon ball, it was certainly a frightful sight though these cases were very rare.

Col. Bartow fell in the thickest of the fight commanding at the time the 7th Ga. Regt. He fell immediately in front of old Mrs. Henry's house, and a small monument has since been erected on the spot.

The dead lay thicker on this part of the field than any other. By the time I reached the field the pockets of all the dead had been rifled. There was any amount of plunder to be had, however, for the picking up. On the next day, however, Major Mounger and myself rode over a part of the field and followed the track of their flight for several miles. Such an amount of plunder was never before seen on this continent.

The enemy seemed to have been frantic with fear and to have thrown away everything which could in the least impede their flight. Arms of every description knapsacks haversacks canteen hats caps coats blankets and shoes covered the ground for miles. From the number of hats and caps and shoes which I saw the Federal army must have entered Washington City bareheaded and barefooted. The Major and myself helped ourselves to some few articles which did not seem to have any particular owner at that time, but we did not go very extensively into this business.

It would be useless for me to give a detailed account of the battle as a reference to the official reports would be much more satisfactory to any one desiring information on the subject. Genl Beauregard in his official report of the battle states that we lost killed three hundred & Sixty nine, and wounded 1483; and estimates the loss of the enemy in killed, wounded and prisoners as near five thousand. Of the killed and wounded on our side about seventy per cent belonged to Johnston's army which had marched to Beauregard's assistance. Johnston's army being situated on the left stood the brunt of the battle.

Both the Generals Patterson and McDowell were superseded in the Northern army because they did not whip out Johnston and Beauregard. Patterson as I have before said ought to have been superseded because he blundered from beginning to end; but it was great injustice to McDowell as no General ever planned a battle better and did his own part better than he did. . . . He deceived Beauregard completely and while

he was looking for an attack in front suddenly fell upon his left flank.
That he was whipped was no fault of his.

THE SPOILERS OF WAR

During the great American war of a century ago the destruction of property belonging to Southerners was not entirely the result of Yankee depredations. Occasionally Confederate soldiers themselves, for one reason or another, would cause property loss to their own people. Sometimes the reason for destruction of a planter's property might be for the practical purpose of satisfying a need. The appropriation of food or stock for their own use by hungry or poorly clothed Johnny Rebs might explain the motivation. At times there might be simply a wild, wanton destruction of property by men too long restrained from satisfying the destructive passion of hate for which they had been trained. But for the most part the Confederate soldier had a reason for playing the role of destroyer.

A letter written from Macon on a Sunday morning, 18 Sept. 1864, by Nathan Monroe to his daughter, Blanche, brings the thought to mind. Blanche, or "Bannie" as her father called her, lived at Sunnyside, near Griffin, and kept her husband's plantation going while he, John McIntosh Kell, was out on the Atlantic on the *Alabama* with Raphael Semmes. After the sinking of the *Alabama* in June 1864, Kell continued in naval service and was away from home throughout the war. Blanche's father, Nathan, wrote her often from their Macon home, "Sylvan Lodge." The house, a one-story Greek Revival structure of great beauty, still stands on Rogers Avenue, though it was modified somewhat in design and turned to face the street when Rogers Avenue was laid out.

On that Sunday morning in September a century ago Nathan was depressed as he wrote to his daughter. "Last evening I took a ride around our premises to see the destruction reported to me by Abram," he wrote, "and found things in a very bad condition." He told her of how he estimated that 300 to 600 yards of the picket fence around the place had been torn down. This may have been thought necessary by the Confederates who were camped in the vicinity because of their need of firewood, but it was considered a great loss to Nathan Monroe. But he went on to say, "They have also set the woods on fire and destroyed some timber." He guessed there were about 800 soldiers camped there, but when he went up to the camp all had left but about 100.

Whether or not the Confederate soldiers who camped around the Monroe place were acting under orders when they tore down the picket fence, I do not know. Sometimes they were ordered to destroy property. A good example of this was the burning of the Virginia town of Hampton, at the mouth of the James River. Can a good reason be found for the destruction of Virginia planters' property at the hands of the Confederates? Let us see. The burning occurred on 7 Aug. 1861. The town was set on fire by order of Gen. John Bankhead Magruder. He was stationed there with a force of about 2,000 men. The Union forces had been pulling back rapidly since the Confederate victory at Manassas, and they evacuated Hampton in great haste. In looking for a reason for this most unusual behavior of Confederates' burning a Virginia town, we get little help from a letter which Capt. Robert A. Smith of the Macon Volunteers wrote to his friend J. W. Burke back home in Macon. He wrote from Sewell's Point on 14 Aug. saying this action was "a military necessity." But what made it a military necessity?

The answer to that question comes from "Prince John" Magruder himself. He explained it by saying he had known "for some time past that Hampton was the harbor of runaway slaves and traitors, and . . . that it could not be held by us even if taken." The Yankees had established a colony of freedmen there. When Magruder saw the "extreme importance" of the place to the Federals and realized that "the town itself would lend great strength to whatever fortifications they might erect around it," he determined to burn it immediately. He claimed that the Hampton residents themselves, who fled from their homes before the fire consumed them, "seemed to concur with me as to the property of this course." One wonders, however, if the "traitors" who were also Virginians, were not provoked, to say the least, at the work of the spoilers who burned their town. To a Northern general, Benjamin F. Butler, the act showed "the spirit in which the war is to be carried on on their part, and . . . perhaps will have a tendency to provoke a corresponding spirit upon our part."

SOUTHERN HOSPITALITY

To go to Confederate prisons such as Andersonville to find examples of Southern hospitality in the matter of treatment of Yankee prisoners may seem strange; and the example, as related in the story I shall tell, is a rare one. But it does illustrate the truth that there are exceptions to all rules, and I hope my Northern friends will see in it the limits to which the warm Southern heart will go. Eliza Andrews (*Wartime Journal of a Georgia Girl*) could not believe Christ meant Yankees when he said "Love your enemies," but Lt. S. F. Mayes, one of the Georgia guards at the gate of the prison at Andersonville, was so well liked by the Federal prisoners under his custody that they found a way to express their appreciation.

William B. Hesseltine, one of the best authorities on the subject, says, "No prisoner loves his jailer," and goes so far as to say, "Rarely, indeed, and then only briefly and under special circumstances—such as those at Ft. Warren early in the conflict—did a few captors fraternize with their charges."

MacKinlay Kantor, in his novel *Andersonville*, in language too obscene for me to repeat, speaks of "The flame-spit of a sentry's gun," a sentry who was trigger-happy and eagerly waiting for a prisoner to cross the "deadline" so he could pop him. And Ovid Futch, who did a serious study of the subject under Bell Wiley at Emory University, quotes inmates of the prison as saying the guards "are the Dambdst set of men I ever had had the luck to fall in with yet. . . ." and "God help the Prisoner when they fall into the hands of the Malishia . . ." and, again, "perched upon the stockade as guards [were] the worst looking scallawags . . . from boys just large enough to handle a gun, to old men who ought to have been dead years ago for the good of their country."

But Lt. Mayes was not treated with contempt as most of the other guards were. Mayes had been in the regular Confederate army, a lieutenant in fact, in Company D of the 7th Georgia Regiment. He was so severely wounded at First Manassas that he was relieved of active service in the field. That is how he came to be stationed at Camp Sumter, or Andersonville as it is now known, stationed at the main entrance to the prison.

In 1907 the old veteran was living at Marietta, Georgia, and at the request of the United Daughters of the Confederacy he released a letter to the press which he had been keeping all through the years since September 1864. He considered it one of his most precious possessions and a reminder of strange friends in a strange situation. Those friends were Francis Fogarittie of the 19th U. S. Infantry, John Foy of the 16th U. S. Infantry, William Hogan of the 14th Conn. Volunteers, T. H. Murphy of the 1st N. Y. Cavalry, H. Rifiley of the 85th Ill. Volunteers, J. H. Friend of the 16th U. S. Cavalry Volunteers, J. Younk of the 2nd Ky. Cavalry Volunteers, Eugene Lewis of the 2nd Mich. Infantry Volunteers, and James Grey of the 4th Iowa Infantry Volunteers.

The letter, dated 20 Sept. 1864, reads as follows:

To Lieut. S. F. Mayes, Second Georgia Infantry

Sir—We, the undersigned prisoners of war, now confined in the Confederate prison for upwards of eleven months, now deem it our duty to present you with a small and trifling testimonial to show you that we appreciate your noble and charitable conduct toward our poor sick brothers as well as the well ones. This watch that we present you with is not as noble as our hearts would be willing to present you with, but it is the best we are able to find. Hoping you may always be able to wear it in remembrance of those Federal prisoners who present you with it; hoping we may be able to enjoy the blessings of a peaceful and happy home, and meet as brothers and not as enemies in a very short time. Believe us, Lieutenant, to be your humble donors.

The letter was signed by the men named above. There is no possible way of knowing how or where they "found" the watch.

WAR PRISON PROBLEMS

Last Sunday I introduced the subject of treatment of Federal prisoners in Confederate prisons. Today I wish to continue along that line of thought and show something of the attitude of civilians toward the Union soldier who became an unwilling visitor to our city. Let me begin with statistics. According to F. C. Ainsworth, adjutant general of the United States in 1903, there were 193,743 Union and 214,865 Confederate soldiers captured and imprisoned. Of the nearly 200,000 Northerners in Southern prisons, more than 30,000 died in the stockades. Of the even greater number of Johnny Rebs in Northern prisons, nearly 26,000 died in captivity. I hold to the view that the 12 percent who died in Northern prisons and the more than 15 percent who died in Southern prisons were the victims not of cruel and inhuman treatment by prison guards who welcomed every opportunity to kill a prisoner, but were the unfortunate victims of uncontrollable conditions such as shortages of medicines and food, and of uncontrolled sanitary conditions. That surely was the situation in Andersonville Prison.

The fantastic story which circulated, at the time, of deliberate poisoning of prisoners by order of the Andersonville authorities was pure falsehood, spawned from the germs of hate and malice. Robert E. Lee released a statement to the press to refute the claim that the prisoners of war at Andersonville had been inoculated with poison in order to relieve the overcrowded conditions there. There is no question but that the captured Federals were disliked, but cruel and inhumane treatment of them and expressions of hatred for the poor unfortunate victims of war is not substantiated by the evidence. Hesseltine, mentioned last week as a recognized authority, blames the atrocity on, first, the politicians who found it advantageous to continue to wave the "bloody shirt," and second, on Union prisoners who after the war wrote vivid tales of mistreatment in order to wring more money from a Congress considering pension claims on the basis of injuries and illnesses resulting from prison treatment.

The following excerpt from the *Macon Daily Telegraph* of 13 May 1862 shows that the people of this city, though much annoyed by the Union policy of refusing to exchange prisoners and realizing the great disadvantages to the South of such a condition, were determined to be charitable toward the poor, hungry, ill-clad, sick, and wounded Union captives with whom they were burdened.

> The eight to nine hundred prisoners now at Camp Oglethorpe in this city, present, as it appears to us, a very inconvenient and expensive problem. The expense attending their subsistence and safe keeping is not short of a thousand dollars per day, and is a good deal more than that of the same number of effective troops in the field. If our country is successful in his war as we expect her to be, and the Lincoln government still refuses an exchange, we shall, in a short time, have on our hands the cost of two armies; and, indeed, we see no reason why the Lincolnites should consent to an exchange with these facts before them. The bulk of their Army being composed of men thrown out of civil employment—men who must be fed by somebody—it is a most economical plan to leave them upon their enemies for support, and there is no difficulty in filling up the vacuum by recruits in like condition. If the 700,000 invaders who are now penetrating our country in all directions,

are successfully repelled (as we do not doubt they are destined to be), it is impossible but that thousands and tens of thousands of them will be cut off, and create a burden upon us as intolerable as the invasion itself. It can scarcely be believed that an enemy who fights us with poisoned balls and medicines, would balk at fighting us with the burden of supporting prisoners taken from their ranks. They have plenty of men of that stamp, and care little for them. They know, too, that food and clothing are scarce in the South. On the other hand, they have plenty of food and clothing and know that we have comparatively few men, and those valued members of society. They can feed and clothe four prisoners for the same money it costs us to maintain one. Why, then, should they favor an exchange of prisoners? The disadvantages are all on our side and there are positive benefits upon their own. We have little idea they will exchange, except in the case of sick and wounded. They could actually conquer us by prisoners and still have an Army in the field.

But if we retain the prisoners, then the obligations of religion and humanity bind us to take proper care of them. Those in Camp Oglethorpe are now nearly naked, and must be clothed. It will take $20,000, as clothing is now valued, to make these men decent and comfortable, and it is time, out of a due respect for the customs of every civilized country, or even of semi-barbarians, that the tailor should be set to work. Wear and tear have already reduced them to very visible extremities.

March 29, 1964

WE ARE ALL BROTHERS

Five thousand people gathered at Andersonville on 12 May 1909 to attend the unveiling cermonies of a monument to Capt. Henry Wirz, the keeper of the Confederate prison where nearly 13,000 prisoners died. Joseph Foraker of Ohio, ex-senator, ex-governor, and ex-captain in the Union army, had made some intemperate remarks about the planting of dynamite under that monument erected to honor a Confederate martyr. But over against that kind of attitude there were those who looked upon the war as a common sorrow to be remembered not in hate but in pity. Among those impressed by the expression of Southern sympathy for the dead Union soldiers buried beneath the Georgia pines was Clara Barton, founder of the American Red Cross.

I have in my files a letter from William D. Conklin, Public Information chairman of the Clara Barton Chapter No. 1 of the American Red Cross, Dansville, New York. In it he quotes from Miss Barton's report on her expedition to Andersonville where she did much work in identifying and marking the graves. The report was published in the *Dansville Advertiser*, March 1866. Miss Barton was impressed by the "humane public-spirited citizen of Fort Valley, Georgia, a Mr. Griffin."

This Mr. Griffin, whom she did not identify, had been

> informed by one of the ever-faithful negroes, that the bodies were becoming exposed, and were rooted up by animals. Having verified this statement, he collected a few negroes, sank the exposed bodies, and covered them to a proper depth. He then reported the facts to Gen. Wilson [James A. Wilson, whose headquarters were in Macon after he captured the city on 20 April 1865], and requested authority to take steps for protecting the grounds. That patriotic officer visited Andersonville in person, appointed Mr. Griffin temporary Superintendent, and gave him such limited faculties as could be furnished in that destitute country . . . We found Mr. Griffin, with a force of about twenty negroes, and a few mules, at work on the grounds.

Miss Barton concluded by saying, "I have understood that that gentleman furnished the labor at his own cost, while General Wilson issued the necessary rations."

The purpose Mr. Conklin had in writing to me was to find out, if possible, who Mr. Griffin was. Mr. Carl W. Schaller, superintendent at Andersonville, had referred him to me. My research took me to N. P. Chipman's *The Tragedy of Andersonville* (San Francisco, 1911), and there I found Joel R. Griffin's testimony as given at the trial of Capt. Wirz. It follows, unabridged.

> The first portion of the past year I was an officer in the Confederate service, colonel of the 8th Georgia Cavalry, Army of Northern Virginia. For the past four months I have had an interest in trying to improve and beautify the Andersonville graveyard; that is, I have aided a brother of mine in trying to improve it. About the 20th of May last, being somewhat disabled, I went down for the purpose of observing matters at Andersonville. I heard that there had been a great deal of distress there, that was the reason I went there. I was ordered by General Wilson to go there to look after the prison. I arrived there about the 20th of May, 1865. I arrived under orders from General Wilson to protect the property there, to improve the graveyard, and to cover bodies that had been somewhat exposed which I did. I found the graveyard in rather a bad condition. It had been disturbed by cows, and part of the graves torn up to some extent, which I had covered. Two of the bodies were exposed; the bodies were placed in lines, and the dirt having been in some instances taken off them in part, the graves were somewhat of-

fensive; that is, of the last bodies buried. No measures had been taken by the rebel government to care for that graveyard that I know of.

I saw no reason at all to believe that the uncovering of those bodies was intentional; it was from want of care. That was three or four weeks, probably, after the Andersonville prison had been broken up.

I have verified the fact that Mr. Griffin was Col. Joel R. Griffin, of the 8th Georgia Cavalry. Mr. Conklin, thanking me for the information I sent him, observed that it was rather surprising that a former colonel in the Confederate army "should take so much trouble in caring for a cemetery of Union prisoners." And he closed with the comment: "He must, indeed, have been 'humane.'"

Well . . . that's the way we are.

THE MARTIAL POETS

April is the month for flowers, and were I a poet I would sing of wondrous beauty and radiant glory shining all 'round. But I am not a poet, and this column aims at keeping the attention of its readers on the ugly scenes of the Civil War. April is the month when we are reminded by the United Daughters of the Confederacy of that war and is the time when we try to draw some lessons from ceremonies of commemoration. April was the month, in 1861, when the young men of this city went hopefully off to Virginia to fight, having learned that

The despot's heel is on thy shore, Maryland!

and knowing full well that if not stopped in Virginia he would advance into Georgia. It was this month 100 years ago that Sherman was gathering 100,000 troops to wage his spring and summer campaign which resulted in the capture of Atlanta.

The horrible and cruel war stirred the emotions of Southern poets and brought forth from their pens the best poetry that the section had produced up to that time. The line above is a reminder of that fact. It is from James Ryder Randall's "Maryland, My Maryland," which the Cary sisters of Baltimore sang to the tune of "Tannenbaum, O Tannenbaum" to a Confederate regiment in New Orleans. It was echoed from the throats of thousands of Johnny Rebs in the camps and on the battlefields during the war. The first verse continues:

> His torch is at thy temple door, Maryland!
> Avenge the patriotic gore
> That flecked the streets of Baltimore
> And be the battle queen of yore,
> Maryland, my Maryland!

The poets—the good ones few and the bad ones countless—not only threw down the gauntlet, as Randall did with his "Battle Cry of the South," Halphin with "God Save the South," and James Barron Hope with his "Oath of Freedom," but also expressed every emotion and every event experienced during those four eventful and emotion-packed years. The newspaper editors were besieged by soldiers and civilians with verses equal to the amount of grape and canister poured into Union lines. In desperation one newspaper slowed down the pace at which it was receiving poems by charging authors the same rate as it charged for obituaries, ten cents a line.

Among the better poets inspired by war themes were Henry Timrod, Francis O. Ticknor, and Father Abram J. Ryan. Timrod spoke to "Carolina" as Randall spoke to "Maryland." Heroes were honored by such poems as Father Ryan's "Sword of Lee" and John W. Palmer's "Stonewall Jackson's Way." Margaret Preston memorialized Jackson's dramatic death in her poem "Under the Shade of the Trees." Ticknor depicted the pathos of the soldier in "Little Giffen of Tennessee."

Many poems showing love of the flag were set to music and became familiar songs. Among these are "The Southern Cross," "Confederate Flag," "The Stars and Bars," and "The Bonnie Blue Flag." The last named was and still is the most popular of all.

It was written in 1861 by Harry B. McCarthy. The first and last verses and the chorus follow.

We are a band of brothers, and native to the soil,
Fighting for our liberty, with treasure, blood and toil;
And when our rights were threatened, the cry rose near and far;
Hurrah for the Bonnie Blue Flag that bears a single star!

(Chorus)
Hurrah! Hurrah! For Southern rights, hurrah!
Hurrah for the Bonnie Blue Flag that bears a single star!

Then, here's to our Confederacy; strong we are and brave,
Like patriots of old we'll fight our heritage to save;
And rather than submit to shame, to die we would prefer—
So cheer again for the Bonnie Blue Flag that bears a single star!

Perhaps the best note to end on is contained in the last verse of Father Ryan's poem "The Sword of Robert Lee."

Forth from its scabbard! All in vain
Bright flashed the sword of Lee;—
'Tis shrouded now in its sheath again,
It sleeps the sleep of our noble slain,
Defeated yet without a stain,
Proudly and peacefully.

ONCE MORE AT HOME

The letter that fills this column today was loaned to me by Miss Newell Mason. It was written by Charles S. Gautier who had gone home to rest after the Red River Campaign. His home was Columbia, Mississippi. He was writing to his aunt, Harriet Newell Mitchell, whose plantation home was near Jackson, Mississippi. The only date on the letter is April 1864 at the top and "25th" above the post script at the bottom. Gautier refers to the death of Gen. Thomas Green. Gen. Green was killed in the Red River Campaign at Blair's Landing, Louisiana, on 12 April so the approximate date is determined. Another general mentioned in the letter should be identified. He was Maj. Gen. John Austin Wharton who also took part in the Red River Campaign, pursuing Gen. Nathaniel P. Banks after that Union general's defeat.

Columbia April 1864

Dear Aunt Hattie

At home again! How sweet those words sounds to an old soldier, who has been battling for his country's rights for two years; and to be seated

by his own fire sides, talking to those loved ones he left before going to
the unholy war, that has been carried on by the ruthless invader for such
a length of time is indeed quite a rare pleasure.

My trip home was attended by no incidents worthy of note, only a
time in trying to pass through the Jayhawkers region without being
molested, which we did with great success; having seen a few of the
unwelcome guest on the road, but they taking fright at us were trying
the speed of their horses, to unveil us from their sight. I wrote you a few
days before reaching the river, and just four days from that time (being
delayed at the river two or three days) we succeeded in crossing the
Mississippi.

All were very well at home now. Sister Harriet having lossed her
youngest child about a month before I arrived and soon after I came two
of her children was taken with the Scarlet fever, but have recovered
enough to be out of danger with careful attention. My visit home was
quite a surprize to all; none having the remotest idea that such meeting
was so close at hand. I did not let them know that I was so close until I
reached the house and dashing in. I made my self known as their long
lost or wished for Brother. You can imagine the meeting better than my
feeble pen can delineate. Success has attend our army over on this side
of the river to such an extent, that Gen. Banks who was in charge of the
Yankee army, have been completely demoralized, and nearly his whole
army captured. We have taken nearly all his artillery, and now are turning our attention to the Gunboats nearly all of which will be destroyed
or captured. Our loss is great, but such a victory is always attended by
sad tidings. The lamented Gen. Green was killed, whose place although
hard to be filled, has left an imperishable name to Texas as one of her
most gallant souls.

It was Gen. Wharton's intention to report to Gen. Kirby Smith before
going home, but after crossing the Mississippi River, and finding the
enemy between him, and our army, started home, and remained only two
days, receiving orders from Gen. Kirby Smith to report at his headquarters. He started for the army to fill the place of Gen. Green—I have
been at home about ten days and intend starting for La. in two or three
days. This part of the world seems to know but little about the trials and
troubles that a war is attended with. We have coffee, sugar and molasses
three great necessarys of life in abundance especially the two last articles.

Well my dear Aunt Hattie I have not been able to find anything yet
as to the whereabouts of your relations, but think more probable that I
shall come in contact with them in northern Texas, or La., where I shall
go. Tell Cousin Eugenia that I mailed her letter, as soon as I arrived at
home, but do not know whether it will reach its point of destination now;
because the enemy is in possession of that country.

Arie is well, and send much love.—Lucy is now on the carpet quite fascinating as the young gentlemen say—(Love to each, and all.) Oh Auntie! I have had the most exquisite pleasure of riding "Cap" a few days ago, she is in fine order, and is as gay as [a] Lark. Sister will add a P.S. so I will bid you good bye, a thousand kisses for Uncle Tom. Love to Cousin Dick's Family and all on the Ridge.

Your most affectionate
Nephew
C. S. GAUTIER

P.S. 25th
I start for the army of La. this morning to report to Gen. Wharton. I shall write to Cousin Mollie Holmes, as soon as I get to La., as I think you would rather hear from me at that place. Answer this Auntie. Love to each and all. Howdy to the blacks.—Charlie.

OH! THE PITY OF IT

Our New York friend whose interest in Clara Barton's comments about the "humane public-spirited citizen from Fort Valley" who covered the open graves at Andersonville has written an interesting letter in which he shares my feeling that "We Are All Brothers" (*Telegraph-News*, 29 March), but he raises some questions which I wish to answer. He cannot understand why Southern people would erect a monument to Capt. Henry Wirz, a prison keeper who was held responsible by the court that tried him as a war criminal under whom nearly 13,000 prisoners died. He admits that "everything I have come across is written from the viewpoint of those who suffered at Andersonville." This makes him wonder why it "seemed appropriate to erect a monument to (Wirz) in 1909."

Southerners moved by pity must have felt horror at what happened at Andersonville. Even if they deplored the penalty imposed on its keeper by the court, why would they wish to memorialize him?

In trying to answer the questions of our New York reader—
whose questions are logical, natural, and understandable in the
light of his admittedly one-sided information—I would say, first,
that surely Southerners were moved by pity. Capt. Wirz himself
was moved by pity. Pleasant A. Stovall of Savannah, who spoke
at the unveiling exercises, pointed out the fact that the prison
keeper paroled the drummer boys so that they might not be
subjected to the privations of prison life, released the brass band
in order that it might add to the entertainment of the men,
allowed the prisoners to rig up their improvised shelters, allowed
the prisoners to go beyond the enclosure and gather fuel, authorized the brewing of corn beer for the refreshment of the men,
and distributed boxes sent from home. I might add that, with
the help of the citizens of the village and the nearby city of
Americus, he provided them what meager food, clothing, and
medicine could be spared. In response to the complaint of one of
the prisoners Wirz answered, "Why sir, my men are short of
rations, and the best I can do is see that your sick comrades are
moved to the hospital. God help you, I cannot."

Why would the United Daughters of the Confederacy erect
a monument at Andersonville, plan an elaborate ceremony, and
invite the martyred captain's daughter to unveil it? Just as the
North had to have a scapegoat and chose Wirz, so did the South
need a symbol. The South needed the consolation that came from
a monument to one who bore the penalty for all. He was a sort
of atonement not only for the trumped up charges of Confederate
atrocities but also for the real burden of sin which lay heavily
upon the hearts of all people with a conscience, North and South.

Emerson had something to say about this theme, though in
a different context, in his essay "Compensation." To the Southern
women who erected the Wirz monument, it represented something of a compensating factor for the Lost Cause. The Orientals
call it "face-saving." Perhaps our Northern friends do not understand face-saving, for they have never had any need for such
therapy.

I believe Americans, whether descendants of Union or Confederate ancestors, will subscribe to the sentiments expressed
by the *Atlanta Constitution* (13 May 1909) which made the fol-

lowing editorial comment on Mr. Stovall's address at the unveiling of the Wirz Monument:

Briefly, but vividly, he pictures the conditions of those days, when passion wrought men's souls to fever pitch and prompted acts which justice and reason would have scorned—when many a life that might have been preserved to future usefulness and happiness and peace was snuffed out upon the altar of the inexorable and unrelenting war god.

And so, we may repeat, viewing it all in the light of written history, in whose pages there can be now no revision—

Oh! The pity of it!

Oh! The pity of it all, let the viewpoint be where it may, whether New England or Georgia, Ohio or Carolina, it matters not; we can only look back, realizing that we cannot change one smallest detail of those days of terror, nor call back a single life they claimed.

History and the survivors have honored the heroes of that conflict. In imperishable print and shafts of stone and bronze the country over, they live. There is no phrase of life or service which is not there set down; all is written and recorded.

Let it therefore, be of history a part.

The time has come to close the book of passion and recrimination.

To open it is but to stir anew the rancors of a past above whose burial place the American people would now erect a shaft whose crowning piece shall be the clasped hands of unity and fraternity.

There is none who will counsel forgetfulness of men and deeds.

But rather will all welcome the dawn of that day, already at hand, when these men, north and south, will live in history as heroes, not of this section nor of that, but of the great American nation.

And when that history is read and its tragedy revealed through the printed lines, the sole emotion that shall stir their souls is that epitomized in Mr. Stovall's brief but potent line:

"Oh! The pity of it!"

ORDEAL OF CAPT. WIRZ

My mind turns again to Andersonville Prison and to that tragic figure, Capt. Henry Wirz, who was executed to atone for the loss of 13,000 Union soldiers who died in his prison camp. Fifty-five years ago, come Tuesday, the United Daughters of the Confederacy unveiled a monument to Capt. Wirz, the only man executed as a war criminal at the end of the Civil War.

Though I have written on Andersonville Prison several times in this column, I have been reminded again of it by a letter from Walter S. McClesky of this city. His forebears served as guards at the prison. Mr. McClesky, a Methodist minister, makes an interesting point when he proves the McCleskys and the Spruills were educated, of good substantial families, and respected citizens of their community. Some of them had been in military service before their assignment at Camp Sumter (Andersonville), and one, James Franklin McClesky, was sheriff of Cobb County at the time of his assignment. This fact helps to refute the claim made by MacKinlay Kantor in his novel, *Anderson-*

ville, that the guards were ignorant, irresponsible, trigger-happy boys.

Descendants of the Andersonville guards might rightly resent insinuations that Georgians were unreasonably cruel and that they took delight in denying the prisoners very badly needed food, clothing, shelter, and medicine; but they might resent even more the fact that a poor German prison keeper was made to pay the supreme penalty for the suffering and death of those prisoners. It is said that Federal authorities would have liked to get bigger game than Wirz and offered him a deal. If he would implicate Jefferson Davis as the instigator of the hardships that resulted in so many deaths then they would free him from the gallows. But the little Swiss-born German would not take that course to save his neck from the rope that snapped out his life in the prison yard at Washington on 10 Nov. 1865. Such a man deserved a monument to his memory.

Rather than go to Kantor's fiction to see the poor victim of sectional hate and bitterness, let us look into the very soul of the captain who had been placed in charge of too many Federal prisoners in a stockade too inadequate to contain them. We can do this by reading a few lines from the pages of his diary kept during his last hours in prison, lines written by his one good hand. In place of the other hand was a stump with the bone protruding through the rotting flesh.

> *I have no desire to live. Perhaps there was never a more willing victim dragged to the scaffold than I. Why should I desire to live? A beggar crippled, with health and spirit broken; why should I want to live?*

His wife was making every effort to see him, but the officer charged with the duty of attending him during visiting hours was sick. Capt. Wirz found it "pretty hard that because a man is sick I have been deprived for two weeks of my only joy—that of seeing my dear wife." He asked for a minister of the gospel, but "for five weeks have I asked in vain . . . " Finally, his request was granted.

On 3 Oct. he wrote: "What a mockery is this trial! I feel at times as if I ought to speak out loud and ask them why they wrong themselves so, and me too . . . " They would not give him more time to arrange his defense, but in a forgiving spirit the doomed prisoner said, "May the day be far distant when General Lew Wallace may plead with grim Death for a day and receive the answer, 'No!' " And again he wrote, "Oh, God, give me the grace and power to bear the cross . . . "

> *Oct. 4: Oh, what a mockery of justice.*
> *Oct. 5: When I left the court room today, I heard a lady say, "I wish I could shoot out his eyes."*

A *New York World* reporter described the execution scene. Twelve hundred people witnessed it.

> The walls of the prison, the adjoining housetops, the windows and trees in the capitol grounds were black with men and women, most of the latter coarse and repulsive creatures who joined the men in making loud and vulgar outcries.

The Confederate martyr died protesting his innocence to the very end. His last words were "I am going before my God who will judge between me and my accusers."

• IV •

MEN
OF
WAR

A Letter to Mr. Lincoln

Humor made the horrors of the Civil War bearable and humor today helps us remember the war with more forbearance and less bitterness. In the tradition of the folk humor of Georgia's well-known writers, Augustus Baldwin Longstreet, Richard Malcolm Johnston, and William Tappan Thompson, was a Rome lawyer who wrote under the name of "Bill Arp." His real name was Charles Henry Smith. He wore the Confederate gray throughout the war, and after it was over he entered politics, serving for a while as state senator and later as mayor of Rome. Many of his humorous sketches appeared in the *Atlanta Constitution*.

When President Lincoln issued his proclamation of 15 April declaring that a state of rebellion existed as a result of the capture of Ft. Sumter, Bill Arp wrote him an open letter which circulated widely in the Southern press at the time.

In his proclamation, Lincoln had ordered the rebels to "disperse and retire peaceably to their respective abodes within twenty days from this date." Here is the way Bill Arp responded to it.

Mr. Linkhorn—Sir: These are to inform you we are all well, and hope these few lines may find you in statusquo. We got your proklamashun, and as you have put us on mity short notis, a few of us boys has concluded to write you, and ax for a little more time. The fact is, we are most obleedged to have a few more days, for the way things are hapinin, its utterly onpossible for us to disperse in 20 days. Old Virginy and Tennessee and North Carolina are continually aggravatin us into tumults and Karousments, and a body cant disperse until you put a stop to sich onruly conduct on their part. I tried my darndest yesterday to disperse and retire, but it was no go; and besides your Marshall here aint doing a darn thing—he dont read the riot act nor remonstrate nor nothing, and ought to be turned out. If you conclude to do so, I am authorized to rekommend to you Capt. Cooper or Mr. McClung, or perhaps myself would attend to the business as well as most anybody. The fact is the boys around here want watchin, or they'll take somethin'. A few days ago I heard they surrounded two of our best citizens because they named Fort and Sumter. Most of them are so hot they fairly siz when you pour water on em, and that's the way they make up their military companies here now—when a man applies to jine the Volunteers, they sprinkle him and if he sizzles they take him, and if he don't they don't.

Mr. Linkhorn, sir, privately speaking, I'm afraid I'll git in a tite place here among these doods and have to elope out of it, and I would like much to have your Scotch cap and cloak, what you traveled to Washington in . . . I want you to write to me immediately about things generally, and let us know where you intend to do your fightin.

Your proklamashun says something about takin possession of the public property at "all Hazzards." We can't find no sich a place on the map. I thought it must be about Charleston, or Savannah, or Harper's Ferry, but they say it ain't anywhere down South. One man said it was a little factory on an island in Lake Champlain, where they made sand bags. My opinion is that sand bags wont pay, and it is a great waste of money. Our boys here carry their sand in their gizzards where it keeps better, and is always handy. I'm afraid your government is given you and your kangaroo a heep of onnecessary trouble, and my humble advice is if things don't work better soon, you'd better grease it or trade the darned old thing off. I'd take rails or anything far it—if I could see you I'd show you a slight of hand trick that would change the whole concern into bottons quick. If you don't trade, or do somethin' else with it soon, it will spile or die on your hands certain.

Give my respects to Bill Suard and the other members of the Kangaroo. What's Hannibal doin? I don't hear anything from him nowadays. Yours with care.

BILL ARP

P.S.—If you can possibly extend that order to 30 days, do so. We have sent you the discount in advance, on a check at Harper's Ferry [who keeps that darned old Ferry now?—it's givin us a heap of trouble] but if you positively won't extend, we'll send you a check, drawn by Jeff Davis, Beauregard endorser, payable on sight anywhere.

Yours,

B. A.

DATA ON JEFFERSON DAVIS

Dear Sir:

I have heard you are a historian. Would you please tell me where I could get some information on Jefferson Davis and his cabinet. I have to write a three hundred word essay on him.

I am ten years old and I go to City Elementary School in Milledgeville.

Yours sincerely,

ALLAN RING

Dear Allan:

I am answering your letter on the eve of the anniversary of the birth of Abraham Lincoln [12 February] whom we should also honor as the president of our entire nation. But Mr. Lincoln will have many to remember him, so you do well to write on the only president the Confederacy ever had.

You asked about Mr. Davis and his cabinet. So I suppose you are interested in the war period only. But I would like to take you back of the war, for it is there that we see the better side of the man. During wartime he was in conflict with his generals and caused the governors of some of the states to hate him. This was especially true of our own Governor Joseph E. Brown who didn't like him at all because he kept trying to take too many Georgia men, guns, and supplies to Virginia when Georgians thought they should be used to protect the state at its borders.

The little baby named Jefferson Davis was born in Kentucky on 3 June 1808, the last year of the presidency of Thomas Jefferson whose ideas about a nation of farmers and the rights of the states were the same as those of his namesake. As the Civil War became more vicious, President Davis attended a very fine college, Transylvania University, at Lexington, Kentucky. There he learned religious tolerance. "My religion is the love of God and man," he said. After he graduated from the Military Academy, the young lieutenant fought Indians in the West, especially old Black Hawk, the terrible Sac chief. It was at this time that Lt. Davis fell in love with Sarah Knox Taylor, the pretty daughter of Colonel Zachary Taylor. The Colonel did not want his daughter to marry a soldier because he knew the wife of an army man could not have a real home with all the moving about. Jefferson loved Sarah so much that he gave up the army. They tried to settle down and make a home on his brother's Mississippi plantation called "Hurricane." But the attempt to become a planter ended soon when Sarah died, just three months after her wedding. They were both very sick with malaria fever; Jefferson was so ill he didn't know when Sarah died. The lonely man had more difficulty recovering from the shock of his wife's death than from getting over the malaria.

Mr. Davis spent several years in retirement, trying to live the life of a country gentleman. Then he married Varina Howell and returned to army life. He fought in the Mexican War under Zachary Taylor, who had become a general by that time. Lt. Davis was wounded and cited for bravery in the Battle of Buena Vista. He served his state and nation as congressman and senator, and as secretary of war under President Franklin Pierce. His service as secretary of war was his greatest service to the Union; his service as president of the Confederacy, his greatest service to his Southern people.

President Davis had very few in his cabinet who stand out as remarkable men and statesmen. Alexander H. Stephens, of our own state, was his vice-president. Stephens was a man of great ability, but he failed to work closely with the president and the government in Richmond. Robert Toombs was the first secretary of state. He was a colorful figure, and he wanted to wear a general's uniform instead of sitting at a desk in Richmond. The "Brains of the Confederacy" was Judah P. Benjamin, a Jew from New Orleans. Benjamin was attorney general, then secretary of war, and finally secretary of state. After the war ended he escaped to England where he won fame as a lawyer. Only two other men served during the entire period of the war. They were Stephen R. Mallory, of Florida, secretary of the navy, and John H. Reagan, of Texas, postmaster general. Reagan was with the president when he fled from Richmond *after General Lee surrendered at Appomattox. He continued with the president in his flight into Georgia. President Davis was captured at Irwinville and was brought through Macon on his way to Fortress Monroe where he spent two years in prison.*

Yours sincerely,

SPENCER B. KING JR.

May 27,1962

LETTER TO GEN. JACKSON

The ghost of
General Thomas J. Jackson
Army of the Valley
Somewhere in the Shenandoah
Dear General:

You will be interested to know that I was one of a small group of Macon citizens who were invited by Col. Richard C. Neeley to visit the 4137th Strategic Wing at Robins Air Force Base last week. Col. Neeley is the commander of this wing, which is one of the units in the Strategic Air Command, a retaliatory wing of the Air Force that is poised and ready to strike enemy, bombing planes when they are detected. SAC, our watch dog, is on alert around the world, every minute of every hour of every day, and packed with more destructive power in terms of TNT than the total explosives used by all nations in World War II.

I felt honored to be invited to visit the Base as the guest of the 4137th Wing of SAC, and a little proud, too, that Col. Neeley had recognized my position as a colonel in the Confederate Air

Force, and as an expert on unusual weapons. Apparently, he had been reading my column in the *Telegraph-News* and had learned about the "Joe Brown Pike," "the Winans Steam Gun," and "the Double-barreled Cannon" and wanted to get some new ideas which might be used to improve SAC's weapons. I went out with my head filled with bright ideas of fantastic weapons like ballistic missiles that could be dropped from the parent plane and guided to an enemy target by remote control, missiles with nuclear warheads that could be directed at a target through calculations by the stars. I conceived the idea of a great refueling plane which could supply the bombers with fuel for almost indefinite lengths of time in the air by contact at 30,000 feet in the sky. But do you know, General, they had already thought up all that, and more besides. The B-52s had the weapons, and the KC-1356 had the fuel. It was frustrating, and I was so overwhelmed by it all that I could not come up with a single new idea. Our tour conductors, Col. Ray B. Sitton and Capt. Willis M. Hodges were considerate, however, and even though I was unable to give them any advice, they treated me with all the respect a colonel in the Confederate Air Force deserves.

As Col. Sitton sat beside me in the cabin of a B-52 explaining the multitude of dials, buttons, and levers that covered the panels in front and overhead and around the sides of the cabin, I thought about the difference between the kind of fighting a boy from Calhoun, Georgia, the colonel's hometown, would experience under you in the Valley and the kind of fighting this airman is doing. My eyes nearly popped out at the sight of the big B-52 with its nuclear "Hounddog" that could chase an enemy plane at a speed faster than sound; at the "Quails," decoys which would fool the adversary and cause him to lose the big bomber as he wasted his missile on the dummy; at the big jet engines that powered the 250-ton bomber.

Our guides took us into the briefing room and showed us more marvelous things. They projected on the screen in the viewing room a B-70 Valkyrie. It has six turbojet engines, and each engine carries 30,000 pounds of thrust that sends it to 70,000 feet at three times the speed of sound. It carries nuclear weapons and launches ballistic missiles.

Security is the chief aim of SAC, and speed is the keyword of its security. As our bus passed the guarded underground barracks of the 4137th squadron, Maj. [sic] Hodges told us the crews of the B-52s could have their great ships in the air in less than fifteen minutes after an alarm, time enough to intercept enemy planes headed for an American city or base.

Col. Sitton explained how they protect themselves against the possibility of accidental war. SAC is in direct contact with the secretary of defense and the president of the United States. Before the nuclear weapons are sent thundering toward what might be enemy planes the president himself has to authorize the pulling of the trigger. All of this is practically instantaneous, but there is time lapse enough to allow for verification of an enemy attack.

General, you who know how to wheel and flank the enemy would be pleased with the speed and efficiency of SAC. You, they say, can be in front of your adversary and almost instantly behind him. But where you are limited in your movements by conditions of the terrain, and would have difficulty in dragging your heavy howitzers and "Napoleons" over muddy roads, the B-52s have no such handicaps, and where you can hurl ball and shrapnel only by the explosive force of gun powder, SAC can hurl nuclear warheads faster than the speed of sound.

General, many decades after you were accidentally shot by your own men, following your great feat of circling Hooker's army at Chancellorsville, the Japanese caught us by surprise at Pearl Harbor, Hawaii, and destroyed our navy, sinking our ships like sitting ducks. After inspecting the 4137th Wing of SAC, I think I can assure you and the ghosts of all our military heroes that we shall never have to experience the humiliation of another Pearl Harbor.

SOME MACONITES OF '63

Between the battles of Fredericksburg, on 13 December 1862—which will be reported in this column next week—and Chancellorsville, the following May, there was very little fighting. Winter had a way of chilling even the enthusiasm of Yanks and Rebs who had dedicated themselves to killing each other. During this period of comparative quiet when battles resulted in no more serious casualties than snowballs might inflict, perhaps it might be well if we become better acquainted with the men of Middle Georgia, and especially of Macon, who played roles of varying degrees of importance and heroism during the war. Beginning soon, then, this column will turn to biography. Readers are requested to help with suggestions and information.

All of Macon's contributions to the war were not in the military field. There were prominent men who played important parts in civil rather than military functions. Clifford Anderson served in the Confederate Congress at Richmond. William B. Johnston was the Depositary of the Confederate Treasury in Macon, which was second only to the one in Richmond. Eugenius A. Nisbet was a member of the Secession Convention at Milledgeville. It was he who introduced the resolution that took Georgia out of the Union. Robert Findley and his sons, James N. and Christopher D., along with Richard M. Cuyler, who moved the Savannah Arsenal to Macon, all were important figures in the business of manufacturing arms and other military equipment.

Macon families, some well-known and some now forgotten, sent their sons to war as soldiers and officers. It is hoped that readers of this column will be able to help the author revive the memory of many of those who have been forgotten and that the next of kin will supply letters, diaries, and information relating to those Macon and Middle Georgia boys who were so well known in the 1860s.

One of the best known of all the Macon boys who fought in the Confederate army was Sidney Lanier, a member of the "Macon Volunteers." One of the best known Georgians, Gen. Howell Cobb, was a native of Athens, but as commander of the Georgia Guards his home and headquarters were in this city at the end of the war. Gen. James Mercer Green, whose home faces the First Baptist Church on Washington Avenue, was superintendent of the Confederate hospitals here. This column will welcome additional names and information along these lines.

The "Gresham Rifles" and the "Lochrane Guards" were in the battle of Fredericksburg. They were commanded by Captains M. R. Rogers and Jackson Barnes, respectively. Capt. Thomas Hardeman, as has been mentioned often in this column, took his "Floyd Rifles" to Virginia at the outbreak of war, and when it and the "Macon Volunteers" became two of the companies of the Second Georgia Batallion, he was made a colonel and put in command. The "Volunteers" were commanded by Capt. R. A. Smith.

J. W. Aderhold's "Independent Volunteers" were in the 1st Georgia; Georgia A. Smith's "Brown Infantry" was also in this regiment. Capt. Lucius M. Lamar's "Macon Guards" were assigned to the 8th Georgia, and Capt. Lamar was made the colonel of the regiment. J. G. Roger's "Central City Blues" were in the 12th Georgia, J. W. Stubbs's "Rutland Guards" were in the 27th, Cicero A. Tharpe's "Huguenin Rifles" were in the 30th, T. W.

Brantley's "Lamar Infantry" was in the 54th, Charles J. Harris's "Lockett Infantry" was in the 59th, and T. J. Pritchett's "Scott Infantry" was in the 74th. J. A. Valkenburg's "Thompson Guards" moved from the 10th to the 13th and, finally, to the 61st Georgia. A Capt. Jones was in command of a company in the 10th Georgia Battalion. But since he was removed from command for cheating his men, perhaps further investigation of him would be inappropriate.

Two companies of cavalry were the "Ocmulgee Rangers," commanded by Capt. Thaddeus Goode Holt, and the "Bibb County Cavalry," under Capt. Samuel S. Dunlap. Capt. Leroy Napier commanded an artillery company that bore his name. It was later under the command of Capt. Henry N. Ellis and was called the "Macon Light Artillery." Theodore W. Parker was captain of the Jackson Artillery. George A. Dure and Thomas L. Massenburg followed Parker, in succession. The "German Artillery" was under the command of F. Burghard. Was this Francis? Perhaps relatives of the Burghard family can supply more information concerning the commander of the "German Artillery." The "Mangham Infantry," the "Ross Volunteers," and the "Sparks Guards" were perhaps home guards. The first was under Capt. Charles J. Williamson, the second under Capt. Richard F. Woolfork, and the third under Capt. J. B. Cumming.

Two Macon men who later became very prominent in the public life had a military service record. They were Sen. A. O. Bacon who served his state and nation in the United States Senate from 1895 to 1914 and James H. Blount who was in the United States Congress from 1873 to 1893.

BELATED BIRTHDAY LETTER

Gen. Robert E. Lee
Lexington, Virginia

Dear General:

You must forgive me for delaying this birthday letter to you, which is now a week and a day past due, but last week my thoughts were on Mercer University, which had just celebrated its 130th anniversary. I think you will not be offended by being put off, knowing your gentle and understanding nature. Then, too, in a way Mercer was the only one of all the colleges to grant you an honorary degree. You may have forgotten that—it was such a long time ago—but your gracious letter of acceptance hangs framed in the Mercer library. That makes you, in a sense, a part of this university, doesn't it?

My first impulse was to address this birthday letter to you in the Wilderness. But it was a hundred years ago that your Army of Northern Virginia was biding its time, waiting for spring and possibly a great battle in the neighborhood of Chancellorsville. If the cloak of secrecy covered your movements from

Burnside and Hooker a century ago, a letter sent to you now would probably not even find your spirit hovering in the headquarters tent from which you sent Longstreet in one direction and Jackson in another—who knows where? Therefore, I had better make its delivery certain by sending it to the chapel at Old Washington College where you were laid to rest in 1870, and where present-day students pledge their devotion to Washington and Lee.

Not only does Mercer University feel a close kinship with you, General, but Georgia lays some claim to you—not just because you belong to the whole South but because in a peculiar way you belong to Georgia. You helped make Ft. Pulaski at Savannah so strong that you, yourself, said the Union shells would never breach the walls. And if the Yankees had not come up with a newfangled rifle cannon, your boast would have held true. I don't think Georgia did it consciously, but this state which held you in such high esteem and which, in turn, was liked by you, chose your birthday, 19 Jan. 1861, to secede from the Union. And when, soon after, Virginia left the Union, you rejected the offer to command the Union armies and chose to take up your sword in defense of your own state.

Col. Garnet Wolseley, the British observer, thought you were "cast in a grander mold and made of different and finer metal than all other men," while a Savannah woman recorded in her diary her opinion that you were too "kidglovish" because you captured more men than you killed in a particular battle. Perhaps your kindness was your disabling weakness, General, but I admire you for these great virtues that you epitomize: gentleness, compassion, and tenderness. Some of your lieutenants were not obedient to your orders, but you showed no malice; your army had too few arms, too few shoes, and never enough supplies, but you controlled your anger; your "right arm"—Jackson—was cut off in the hour of victory, but you mastered your grief. Remember the time on the field of battle when you heard a wounded Yankee raise his defiant voice in a "Hurrah for the Union," how you went over to assist him, how he thought you had come to finish him off with your sword, and how relieved he was when you took his hand saying, "My son, I wish you well"? Remember the time when you put Hood under arrest for insubordination after Second Manassas and yet, at South Mountain when his Texas brigade demanded it, you relented and placed him back in command of his troops? How could one so considerate of his enemies deal severely with his own officers? Such tenderness was recompensed with pain and suffering, the pain of grief, anxiety, remorse, uncertainty and, finally, certainty—the certainty of defeat.

Some of your officers and men suffered the pain of cowardice, but not you who considered "duty" to be the most sublime word in the English language. Sometimes your courage made you reckless and your men, finding you in the line of danger, would shout, "Go back, General, go back!" Yet, your courage aroused them. You inspired a Texas brigade to charge by raising yourself in the stirrups to wave the Texans on and were answered by the rebel yell. Smothered by the yell was a voice saying, "I would charge hell itself for that old man!"

Yes, your strength lay in your skill and courage, and your weakness in kindness and compassion. Even that was a sort of spiritual strength, was it not? You put it in these words in your General Orders on 13 August 1863.

> Soldiers! we have sinned against Almighty God. We have forgotten his signal mercies, and have cultivated a revengeful, haughty and boastful spirit . . . and we have relied too much on our own arms for the achievement of our independence. God is our only refuge and our strength.

Now, 92 years after your burial and a century after Col. Wolseley paid you his great compliment, we, Americans all, honor you on the 156th anniversary of your birth. You were a great general, but, what is more, you were "cast in a finer mold" than most men.

February 10, 1963

ABE LINCOLN'S BIRTHDAY

On Tuesday the nation will celebrate Lincoln's birthday, and this is an appropriate time to reflect upon "The Great Emancipator." Especially appropriate is the celebration this year, for it marks the centennial of the "Emancipation Proclamation."

In years gone by I have treated Abraham Lincoln rather shabbily. Usually, I crowd his birthday off the calendar by celebrating "Georgia Day," which happens to come at the very same time. This year, in honor of the centennial of "Emancipation," I am paying greater respect to one of our greatest presidents. But even in this tribute, I am honoring Daniel Chester French's "Lincoln"—carved from Georgia white marble and seated 19 feet high within the shadows of 36 great white marble fluted Doric columns on the bank of the Potomac River—more than I am the man. The reason for this is not that I do not admire one who was, as James A. Garfield said,

born . . . to an inheritance of extreme poverty; surrounded by the rude forces of the wilderness; wholly unaided by parents; only one year of school; never, for a day, master of his own time until he reached his majority; making his way to the profession of law by the hardest and

roughest road; yet by force of unconquerable will and persistent, patient
work he attained a foremost place in his profession,

And, moving up from high to higher,
Became on Fortune's crowning slope
The pillar of a people's hope,
The center of a world's desire.

Indeed, I accept all that. Lincoln, the man, was worthy of all
the honor that America will bestow upon him come Tuesday.
The Lincoln who is really being honored, however, is not the
flesh and blood Lincoln but the myth symbolized in the great
figure seated in the Lincoln Memorial. He is not Whitman's
Captain who fell even as the "prize was won." The "prize" was
not really won when Walt Whitman wrote his famous poem.

O Captain! My Captain! Our fearful trip is done,
The ship has weather'd every rack, the prize we sought is won,
The port is near, the bells I hear, the people all exulting,
While follow eyes the steady keel, the vessel grim and daring;
But O heart! heart! heart!
O the bleeding drops of red,
Where on the deck my Captain lies,
Fallen cold and dead.

That Captain is "cold and dead," but the myth symbolized in the
monument will persist as long as men long for, struggle for, and
preserve freedom.

The myth is more enduring than the man; the myth is as
eternal as hope. Lincoln the man, the president, was not truly
"The Emancipator." He issued the Proclamation as a matter of
expediency, and the radicals made it a symbol of freedom. The
Proclamation did not abolish slavery, it simply declared that
"All persons held as slaves within any State or designated part
of a State the people whereof shall then be in rebellion against
the United States shall be, thenceforward, and forever free."
What of the slaves in Maryland and Kentucky and other places
not in a state of rebellion, Mr. Lincoln? As the British viewed
it, President Lincoln was freeing slaves in areas where he had
no jurisdiction and keeping slavery in areas where he did have
jurisdiction. Slavery was abolished by the Thirteenth Amend-

ment, which Southern states ratified as a condition of restoration to the Union, as every school boy knows.

The president was committed with the force of his whole being to the preservation of the Union. He said, "My paramount object is to save the Union, and not either to save or to destroy slavery." That was the real Lincoln which America will honor on Tuesday. All America can love him for that. But the mythical Lincoln that sits on the bank of the Potomac can be honored, too, for that marble Lincoln is identified with the idea of an indestructible Union, whose government is of all the people, by all the people, and for all the people. As the myth is interpreted then, it becomes even greater than the man, more eternal—and more true. It stands for freedom for all races, all creeds.

The captain fell and died, but his ship, "weathered every rack," you say? This, too, is part fact, part fiction. The captain fell with no malice in his great heart, but the ship has been tossed upon the rocks of race prejudice and sectional hatred for many a year. Nevertheless, the mythical symbol of freedom will ride that ship through the rough waters until it finally reaches a safe port. And the myth of Lincoln will not be seated in the Lincoln Memorial, but will be standing at the prow of freedom's ship—tall and straight.

COL. TOM HARDEMAN, JR.

It is appropriate that this series of biographical sketches of Macon people in the Civil War include at this time Col. Thomas Hardeman, Jr., for Memorial Day, which was observed last Friday, originated under the leadership of his wife, Jane Lumsden. According to the marker at Rose Hill Cemetery, Mrs. Hardeman organized the Ladies Memorial Association of Macon in March 1866 and was its first president. These ladies, assisted by young men "with hoes, rakes, and spades," cleaned the graves of the Confederate soldiers at Rose Hill and the old cemetery at Seventh and Cherry streets and decorated them with flowers brought by the children.

Thomas Hardeman, Jr., was born in Eatonton on 12 Jan. 1825. Twenty years later he graduated from Emory College and began the study of law, being admitted to the bar in 1847. Soon after, however, he turned to business, managing a warehouse and commission firm. In 1854 he became captain of the Floyd Rifles, a local military company named after Gen. Charles R. Floyd. This company had been organized in 1841. Headquarters were at the Floyd House, the leading hotel at the time, located at Mulberry and Third streets.

Hardeman's political career began in the state House of Representatives in 1853. After several terms in the General Assembly of Georgia, he was elected as a Democrat to the 36th Congress of the United States. He served from 4 Mar. 1859 until 23 Jan. 1861, when he withdrew following the secession of Georgia from the Union. He was not a "hotheaded" secessionist, but reluctantly came home with other representatives of Georgia, and Senators Toombs and Iverson.

On 20 April 1861, a few days after President Lincoln had called for volunteers to put down "armed rebellion in the South," Gov. Joseph E. Brown offered to the Confederacy four companies for immediate service in Virginia. They were the Floyd Rifles, Capt. Thomas Hardeman; the Macon Volunteers, Capt. Robert A. Smith; the Columbus Light Guards, Capt. P. H. Colquitt; and the Spalding Grays, Capt. L. T. Doyal. Gov. Brown, in a letter of that date, said to L. P. Walker, secretary of war, "they are all excellent companies, well drilled [and] all ready to start tonight . . . " On reaching Norfolk they were quickly organized into the Second Georgia Battalion. Hardeman was made commander with the rank of major.

Maj. Hardeman was commissioned a colonel on 18 Feb. 1862 with orders to command the 45th Georgia Regiment. Before his transfer to the new command, the Second Georgia Battalion's commander encamped with his troops on the Newbern, North Carolina, road after being driven out of that town by Federal forces. The Battalion's term of service would have a short rest in their respective cities before returning to the Virginia front. Col. Hardeman bade farewell to his old command at Greensboro and assumed command of the 45th Georgia. Col. Doyal then took command of the Second Georgia Battalion and later commanded the 53rd Georgia Regiment.

In the Seven Days' Battles of mid-summer 1862, Col. Hardeman's 45th stood its ground so well in one engagement that it attracted the attention of fellow officers. In a report to Maj. R. C. Morgan, Col. E. L. Thomas wrote, "I have been informed that the 45th Georgia Regiment, Col. Thomas Hardeman, held his [*sic*] position on the left of the brigade until all except the 35th Georgia had retired."

Toward the end of the war we find Col. Hardeman back in Georgia, serving his state again in the General Assembly. He was speaker of the house on 24 Nov. 1863 when that body expressed a determination to prosecute the war with "the utmost vigor and energy," and again on 19 Mar. 1864 when the House adopted resolutions showing where the Confederate States stood in the war and the terms on which peace should be offered to the enemy. But he also served as adjutant general in the First Brigade of the Georgia Militia in the fall of 1864. We find him at Macon on 22 Nov. congratulating Brig. Gen. P. J. Phillips of the Second Brigade, Georgia Militia, for his successful stand at Griswoldville. Phillips, after holding from 3:00 P.M. until dark, fell back only after being ordered to do so by Maj. Gen. Gustavus W. Smith. On receiving Phillips's report, Col. Hardeman replied, "The Major-General takes this method of tendering you and the troops of your command his grateful acknowledgments for their gallant conduct . . . and is gratified at your success in driving before you the enemies of your country. . . ."

Col. Hardeman was pardoned by President Johnson on 28 Aug. 1865 and returned to the United States Congress in 1883. At the end of the 48th Congress he returned to Macon and served the city as Post Master. Death came in 1891, and the old soldier was buried in Rose Hill Cemetery along with the more than 500 soldiers who fought for the same cause.

CAPT. ROBERT A. SMITH

When the Macon Volunteers went off with the Floyd Rifles from Macon to Virginia to make up two of the companies of the Second Georgia Battalion, their captain was Robert A. Smith. Smith's record as a Confederate officer was short but impressive. He entered the army in April 1861, and on 26 June the next year, according to the "History of the Doles-Cook Brigade," he "gave his life on the altar of his country," in the battle of Ellison's Mill, near Richmond. Just prior to this battle he had been promoted to the rank of colonel and given the command of a newly organized regiment, the 44th Georgia. According to the same source, he was so weak at the time of the call to mount for the charge at Ellison's Mill that he had to be lifted upon his horse. During the fury of battle he was wounded three times before being taken off the field. He died two days later.

Capt. Smith wrote to his good friend in Macon, the Rev. John W. Burke. His letter was dated Sewell's Point, Virginia, 14 Aug. 1861. He had received some news from Macon that did not cheer him. He was concerned about the "low ebb" of religion in Macon [see this column, *Telegraph-News*, 9 July 1961], and he regretted "to learn that the Depository is not flourishing." Burke published religious papers for the Methodist Church and sold books and pamphlets of a religious nature. Capt. Smith advised the minister "to look to God for both guidance and comfort as well as support. You are embarked in God's own cause and may well trust in Him to sustain the Same." And again he urged "Brother" Burke to "Stir up the pure minds of the brethren . . . for without God we can do nothing."

Health was a universal subject of discussion and most all soldiers' letters dealt with it in varying degrees. Capt. Smith's was no exception. He wrote,

> *Corporal Sisson has been restored to health but as yet not to his former strength. There have been a large number of my company sick during the last two weeks but all of them are convalescent. God has wonderfully helped us in this regard. Nearly all the Regiments in and near Norfolk Harbor have suffered much from sickness and several of them have had a number of deaths. But our Battalion of 433 men has lost but one man by death. The 3rd North Carolina Regiment of 13 companies between us and Norfolk have 400 men sick. At Yorktown the sickness is more general. At Rigs Point there has been much Sickness but on the whole, considering the season and the localities of our Georgia troops, the Georgians have been very fortunate indeed. The Alabamians much less so.*

His reference to "a large number" being sick in his company reminds one of the fact that Sidney Lanier, whose health was not improved by his war experiences, was one of the men in Capt. Smith's company. The Macon Volunteers was Co. D of the Second Georgia Battalion.

The town of Hampton was burned by the Confederates and Capt. Smith defended the action as a " military necessity." Here is the way he explained it to Rev. Burke.

> *Since I last wrote, Genl Magruder has approached near to Fortress Monroe and caused the Cavalry portion of his command to burn the town of Hampton which the enemy had evacuated in great haste. We distinctly gave the fire and have clearly seen the chimneys left standing since the fire of that once flourishing village. The burning of Hampton was a military necessity. Magruder tried after firing Hampton to draw the forces at Fortress Monroe into an engagement but he could not tempt them out of their stronghold. He will continue to annoy them on that side of the river. In the meantime Genl Huger is getting ready to annoy them from this side of the river. The North Carolina 3rd Regiment will reinforce*

us this week. Rifled Cannon, shooting 6 miles will be sent to Sewell's Point very Soon and Genl Huger is going to tent near here in order to have ample preparation made to annoy Ships of the enemy.

From our beach to Fortress Monroe is 3 1/2 miles. . . . The war vessels are nearer to us than the Fortress. Our rifled Cannon will reach not only the Ships but the front gate of the Fortress. So you See that we shall not be wholly inactive at this Point. Genl Huger told me a few days Since that he intended to provoke the enemy to a fight if possible. It will be difficult to do. The Northern papers says that Genl Butler has only 6,000 troops at Newport News and at Fortress Monroe.

Near the end of the letter Capt. Smith speaks of Macon friends who have visited him: Dr. Strohecher, Mills, Bass, Holmes, and others. "Every face cheers us," he wrote. He requested Rev. Burke to send him the *New York Herald* if possible. He had heard rumors that Johnston and Beauregard would not make an attack on Washington any time soon. "The prospects are that the war will continue through the coming winter." He closed with a prayer for "peace and our success in arms."

GEN. ROBERT E. LEE

A high sense of duty, fidelity, and affection towards his wife and children; a love for his soldiers, which was reciprocated generously; gentle, moderate in habits; deeply religious yet tolerant towards his officers, his men, and even his enemies; unselfish, never yielding to the temptation to shift blame for failures to subordinates or superiors; all these and more make up the qualities of Robert E. Lee, who was born on this day 157 years ago.

Bell Wiley, in an address on Lee delivered at Mercer University on 19 Jan. 1961, told a story that illustrates the affection his soldiers had for him.

A short time after Appomattox, a tattered soldier of Hood's Texas Brigade called at Lee's residence in Richmond and asked to see the general. He was told that Lee was busy and could not be disturbed. As the Texan turned to leave he remarked that he had followed Gen. Lee for four years and had hoped before he began his long walk to Texas to shake his old commander by the hand and bid him goodbye. The general's aide then told the soldier to wait a moment while he went upstairs. Presently Gen. Lee came down the steps, walked up to the soldier and extended his hand. One who observed the scene wrote, "The poor fellow grasped it, looked Gen. Lee straight in the eye, struggled to say something, but choked and could not and wringing Lee's hand, he dropped it as he burst into tears: Then, covering his face with his arm, he turned away and walked out of the room and the house. Gen. Lee gazed after him for a few moments motionless, his fine, deep, dark eyes suffused and darkened with emotion, and then again gravely bowing to me he left the room and returned upstairs. Not a single word was spoken during the meeting."

The emotional experience of Lee's loyal soldier is still vicariously felt by Southerners—let us say Americans—who revere his memory and cherish those qualities with which he was endowed.

In his tribute to Lee, Wiley injected a message which I think is needed at this time of remembering the hate that divided our nation into two antagonistic societies, each bent on destroying the other. He made his point by relating an incident which occurred after Lee accepted the presidency of Washington College. One of his faculty members spoke in adverse criticism of Gen. Grant, whereupon Lee rebuked him with these stern words, "Sir, if you presume ever again to speak disrespectfully of General Grant in my presence, either you or I will sever his connection with this University." And Wiley made his point even more lucid in his closing remarks when he said, "It is inconceivable that Lee, if he were alive today, would advocate resistance to national authority or in any way abet social turmoil or racial hatred." There were those who thought Wiley had misused the greatest hero of the Confederacy and had tricked the dead and helpless general into a state of reluctant submission to national supremacy. But Wiley didn't trick Lee: the general made his own decision concerning that question at Appomattox.

GEN. "BEAST" BUTLER

In previous articles, I have cited instances of Confederates' destroying property belonging to Southerners, and I called these soldiers spoilers. Now I wish to present a spoiler from the other camp, one who truly deserves the title. Mary Boykin Chestnut (*A Diary from Dixie*) called him harsher names. To her he was a "hideous, cross-eyed beast." His name was Benjamin F. Butler, but Southern newspapers spelled it "Bombastes Furioso" Butler. The *Macon Daily Telegraph* on 22 May 1862 reported,

> Bombastes Furioso Butler has been playing thunder at New Orleans, robbing the Consul of the Netherlands of $800,000 deposited for the eminent Banking House of Hope of Amsterdam, inciting the poor against the rich . . . and we see by a notice in an exchange [that he] has opened the St. Charles Hotel for the reception of customers, flattering himself that he can keep a hotel. He will be happy to take in his friends and the public generally. The best of liquors to be found at his bar, and all valuables to be deposited with him for safe keeping [so safe that the owners could never get at them again].

One of the "poor," apparently, was his own brother whom he

permitted, according to the best authorities on the subject, to reap "ungodly millions of profit in cotton."

Property was not all this spoiler would take from the citizens of the conquered Crescent City; he would, by insinuation, take from Southern women the respect that was due them. Some of the New Orleans women provoked him and his soldiers who occupied their old city, I am sure, but the retaliatory measure he finally took to subdue the ladies and force them to give up their haughty ways was beyond all reason. He issued an order that condemned any female in the city who insulted a Union officer or soldier. She was to "be regarded and held liable to be treated as a woman of the town plying her avocation."

Mrs. Chestnut interpreted it as an order "turning over the women of New Orleans to his soldiers," and though Gen. Butler insisted that such an interpretation was entirely foreign to his intention, many Southerners of both sexes were terribly shocked by it. At Corinth, Mississippi, where the Confederates were waiting for the Yankees who had driven them from Shiloh, but were too tired to follow immediately, they heard about the infamous order of Butler. A dispatch from that city told of the indignation with which the news was received in the Confederate camp. As if in answer to the shocking announcement, the dispatch closed with the statement, "A federal spy will be shot today."

Ben Ames Williams, who edited the latest edition of Mrs. Chestnut's diary, says Butler's men and officers "suffered no further discourtesy from the women of New Orleans" after he issued his "Woman Order," but the facts do not support this. A dispatch from New Orleans dated 2 June and published in the *Charleston Mercury* was copied in the *Macon Telegraph*. If the report from New Orleans was correct, then Williams drew a false conclusion. The dispatch reads as follows.

> No doubt you have heard of Butler's proclamation concerning our ladies, and I guess he regrets it very much. Our ladies now wear a neat little secession flag sewed on their bosoms, and they plainly show a revolver in the right side of their belt and a small dirk in the left, and in many cases they are seen turning up their noses, with a peculiar pout, and an insignificant shake of the head—"You nasty Yankee, you," and pass on.

The reporter closed by remarking, "I am glad to say the ladies of this city have taken a bold and decided stand." It is also true that Butler was so uneasy for his own safety that he stationed a guard of 500 soldiers around his hotel to protect himself.

Butler's order was considered to be "an unspeakable infamy" not only at home but abroad. Many English people were ready to denounce their kinship with the Americans who could produce a man so vile as to issue such an order. Lord Palmerston has been quoted as saying, "Any Englishman must blush to think that such an act has been committed by one belonging to the Anglo-Saxon race."

Richmond, Charleston, and many other Southern papers carried the following acrostic, which E. M. Coulter (*The Confederate States of America*) says expressed the attitude of Southerners.

Brutal and vulgar, a coward and knave;
Famed for no action, noble or brave;
Beastly by instinct, a drunkard and sot;
Ugly and venomous, on mankind a blot;
Thief, liar and scoundrel in highest degree;
Let Yankeedom boast of such hero[e]s as thee;
Every woman and child shall for ages to come,
Remember thee, monster, thou vilest of scum.

A SAINT OR A SINNER?

Next Wednesday is Lincoln's birthday, and having honored Robert E. Lee recently on his birthday, this column would not be so disloyal as to ignore the president who held the Union together. To hold the Union together and successfully carry on a war which accomplished that, Lincoln had to resort to unusual methods and even exercise executive powers not given to him before he acted. The question may well be asked then, was he not a dictator? But he issued the Emancipation Proclamation, which made millions of black men free. Therefore, was he not conducting a war for freedom and equality for all men, and in winning that war, did he not prove himself to have been a democrat? What was he, then, a dictator or a democrat?

On the eve of Lincoln's birthday last year, this column dealt critically with the scope of the Emancipation Proclamation and pointed out the fact that "The Emancipator" did not really free all the slaves. It took ratification by the slave states to pass that amendment! Nevertheless, it is conceded without any strain on my part that the image of Lincoln as a democrat is deserved. Without lessening respect for the great president who held the

Union together, I wish now to talk about Lincoln and the expansion of executive powers, taking a look, too, at the significance of Lincoln's assumption of broad powers upon future developments in our governmental system.

Never before, not in the War of 1812 nor the Mexican War, had the president gone beyond war powers clearly given to him either by the Constitution or by statute. But in 1861 the debate on the question of the war powers of the executive moved out of the academic circle and into the practical arena, with Congress challenging the dictatorial actions of the president. Perhaps it took speed and decisiveness on the part of Lincoln to wage and win a war for union, but it created serious questions of constitutionality; that is, until Congress yielded, and the Supreme Court accepted the principle of wartime dictatorship.

Immediately after the Confederate attack on Ft. Sumter and its surrender, Lincoln called a special session of Congress, but he set the date for 4 July, eighty days away! During those 80 days the president moved with a free hand and much of what he did, since he had no statutory or constitutional authority, was arbitrary. It is true that he justified his every act. And surely neither Woodrow Wilson nor Franklin D. Roosevelt regretted Lincoln's precedent when they faced the necessity of decisive action in the twentieth century. The difference, however, lies in the fact that both Wilson and Roosevelt were wise enough to use their added powers with prior Congressional approval. It can be said, nevertheless, that Lincoln made it easier for his successors to move decisively when those successors were strong personalities or when they had to meet serious problems of an emergency nature, as did President John F. Kennedy in the Cuban crisis.

Specifically, what was Lincoln's course of action during his 80 days of dictatorship? There is no question that the circumstances called for drastic action. When Lincoln took office, seven states were out of the Union. He was determined to hold the Union together at any cost, and he did not believe he could trust a states' rights Congress to hold it. The fact was, Congress had not succeeded in doing it under Buchanan. When the Confederates seized Sumter, Lincoln issued a proclamation of rebellion, and yet held Congress off for 80 days while he called up the militia to suppress it. He also issued a proclamation of blockade—legally a recognition of war between belligerents, though he persisted in arguing that the Union was not, could not, be divided. He issued a call for volunteers for three years of active duty, without statutory authority. He directed large additions to be made to the regular army and navy, without enabling legislation. He ordered $2 million paid out of the treasury and pledged the government's credit for $250 million, empowered by no law to do so. He violated civil rights by suspending the writ of habeas corpus.

The president recognized the doubtful legality of such acts, but justified them on the basis of "public necessity" and "popular demand." His attorney general agreed that this power stemmed from his presidential oath to uphold the Constitution, saying that oath required his using any means necessary to suppress the rebellion. The majority of the justices of the Supreme Court upheld this view in the Prize Cases (1863).

Let the Negroes honor Lincoln as the Great Emancipator if they wish, there is no real harm in holding to that half-truth; but now on the eve of the anniversary of his birth, let all Americans, white and black, honor him for holding the nation together. Let us also be thankful that we still have a system of government that gives the president additional powers when needed, and only through the legislative process, not by surrender to dictatorship.

March 22, 1964

LINCOLN'S GREAT HUMOR

After examining what appears to be all possible reasons why Lincoln won over Davis in an argument in which mighty armies took part, I have concluded that Lincoln's sense of humor was the decisive factor in his victory. It was his ability to laugh, and even to laugh at himself, that tipped the scales in favor of Union victory over the Confederacy. I know the history books show that Lincoln had superior numbers, greater industrial strength, more resources, greater wealth, a navy to blockade Southern ports, and diplomats with the skill to keep European powers from making war on the United States. These and other points of strength assured Lincoln of victory. Any one of these advantages shifted to the other side might have reversed the decision. But the final factor in Lincoln's victory, his humor, has never been given the credit it deserves. If Davis had been blessed with it and Lincoln denied it, who knows, perhaps the result might have been different.

This thought occurred to me again the other day when I read one of the old familiar stories of Lincoln's retort to a heckler who accused him of being two-faced. His reply was, "If the good Lord

had given me two faces, do you think I'd be wearing this one?"
This idea was put into verse, which I believe is also attributed
to Lincoln.

My face misses the mark of beauty by far,
But I don't mind it
Because I'm behind it;
It's the folks in front who get the jar.

Humorous stories, some racy, credited to the president, circulated widely in Lincoln's day. The president of the Confederacy
never told jokes on himself or even circulated bits of humor, racy
or otherwise, about his generals or cabinet members, or anyone
else. He perhaps would have liked very much to get off some
good jokes on people like Joe Brown and Zeb Vance, governors
of Georgia and North Carolina, but I do not know of any occasion
where he indulged in such a pastime. He may have been too
worried by such thorns in the flesh to be frivolous, but I think
a laugh now and then would have helped ease the tension and
improve many a bad situation. At least, it would have been worth
a try.

Concerning jokes about Lincoln's generals, the one on Grant
comes to mind. Some ministers protested to the president that
Grant should not be entrusted with the command of the Union
forces in the field because he indulged too often in bending an
elbow. Everyone knows the president's quick retort: "Find out
what brand of liquor he uses and send a keg of it to each one of
my generals!"

The *New York Evening Post* published a collection of "racy
little jokes and stories" by the president in election year 1864.
Whether the Lincoln stories caused him to win the election in
November or Sherman's victory at Atlanta was more responsible
for it, I cannot tell, but the Lincoln humor did not hurt his cause.

Even Southern papers copied the stories circulated by the
Evening Post. Among those reprinted in the *Macon Telegraph*
are the following, with one or two extra ones that I threw in for
good measure. The *Telegraph* a century ago did not copy any of
the racy ones, and I certainly shall not besmirch its good name
today.

Lincoln often sank to the lowest level of humor, the pun. One of the best, picked from a bunch of bad ones, is the story of a paymaster who met the president at a reception one evening. Lincoln had been getting reports of discontent among the soldiers in the West because of late payments. When the visiting paymaster announced to him that he had come to pay his respects, Lincoln replied, "From the complaints of the soldiers I guess that's about all any of you do pay."

The office seekers hounded Lincoln, as they hound all presidents. Once when Lincoln became the victim of some contagious disease, he remarked to his doctor, "I've got something now that I can give to everybody." When an eager office seeker began to tell the president what he had done to get him elected, Lincoln asked, "You made me President?" "I think I did," the hopeful applicant answered. "Then a precious mess you've got me into," the president said as he turned to the next visitor.

I close with Lincoln's reply to a heckler who tried to tease him about his long legs: "How long should a man's legs be?" asked the heckler. "Long enough to reach the ground," Lincoln replied.

Figuratively, the legs of the president of the Confederacy were not quite long enough to reach the ground. The president of the United States, on the other hand, walked, talked, and laughed with the common man.

• V •

THE
HOME FRONT

MERCER DURING WARTIME

The Civil War affected every phase of life in the South, and the colleges felt the full impact of faculty and student withdrawals. Mercer University, then at Penfield, in Green County, was the only college in Georgia, except the women's colleges, that did not close during the war. This fact would cause one to doubt the loyalty of the institution toward the Confederacy if it were not noted that, of the twelve who enrolled in 1863 to keep the little college alive under the tutelage of two faithful professors, nine were in Confederate service before the year ended. According to Spright Dowell's *A History of Mercer University*, the Georgia Baptists, in their annual meeting in Athens in 1861, and the Southern Baptists, in their meeting in Savannah the same year, strongly endorsed the action of the seceding states.

Mercer, in harmony with the attitude of the Baptists, was ready to defend the South in its struggle for independence. Indeed, on the eve of the war the catalog announced the addition of a course in the art of debating to train the Mercer men to defend the South's institutions properly. And the catalog of 1860-1861 made the following pronouncement: "Southern students ought not to be sent to school in a foreign nation." Most of the Southern boys had already returned home from the foreign Yankee land by that time.

The faculty quickly dwindled to three professors, President Nathaniel M. Crawford, Shelton P. Sanford, and Joseph E. Willet. Prof. Sanford drilled the Mercer cadets in preparation for military service. Soon they were gone. Gone too was Prof. Willet, to Atlanta to serve the Confederacy as a chemist. Twenty-nine of the Mercer boys who fought for Southern independence died in service.

A letter from one of the Mercer students, R. H. L. Clack of Madison, written to his brother, reflects the conditions at the time. The original letter is in the S. C. Candler collection at Madison. I am indebted to *The Madisonian* for permission to reprint the letter, which appeared in its 20 April issue.

To: Mr. James J. Clack,
Ebenezer,
Morgan County, Georgia

Penfield, Ga.
April 16th 1861

Dear Bro.

I seat myself tonight to write you a few lines to let you know that I am well, and hope that these few lines may reach you in good health.

I expect to be in Madison Wednesday—night—the 24th. Send out there after me on a mule as I do not expect to bring my trunk. If it so happens that I cannot be there that night send for me the next. There is some excitement here concerning the political affair of the country. Lincoln has issued a proclamation commanding the Southern Confederacy to surrender their arms in 20 days if not he will raise an army of 75,000 men and take possession of all the forts and public property that belongs to United States. Fort Sumter has been taken and Maj. Anderson left it in tears. I expect the Senior Class will leave here in a few days. They say that Dr. Crawford has promised to give them diplomas as soon as they will started their examinations [which they will do in a few days] and discharge them. They expect to go to Fort Pickens [Pensacola]. Florence makes out he is going. He is on the fence in respect to it. Mercer Cadets have received their guns. Your Bros.

R. H. L. Clack

SOLDIERS' RELIEF SOCIETY

Almost simultaneously with the mobilization of troops in the Confederacy, the women organized themselves for the purpose of making needed clothing and such equipment for the soldiers as their skilled hands could produce. Unlike the War Manpower Commission of World War II, which controlled labor as a governmental function, the ladies' societies in the War for Southern Independence were strictly voluntary and not governmental in character.

Work was carried on by local groups with various names, such as soldiers' aid societies, ladies' aid associations, or as in Macon, the "Soldiers' Relief Society." Indeed, there was no uniformity in the designation of these groups; there were ladies' knitting clubs, humane societies, and clothing societies. But by whatever name they were known, the Macon Soldiers' Relief Society stated its purpose to be "the making of clothing and such other necessary articles as may be needful for the soldiers who have been or may be called into the service of the country."

E. M. Coulter, in *The Confederate States of America*, quotes a contemporary as saying, "Heaven only knows what the soldiers of the South would have done without the exertions of the women in their behalf." T. Conn Bryan says in *Confederate Georgia*, "There is no way of estimating the total value of the contributions made by the Georgia societies." A good example of the self-sacrificing devotion of the women is seen in the fact that the Soldiers' Aid Society of West Point worked all day on Sunday to have 40 coats ready for a company they heard was to come through town on Monday and was reported to be in great need of such clothing.

The ladies did not stop with simply making wearing apparel. Bryan quotes Martha Low Fort of Milledgeville as saying that her mother's society made shirts, coats, socks, and even cartridges for the army. The ladies of Macon celebrated one 4th of July by making 3,000 cartridges. Some showed a spirit of ingenuity and even inventiveness. Julia Stanford, a teacher at the Monroe Female University (Tift College), entered the following note in her diary on 21 June 1861: "While in Macon I obtained a new idea—cover the canteens with woolen cloth to prevent the rapid conduction of heat. Keeps the water much cooler."

The Macon society was one of the earlier ones, being formed on 27 April 1861. The prominent female citizens of Macon met at Concert Hall that day to elect their officers and begin their work. Mrs. Washington Poe was chosen president; Mrs. Thomas Hardeman, Jr., vice-president; Miss Julia Wrigby, treasurer; and Miss M. E. Bass, secretary. Each member of the society was to pay an initiation fee of 50 cents, or its equivalent in work. The citizens of Macon "friendly to the object of the society" were requested to contribute to it.

One of the ladies, known to this writer only as "Polly," was somewhat concerned about the absent soldier boys' faithfulness in remembering the girls back home. In her letter she said,

> I was startled the other day on learning from your columns that our "Charlies" and "Willies" had forgotten us amid ther pleasures, while we are at home bemoaning their sad condition on being called from the presence of a circle of loving friends, and many endearments. Never mind, those of us who have sweethearts in the army will be remembered when their shirts begin to wear thin, their coats are threadbare, and piercing winter winds whistle through the crevices of their tents. Yes, they will

*remember us, and will be glad to share the benefits of our newly organized
association, "The Soldiers' Relief Society." What has produced so many
ready and willing hands in this new work if it is not the love we bear to
them? They may lavish their smiles upon the "Virigina lassier," but when
the tug of war comes on they will think of "home, sweet home," and the
"Pollies" and "Susies," who are industriously persevering in preparing
comforts for them. Then, too, they will appreciate those beautiful lines of
poetry which constantly appear in your columns, designed to cheer their
hearts and to tell them they are not forgotten.*

The "Charlies" and "Willies" were grateful for what the ladies did for them. A letter to the *Telegraph* from one who signed
it simply "K" expressed their gratitude. He said,

The Rifles received a fine lot of woolen shirts from the Ladies' Soldiers' Relief Society of Macon today, and I can assure you that they
were thankfully received, and the fair donors will be gratefully
remembered.

WHAT PRICE SECESSION?

"They refuse to treat us as belligerents, but hold us as rebels and traitors, for whom the gibbet waits," complained the *Richmond Whig* in response to the Federal policy of nonrecognition of the Confederacy. In this statement lies a basic point in the sectional conflict during the American Civil War. The Southerners could never understand the Union point of view, and the Northerners could never understand the philosophy by which the Rebels asserted the right of the slave states to establish a separate nation on the principle of states' rights.

Acting on the theory that secession was rebellion and that the penalty for treason should be loss of property, the Radicals pushed a confiscation act through the Federal Congress on 6 Aug. 1861. The primary objective of the act was emancipation, and the measure declared that slaves used against the United States would be freed. Later a second act went to the point of freeing the slaves of all persons who committed treason or supported the rebellion.

The confiscation acts did much to break the morale of the Confederacy, but early reaction to that policy was one of defiance and ridicule. Southern editors were especially verbose in their editorials condemning what they considered a flagrant violation of property rights.

Typical of newspaper response to the First Confiscation Act was the following editorial, which appeared in the Macon paper on 7 August. Space does not allow its reproduction in full, but the selected excerpts are sufficient to indicate a mixed feeling of fear concerning the application of the law and both contempt and defiance of a government that would have the audacity to threaten citizens of the Confederacy with loss of their property.

> Did any reader of the *Telegraph*, about high noon day before yesterday, feel a sudden, desolating, lightning stroke of poverty hitting him directly on the caput, and thence diverging in two columns of the fluid directly through both pockets, making a big hole in each and carrying off every cent of loose change? Did he see a big red breeched Fire Zouave running off with the title papers to his plantation, a regiment of Connecticut and Massachusetts Hessians marching off his unhappy, darkies to Cuba, bent on a "spekalation," a New York Five Point Ranger disporting himself with Madam's carriage and pair of bays, an Illinois Sucker packing up Misses' piano for the entertainment of his young prairie wolves, a red-eyed Wolverine saturating his ugly carcass with the best Burgundy in the cellar, the Pennsylvanian robbing the hen roosts, and the hosts of the feminine camp-followers . . . stripping the cupboards of the silver, and the "chaney" making love to the books and pictures and stealing the linen? . . . If not let us assure him it is only our good army on the Potamac which prevents all this from being done . . .
>
> Let every man lay these facts to heart, and stand in his lot ready to pour out every dollar he can raise, if need be, to back our struggle for all we have and all we are—for liberty, life, property, for wife, children and servants. . . .
>
> We smile with contempt at the insane rage of the Lincoln Congress which has passed this sweeping enactment of confiscation . . . and the confiscation bill of the infamous Lincoln Congress, though backed with their boasted half million troops, shall be as harmless as the courses of the decrepid giants upon the heads of Bunyan's pilgrims.
>
> In fact, the passage of this bill will help our cause. It is of a piece with most of the Lincoln Legislation in regard to this war—it is suicidal. It not only displays a dastardly and impotent malice, at which the outside world will revolt, but in so far as it threatens the existence of the Southern people and Southern society and industry, it jeopards the prosperity and peace of the world. The world cannot, with any kind of

convenience, comfort or security get along without us, just now; and no
matter how rampant may be the negrophilism of England and France,
their political and industrial interests . . .[will cause them to] take up
the cudgels with Lincolndom in behalf of an unrestricted trade and
commerce with the South.

This hope died, however, for the Union won out in the contest
for official favors of England and the European powers. The
reasons for the failure of King Cotton diplomacy will be examined more closely at a later time.

LONG LETTER FROM HOME

Letters from Johnny Rebs away at camp have been preserved by the children and grandchildren of those soldiers in great quantity and will be the chief interest of this column for a while. Requests made for such letters have brought a good response, and my file of them is growing larger week by week.

The parents, especially the mothers of those Johnny Rebs, probably wrote as frequently to their soldier boys as their sons wrote to them, but such letters were not as carefully preserved. The following one is an exception. William J. Mosely received it from his mother while he was at a camp near Savannah. Mosely was sergeant major of the 10th Georgia Infantry Battalion, Anderson's brigade. He was in D Company. His home was in the Hazzard district of Bibb County. He not only carefully kept all the letters he received and carried them home after the war, he also requested his parents to keep all of his, which they did. His son, T. H. Mosely, who lives on Stanislaus Circle in this city, has the entire collection of more than 200 items. He keeps them in a beautiful wooden casket, reinforced with brass, which Sgt. Mosely made after the war. The mother's letter follows,

along with an added note from his eleven-year-old brother
James.

Georgia, Bibb county
December the 11th 1861

Deare sone

   *after my compliments to you wee are all well at present hoping these
few lines will find you in the same blessing of life wee received your letter
dated November the 20th December the 1 and 2 which was greate satisfaction to heare from you and to heare you was well wee would have
written to you before now but wee started a letter the same day you started
yours by Mr. Seth Gates wee had some rane heare as well as you did
William you did not say a word about coming home but i want you to
come home a christmas if you can any how in the world i dont want you
to go to the confederate armey if you can help it i wont you at home bad
enough i aim to send you some biscuit and ginger cakes by Mr. Chamless
i would bake you some other cakes but i am nearly out of shugar and
there is so many wanting him to carry something for them i want to send
you a gug of syrup but i am afrade it would bee too much truble to Mr.
Chamless so i will [keep?] it until you come then i want you to carry
some with you your pa is gathering corn to day in this field at the house
hee has got this field and the rockmore field to gather yet hee has got the
swamp corn in the crib at last hee has been sowing wheat all the weake
untill now hee has soad in the swamp untill it is so muddy hee has to
wate a while for it to dry before hee can finish it if it doesnt rain a gane
it is warm and cloudy georgia [William's seven-year-old sister] ses shee
is well and fater than you ever saw her and shee wants to see you the
worst kind the children all wants christmas to come so you can come
home your grand ma has got well the family connection is all well as far
as i know i aimed to wright to you last sunday but wee had company
you aught to have bin home last saturday and sunday Mary and the Miss
Chamless girls was hear alittle while a saturday night Johnny Parker
was with them James Knight was hear a sunday all was well Mrs elisha
Nowels and Mrs luke Nowels and all bill Nowels foalks was hear in the
evening to ses shee thinks enough of you to wright to you but shee cannot
wright now if you neede any thing let mee know and you shall have it
jimma ses hee is going to wright some so i will leave rom so i will give
you my best love and respects so good by your affection Mother wright
soon*

MARYANN E MOSELY

*Dear Brother i now tak my pen in hand to let you know i havent forgotten
you yet as you requested mee to wright you a few lines to let you know i
can kill two birds at one shoot when i did not see but one of them i want*

you to come to eate some egg nog A christmas so i must come to a close so i can go to pulling corn so good by your very Affectioneate brother

JAMES H MOSELY

CHRISTMAS HOPES: 1861

Hopes for ultimate victory ran high in the Confederacy at Christmas time in 1861, but no one dared venture a guess as to how long it would take. Facing the realities of the situation, Southerners had to project their hopes into a dim future. Joseph Clisby, then editor of this paper, could only wish his readers "A hopeful and cheerful Christmas . . . we cannot expect a merry one."

The main hope of the men in the camps was to get home for Christmas. Many soldiers were way off in the mountain regions of western Virginia and had no encouragement from their officers in seeking furloughs. Others closer home, such as William Mosely and his comrades defending the coast at Camp Jasper near Savannah, hoped for permission to go home, and some got furloughs—but not Sgt. Mosely. The letter Mosely got from his mother [quoted in the previous essay] had made him very homesick, and he wrote as follows on Christmas Eve:

> *This being the evening of the 24th I resume my seat to finish my letter as we have just opened our box which was very acceptable being as Christmas is close at hand the captain says he is going to give us all an*

egg nog so cake and egg nog will go pretty well together but it will not be as much of a Christmas here with both as it would be with egg nog by its self made of the eggs that Georgia [his little sister] is saving for me.

Editor Clisby's hope for ultimate success was based on a comparatively good year for the Confederacy. Though Lee had failed in his western Virginia campaign the Federals had not won any significant battle nor captured any important city. Clisby put it this way:

We have, thank heaven, much reason for gratitude in the present and cheerful hope for the future. What man is there in the South . . . who, if he had a year ago been told that ere another Christmas festival, the whole power of the Federal army and navy would have been employed in a remorseless effort to destroy us—that fleets of hundreds of ships would have been sent to ravage our coasts—and armies comprising seven hundred thousand men to plunder, burn and destroy our interior, would not have anticipated a year of woe and trouble? What man with these facts before him, would have predicted that next Christmas would find our soil substantially clear of the enemy—their forces all held in check—not a town lost—the South strong and confident—the North faltering and hesitating?

Clisby expressed the hope that the next Christmas would "find us, by God's help, in the employment of peace. . . ."

And, of course, the hope of children is universal and eternal. The Macon Christmas tree "managers" would see to it that their hopes were not in vain in this year of war. A bazaar was planned for the benefit of the families of the absent soldiers. It was held on the second floor of the Ayres Building over Mrs. Dessau's shop. The location was at Cherry and Second where Roy G. William's drug store now stands. In announcing the sale the ladies said,

We have received a private telegram from Santa Claus, saying his jolly old soul had been filled with patriotism, and this Christmas, in consequence of the war times, he would visit no firesides, nor extravagantly spoil a suit of clothes scrambling down chimneys, but would drive directly to Ayres' rooms and there deposit his wares, and let the ladies sell them for the pleasure of his young friends and the benefit of the soldiers.

So, the children hoped for toys and gifts, the soldiers hoped for the sight of loved ones, the generals hoped for victory, and all the people joined in with editor Clisby in the hope for peace; but every dream and every prayer had to be tempered with realism and more than one Christmas would pass before peace would come and lonesome soldiers would return to their firesides to play Santa Claus. As for the generals' hopes, victories would come, but the final and complete victory would elude them, unless they could look down the corridor of time and interpret their own defeat as the final and complete victory.

"A Merry Christmas"

On the eve of Christmas Eve this column wishes to send Season's Greetings to all devotees of the Civil War who by this common bond are drawn into a bond of friendship. This Christmas is a far, far better one than Christmas a hundred years ago, but the spirit is the same. Those who have much feel impelled to share with those who have so much need. Even as Mary Day and many other well-known people of Macon then organized committees to "prepare Christmas cheer for soldiers and the poor," so today do religious and civic groups feel the tug of charity in our community.

I can think of no better way to commemorate the season under the title of this column than to quote Joseph Clisby's Christmas editorial of a century ago.

A MERRY CHRISTMAS

To our readers, one and all! The stereotyped greeting of this festal day, will fall coldly and repulsively on many an ear, and bring tears to the eye of the saddened mourner, as he thinks of a place made vacant since the last Festival. Thousands, too, more blessed, and able yet to number all their loved among the living, will send many a pensive thought to the "dwellers in tents," whose manly voices and hilarious laughs were wont to cheer the hallowed hours of Christmas. God send that, before another year, those sounds may again become familiar, and the heroes of the war return once more to bless their households and reap for the remainder of their days the honors of the patriot hero.

We devoutly hope that we are in the last year of this war. That a few more months will see this terrible struggle over, and the independence of the South acknowledged by the whole world. True, many are still looking for long years of war, and they may come. There are, at present, no certain indications of peace.

But we assume that no such struggle as this can be long continued after its grand object has become manifestly hopeless. We see no reason why the North should protract the war merely to lose men and money; and that it can be attended with no other result, we believe is now the conclusion of all men of sense. It is also true that the government of the Federal Union is not now controlled by suggestions of either reason or patriotism; but it seems to us, nevertheless, that the common sense of the North will soon assert itself in spite of the Government. The indications of a violent collision between common sense and fanaticism are apparent and increasing. One or the other will be put down in the course of another year, and we do not think Black Republicanism is in the road to victory.

In the light of the present and in the glorious record of the past year, there is so much reason for satisfaction and gratitude, that our Christmas will at least be hopeful if not buoyant. As a people we have suffered much, but, under God, have won a glorious reputation. It is not too much to say that the toils, struggles, dangers and victories of the past two years have done more to vindicate our character and our institutions in the face of a slanderous world, than a century of quiet and easy prosperity. In these two years of suffering, we have shaken off the bad, but common reputation of a slothful, vicious, effeminate, inadventurous people, "embruited and emasculated by slavery," and have been publicly acknowledged by the leading papers of the world, as the most hardy, constant, valiant and heroic people under the sun.

Within that time all the social theories of rampant radicals, infidels, and negrophilizing philosophers, have been scattered to the winds by the stern logic of Southern arms and Southern valor. Even the mildest forms of abolition philosophy have been startled and confounded by the events of this short time. We have great reason, in the midst of tears of bereavement, to thank God for his mercies, and to take a strong, bold and hopeful courage for the future. We can see bright sun-light ahead. The independence of the Confederate States is no longer doubtful. God is opening to us and our children the bright promise of a happy, prosperous and honorable future, and inviting us by our patience, moderation and steadfast adherence to religion, and law, to prove ourselves worthy of it. God is confounding our enemies, as much as he did the Anaks of the olden time, and working for us with an evident hand. Let us, then, on this happy day, renew our vows of piety, patience and patriotism, and go forward with cheerful hearts to enjoy, to do and to suffer whatever the Almighty may have in store for us.

HIGH HOPES FOR 1863

Looking back from the vantage point of 1963, the year 1863 is seen as one of tragedy for the Southern Confederacy. It was the year the tide turned against the Southern armies. However, Southern people looked forward with optimism as the year dawned. Joseph Clisby, editor of the *Macon Daily Telegraph*, believing there was "luck in odd numbers," hoped the new year would bring peace.

The editor viewed the previous year and found much to encourage him in the belief that peace and victory would be accomplished in the year that had begun so hopefully. But he warned the people of Macon that such an accomplishment would demand untiring and united efforts on the part of all. "United and prudent, we may exceed in progress and development any land the sun ever shone upon," he said, "but discordant, factious and demagogical, we shall sink to ruin more rapidly still." He was certain that "heaven will most assuredly, place our fate as a people in our hands, and leave us to work it out for weel or woe."

His editorial reflects something of the confidence gained by
Lee and Jackson's victory over Burnside's Union army at Fredericksburg the previous month. But at the very time Clisby was
writing his New Year's editorial, Rosecrans was taking control
of central Tennessee away from Bragg at Murfreesboro. Editor
Clisby anticipated victory there. "As we write," he said, "news
comes of the great fight of the 30th at Murfreesboro, but no
tidings of the result of the conflict. We are confident, however,
that another victory awaits our arms, and that not a word of
this editorial will need a change by the result." By January 3rd
the battle had ended and, though the number killed was greater
in the Union forces than in the Confederate army, Bragg lost
control of the area.

Joseph Clisby could not know at the time he wrote what the
outcome of Murfreesboro would be. As he saw it, "the tide of
Confederate success has rolled on without interruption." The
enemy's advance into the Confederacy had been, in his opinion,
"but an advance to defeat and exhaustion." He said, "every effort
of our troops to harrass the [enemy's] rear, cut his lines of communication and destroy his supplies has been attended with
wonderful success, while every attack upon his front, with one
exception, has been a victory." The exception was a most significant one, being the Battle of Antietam, where Lee's invasion
of Maryland had been turned back. Here, near Sharpsburg,
McClellan had turned Lee, and had given Lincoln the needed
impetus to announce his plan to emancipate the slaves.

The formal proclamation was issued on 1 January, and editor
Clisby treated it with sarcasm and scorn. Looking back at the
emancipation one can see what a tremendous effect it had in
turning the weight of public opinion in England away from the
Confederacy and, thereby, giving great advantage to the Union.
But, here again, hindsight is better than foresight, and Clisby
would not let such factors weaken his faith in ultimate victory
for the Confederacy.

Lincoln "must have grinned horribly when he put his name
to the proclamation," wrote the editor. He observed that the
Northern press had to publish the proclamation alongside news
of Rosecrans's defeat—at that time the Union general was hav-

ing the worst of it—and the editor opined, "the people of the North may cry on one side of their faces and laugh in scorn of such impotence and imbecility on the other."

In his imagination he could see

a ghastly smile o'erspread many a Northern countenance when the document found its way into the morning papers. They did not count upon such a compunction when Lincoln committed himself to this policy. They felt sure that with their million men, by the time January rolled round they would have penetrated the vitals of the South and the Proclamation would then have struck terror to the rebels. But now it is such transparent bosh as to provoke only the contempt even of its original advocates, and add, if possible, to the public scorn and devastation in which the Lincoln administration is held.

He closed by saying,

The renegades in the Yankee Congress who are representing Missouri, Louisiana, Virginia and North Carolina, in the Lincoln Congress will find matter for serious reflection in the present aspects of the situation.

Serious reflection now, a hundred years later, leads one to conclude that Lincoln saw further than did editor Clisby, and that the door he opened with the Emancipation Proclamation gave the Negro entrance to a road on which he is traveling to that final goal of dignity and responsibility that comes with full citizenship.

ERSATZ IN CONFEDERACY

In past columns I have referred to Mary Elizabeth Massey's book *Ersatz in the Confederacy,* in which she discussed reasons for shortages in the South during the Civil War. The term "ersatz" was not used during that war, to my knowledge, but was one we heard often during World War II. It is a German word meaning substitute. All nations engaged in the great conflict of the 1940s learned a great deal about substitutes, and the development of synthetics was due in large measure to the fact that the usual source of the raw material for a particular product was cut off. A good example in the United States is rubber. When raw rubber became unavailable American ingenuity brought synthetic rubber into commercial use.

I shall devote several of these columns to the subject of shortages and substitutes during the Civil War as experienced both by the soldiers in camp and the people at home. This week's example of shortages in the Confederacy is an old newspaper dated Vicksburg, Mississippi, 2 July 1863, but printed two days later by Federal troops after Grant had forced the surrender of the beleaguered city. So short were they of newsprint in Vicksburg that they ran copies off on the back side of wallpaper.

I have a copy of that paper hanging on my office wall, framed with glass on both sides so that *The Daily Citizen* is seen on one side and the leaf and flower design on the other. But there is a story behind this old newspaper; and, in all truth, I must confess it is not an original. To look at it, one could not tell it is a reprint of the original. It looks genuine, and when I acquired it many years ago I thought it was an original. But when I checked it against an original at the Library of Congress where they have a genuine copy in the Manuscripts Division, I found that those who reproduced it, though they labored hard to reproduce it faithfully to conform to the original in every respect, failed to catch some minute details. Nevertheless, it serves well as an illustration of the resourcefulness of the soldiers in Vicksburg who took over the newspaper shop.

I had never seen any original outside the Library of Congress until last week when a person, who will for the present remain anonymous, brought a copy into my office for me to see. He and I both became very excited when, on comparing his copy with mine, we observed they were not exactly similar. As well as I could remember his copy conformed to the letter in comparison with the genuine copy I saw several years ago in Washington. Of course, he has rushed a thermofax copy to the Library of Congress to verify it.

Not only is there external evidence in the document itself of the wartime shortages and the ingenuity of people in meeting such a situation, but there is internal evidence in the text of the newspaper of suffering due to shortage of food and of desperation that drove hungry people to find any possible way for survival in a city that was under siege until starved into submission. Two items from this newspaper will show vividly to what extremes the citizens were driven. They are quoted here verbatim.

ITEM: We are indebted to Major Gillespie for a steak of Confederate beef ALIAS mule meat. We have tried it, and can assure our friends that if it is rendered necessary, they need have no scruples at eating the meat. It is sweet, savory, and tender, and so long as we have a mule left we are satisfied our soldiers will be content to subsist on it.

ITEM: We learn of an instance wherein a "knight of the quill" and a "disciple of the black art," with malice in their hearts and vengeance in their eyes, ruthlessly put a period to the existence of a venerable feline that has for a time, not within the recollection of the "oldest inhabitant," faithfully discharged the duties to be expected of him to the terror of sundry vermin in his neighborhood. Poor, defunct Thomas was then prepared, not for the grave, but for the pot, and several friends invited to partake of a nice "rabbit." As a matter of course, no one would offend the feelings of another, especially in these times, by refusing a cordial invitation to dinner, and the guests assisted in consuming the poor animal with a relish that did honor to their epicurean taste. The "sold" assure us the meat was delicious, and that pussy must look out for her safety.

THE CUISINE IN WARTIME

Trade between the Confederacy and the United States was not entirely cut off during the Civil War, but it was reduced to a negligible quantity; neither was the flow of goods from across the Atlantic entirely stopped by the Union blockade of Southern ports, but the sources of livelihood to which Southerners had been accustomed were reduced to a minimum, especially those from England and other foreign countries. Not only was the quantity of supplies reduced almost to the vanishing point because of these conditions, but there existed a poorer quality of foods, wearing apparel, household furnishings, medicines, and many other things that went toward making the life of the Southerners comfortable. This forced the people of the Confederacy to stretch their ingenuity to the limit to find substitutes for the essentials. Luxuries had to be given up for the period of the war—and during those hard days beyond.

This installment of the series of essays on shortages and substitutes is concerned with food shortages and the unique ways the people of the South made the best of what they had. When they had nothing, they found something to take its place, if possible, and if not did without.

One of my sources for this essay is a reprint of an old and long-forgotten cookbook originally published by West and Johnston in 1863 in Richmond, Virginia, entitled *Confederate Receipt Book A Compilation of Over One Hundred Receipts, Adapted to the Times.* It was reprinted by the University of Georgia Press (Athens, 1960). E. M. Coulter says in the introduction, "The little book of recipes"—note the change in the spelling of "receipts"— "may have as much quaint and amusing appeal to present-day readers as it had practical value to a beleaguered people fighting for their national independence, which they finally lost after four years of struggle."

The little book, which had been almost extinct until the University of Georgia reprinted it, also has a section on "Remedies," but our interest at the moment is the "Culinary Receipts." Salt was such a scarce item that many of the recipes called for "little salt," some even were without salt altogether. To make an apple pie without apples sounds like an impossible feat, but here is the way it was to be made: the basic ingredient was a small bowl of crackers which were to be soaked until soft. One teaspoonful of tartaric acid, some sweetening—syrup, if sugar was not available—was to be added to suit the taste, a little butter, and "a very little nutmeg." And there you have an apple pie!

Or, is it artificial oysters you desire? Here the basic ingredient is young green corn. Grate it, then add one egg, "well beaten, a small teacup of flour, two or three tablespoonfuls of butter, some salt and pepper, mix them all together." A tablespoon of batter fried a light brown and buttered would look very much like an oyster. Taste? Well, perhaps the imagination would have to determine the degree of authenticity.

The problem of raisin bread without yeast called for some brain searching, but someone came up with an answer: "Mix in your flour subcarbonate of soda, two parts, tartaric acid one part, both finely powdered. Mix up your bread with warm water, adding but little at a time, and bake soon."

Indian bread was made by adding a quart of buttermilk to one quart of cornmeal and one quart of coarse flour. A cup of molasses and a "little" soda and salt completed the mixture. My wife tried this one soon after the little book came from the press and we found it "tolerable," but we could not agree with Coulter who said, "experimenting with some of the recipes may offer exhilarating flavors for those who would rather taste of the Confederate times than read about them."

Perhaps Coulter was thinking more about the recipes for beverages than for breads, pies, and such. Table beer was made by adding to eight quarts of boiling water "a pound of treacle, a quarter of an ounce of ginger and two bay leaves." This was to boil for 15 minutes, then after it cooled it was to be worked "with yeast as other beer."

Space limitations allow for only one more "receipt." I shall choose blackberry wine.

> Measure your berries and bruise them; to every gallon add one quart of boiling water, let mixture stand twenty-four hours, stirring occasionally, then strain off the liquor into a cask; to every gallon add two pounds of sugar, cork tight, and let stand till following October, and you will have wine ready for use without any further straining or boiling, that will make lips smack as they never smacked under similar influence before.

NEWS OF LINCOLN'S DEATH

Austrian-born chemist and popular writer Otto Eisenschiml, or O. E. as he is called, has just come out with a new book on the Civil War to add to his ten others. This one, published by Bobbs Merrill just last month, is entitled *Historian Without an Armchair*. It contains a number of interesting stories, the most interesting to Macon readers being "The Strange Case of the *Macon Daily Evening News*." Editor Joe Parham sent the book to me after his paper ran a story on it [see the *Macon News*, 15 April 1963].

The *Macon Daily Evening News*, related in no way to the present Macon afternoon paper, had a short run in April and May 1865 after Union forces under Gen. James Harrison Wilson had captured the city on 20 April. The earliest issue extant to my knowledge, and confirmed by Gregory's *Union List of Newspapers*, is 26 April. This issue carried news of Lincoln's death. In his story, which he admits is "much ado about very little," O. E. concludes that neither the Macon people nor Gen. Wilson and his 9,000 horsemen knew Lincoln had been assassinated until that date.

The reason he assumes that Macon was ignorant of the fact 12 days after the event, when Atlanta and other places had known it for days, is because he could find no record of it among the Macon papers. But the reason he could not find any Macon papers dated prior to 26 April is there are none to be found. Two other papers, the *Journal and Messenger* and the *Daily Herald*, appeared before the *Telegraph* resumed on 11 May, but there are no known issues of these papers dated before 26 April.

Otto Eisenschiml is a highly respected chemist and a widely read author of Civil War stories, but as a historian-detective his logic is faulty when he concludes that the Macon people and their unwelcomed guests did not know of the death of Lincoln until 26 April simply because he knows of no Macon paper that reported it before that date. He guesses that Wilson received a shock when he received a telegram from Sherman—presumably on the 26th, since it was sent three days earlier and a previous one had taken that long to reach Wilson at Macon—that referred to "our new President."

Our historian-detective received a letter from a Macon man, the late Oliver Orr, saying there was no mention of Lincoln's death in the *News* on the 25th. Orr may have had a copy dated 25 April, but it has long since been lost, and apparently Eisenschiml never saw it. But let us assume for the moment, and it might very well be true, that there was an issue of 25 April, and that it did not carry the story of Lincoln's death. Nevertheless, it could have carried the story because the story was out in Macon, as I can prove. Remember, the *News* was appearing sporadically and was concerned primarily with orders from the commander of the post instructing the Macon citizens on how to conduct themselves under Federal control. But for Eisenschiml to conclude that it was not known in Macon before 26 April is faulty reasoning, and I shall now introduce new evidence to show that the announcement was received in Macon on 23 April and confirmed the next day.

Before I call my star witness, however, I would like to suggest there is some evidence that news of Lincoln's death caused excitement throughout Georgia within a week after John Wilkes Booth's bullet struck him down in Ford's Theatre. On 21 April,

Eliza Andrews and her sister Metta were on their way from Macon to their home in Washington, Georgia. They had been visiting their sister Cora, mistress of the Troup Butler plantation near Albany. Eliza records in her journal: "We reached Camack [on the Georgia Railroad] in time for the train from Augusta, and as we drew up at the platform, somebody thrust his head in at the window and shouted: 'Lincoln's been assassinated.' " There were people there going in all directions, north, east, west, south. Surely, some were going to Macon and would carry the news back with them.

Now, for my star witness. Here, to my way of thinking, is evidence much stronger than simply the omission of news in local newspapers. It comes from one of Gen. Wilson's soldiers during the occupation of Macon. It is a copy of a diary of E. N. Gilpin, of the Third Iowa Cavalry. This soldier was with Gen. Wilson on his raid from Selma, Alabama, to Macon. The diary is a reprint of a copy autographed, by the way, by none other than James Harrison Wilson himself. Gilpin's entry for 23 April reads as follows: " . . . the rumor has just reached us of the assassination of President Lincoln! We cannot believe it." And the next entry: "April 24. News of Lincoln's murder confirmed. It comes like a stunning blow. The soldiers loved him, and grieve for him as though they had lost a father. . . . "

THE *DAILY EVENING NEWS*

Despite my good intentions not to make dogmatic statements, I slip occasionally and commit the sin that no historian should ever commit. Three weeks ago within an hour after Giles H. O'Neal, a former student of mine, read this column [12 May 1963], I had a telephone call from him informing me that he had a copy of the 25 April issue of the *Macon Daily Evening News* of that eventful year 1865. I had said none were to be found prior to 26 April.

It all started, you remember, when I took Otto Eisenschmil to task for drawing the conclusion that Macon did not know of the assassination of Lincoln until it appeared in the 26 April issue of the short-lived news sheet that appeared sporadically during the period of occupation by Union forces following Gen. James H. Wilson's capture of the city.

I wish to confess my error, and I want to make it clear to those who are interested that there is a 25 April issue of this old newspaper in existence. Of course, I had not denied that it had been published, merely that it did not now exist. But Giles O'Neal has proven me wrong; it does exist and he has a copy framed under glass. The point of my challenge to Eisenschiml was not, however, the date of the first issue—we both accepted the fact that there was no local newspaper report of Lincoln's death prior to 26 April—my point was that Otto Eisenschiml should not conclude that Macon did not know of the assassination on 25 April simply because it did not appear in the paper that day.

I cannot believe our town did not know of Lincoln's assassination by 25 April 1865. The news was general throughout Georgia, as Eisenschiml himself says in his story, "The Strange Case of the *Macon Daily Evening News*." He cited several Georgia papers that carried the news as early as 20 April. Could it be that the *News*, if it was in the free hands of local citizens, which I doubt, was indifferent to the assassination of a foreign ruler. I do not find any reports of assassinations of other foreign potentates in this Southern newspaper! In fact, the only foreign news I note is a story about the "poor daughters of China" who, "a sad and isolated lot," are compelled to "remain shut up in the parental mansion, solely occupied with sewing and housewifery."

But to come back to a serious vein: I cannot explain to my satisfaction, and certainly not to Otto Eisenschiml's, why the *Daily Evening News* did not carry the story of Lincoln's assassination one day—25 April—and did carry it the next day. But I am certain that Macon did know about that great tragic event earlier than its publication in the local paper.

The paper—it lies before me, thanks to Giles O'Neal—is one sheet, printed in four columns on each side. The front side contains two columns on the surrender of Lee, the third column carries Lee's farewell to his troops and information concerning paroles, and the last column contains Col. J. G. Vail's orders. Vail was the Federal officer in command of the post under Gen. Wilson's orders. The masthead on the reverse side carries only the paper's name, *The Evening News*, and the date, 25 April 1865. No editor or publisher is mentioned. Most of the copy on the backside is filler, such as the "Daughters of China" already mentioned. There is a notice that the "Southern Express" is "now open" in Atlanta. The last column contains advertisements. The

administrator of an estate in Jonesboro who could not accept the
fact of the Emancipation Proclamation offered for sale "to the
highest bidder" all the Negroes—"men, women, boys and girls,
most of them young and likely. . . . At the same time, a gold
Watch will be sold."

A sensational rumor of a naval engagement between United
States and French vessels is mentioned in column one of the
reverse side. There is no dateline for that story. The fact that
there are no items in the paper that are dated after Lincoln's
assassination makes me think those who had the makeup of the
paper in their hands probably had no intention of pulling the
galleys and setting new type again. Typesetting by hand was
very slow, and perhaps the 25 April issue had taken several days
to make up, quite a contrast to the fast line-o-type machines of
today. Let it be said to the credit of whoever put out this little
sheet, he did publish the acount of Lincoln's assassination the
next day. And that made it official in Macon, Georgia.

Let it be said, also, that I am grateful to Giles O'Neal for
turning up this interesting issue of that old newspaper. He has
promised to place photostatic copies in our libraries. Thank you,
Giles.

"CONFEDERATE CATECHISM"

A friend has sent me a copy of L. G. Tyler's "A Confederate Catechism" taken from the *Southern Churchman*, 22 Feb. 1930. This was just one of the media through which circulated Dr. Tyler's views on the causes of secession and the war. He printed it in pamphlet form also. His strong pro-Southern position, reminiscent of Miss Millie Rutherford's "Righting the Wrongs of History" and other writings of many "unreconstructed rebels," gives me a fine opportunity to reflect now, a generation later, on the causes and consequences of disunion a century ago.

Lyon Gardner Tyler's views should be examined against the environment and background of the man. When one observes the geographical boundaries and intellectual atmosphere in which he moved, the direction of his thinking can be anticipated. I do not intend to deal with his attitude in a violently antagonistic manner, rather with sympathy and understanding, but with the detachment of one farther removed—a generation at least—and one who, though not claiming the prestige of the president of William and Mary College, nevertheless, has spent some time reading and thinking about the subject under discussion.

Lyon Tyler was a six-year-old boy when the great American war began and twelve when it ended. Therefore, he grew to manhood during the period of Reconstruction when sectional bitterness was most intense. Furthermore, he was a Virginian, the son of President John T. Tyler, fifth in the line of Virginia's sons who reached the nation's highest elective office. But his father was a pro-Southern man whose sentiments were more with Virginia and the planter interests than with the Whigs who had to endure him after the death of William Henry Harrison, exponent of nationalism and hero of Tippecanoe. In the year that marked the end of Federal control in the South— 1877—Professor Tyler was teaching belles-lettres at William and Mary, he then practiced law for six years in Richmond, and finally returned to William and Mary in 1888 to take the presidency, which he held until 1919. It is against this background that we read his "Confederate Catechism." Excerpts from it would fill this column, but some are omitted to make space for an opinion or two of my own.

What was the cause of secession in 1861? It was the fact that the Union consisted of two jarring nations having different interests, which were brought to the breaking point in 1861 by the intemperate agitation in the North against everything Southern. . . . Was slavery the cause of secession or the war? No. Slavery existed previous to the Constitution, and the Union was formed in spite of it. . . . Was Secession the cause of the war? No, secession is a mere civil process having no necessary connection with war. Norway seceded from Sweden, and there was no war. . . . What then was the cause of the war? The cause of the war was the denial of self-government, by Lincoln to 8,000,000 people, occupying a territory half the size of Europe. . . . Did the South fight for slavery or the extension of slavery? No, for had Lincoln not sent armies to the South, that country would have done no fighting at all. . . . Did the South fight for the overthrow of the United States Government? No, the South fought to establish its own government. . . . What did the South fight for? It fought to repel invasion and for self-government, just as the fathers of the American Revolution had done. . . . Did the South in firing on Fort Sumter begin the war? No, Lincoln began the war by attempting to land troops at Fort Pickens, in Florida, in violation of a truce existing between the Federals and Confederates at that place.

This was long before Fort Sumter was fired on, and Fort Sumter was fired on only after Lincoln had sent an armed squadron to supply and strengthen that Fort. . . . Did Lincoln carry on the war for the purpose of freeing the slaves? No, he frequently denied that that was his purpose in waging war. He claimed that he fought the South in order to preserve the Union. . . . Did Lincoln, by his conquest of the South, save the Union? No, the old Union was a union based on consent; the present Union is a great Northern nation based on force and controlled by Northern majorities, to which the South, as a conquered province, has had to conform all its policies and ideals. The national authority is only Northern authority. . . .

And so it goes, the argument we have heard from Southern writers through a long period that has not entirely closed. Nevertheless, a crop of revisionists has risen in the South who look at it with much less Southern prejudice.

I am inclined to agree with Tyler, however, when he places emphasis on the constitutional interpretation of the war. I do believe the struggle for states' rights culminated in secession and the war that followed, and that issue, though settled legally by a Union victory, was, and is, a fundamental question in determining the nature of our union. On the other hand, I believe fanaticism, as J. B. Randall so pointedly says, was the reason for the war that divided our nation. Fanatical reform efforts from above the Mason-Dixon line and fanatical efforts to maintain the status quo below the line caused the war. Slavery was the theme that was heard from the trumpets that blasted out the discord of fanaticism from both sides. As for the consequences: well, let us just say that we admire the brave fight the Rebels made for "self-determination," but deep down we realize there are some things out there in the future that are actually better than things as they are, even though we cannot always see it at the time.

AUTHOR OTTO EISENSCHIML

This column is honored to have as its guest today Otto Eisenschiml, well known among Civil War fans for his *Why Was Lincoln Murdered?* and many other books on that period. He has already been introduced in this column [see issues of 12 May and 2 June 1963] and, therefore, is no stranger to its readers. Those who have read his Civil War books or who know him for his contributions in the field of chemistry will have the pleasure of hearing him here in Macon as he speaks at Mercer University on Tuesday morning of this week. This author, whose investigation showed our sleepy little town so slow that it did not learn of Lincoln's death until two weeks after he was shot, will find when he arrives here that it has grown into a city "on the move." This Austrian-born chemist who lives in Chicago is a marvelous storyteller, and what he says here has been written especially for our readers.

It will be a special treat for me to address my audience in Macon on 8 October. I have repeatedly spoken in Savannah, Atlanta, Marietta, Rome, and Columbus, but to my regret your city never was on my itinerary, although it played such an important and praiseworthy part in the Civil War.

In a forthcoming review of my latest book, "O. E.: Historian Without An Armchair," a prominent Southern writer refers to me as "although a Chicagoan and a son of a Union officer, [he] is a fair friend of the Southern viewpoint toward all things Confederate." I should like to elucidate this remark.

My father was a rebel in the revolution that swept through Europe in 1848, and his rebellious blood flows in my veins. Unfortunately, the revolution in which he fought was squelched, he had to flee to America, and became one of the '49er gold diggers in California, where he stayed for 10 years. In 1859 he settled in Chicago, opened a business, and caught in the excitement of 1861, enlisted as a captain in an Illinois regiment. His first battle was Shiloh, and in his estate [I was only 7 years old when he died], I found a letter, from which I shall quote:

> We captured some Confederates, and I was surprised to find that these boys are just like ourselves and, except that they talk differently, might just as well be members of our family. I swear that hereafter I shall never fire a shot at any Confederate, and will have myself transferred out West. If I have to kill someone, it will be an Indian, not a Southerner.

His transfer was duly effected, and he finished the war out West.

My soft spot for the South, however, hasn't always been reciprocated. I happen to be a member of the Cobb County [Marietta] Historical Society, and have attended and spoken at many of its meetings. At one time, traveling by automobile, I strayed from the paved road and got lost. I asked the first native I met to show me the way to Atlanta. He looked at my license and drawled, "So you are from Illinois, eh? Well, you fellows found your way to Atlanta in 1864 without our help, now go and find it for yourself the way they did." Frankly, I might have said the same thing in his place.

I have never used the word "rebel" in my writings. The word is not only morally, but also legally wrong, for when Lincoln imposed a blockade on all Southern ports in April 1861, he unknowingly bestowed on the seceded states the status of belligerency, and a belligerent cannot possibly be a rebel. He has to be one or the other. As a lawyer Lincoln should have known this, but nevertheless used the word "rebel" regularly in his official proclamations, and it always has irritated me. Would it not be a good idea to have someone who has been called a rebel take legal action, and have the matter officially decided?

A Southern friend of mine once told me that no one should write about the Civil War, unless he was on one side or the other. I beg to differ. On the contrary, I think that no one should write history, unless he takes a scientific attitude and suppresses his own feelings. Emotional history is one thing, factual history is something else again. I prefer facts to emotions because, being a chemist by profession, I have taken an implied oath to stick to the truth, no matter what. This attitude also applies to a forthcoming article of mine in *Civil War Times Illustrated*, entitled "William T. Sherman—Hero or War Criminal?" I shall not divulge my answer to this question, except to say that I expect to lose some more of my Northern friends. If I do, so be it.

On my pending trip to Macon I shall fly in fear that if I traveled by auto, I might get lost again and meet another native who would refuse to put me back on the path to my destination.

SANTA WAS A YANKEE

The story I am about to tell should have been in this column last Sunday, but I did not want to break the series then running. Lt. A. O. Bacon's memoirs having now ended, the column will be devoted largely to the events of 1864, the year that began with Sherman at one end of the state and ended with him at the other end, Savannah, to be exact.

And speaking of Sherman, the story concerns itself with Sherman's army in Savannah, at least with one of his noncommissioned officers, a sergeant. I am relating the story as I remember it from reading it, and I cannot remember the sergeant's name. But let me insist, the story is altogether true! And I think the implication in the story is true also. I shall let the reader be the judge of that, however.

In spite of the efforts of the historians, both Northern and Southern, to get at the truth of history, many good people here in the Deep South cannot free themselves from the attitude that Sherman's bite was as bad as his bark. The wide swath that he cut through Georgia, in their way of thinking, was one long path of blackened chimneys and smoking ruins. They think he never left a private dwelling standing unless it happened to be the home of a Mason; and in that case, of course, he always ordered it to be saved!

Well, my story shows a different side of the least-liked man who ever marched through Georgia. It is a Christmas story, and, therefore, since we are still in the season of joy and merriment and peace on earth goodwill toward men, it is appropriate at this time. But how could a Christmas story have anything to do with a man who succeeded in his determination to make war, in his own words, a hell for the Georgia people? But it does, for it is a tale of Sherman's playing Santa Claus. That is to say, it is a tale of one of Sherman's Yankee sergeant's playing Santa Claus. And not only with Sherman's permission, but with his blessing!

The long narrative of how Sherman with his 60,000 Yankee troops battled his way around Joe Johnston's army at Kennesaw Mountain, beat Hood at Atlanta, and then burned the city and marched toward a city too beautiful to destroy, will take the entire year 1964 to tell in detail. This column will use many of the coming Sundays to tell it. But in the spirit of the present Christmas season let us flip the pages of the 1864 calendar down to the last page and find . . . a Yankee Santa Claus.

When Sherman's army reached Savannah on 20 December 1864, just four days before Christmas, he sent President Lincoln his famous message which said, in substance, that he was presenting the city of Savannah to Mr. Lincoln as a Christmas present. But the same general who gave the Union president the city of Savannah also arranged to have Santa Claus visit the children of that conquered city.

It happened in this manner. The Union soldiers were far away from home and many of them were fathers of little children who themselves would have a visit from Santa even though their dads were far away in the Southland. These soldiers missed their families. They were in a desolate city that had been battered from the gunboats at sea and blockaded since April of 1862. The chances were small, indeed, that the little kids of Savannah could have the things that bring joy, the things that were bringing joy to Yankee kids.

One company of occupying troops talked it over and decided that to the best of their ability they would bring some joy to the Savannah children. They went to work improvising dolls from rags, making crude toys with their rough hands, taking food from their own rations, admittedly stolen in raids on Georgia farms. All this they gathered up and placed on a wagon, which they decorated in gay colors, making it look as much like Santa's sleigh as possible. The mules that pulled the wagon were even fitted with improvised antlers to resemble, not too closely, reindeer. They picked by lot a sergeant of the company to dress as Santa Claus and drive the wagon about the town delivering the presents and food to the homes in the city. I know there are those skeptics who will charge me with inventing a falsehood but, so help me, it is true. If I could get to my files I could document this story, but it happens that I am celebrating my Christmas by staying out of my office. So, dear friends, you will just have to take my word for it that Sherman permitted one of his sergeants to play Santa Claus for the Savannah children and thus turned their Christmas from one of want to one of merriment, such as it was.

SOUTH'S FARE SKIMPY

Today I yield this column to one of my students at Mercer University. Rose Marie Morris takes a look at shortages during the Civil War through the eyes of several women whose wartime diaries are well known today. Her essay follows.

The shortage of food was a problem the Southerners had to deal with throughout the Civil War. Even as early as 1861 a woman in Mississippi wrote: "Flour was almost unknown in that part of the Confederacy. Coffee and sugar were about as scarce as flour. We had coffee made of peanuts, black tea made of blackberry leaves, and green tea made of Holly leaves."

Coffee was probably the one item missed most when the blockade prevented importation. The poor Southerners tried innumerable substitues for the flavorful bean—parched corn, rye, wheat, okra seed, acorns, dandelion roots, sugar cane, parched rice, cotton seed, sorghum molasses, English peas, peanuts, and beans. These were used alone and in combinations to make a brew that would hopefully resemble that aromatic beverage.

White sugar was another luxury often found missing from the Southern pantries. Eliza Andrews in 1865 wrote of a relative bringing her candy obtained from a blockade runner. This was the first time in four years she had tasted candy except homemade, and that generally made from sorghum.

Mary Boykin Chesnut's diary records a letter from a friend in Lincolnton, North Carolina, who had a unique method for satisfying a sweet tooth: "We keep a cookery book on the mantelpiece and when our dinner is deficient we read a pudding or a creme. It does not entirely satisfy the appetite, this dessert is imagination, but perhaps it is good for the digestion."

Fresh meat became extremely scarce toward the end of the war. In 1864 one ounce of meat per person per day was considered ample. President Davis is reported to have advocated eating rats to supplement the short rations—"I don't see why rats, if fat, are not as good as squirrels. Our men did eat mule meat at Vicksburg, but it would be an expensive luxury now."

Eliza Andrews of Washington, Georgia, wrote of serving barbecued lamb to her dinner guests one evening. No one seemed to mind that the main course of the meal had been "Mary Lizzie," the pet of her younger brother, Marsh. " . . . the wolf in the fable never fell upon his victim more ravenously as we did upon poor little Mary Lizzie," she wrote.

The area Sherman left behind was naturally the most destitute. Mary A. H. Gay, a DeKalb County woman, kept a diary of the extreme hardships of this ravaged land. She told of spending a whole day picking grains of corn out of bureau drawers and other improvised troughs the Federals had used for feeding their horses. Her labor yielded about a half bushel of grain, which she had washed and ground. From this meal she made mush and hotcakes to ward off starvation. In the bitter cold of November 1864 Mrs. Gay gathered scrap metal from the battlefield of Atlanta until her hands bled. She exchanged the metal at the commissary for much-needed food.

Eliza Andrews's hometown of Washington was not directly in the path of Sherman, so food was not scarce enough to cause starvation, but the meals were monotonous, to say the least. Eliza, who had never known hunger before the war, wrote: "We have nothing but ham, ham, ham every day—ham and cornfield peas one day, cornfield peas and ham the next, is the tedious menu. Mother does her best by making Emily give us every variation on peas that was ever heard of; one day we have pea soup, another pea croquettes, then baked peas and ham and so on, through the whole gamut, but alas! they are cornfield peas still and often not enough of them!"

The short supplies of food and the stream of visitors through the Andrews' home were a source of embarrassment to Eliza. She had always been accustomed to practicing Southern hospitality in its most gracious fashion, and now her family had to resort to conspiracy to hide their desperate situation: "We have so much company that it is necessary to keep up appearances—We eat as little as we can do with ourselves, but we don't want father's guests to suspect that we are stinted, so Metta [her sister] pretends to a loss of appetite while I profess a great fondness for whatever happens to be most abundant, which is sure to be cornfield peas or some other coarse rank thing I detest. Metta's delicate appetite and my affection for cornfield peas are a standing joke between us." Eliza's indomitable sense of humor served to lessen her suffering during a tragic era.

HABEAS CORPUS WRIT

The writ of habeas corpus, a cherished freedom written into the Constitution of the United States and with roots lying deep in British soil, was not only suspended by President Lincoln, but his action was ratified by Congress on 3 March 1863. Lincoln argued the military necessity of such an action, of course. I am not going into the constitutional question of which branch of the federal government, executive or legislative, has the power to suspend the writ as provided in the clause, " . . . unless when in Cases of Rebellion or Invasion the Public Safety may require it" (Art. 1, Sec. 9). The purpose of this column today is not to press the matter as it related to Lincoln at all or to argue the right or wrong of it, but to deal with a similar problem confronting President Davis and his Congress.

Jefferson Davis, with exactly the same consitutional limitation that bound Lincoln, asked for and got from the Confederate Congress the right to suspend the writ of habeas corpus, just as Lincoln did. He, like Lincoln, wanted a tighter control over persons suspected of obstructing the government in its war effort. Congress gave him that power, first on 27 February 1862, again on 13 October 1862, and a third time on 15 February 1864. The duration lasted for about seven months the first time, four months the second time, and five and a half months the last time.

Many Southerners were particularly alarmed over the passage of the third act. Led by Gov. Joe Brown, whose objection is not surprising, Georgians were disturbed. Alexander H. Stephens, the vice-president, was concerned about such a bold step by the president. This, too, is understandable when one inquires into the relationship between the two top men in the Confederacy.

Gov. Brown issued a call for a special session of the Georgia Legislature for March 10th. Though the act of February 15th was not stated to have been the reason for the call, many thought the talk of currency matters was merely to hide the real reason for the meeting. The governor's message of the 10th calling the special sessions shows his concern regarding the suspension of the writ of habeas corpus.

> I cannot withhold the expression of the deep mortification I feel at the action of Congress in attempting to suspend the writ of habeas corpus, and to confer upon the President powers expressly denied to him by the Constitution of the Confederate States. Under protest of a necessity which our people know does not exist in this case, whatever may have been the motive, our Congress with the assent and at the request of the Executive, has struck a fell blow at the liberties of the people of these States.

Stephens's half-brother, Linton, who was a member of the legislature, spoke vigorously against the act, but L. Q. C. Lamar supported the action of the Confederate Congress, much to the delight of Joseph Clisby, editor of the *Macon Telegraph*. Lamar spoke as a visitor to the legislature at Milledgeville and again to a large audience in Macon. According to the *Telegraph*, he spoke for two hours without wearing out the patience of the receptive audience. The *Telegraph* found it

> gratifying to see so universal and enthusiastic response upon the part of the audience to the policy of sustaining the Confederate government; and such unerring indications that the course of the nullifiers meets with no support from the people.

Just how accurate this paper was in appraising the mood and attitude of the audience, one can only guess.

Alexander H. Stephens did not take a very strong position against the Confederate government. This would be expected, not only in the light of his position, but also because of the nature of the man and the record of his compromising of issues generally. Nevertheless, though not as strong an opponent of the Davis government as his half-brother and not nearly so violent in opposition as Brown, the vice-president was not happy at the turn of events. But his mild position pleased editor Clisby. Speaking of Stephens's Milledgeville speech, Clisby said,

> Mr. Stephens takes the ground that was most commonly anticipated. He goes for splitting the difference between the nullifiers on the one hand, and the uncompromising administration man on the other, and subsides into a protest. This, indeed, would be a far more prudent and seemly course; and it certainly would have been an extraordinary spectacle for the second officer of the Confederate Government to be seen exciting a State Legislature by inflammatory appeals to set at naught the laws and authority of the general government.

THE BELLIGERENT SEX

"If I were a man, I should be in the foremost ranks of those who are fighting for rights guaranteed by the Constitution of the United States."

Thus spoke Mary Gay of Decatur. This spirited young woman, who was born in Jones County but had moved to Decatur, had been ordered out of her home by the red-headed general who thought of war as hell. The belligerent women had much to do with making the general's concept of war what it was.

I spoke on this subject recently in Atlanta at the seventh national assembly of the United States Civil War Centennial Commission. A few of the Yankees there complimented me by asking for a copy of my manuscript. Since I spoke from notes, I could not comply, but through this column I shall incorporate much of what I said in Atlanta and I shall send clippings to those new-found friends who live as far away as Michigan, New Hampshire, and Vermont. The Northern "buffs" especially seemed to like the spirit of the Southern women. They even took Eliza Andrews's comment with a grin: "Surely Christ didn't mean Yankees when he said, 'Love your enemies.' "

As the war drew toward a close, and with Sherman's armies surging toward Atlanta, the women of the South had more and more difficulty in suppressing emotions of fright and despair. Francis Butler Simkins and James Patton, who wrote a thoughtful work entitled *Women of the Confederacy* (1936), said the women had to struggle "valiantly" to keep fear and despair from overcoming their patriotic emotions. But as I read the many diaries and journals of the women who faced certain defeat and loss of property and, worse still, loss of sons, husbands, sweethearts, and fathers, I am convinced that most of the Confederate women showed a spirit of patriotism to the very end.

Their loyalty to the Confederacy may have been subjective and a bit naive, but it was genuine, nevertheless. Eliza Andrews of Washington, Georgia, whose popular journal is well known, wrote, "I would rather be wrong with Lee and his glorious army than right with a gang of fanatics that have come down here to plunder and oppress us in the name of liberty." And Kate Cumming (*The Journal of a Confederate Nurse*, edited by Richard Harwell, 1959), who disapproved heartily of Georgians Joseph E. Brown and Alexander H. Stephens when they criticized the Confederate government, expressed her philosophy in the following words: "My country right, my country wrong, but still my country."

That patriotism often burst out in defiant words and deeds. John L. Underwood (*Women of the Confederacy*, 1906) tells how a soldier at Resaca observed a wagonload of women refugees fleeing from the Federal troops. As they passed him the soldier saw one of the young women stand erect in the wagon and wave her large hat, bedecked with red ribbons. Such defiance of the enemy made the soldier say, "For that a man could freely die."

When Sherman's troops entered her town, Anna Maria Greene recorded in her diary (*Journal of a Milledgeville Girl*, edited by J. C. Bonner, 1964) the following note: "We went through the house singing 'We live and die with Davis.'" Down in Savannah, when Sherman reached that city, one of his officers called upon Fanny Cohen, presumably on business for his superior. Fanny received him in the parlor but did not offer him a seat. Finally, she said, the interview ended. She opened the front door for him and "he walked out like a well-bred dog."

The belligerent ladies teased their men into joining the army. Or, if that didn't work, they shamed them into showing a patriotism that was not always strongly felt. A story illustrative of this is one told by D. W. Standard in his little but significant book, *Columbus, Georgia, in the Confederacy* (1954). He says the young women of that city organized a Home Guard for the stated purpose of protecting the men who refused to join the army!

War weariness at home, as well as on battlefields that were strewn with dead and dying, sometimes caused a break in morale. Maryann Mosely of Macon wrote to her son William begging him to come home "a Christmas." She didn't want him "to go to the Confederate armey." Kate Cumming recorded the opinion of one of the doctors that it was the earnest appeal of the wife of a private of their acquaintance that caused him to desert. Simkins and Patton quote Anne Perkins, a Virginia girl, as giving the following reasons why she wanted her husband to come home: she and the children were ill, he was not strong enough for camp life, his life was in danger of enemy bullets, he could get a discharge without dishonor, and "most important of all, because his absence was breaking her heart."

But there were more women who were dominated by their fighting spirit and who held their men loyal to the Cause than there were of the other kind.

THE HORRORS OF WAR

The fighting spirit of the Confederate women was whetted by acts of vandalism by "those vile wretches," the Union soldiers, and by the hardships that Yankee depredations forced those women to endure. Perhaps the diarists, in their emotional reactions to plundering and pillaging Union men, were prone to exaggerate occasionally, but there was much truth in their vivid accounts of atrocities and ruthless violations of property rights. On the other hand, there is very little evidence of violation of women's honor, or even of ruthless destruction of their homes. Of course, if the eyes and ears of the Rebel women were not deceiving them, there were exceptions. The attitude of the Union soldiers that the Southerners were, after all, rebels and deserved nothing less than to lose their property is compatible with Northern sentiment that prompted the passage of confiscation laws by the United States Congress.

Lincoln's Emancipation Proclamation was another factor indirectly contributing to the loss of Confederate property. Encouraged by the proclamation, slaves sometimes ran away, causing great hardships for the women who were trying desperately to run their farms while their men were away at camp or in line of battle. Betty Maury in Richmond recorded in her diary (manuscript in the Library of Congress) on 18 February 1863: "I don't feel very well this morning all my niggers have run away and left me."

Perhaps nothing angered the Confederate women more than the fact that Northern women were encouraging their men to bring back treasures from the South. Kate Cumming recorded in her journal that letters found on dead Union soldiers on the battlefields contained

> *petitions from the women to send them valuables from the South. One says she wants a silk dress, another a watch, and one writer told her husband that now was the time to get a piano, as they could not afford to buy one.*

Miriam Morgan fled from her home in Baton Rouge, Louisiana, to Linwood to tell her sister Sarah how the soldiers plundered their home. The soldiers had cut the portrait of the girls' mother from its frame, and

> *Margaret, who was present at the sacking told how she had saved father's. It seems that those who wrought destruction in our house were all officers. One jumped on the sofa to cut the picture down when Margaret cried, "For God's sake, gentlemen, let it be! I'll help you to anything here. He's dead, and the young ladies would rather see the house burn than lose it!"*
>
> *"I'll blow your damned brains out," was the "gentleman's" answer as he put a pistol to her head, which a brother officer dashed away, and the picture was abandoned for the finer sport.* (Sarah Morgan Dawson, *A Confederate Girl's Diary*, 1913.)

One observer told of what he considered the "crowning act of vandalism" in South Carolina, the destruction of the Ursuline Convent School (David P. Cunningham, *Sherman's March Through the South*, 1867). After destroying the trunks and piano with hatchets and crowbars, one burly soldier carried a holy water font about and shook it in the face of one of the nuns. They set fire to the buildings and the sad scene the next morning was one of "groups of crouching, weeping, helpless women and children" among the ashes of what had been their home.

Eliza Andrews said the Union soldiers were so angry at being fed on her porch instead of in the dining room that "Mammy said they cursed her and said Judge Andrews was a damned old aristocrat who deserved to have his house burned." They did not burn it, however.

But neither were all the Rebels angels. Kate Cumming, writing from north Georgia in January 1864, said, "Our cavalry behave very badly, taking everything they can lay their hands on." The most shocking revelation of Confederate atrocities was Kate Cumming's account of a Confederate captain in Atlanta who, when entrusted with a Federal prisoner, took his captive into the woods and shot him because, as he said, of the way his mother and sisters had been treated by Federal soldiers.

A WOMAN'S INGENUITY

In wrath and defiance they boldly arose,
And scorned to concede one inch to their foes.

That was the way an anonymous poet, writing under the pen name of Tenella, expressed the sentiments of the Confederate women who have been designated in this column as "the belligerent sex." We have seen how the women's defiance was expressed in patriotic declarations. Now we shall see how that defiance, intensified by Yankee depredations, stirred them to exert their best efforts to find new and unique ways to thwart the enemy.

I am sure Tenella, from whose poem "A Lament for New Orleans" the lines quoted above are taken, must have been a woman. (This poem first appeared in the *Southern Literary Messenger* in July 1863.) Tenella and her Southern kin could match the Yankees trick for trick when it came to ingenuity. Dr. Hanson Hard told in his journal (manuscript is in the Library of Congress) how the Federal surgeons at one of the hospitals in Paducah, Kentucky, fooled the Rebels who were bent on looting the place by making them think an epidemic of smallpox had broken out there. But Tenella and the Southern women had some tricks of their own. One story told by John L. Underwood in his *Women of the Confederacy* (1906) is of a Mississippi woman who bored holes in the hams that she took from the smoke house and scattered about the yard. The invading soldiers, thinking the meat was poisoned and determined not to be fooled into making a fatal mistake by eating it, passed up the good hams. She then gathered them up again and hung them back in their proper place.

Francis B. Simkins and James W. Patton, in their excellent study, *The Women of the Confederacy* (1936), describe many clever ways that the women discovered to hide their valuables. One of the cleverest, I think, was the trick of building a dam to divert the course of a small stream, and after making a package of the silver or other valuables as watertight as possible, they would fasten it firmly to a root in the bed of the stream. They would then break the dam to let the water resume its original course.

The women had to stretch their ingenuity to the limit to protect their valuables because the invading soldiers and "bummers" who foraged about the countryside were keen-eyed. Tenella, our anonymous (lady?) poet, was prompted by Union raids in Maryland to write a long poem for the *Gray Jacket* under the title, "The Rebel Sock."

> *From right to left, from house to house,*
> *The little army rides.*
> *In every lady's wardrobe look*
> *To see what there she hides;*
> *They peep in closets, trunks and drawers,*
> *Examine every box;*
> *Not rebel soldiers now they seek,*
> *But rebel soldiers' socks!*
> *But all in vain—too keen for them*
> *Were those dear ladies there,*
> *And not a sock or flannel shirt*
> *Was taken anywhere.*

Emma Manley of Griffin told the Daughters of the Confederacy of that city in 1921 a story that shows the clever ingenuity of one of the Negro slave women. When Sherman's blue coats appeared, hot on the trail of the Rebel soldiers who had hurried away ahead of them, Manda ran up the road shouting, "Come back, Marse Taylor, and give up, those Yankees will kill you." The soldiers galloped off after them—in the wrong direction!

Sometimes the Confederate ladies were not quick enough to save everything. Dolly Burge (*A Woman's Wartime Journal*, 1927) described how a captain from Illinois came through Covington and into her house during Sherman's march through Georgia. He was acquainted with her brother, and on that basis she appealed to him to protect her home. "He promised to do this," she wrote, "and comforted me with the assurance that my dwelling-house would not be burned, though my outbuildings might." She was concerned about her little daughter, nine years of age.

> Poor little Sadai went crying to (the Union captain) as to a friend and told him they had taken her doll, Nancy. He begged her to come to see him and he would give her a fine waxen one.

The ingenuity of the women served them well, too, in finding solutions to their problem of shortages. Mrs. Jefferson Davis wrote to John L. Underwood on 25 October 1905, as follows:

> The ladies picked their old silk pieces into fragments and spun them into gloves, stockings and scarfs for the soldier's necks . . . cut up their house linen and scraped it into lint; tore up their sheets and rolled them into bandages. . . . They covered their old shoes with old kid gloves or pieces of silk and their little feet looked charming and natty in them. In the country they made their own candles, and one lady sent me three cakes of sweet soap and a small jar of soft soap made from the skin, bones and refuse bits of hams boiled for her family. Another sent the most exquisite unbleached flax thread, of the smoothest and finest quality, spun by herself.

As the soldiers grew more weary of war and as the hardships and suffering became greater at home, the morale of the women, which had sustained the fighting men for four years, began to break. Finally, there came the realization that theirs was a Lost Cause.

A BITTER REALIZATION

The bitter truth that the soldiers had, perhaps, already faced suddenly confronted the women, and they realized that their cause was lost. Susan Bradford was attending a town gathering at the Florida capitol in Tallahassee when the news of surrender came. A quartet was singing "The Southern Marseillaise" when a man came in with a telegram. He read in an emotion-choked voice: "General Lee has surrendered the army of Northern Virginia today at Appomattox." To Susan and to the courageous Southern women who had urged their men to continue the fight against the hated foe, that message was "the death knell" of all their hopes. Susan described the scene at the Florida capitol.

> . . . for a moment a silence of the grave filled the hall; then followed such a scene as we pray we may never see repeated—tears and cries and lamentation, the bitterness of heart-broken woe. Men, women, and children wept as they realized the calamity which had befallen us.

Florida Clemson, John C. Calhoun's granddaughter, wrote in her diary (*A Rebel Came Home*, 1961) on 1 May 1865: "I had a good cry Saturday night on hearing that peace had been declared." Kate Stone of Brokenburn cried, "God spare us from this crushing blow and save our country." But some thought God had deserted them. Cornelia Phillips Spencer of North Carolina said she had lost the incentive to pray, and Betty Maury of Virginia wrote, "my faith and trust are weak. I feel as if God has hidden His face from us."

The impact of the war and the shock of defeat affected some of the women in such a manner as to intensify their hatred of the Yankees, left them resentful and unforgiving. Eliza Andrews, who lost no one as close as brother or father, and who had no husband to lose, could not forgive easily. She had difficulty in changing from her attitude that Christ could not have meant Yankees when he said "Love your enemies!" But even this fire-eater softened a little. She thought perhaps she might be willing to shake hands with a certain colonel in her town during the Federal occupation, and she even saw "instincts of a gentleman" in a captain who apologized for a raid upon the Toombs's home.

Other women were humbled by defeat, and sorrow made them more tender. Some who lost most heavily seemed to be more contrite than the more fortunate ones. Josephine Habersham of Savannah, who had been outspoken in her hatred of the Yankees all through her diary, which she kept during the year 1863 (*Ebb Tide*, 1958), was brought face to face with tragedy on 22 July 1864 when her sons, Joseph Clay and William Neyle, were killed in the heavy fighting in Atlanta. Willie's friend saw him die and wrote Josephine about it, describing the bravery of her son and expressing his sadness at the loss of a friend. The mother, whose sons "in death . . . were not divided," wrote Willie's companion saying, "Believe me, young friend, that the true secret of Life's happiness is to be able to say, 'Thy will, not mine, be done.' " Here, as in so many cases, a mother's hate for the enemy is softened. Her faith was strong enough to sustain her in that moment of tragedy and loss.

Lilla, ten-year-old sister of the two boys, could not accept the experience with her mother's spirit of submission. There was no rebellion in the simple little poem she wrote, but neither was there a spirit of resignation when she penned the words

From our home we'll miss them sadly,
When the winter's drawing near;
Oh how sad it is to think
That we will not have them here.

Wars, as horrible as they are, bring some good. This seems paradoxical, but it is true. Simkins and Patton, in their *Women of the Confederacy,* quote Cornelia Phillips Spencer as saying, "Heaven forbid that we should forget the good the war has brought us." Such good, in her opinion, was faith and courage, patience, charity . . . a unity inspired by a common purpose and by the splendid gallantry of the soldiers. The tears they shed were "proud tears."

• VI •

MEANING
AND
PURPOSE

CELEBRATING "LOST CAUSE"

At a most enjoyable dinner one evening not long ago with a group of my friends, one of them asked me a question that many are now asking: "Why are you celebrating the beginning of the Civil War—why are you writing so much on something a hundred years old which 'twould be better to forget?"

My reply to him was, "We are celebrating the beginning of the war because we cannot celebrate the end of it; so, naturally, we must get our licks in before the bragging turns sour."

The answer was, of course, facetious. And yet perhaps not so facetious, when you think about it. Although the Civil War Commission charges us to commemorate rather than celebrate the centennial, we feel that we have some right to a little compensation for the "Lost Cause." Neither North nor South should make light of a war that was so useless, so tragic, and so destructive. And yet it is in our very nature, the victor and the vanquished, to find the lighter side of what was a glorious victory for one and a traumatic experience for the other. The South should be forgiven if it brags a little.

After all, there was little left for the boys in gray but the comfort that comes from the memory of bravery and courage that made the home folks proud of them in victory and defeat; and some of that comfort is claimed today by their descendants. The North can well boast of final victory, and the South can find some comfort in remembering victories at Manassas, Fredericksburg, Chancellorsville, and Chickamauga. In the South, then, we can find our best chance to joke and laugh with Johnny Reb before the rations get short, his comrades in arms fall all around him, and Sherman marches to the sea.

I am reminded of the story of the Confederate veteran who lost a leg at Chickamauga. After the war he ran a little general store near the spot where he had been wounded in that bloody battle that had resulted in a victory for the Confederates. He loved to boast to his neighbors, "we Rebs sure gave those Yankees a beating that day." A Union officer put a stop to his bragging one day by making him sign a loyalty oath declaring he would never again speak against the Union. He was as good as his word. From that time on he considered himself a good loyal citizen of the United States. Now he took a new view of that battle. As his neighbors gathered around the pot-bellied stove in his little store they heard him say, "You Rebs sure gave us Yankees a helluva licking at Chickamauga."

Last month it was my pleasure to speak at Milledgeville at a luncheon that began a three-day commemoration of the centennial of the secession of the state of Georgia. For me it was an occasion mixed with emotions of gaiety and sadness. The celebration caught something of the spirit of independence existing in that town a hundred years ago—a spirit impelled toward defense and defiance by recent events culminating a long chain of federal-state quarrels.

Many visible reminders of 1861 were all around me. The restored Statehouse on Capitol Square where the cadets of the Georgia Military College drilled, the white-columned homes and broad streets shaded by ancient oak trees, the bearded gentlemen and lovely ladies in their hoop skirts, the Confederate flags, the parade, pageant, and fireworks, and the grand old-fashioned ball, all gave a festive air to the former capital of our state. But

through it all, and even at the height of celebration, there was
a question in the minds of the more thoughtful, an unspoken
question, but, nevertheless, a wondering about what it all means.
I was reminded again of the question my friend asked me: "Why
the celebration?"

As I joined in wholeheartedly with the fun and tried to lift
my voice with the crowd in a Rebel Yell at Milledgeville, I tried
to find the meaning of it all, to learn the lessons that The Great
American Tragedy teaches: lessons of courage and hope, the
rewards that come from endurance in the time of trial, appreciation for the great heritage that is ours, the humility that
comes not in the gloating of victory but in the discipline of defeat,
and faith in the true greatness of a united nation praying and
working for peace and goodwill throughout the whole world.

A LESSON IN ENDURANCE

In my essay of 26 Feb., I sought reasons for observing the centennial of the greatest mistake our nation ever made which we would like to forget ever happened. In this installment and the next, I want to search out its meaning to see if there are not some lessons that we should learn from that terrible fratricidal war, which resulted from fanaticism on both sides and which we are now so ashamed of that we want to put it out of our memory.

In the first place, let me say to my friends who prefer not to remember the war, we cannot eliminate history. History will not leave us alone; we have to live with it. We will not change the past by blotting it out of memory. Though some cynic has said, "All we learn from history is we do not learn from history," I say we must learn from the past. We must equip ourselves for the future with the judgment that comes from learning. And the learning comes from recognition of the mistakes of the past.

In the column referred to above, I spoke of the lessons of courage and endurance. Let me elaborate on these a little more. Bell Wiley, a member of the National Civil War Centennial

Commission, says the greatness demonstrated by our forefathers
a century ago

> is indeed a precious heritage, for it enables us to look forward with calm
> confidence to the crises which confront us and our children. Because
> our forefathers endured, we know that we can endure. Their strength
> is our strength and their example should be our standard.

Winston Churchill marveled at the courage and endurance of
the Rebels of 1863, who though certain of defeat, continued on
in stubborn resistance almost two years longer.

I think there is an even greater lesson to be learned. That
lesson is faith in the ultimate triumph of good that comes
through submission to a will beyond and above the will of men.
Syngman Rhee, president of the Republic of South Korea, once
said to an American visitor, "The trouble with you Americans
is you have never known defeat, you have never had to suffer
the shame of bloody boots tramping upon your soil." This is true
of America, yes, but is different with the South. The South in
remembering the days of the invader is disciplined by the
thought. When the mother of two Confederate sons learned that
they had both died one afternoon in the Battle of Atlanta, her
anger vanished in sorrow and submissively she said, "Thy will
be done."

We, as a nation, have nothing to gain but enemies by vain
boasting. Joseph G. Harrison wrote in the *Atlanta Journal-Constitution*, Sunday, 5 Feb., "Many have long wondered whether
an America uniquely prosperous and secure, really understands
the fears, desires and needs of the two-thirds of the world which
is desperately poor, backward and uncertain of the future." What
assurance is there that we have earned permanent success and
prosperity? How do we know that we shall always be showered
with heaven's blessings and feel the warm smile of providence?
The old saying, "pride goes before a fall," may be unpopular, but
it is still true. A study of past ages teaches us that great civilizations that once ruled the world are now remembered only in
history. The humility that replaced hate in a mother's heart
when she faced the loss of her sons can apply to the South as a
whole. There is a kindred feeling between the region once known

as the Confederacy and nations that have experienced occupation by the conqueror. This should bring about a feeling of broth-
erhood and goodwill between all Americans and peoples of other
lands. And it can if the nation will apply the lesson forced by
the bayonet upon the South so long ago.

If America can learn to be proud without being guilty of false
pride, the commemoration of the Civil War will be worth the
effort. Otherwise, it would be better forgotten.

MEANING OF SOVEREIGNTY

An important lesson to be learned from the Civil War is the supremacy of the national authority. Whatever historic validity Calhoun's "compact theory" might have once had, the majority of Americans know the Constitution of the United States of America is the fundamental law that "we the people" made, not one made by 50 states. Less than one-fourth of these states were brought into being by the federal government, all others were created by the Congress. Sovereignty lies in the American people, the whole people, and not in one unit of the federal system, nor in any number of units combined in opposition to the national will.

The nation is united and sovereign today regardless of what our forefathers desired to make it a hundred years ago. And let me hurry to say they believed what they were fighting for was right. I respect their sincerity. Nevertheless, as there is no earthly power outside America that has authority over the nation, there is no power within the country that is greater than the national will. This principle was put through its greatest test in the great sectional conflict of the nineteenth century. It was not the result of that conflict, but, as Ralph McGill said recently, it was merely confirmed by the Union victory in the Civil War.

That is not to say all rights of the individual states are to be surrendered. Certain immunities, rights, and privileges of the states are guaranteed by the Constitution. These should be jealously guarded, and the states should be vigilant in seeing that their constitutional rights are preserved. But there is a difference between states' rights and sovereignty. The federal government has no right to invade areas that are reserved to the states, but neither have the states power to deny any American citizen rights guaranteed to him under the Constitution of the United States.

Sovereignty cannot be divided. When in conflict with a state or group of states, the nation is supreme. The logical end of state sovereignty is anarchy, for if a state can oppose the authority of the national government then a county could oppose the authority of the state, a town oppose the county, a street oppose the town, and so on, down to the individual. Individual sovereignty is an ideal. Locke, Jefferson, and Rousseau could do much with it, but it exists only in a state of nature. In the nation, there must be law, authority, and undivided sovereignty. Liberty is good, a precious thing, but where there is no law there is no liberty. This we should learn from the Civil War.

In a recent editorial in this paper it was pointed out that the theme of the centennial observance is "peace, goodwill, and binding faith." We are one people, regardless of our differences. No one in his right mind would deny that. But the differences between sections have been and can continue to be compromised. The South protests against the demands made upon it to change its cultural, social, and economic way of life. But this must not lead to fanaticism. The emotionalism of 1861 led to a divided nation, and Southerners who have learned the real meaning of sovereignty will not permit fanaticism to cause history to repeat itself.

Recently I received a letter from a man, whom I did not know, in Albany, New York. He had written a book purporting that a conflict of cultures was the major factor in the sectional dispute before, during, and since the Civil War. He said, "There have been only two cultures in this country, that of the old South and that of New England." He went on to say they were and are "as different as rival nationalities in Europe." I cannot agree with him. I think there has been some "merging" of cultures in America ever since John Rolfe married Pocahontas. The American nation is made up of peoples from all nations, plus those noble savages who first owned the land.

As for any danger of a rupture in our nation between the sections over economic or cultural differences, I shall only say, the nation was born in compromise, has lived through compromise, and will continue to harmonize its differences by compromise. As long as America remains united and strong in its binding faith, our future is as certain as tomorrow's sunrise.

A NAME FOR THE CONFLICT

Here we are on the eve of the centennial of the capture of Ft. Sumter. The Confederacy's decisive action could only have had one result—war. We have already discussed the causes of the war and have tried to understand what it means to us today. It is necessary now to think about a name for the war, which we shall follow in retrospect over the next four years.

This column runs under the title "Civil War." I use this designation here and in all references to it, except when speaking to my UDC friends. Then, out of respect for their wishes, I use Alexander H. Stephens's name for it, "The War Between the States." I once promised the United Daughters of the Confederacy that I would never, in their presence, call the Civil War the "Civil War," but whenever I mentioned the Civil War I would use their name for it, and not refer to it as the "Civil War."

Perhaps my best defense for the short name is its brevity. As James Street said, it saves type. I not only think "The War Between the States" is too long a name, but English teachers, who know better than I, say "between" cannot be used in the sense of "between the states." Since there were 11 Southern states affirming states' rights and 22 other states loyal to the Union, perhaps "War Among the States" would be more correct grammatically. Or, perhaps E. Merlton Coulter, who found a score of names for the war, has the better name for it when he calls it "The War Against the States."

Many students have observed that Confederate leaders of that day referred to the war as the "Civil War," among them Jefferson Davis, Robert E. Lee, James Longstreet, and John B. Gordon. Even Stephens, who later gave it the popular Southern name, called it "a civil war." Lincoln and his government, trying to deny it was a war at all, called it a "Rebellion," but conducted it as though the United States were at war with a foreign country.

Years ago I helped prepare a history of the United States. When faced with the problem of naming the war and not wanting to offend either North or South, we called it "The War for Southern Independence." That is really what it was, and contemporaries called it that. The Confederate States were fighting for independence just as surely as the original colonies of the British empire in America were fighting for independence. In the second struggle the rebels failed. Whatever Charles Beard, twentieth-century historian, meant by the "Second American Revolution," we know he did not mean a second rebel victory.

Some of the less popular names among Southerners are "The War Against Slavery," "The War for Democracy," "The Insurrection," and "The War of the Rebellion." Coulter tells the story of Miss Mildred Rutherford, who "presided" over the library of Lucy Cobb Institute in Athens. She was so terribly offended by the title on her set of the "Official Records" that she had the "War of of the Rebellion" painted over on every one of the more than 100 volumes and substituted a new title to protect her girls from a "pitfall." Miss Rutherford's new title was "The Official Records of the Armies of the Union and Confederate Armies in the War Between the States."

The Northern people dislike with equal vehemence such Southern designations as "The War of the Abolition Party Against the Principles of the Constitution of the United States," "The War for Southern Freedom," or "The War of Coercion."

There are neutral terms that might be mentioned, such as "The Late War" and Winston Churchill's "noblest war—the last war between gentlemen." As for the former, that is meaningless now, and as for the latter, I share with James Street the thought that the bloodiest war in United States history could hardly be called a "gentleman's war." I know the soldiers in blue and those in gray traded tobacco and newspapers and sometimes stopped fighting long enough to bury their dead. Nevertheless, the war was as ruthless and cruel as the weapons of that time could make it. And I imagine the lack of painkilling and miracle drugs made the collective suffering greater than any war since. One of the most neutral terms for the Civil War was the one used by Mrs. Roger A. Pryor when in her reminiscences she called it "The War Between the Northern and Southern States of America."

Whatever we might call that "late Unpleasantness," we can be sure it was more of an "Uncivil War" than a civil one.

THE LEGACY OF THE WAR

In a previous essay I alluded to America's power and prestige as a heritage of the Civil War. This is part of the legacy of that war, which Robert Penn Warren discusses in his provocative essay, "The Legacy of the Civil War" (Random House, 1961), on how that conflict affected the American people. Today I wish to indulge in some meditations on Mr. Warren's "Meditations on the Centennial."

To begin with, the poet-novelist sees the American Civil War—"the War"—as the greatest single event of our history: "it is our history." He says we had no history "in the deepest sense" before 1865. The American Revolution merely created a nation "on paper," but the Civil War changed "an idea, an ideal," into the reality of union. Now, he says, "for better or worse," we are one nation in its true and full sense. This, to him, is the most obvious fact among many "clear and objective facts" to be gleaned from the war. Among these are, as is well known, the abolition of slavery—"even if it did little or nothing to abolish racism"; the reclaiming by the parent of authority over the children who had run away—"but in so doing it made them more

Southern"; the formulation of the American concept of war; and the "enormous stimulation of technology and production."

Robert Penn Warren also sees the Civil War as having created a climate favorable to the formulation of the pragmatic philosophy. He quotes historians David Donald ("Lincoln and the Pragmatic Tradition") and T. Harry Williams—"the position he [Lincoln] took on specific political issues was always a pragmatic one"—to illustrate the truth of this. And he turns to Sidney Hook who quotes Lincoln's message to Congress in 1862 in which he said, "The dogmas of the quiet past are inadequate to the stormy present . . . As our case is new, we must think anew and act anew."

It also brought about a "collision between two absolutes," that is "higher law"—to which Garrison dedicated *The Liberator*—and "legalism"—to which the South held firmly until John Brown's raid and Lincoln's election led it into a Second War for Independence.

Warren uses phrases that linger in the mind and convey ideas that take root—"power and prestige," "higher law," "legalism." When he comes to the psychological results he uses the terms "the Great Alibi" and "the Treasury of Virtue." The war gave the South "the Great Alibi" by which Southerners "explain and condone everything"; and it gave the North a "Treasury of Virtue" which, he says, is equally unlovely, and it may ultimately be "equally corrosive of national and personal integrity."

He has much to say about "power and prestige." Victor and vanquished alike find pleasure in the fact that our nation is the most powerful and wealthy on earth. "Even the most disgruntled Southerner," he says, "no matter how much he may damn the Yankee and his works, loves as well as the next man to bask in the beams of power and prestige."

Finally, he comes to causality. In meditating upon the lively question of the inevitability of the Civil War, Warren moves on to the bigger question of causality in history. He moves from the academic to the practical, from the abstract to the concrete, by applying the question to the present world situation. Using the words of Arthur M. Schlessinger, Jr., who saw in our great crisis of 1860 an inevitable collision, he asks, "Does a society like the USSR 'closed in the defense of evil institutions,' create 'moral differences far too profound to be solved by compromise'?" I do not think the Civil War can be explained simply as a clash of morals, but the question as applied to our adversary today is one with which we shall have to deal, and how we deal with it will determine our future.

Warren's penetrating essay convinces me that some poets do occasionally interpret history more clearly than some historians.

A STATEMENT OF PURPOSE

The first year of the Civil War Centennial has closed, and with its closing, memories of Ft. Sumter and First Manassas linger in Southern minds; but a review of the year 1861 shows ups and downs—the western Virginia campaign was not considered a success. And ups and downs it was, too, with the Civil War Centennial Commission, which officially launched the observance of the centennial a year ago on a hopeful and optimistic note. Ceremonies at the mausoleum of Gen. Robert E. Lee at Lexington, Virginia, and at the tomb of Gen. Ulysses S. Grant in New York emphasized the theme of unity. Lee's grandson paid tribute to Grant and Grant's grandson honored Lee. This newspaper asked editorially on 7 January, "What better symbol that the wounds of a century ago have healed?"

We were not so sure that the wounds had entirely healed when the segregation issue flared up within the Commission as it met in Charleston, South Carolina, in April to celebrate the seizure of Ft. Sumter by Confederate forces. Before the year had ended the chairman of the Commission had resigned and another had been elected. I shall not go into the problems related to the internal affairs of the Commission, but rather point out the fact that with the new chairman, Allan Nevins, the original aims of unity and truth and historical scholarship have a pretty good chance of being accomplished.

The burden rests, however, upon the states and upon those on the local level who assume leadership in the commemoration of the Civil War. I hope sincerely that Georgia will rise to the challenge issued by the new chairman: less propaganda and more publications that will stand the critical eye of scholarship; less pompous pageantry and more preservation of historical records; less celebration and more commemoration. This only will justify the time, effort, and money spent on the national and state level during these centennial years.

Georgia has been dragging her feet in regard to publications of worth. Some celebrations have been held, some pageants and public meetings have taken place, and some good has come from such stimulation, but unless more good history is written and more and clearer understanding of purpose is manifested, the observance will have to be written off as a failure. The greatest good yet accomplished in our state is that many of our people have been encouraged to rediscover family records and have made efforts to permanently preserve them in libraries and archives.

I am keenly aware of the failure to publish more than we have in our first year of the centennial in Georgia. This has been due largely to a lack of coordination of effort. As chairman of the Publications Committee of the Georgia Commission I shall do all I can this year to see that Dr. Nevins's promise to "promote the publication of books and the collection of sources" will be kept. I quote in full below his statement issued on taking the office of chairman of the Civil War Centennial Commission.

> We shall use our energies and influence to help make the national commemoration of the Civil War both instructive and constructive.
>
> To this end we shall discourage observances that are cheap and tawdry, or that are divisive in temper, or that in any other respect fall short of expressing the magnanimity of spirit shown by Lincoln and Lee, that fall short of honoring the heroism of the 600,000 men who gave their lives. We shall encourage observances which will assist the

American people in understanding the mingled tragedy and exaltation of the war, and to draw from it lessons both practical and moral commensurate with its importance.

We shall promote the publication of books and the collection of sources, which will stand as a permanent memorial of this commemoration. We shall do what we can to make the principal events of the war, civil and military, more meaningful to teachers and students in the schools of the Nation. We well realize that by use of the mass media we can give observances otherwise merely local a national interest and impact. We hope to enlist in our work the poets, the essayists, the novelists, and the composers of the country.

Above all our central theme will be unity, not division, for out of the brothers' war slowly emerged the basis of firm union of hearts instead of an uncertain union of jarring political elements. So far as we can, we shall allow the just pride of no national group to be belittled or besmirched. A host of white Southerners died for what they believed a just cause; a host of white Northerners died for what they held a sacred duty; a host of Negroes died, many in the uniform of the United States, for the achievement of freedom and human equality. We must honor them all. When we finally reach the commemoration of Appomattox, we shall treat it not as victory or defeat, but as a beginning—the beginning of a century of increasing concord, mutual understanding, and fraternal affection among all the sections and social groups of the republic.

STRENGTH FROM HARDSHIP

"In his recollections, George Cary Eggleston, who witnessed the drama at Appomattox, said,

> I think we must have known from the beginning of the campaign of 1864 that the end was approaching, and that it could not be other than a disastrous one . . . [but] we had to shut our eyes to the facts very resolutely, that we might not see how certainly we were to be crushed. And we did shut our eyes so successfully as to hope in a vague, irrational way for the impossible to the very end.

Winston Churchill, who examined the American Civil War, as the English are wont to do, marveled at the courage of the Southern Rebels, which caused them to fight on for two more years after they knew their cause was hopeless. This, to Churchill, is 'one of the enduring glories of the American people.' "

This is the way I began my address at the Memorial Day program held 26 April at the Reynolds High School. The program was sponsored by the Gordon-Carson Chapter of Taylor County and the Daughters of the Confederacy from Macon County. It gave me an opportunity to retell the familiar story of Gen. Gordon's bold attack at Ft. Stedman just before Lee began his retreat

to Appomattox. But the real hero of the story was Capt. Joseph
P. Carson, of Taylor County, captain of the Sharpshooters, 4th
Georgia.

The message I tried to get across was simple: the worth-
whileness of striving for what appears to be the impossible. The
real victory is not in the gain, but in the effort.

> The glory of striving for an ideal against impossible odds is perhaps
> the greatest joy we should get from the observance of the Centennial
> of America's most useless, yet most ennobling of all wars. To endure
> hardships and to keep one's faith in his ideal, in himself, and the col-
> lective effort, under God, of his people to fight for the right as they see
> the right is our legacy from the War Between the States.

> The stubborn courage of the Southern boys fighting for their rights
> as they saw them, fighting for their homes and the loved ones sheltered
> there, fighting for glory and honor—that dogged determination is re-
> flected in the Resolutions of McGowan's Brigade which closed with these
> words: "Therefore, unsubdued by past reverses, and unawed by future
> dangers, we declare our determination to battle to the end, and not to
> lay down our arms until independence is secured. Is life so dear, or peace
> so sweet, as to be purchased at the price of chains and slavery? Forbid
> it Heaven!"

> Everything had been exhausted by the spring of '65, except, as Gen.
> Gordon said, "devotion and valor"; and it was a reckless and impossible
> thing Gordon wanted to do. But Gen. Lee, himself, had said he thought
> "the sorely tried people could be induced to make one more effort." So,
> Lee consented. Capt. Carson and his expert marksmen were chosen to
> lead the assault in the darkness of pre-dawn. Carson was described as
> a large, strong man, "erect as an Indian." His square face "was relieved
> by a tawny mustache and wavy hair. He had a pleasant voice, and
> smiling steely blue eyes. And every ounce of him was courage."

> The attack—across a cornfield only 150 yards in width—was tem-
> porarily successful, but Pickett failed to come up, as had been hoped,
> and the captured fort had to be abandoned in a hail of bullets. Capt.
> Carson and another soldier carried "Bob" Carson's body through the
> fire. Carson's young brother had been urged not to make the charge.
> Carson was the only one of the four brothers to return home.

This, in sketchy outline, is the story I told at Reynolds to
illustrate the war's lesson of endurance. Then I closed with a
more personal story.

> When I was at Mercer University as a student in 1925, the football
> team was captained by Clyde Bryan Carson, of Taylor County. We called

him "Bo-Dick." He was quiet and soft spoken, yet strong and "erect as an Indian." And "every ounce of him was courage." He led the Mercer Bears to a 21 to 6 victory over the Petrels of Oglethorpe University that year. All bets were on the stronger Petrels, but Capt. Carson, "the scrappiest center in the S.I.A.A.," inspired his team to do the impossible. The Capt. Carson I knew in 1925 was the grandnephew of the hero of Ft. Stedman; and the glory that seemed to fade in 1865 was restored somehow that day when Capt. Carson led his team to victory.

So it is today. Ours is not just a memory of past glory, but a strength that comes from enduring hardships; a courage inspired by Capt. Carson and his Sharpshooters at Ft. Stedman; a faith in our ability as a people to do the impossible; a confidence that in spite of the dark clouds that hover over us we will, with God's help, survive and succeed. And, as Capt. "Bo-Dick" Carson revived the glory of '65, so do we today enjoy the legacy of an enduring glory.

BEHIND 14TH AMENDMENT

This essay is being written during the heat of excitement over the conflict between the state of Mississippi and the federal government. By the time it appears in print I earnestly hope much of the tension will have passed. Nevertheless, the basic conflict between law and liberty will not have been solved; indeed, this problem is one that began to disturb the American people at the time of the founding of the federal system, rose higher in 1814 when the New England states opposed the nationalism reflected in the war of 1812, became more intense in 1830 when Southern states attempted to nullify a federal tariff law, burst into a great four-year sectional war in the 1860s, and now comes full circle to confuse and divide us.

A letter from a former student is before me. He had read an article that bothered him. I am sure it must have been David Lawrence's "Illegality Breeds Illegality," appearing in a recent issue of *U. S. News & World Report.* The student wanted to know if it is true that the 14th Amendment was adopted illegally. Then he asked, "Why has it remained illegal?"

In answer to his double-barreled question, I would say, though it was illegally adopted it has not remained illegal. On the first point I fully agree with Mr. Lawrence that the amendment was forced and, therefore, illegal and unconstitutional. But when he contends that the amendment "is not valid" today, I disagree.

I would say the amendment on which the federal government bases its authority to coerce the state of Mississippi by armed force was not lawfully sanctioned when written and, therefore, was unconstitutional. But I would insist that the amendment, which protects "life, liberty, and property," is today neither unwanted nor unconstitutional, for the Constitution of the United States is what the Supreme Court plus the majority of the people say it is. Of course, the Supreme Court sometimes speaks ahead of some of the people and sometimes speaks behind some of the people as it assumes the Constitution to be what the court says it is; but in the final analysis sovereignty lies with the people.

My reason for saying the 14th Amendment, though admittedly adopted by illegal means, is now legal by the will of the people, rests on the fact that the Constitution is the will of the people. It changes not only by formal amendment but by usage and interpretation. It changes when the president of the United States interprets it at a certain time to meet a particular situation. It changed when George Washington decided not to seek the advice of the Senate in treaty making despite the fact that the Constitution clearly gave that body an advisory function and when Andrew Jackson let the state of Georgia defy John Marshall's decision in favor of the Cherokee Indians. It also changed when the Supreme Court under Marshall assumed the right of judicial review. One could cite the written document to prove the court had not been given that power specifically, but the court went on setting aside act after act of the federal Congress and the people came to accept its decisions. It changed when the court reversed itself after a half century and declared the "separate but equal" principle no longer consitutional.

The state of Mississippi has not yet come to accept the court's racial position, nor has the state of Alabama, nor South Carolina, but Southern people are gradually accepting the ruling of the court. And though the court's function is to interpret law rather than enact it, it seems that the time has come when the sovereign people themselves are determined to accept this principle. And when the people accept it, it becomes the law of the land—not before.

The party system is another example of a change in the operation of our government that was brought about not with constitutional authority, but as the result of custom. The Constitution itself was illegally adopted. Here is the way it came about. When the Founding Fathers met in Philadelphia in 1787 they were authorized by the Congress of the Confederation to propose amendments to the Articles of the Confederation. No alteration was to be made in the Articles—which recognized the sovereignty of each state—unless there was unanimous consent of the states to the proposed changes. The Convention voted to violate the Articles by establishing a government of the people when as many as three-fourths of the states ratified the federal constitution. This was unconstitutional, but it became, in time, the will of the people. And so have the amendments, and even the unwritten innovations, that have come to be accepted by a majority of the people.

True liberty comes only through security and stability under law, the "natural rights" philosophers notwithstanding. But it is alarming to have to admit that law and order has to be maintained by military force rather than by legal procedure.

CIVIL AUTHORITY SUPREME

Last week this column dealt with the basic problem of constitutionality. The question was whether federal law should prevail in Mississippi or whether that state should be free from the coercive power of the federal government—a coercion and restraint backed up with military power. I answered the question in favor of national supremacy. Unfortunately, violence and disorder made it necessary. If the Civil War means anything constructive, it means that this nation is "one and indivisible." There is no other answer: the federal power supercedes state power; the whole is greater than any of its parts; the "indestructible" states are gathered together into an 'indestructible" union.

But even as I argue that the federal government has supremacy over state authority, I deplore the fact that it has to be demonstrated by the use of the military forces of the United States. That is the way Latin American generals rule their people, that was the way the Nazi rulers controlled their people before the democratic nations joined together to put them down, and that is the way the Communist dictators keep their people in subjection today.

One of the principles emphasized by Jefferson in his inaugural address in 1801 is "the supremacy of the civil over the military authority." We can accept the growth of central power when it comes through legal and constitutional means. We can accept the increase of executive power when the people's representatives make it possible through legislation resulting from long and thoughtful deliberation, debate, and decision. But the use of troops to support the position of the attorney general of the United States before all legal means have been exhausted is, in my opinion, an admission of the failure of jurisprudence and will, if not checked, lead to the final and complete breakdown of the principle enunciated by Jefferson a century and a half ago.

The principle was upheld by the Supreme Court of the United States in 1866 in the case *ex parte* Milligan which declared that neither the Congress nor the president has the legal power to set up a military commission to sit in judgment over civilians where the civil courts are open.

The fact that the situation in Mississippi reached the point of violence and bloodshed, resulting in the use of federal troops and the nationalizing of the state troops to suppress it, is an admission of a lack of maturity and statesmanship on both sides.

One would think our politicians on the state and federal level would have learned something from the study of American history. What lesson does the Civil War teach them—that "the only lesson we learn from history is that we cannot learn from history?"

The president's use of force may have been necessary, but was it the only way out of the dilemma? And will the use of federal troops to enforce federal law become more and more the accepted pattern? Will it be the answer every time the federal government finds itself set against a state or a group? It is the implication in this easy and quick way out of a difficult situation that disturbs me.

I know there is a precedent for it. President Washington resorted to the use of military force in order to enforce the Whiskey Tax in Pennsylvania in 1795. Andrew Jackson, when faced by a rebellious South Carolina that refused to obey the federal tariff law of 1828, threatened to use the bayonet. He was saved from having to carry out out his threat by signing a compromise bill into law. Lincoln exercised the power of a dictator during the Civil War in restraining civilians by force. In 1892, President Cleveland sent a regiment of troops into Chicago to enforce the delivery of U. S. mail in the state of Illinois when the Pullman strike disrupted the mail service. There is no doubt that Republican President Eisenhower had the power to send airborne troops to Little Rock in 1957. Democrat Kennedy's power to follow this Republican's example in Mississippi is founded on precedent. But every time a president solves the continuing problem of federal-state relationship with armed force, he moves our nation another step further away from good and orderly government under law and makes it easier for the next president to adopt the dictator's method of securing orderly government through military force.

There is something ominous in the fact that an order from the chief executive can turn the loyalty of Mississippi's soldiers into an army of the United States, ready to march against neighbors and kin and shoot them down if necessary in order to prove to the world where supremacy lies in America.

I abhor the violence that necessitated the use of arms in Oxford and take comfort in the sense of security this use of military gives me, but I fear the consequences of the president's interpretation of the Constitution that clearly gives to Congress the power "to provide for the calling forth of the Militia" and gives to the president the power only to command.

THE ROAD TO REUNION

Item: On 1 April 1861—and this was no April Fool's joke—
William H. Seward, secretary of state, handed Lincoln a paper
containing his "Thoughts for the President's Consideration." In
it he proposed a quarrel with some foreign power in order to
unite the divided nation.

Big events have occurred so rapidly lately that if we should
stop to reflect upon them history would leave us far behind. It
is hard to keep pace with our changing world. It's like the Queen
told Alice, "Now, here, you see, it takes all the running you can
do, to keep in the same place. If you want to get somewhere else,
you must run at least twice as fast as that."

And while we were running ourselves out of breath on our
treadmills, the news shifted from integration in Mississippi to
intervention in Cuba, which shut out news temporarily from the
Far East, the November elections, and Berlin. Heaven only
knows what major crisis will be crowded out of the banner head-
line at the time we, or the Russians, land on the moon. We will
still be on our little treadmill perhaps, running too fast to stop

for reflection. Does anyone wonder why this column stays most of the time in the nineteenth century? To see how much the acceleration has increased in the past 100 years observe the speed with which we traveled the road to reunion in October and compare that with the slow journey our grandfathers made up that road after Appomattox. One moment we were worried about federal troops in Mississippi, and the next we were alarmed over the Russian missiles in Cuba. It was a full generation after the Civil War that signs of sectional amalgamation began to appear, though some, like poet A. J. Ryan, felt the pull toward unity earlier. The yellow fever epidemic, which struck the South a heavy blow in 1878, brought aid and sympathy from the richer North and prompted Father Ryan to write:

> For at the touch of Mercy's hand
> The North and South stood side by side.

One might say we were well on the road to reunion when we fought Spain in 1898. Indeed, Paul H. Buck does so in a book of that title (*The Road to Reunion*, Boston, 1938). War has a way of making us forget our differences. At least the Southern boys who fought in Cuba and the Philippines showed their loyalty to the "Stars and Stripes." It is true that some of their fathers who had fought under the "Stars and Bars" of the Confederacy and were fighting again as American soldiers forgot old loyalties slowly. Such was the case with ex-Confederate general Joe Wheeler who ordered his United States Cavalry in Cuba to "Charge the Damnyankees!"

World War I carried us farther up this patriotic road, and subsequent wars and crises had just about carried us to the ultimate goal. Then the Supreme Court moved nearer and nearer the Civil Rights goal recommended by President Truman's Commission in 1946, until it finally reached the doctrine of racial integration in its famous 1954 ruling in Brown v. Topeka Board of Education. With the federal executive determined to execute this "new" law of the land, the South was driven back to the position it held in 1860—at least in emotional response. The Mississippi crisis was the boiling-over point in the twentieth-century sectional dispute. But before we could analyze the situation properly the sudden, startling, and shocking fact of Russian missile bases in Cuba, 90 miles off the Florida coast, shook the South and made us forget the "little unpleasantness" between North and South. Suddenly we were one.

President Kennedy, in 18 minutes on Monday evening of 22 Oct., made us forget sectional differences, as he himself forgot all about his war against the Republicans. All of the sudden, North and South were reunited. White man and Negro were both American citizens, both wondering how long their children would have pure air to breathe and share in common, both wondering at what moment a hot scorching blast might burn their white and black children to charred masses of flesh so that none could tell which was white and which was black. White man and black man made peace; Yankee and Rebel became brothers; and the Donkey and the Elephant were content to lie down together—at least for a little while.

IT WON'T HAPPEN HERE

The Constitution of the United States has been the central theme of this column for the month of November. In rereading my recent essays I find that I let the Mississippi race problem, which brought federal-state relations to a serious crisis, and the Cuban situation, which sparked an even more serious international crisis, force me far beyond the problems of the 1860s. Yet, both the domestic and the foreign crises, which caused me to examine our federal Constitution more closely, were examined in the light of the great American War of 1861-1865. It is through such a device that I can justify discussion of present-day problems under the title of this column.

One evening recently I was discussing the growth of executive power with some of my colleagues. That, along with the growth of federal power, has been one of the trends in government that has caused concern recently. This column last week revealed how quickly one man—our president—could bring a nation divided over the race issue back to unity; the week before it showed how strong the federal government was in its military power, a power exercised through the authority of the president.

Let me continue to follow this line of thinking. It might seem, from what has been said in the previous essays, that I would advocate a weak executive. Just the contrary. I think a weak executive in a time like this, or in a nation that has developed along the lines that ours has, is undesirable. The thing we must be sure of is that the president, strong as he must be, must be fully conscious of the basic right of the people to enact the laws under which they live. This they have the constitutional right to do through their representatives; neither the executive nor the judiciary has a constitutional right to do so. We need a strong president who can execute the laws and can defend the Constitution as he has sworn he will do. A weak president might not be able to withstand a group, one with a military-industrial complex to use Gen. Eisenhower's words, which might fear for the nation's security so much that they would be tempted to take the government over and set up a dictatorship. Actually, we might have more cause to fear a weak president than to fear a strong one. A strong executive committed to upholding the Constitution, with its checks and balances, might protect the nation from a would-be military dictator.

This might seem too far-fetched to warrant serious discussion, but it is the theme of one of the leading bestsellers at the moment. The book is *Seven Days in May* (Harper and Row, 1962), a novel by Fletcher Knebel and Charles W. Bailey II, both of the Washington Bureau of Cowles Publications. Since writing my last week's column I have read this fantastic tale of an attempted army coup to overthrow the government. The setting is the United States, 1976. It is frightening to see how close a strong man, who fears for his country's safety, comes to taking the government away from a weak man, who is responsible for upholding the Constitution and defending the citizens, not only from an outside enemy but also from self-destruction through submission to a military dictatorship. Unlimited nuclear power and a push-button system make the fear a very real one. If I interpret the novel correctly, the decisive factor that brought about the defeat of the plot was that a few of the intimate friends of the president believed in the American democratic system, which places the civil over the military! Another factor was a final gathering of courage on the part of that president to defend the Constitution, which he was oath-bound to do. It is not easy to erase two hundred years of patriotic loyalty to a "government of the people, by the people, and for the people."

In 1885, a young student at Johns Hopkins University wrote:

> As at present constituted, the federal government lacks strength because its powers are divided, lacks promptness because its authorities are multiplied, lacks wieldiness because its processes are roundabout lacks efficiency because its responsibility is indistinct and its action without competent direction.

In time that young student became president of the United States and did much to strengthen his government, as did Theodore Roosevelt before him and as did Franklin D. Roosevelt and others after him. Woodrow Wilson knew the Constitution, knew its weaknesses, knew how to use the power it gave him. So must it be with all presidents. We could not afford a weak president now or at anytime in the future. Our push-button world will not permit it. As Richard E. Neustadt, consultant to President Kennedy, says, the presidency "is not a place for amateurs."

STUDENT VIEWS THE WAR

Occasionally, I throw out to my classes at Mercer University a challenge to interpret the American Civil War, and, occasionally, I get a response that I think is provocative enough to share with the readers of this column. Thus, Miss Jacqueline Dean, a sophomore from Perry, becomes my guest contributor today with her essay, "The Far Reaching Results of the Civil War." Miss Dean, like most of my students, reflects a "Southern attitude."

It was 12 April 1861 when the shots that signaled the beginning of the Civil War were fired. Yet today the deep scars of that great conflict still remain even though the scars of two world wars have faded. . . .

After the United States helped overcome Germany and Japan in World War II, great efforts were made to lighten the burden of defeat for the nations. However, after the Civil War in the South, Reconstruction was imposed instead of a Marshall Plan. Although the South was prostrate, the North imposed 12 years of military occupation upon the states. There were no great relief efforts and more than a million people faced starvation. The Freedman's Bureau, created by the government in Washington, profited four dollars in taxes on cotton for each dollar it gave for the relief of the freed slaves. Funds from private charities from the North were pathetically small. The South's capital went up in smoke along with cities, farms, and industries.

The United States helped to create an international bank and international monetary funds to stabilize world currency and stimulate the flow of money abroad after World War II. However, in 1865, the United States Treasury agents, Northern carpetbaggers, and Southern scalawags poured into the South, captured state and local governments by using the votes of Negroes, and squeezed hundreds of millions of dollars out of the South in graft and taxes. . . .

The one-party system stems from the Reconstruction period. There was a sizable Whig party in the South prior to the Civil War and Abraham Lincoln found enough Republican support to begin reconstruction in several Southern states before his death. Nevertheless, the frauds and corruption that filled Southern statehouses under the Northern occupation led the native white population to quit the Republican party in large numbers. In later years, Southern Democratic leaders sided with Negroes to remain in control of Republican party organization, thus word spread that the Republican party was a Negro party in the South. This prevented the rise of the Republican party and accounted for the one-party system. The stigma of Reconstruction with Republicans and Negroes ruling the South has not fully been forgotten.

Segregation, too, has its roots in the Reconstruction era. There was little segregation in the South for many years after Reconstruction, and it was not until the 1890s that segregation laws were fully developed. They were largely a defense movement by the whites who feared that if the barriers remained down, social equality would develop. Before the war the Negroes posed no problem, but after the war, at the prodding of Northerners, the relations between Southern whites and the Negroes became more strained.

The lawsuits, demonstrations, and disturbances against school desegregation are also outgrowths of the Reconstruction. Four thousand schools for Negroes were established in the South by the Freedman's Bureau while none were built for the white people. The white people had to support schools for their children as best they could. After Reconstruction, there was an effort to give separate but equal education to both races in spite of the poverty that was a hindrance to Southern education for 80 years.

Southern economy suffered extensively for many years after the Reconstruction days. Immediately after the war, there were no government crop loans, no new farm implements, and no free seed, but there was a host of freed slaves for the returning Southern soldiers to feed. Sharecropping developed but both Negroes and the white farmers were caught in grinding poverty that deepened for years. Not until World War II did any real relief occur. In fact, World War II did for the South what the Civil War had done for the North in regard to industrial development.

Yes, the South felt the effects of the Civil War for 75 years until World War II initiated changes. Now, a century later, the Southern states are out from under the cloud of the Civil War and Reconstruction with many new Southern industries and a Negro problem that is gradually moving North.

A STRANGE
SENSE OF HUMOR

What the Abolitionists were advocating—liberation of the
Negro slaves—two Union generals were putting into practice
before Lincoln issued his Emancipation Proclamation. These two
generals were John C. Fremont in Missouri and David Hunter
on the South Atlantic coast. Hunter's headquarters was at Hilton
Head, South Carolina. From March 1862 to June 1863 he was
commander of the Southern Department, which took in the
states of South Carolina, Georgia, and Florida. One cannot talk
about Hunter without bringing his Irish adjutant into the story.

It can be seen by observing the dates of Hunter's command
of the Southern Department that his emancipation proclamation
was ahead of Lincoln's. So was Fremont's, for that matter. Lincoln was unhappy about both Fremont and Hunter's proclamations of emancipation. The reason will soon be evident.

About a month after Gen. Hunter took command of Ft. Pulaski, which protected Savannah, the city surrendered to Union
forces. That was on 11 April, and the very next day Hunter issued
an order liberating the slaves who had fallen into Federal hands.
Then, on 9 May, he issued his proclamation freeing all the slaves

in his department, which consisted of the three South Atlantic states already mentioned. The freed slaves were being organized under a New England abolitionist minister, Thomas Wentworth Higginson. Later, a Kansas abolitionist named James Montgomery formed colored regiments to disrupt the life of the Southerners and thus liberate Southern Negroes. A Boston-born white colonel, Robert G. Shaw, brought a large regiment of Negro troops down from Massachusetts to assist in setting the slaves free.

On 11 June, the town of Darien, Georgia, on the Altamaha River, was completely destroyed, having been burned by the Negro troops. Immediately after that Lincoln replaced Hunter. The order from the president had been issued before Darien was burned, but Lincoln's fear of and opposition to servile insurrection had caused him to countermand Hunter's emancipation proclamation, and the destruction of homes, schools, and churches was displeasing to him. Hunter, who knew Lincoln personally— had even slept in the East Room of the White House to protect the president during the first days of Lincoln's occupancy— seems to be the villain of the piece. Actually, Montgomery, the Kansas Jayhawker, was the villain at Darien. But that is another story.

As bad as Hunter looks to Southerners who shudder at the thought of liberated slaves armed and in a state of insurrection in 1863, Col. Halpine, Hunter's adjutant, might look even more despicable to Negroes today who would fail to see any humor in Halpine's poem quoted here.

Halpine, Irish-born poet, journalist, and would-be humorist, spent much of his time at Hilton Head sending anonymous poems to the *New York Herald*. Under the pen name of Pvt. Miles O'Reilly, he wrote this poem. It loses its humor when read by Negroes today, and I imagine it caused very few chuckles among the Negroes of that day. Perhaps I should let it die buried in the dust of the past, but because a Union officer ostensibly fighting for Negro freedom wrote it, I think we Southerners, white and black, should take a look at it.

SAMBO'S RIGHT TO BE KILT

Some tell us 'tis a burnin' shame
To make the naygers fight;
And that the thrade of bein' kilt
Belongs but to the white:
But as for me, upon my sowl!
So liberal are we here,
I'll let Sambo be murthered instead of myself,
On every day in the year.
On every day in the year, boys,
And in every hour of the day;
The right to be kilt I'll divide wid him,
And divil a word I'll say.

In battle's wild commotion
I shouldn't at all object
If Sambo's body should stop a ball
That was comin' for me direct;
And the prod of a Southern bagnet,
So ginerous are we here,
I'll resign, and let Sambo take it
On every day in the year.
On every day in the year, boys,
And wid none o' your nasty pride,
All my right in a Southern bagnet prod,
Wid Sambo I'll divide.

The men who object to Sambo
Should take his place and fight;
And it's betther to have a nayger's hue
Than a liver that's wake and white.
Though Sambo's black as the ace of spades,
His finger a thrigger can pull,
And his eye runs straight on the barrel-sights
From undher its thatch of wool.
So hear me all, boys darlin',
Don't think I'm tippin' and chaff,
The right to be kilt we'll divide wid him,
And give him the largest half!

April 26, 1964

QUICK AND THE DEAD

The story is a familiar one. There were two men, one a hero and the other a deserter. The first gave his life for a lost cause, the other turned away and lived to fight a different kind of battle. The hero who died believed in the Southern Confederacy for which he fought, was captured, wasted away in Northern prison camps, and was allowed to go home to die. The one who ran away was perhaps no less brave, and he suffered too in his running, but he lived to build the great city of Atlanta from the ashes to which Sherman reduced it in 1864.

Now these two men are not fictitious characters. They actually existed. They are not created as symbols of the quick and the dead—the hero and the coward. One cannot be sure of the heroism or cowardice of men who fight and men who run. But these flesh and blood men of a century ago are very truly symbols, the one of men who would destroy the enemy and in the attempt destroy themselves, and the other of men who would avoid acts of destruction and refuse to fight for a cause in which they do not believe.

Theodorick Montfort was the hero. He symbolizes futility. He died for a cause worthy of his "last full measure of devotion," but he was dead, as dead as the cause for which he fought. Yet in the very effort there was a certain virtue. He perhaps would have protested the useless waste, even as I protest it, were he to choose the course for another; but for himself, he would make no other choice. Will Parkins was the deserter. He knew his choice. There was no hesitation, no uncertainty. He could not bring himself to fight against his country, and his country was America. His choice was to run away to live and fight the constructive battle, to build back, to create beauty where war had left only ugly scars and human debris.

It was not for the hero to have a part in building. He gave his life, not in a sudden glorious bursting of a shell or the zing of a bullet in a victorious assault, but little by little, day by day, in Federal prisons. Lt. Montfort, a young lawyer from Oglethorpe, joined the "Wise Guards" when the wars started and went off quickly to the mountains of western Virginia. He proudly marched away with his company. The only legal work remaining for the young lawyer was the writing of wills for his comrades. He left his wife, Louise, and their children, David, 13 years of age—old enough to help out at home—and the younger ones, Mollie, "Tebo," and "Pink," the baby.

Will Parkins had a vastly different background. He was born in New York State but had moved to Columbia, South Carolina. He was living happily there with his wife and child when his adopted state seceded. He was not at all sympathetic to the action that South Carolina took, and he resolved not to have any thing to do with it. He was drafted into service against his will, but managed to escape, and after many weary months of dodging through the Confederate lines he reached his parents' home.

In the meantime, Lt. Montfort, whose company had been sent to Ft. Pulaski to defend Georgia from attack by the sea, had been captured when that fort fell and was sent to a New York prison. The sick and weary soldier was released to go home. He reached his home to receive a hero's reward, three days with his family. Then he died. To Will Parkins such a futile waste of human life was useless. Lt. Montfort would disagree were he alive, but dead men are seldom heard by the living.

After the war was over Will Parkins returned to the South. His family was now reunited. He came to Atlanta in time to start the city on the long road upward from the ashes. He was the first and foremost architect of Atlanta in the Reconstruction period. He designed the Kimball House, "the finest hotel south of New York City." Among his churches, his first was the Catholic Church of the Immaculate Conception, which still stands on Hunter Street near the Capitol. He designed First Methodist at Peachtree and Houston and Second Methodist on Whitewall. I can remember well those beautiful Gothic Revival structures with their tall spires. One of his finest office buildings was the Healy Building, which stood at Five Points. His cultural interests were reflected in his efforts in organizing the library and in his services as organist to St. Philip's Episcopal Church. His fame as an architect was Southwide. When Wesleyan College wanted to change the grand old classical building, which Elam Alexander had designed, by making it conform to the popular Victorian style, Will Parkins was chosen to design it.

Some men are born to create, some to destroy. Lt. Montfort never intended to destroy anything, much less himself. He meant only to preserve and protect his home, his land, his way of life. Will Parkins was a practical man. Let others die for their ideals, he would live for his. Was he a coward? I leave the answer to the reader. The deserter is never glorified. But Will Parkins lived to create, to build beautiful things, to play lovely music, to encourage the improvement of the mind through books. Dead men have their monuments erected for them, live men build their own.

• VII •

JOURNEYS

A JOURNEY INTO THE PAST

Kay Tipton had invited me to speak to the Madison Kiwanis Club at their annual ladies' night banquet. Mrs. King and our daughter Jan went with me. It was like a journey into the past. The quaint and beautiful old town in Morgan County has an abundance of Greek Revival homes. Every crowded minute was exciting, and the memory of friendly people and lovely Snow Hill, Bonar Hall, Thurleston, Honeymoon House, McHenry House, Green Oaks, and Joshua Hill's home have now become a part of the treasured images of my mind.

We were to start with coffee at the fluted-columned cottage of the Tiptons. Not knowing our way around, we inquired at the the office of *The Madisonian*, that modern newspaper whose history dates back to William Tappan Thompson and his *Southern Miscellany* of the 1840s. It was there with publisher Graham Ponder and his "Editor-of-the-Week" wife, Adelaide, that we began to get the feel of the rich heritage that Madison has. Graham escorted us to the Tipton home. The tulips were in bloom. Adelaide took us to see the fine old building that the Morgan County Foundation has restored for library and civic use. Nelle Bateman told us about the expanding services of the Uncle Remus Regional Library.

Then, in a tea room in the cellar of a building that is older than the Democratic party, we met leading citizens of the town and talked with them about preservation of the old homes, relics, and documents. Louise Hicky gave me a copy of her booklet on the history of Morgan County. The tea room was filled with relics and curios. I saw wooden nails for the first time in my life—not pegs, but nails, sharp and strong enough to be driven into planks with a lesser degree of hardness than the nails. These heart pine nails had become even harder with age. We wondered if the original builder had not fudged a little by boring holes to receive the sharp wooden spikes. I plan to go back to Madison many times, and I must see the gun collection, which we failed to see because of lack of time

In the custody of Mrs. Lowry W. Hunt, chairman of the Morgan County Civil War Centennial Committee, we rode about the town seeing the magnificent residences and the wide, shaded streets. Many legends surround those homes. There was one about the lady who inherited a house, but because of the law then in effect that made a woman the legal ward of her husband, the master of the house lost it one night in a card game. This led to a change in the law so that a married woman could own property in her own name.

In the Barnett-Stokes house we found a lovely portrait of Eliza Fannin Walker, half sister of Col. James Fannin who fought for Texas independence under Sam Houston. There is a cracked door in that house that Katie Barnett and Fannin Stokes will not repair because the scar reminds them of the time a Yankee soldier split it with his sword. Many letters, preserved and in good condition, tell of love and hate and suffering in wartime. One of the treasured items we heard of is a quilt lined with such letters. One of the stories that appealed to me most was the one about the young mother whose husband was away at some Confederate army camp. She prepared a corn pone, and before putting it in the oven, she pressed the little child's foot into the soft mixture. She then sent the hard baked bread to the baby's father to show him how much his little daughter had grown.

Another story that might be paralleled in many a community throughout the South was the one about the soldier who lost an arm in battle. He was sent home to have his well-earned rest. But he could not remain inactive, so he organized a company of indigent ex-soldiers and old men for defense against Sherman's bummers.

Caroline Hunt and her committee are working enthusiastically collecting items for a museum of the Civil War period. They hope to acquire a house of the period and fill it with Civil War implements, tools, and weapons. They are conducting a house-to-house canvas. They tell me the Negroes are cooperating wonderfully well by contributing churns that date back of the Civil War, old coffee mills, charcoal-burning flatirons, and such things.

The collection of letters is growing fast, and one fascinating diary has already been uncovered. Soon they will have enough documents to invite Mary Bryan and her staff at the state archives to come to Madison and microfilm them all. Out of all this may come, should come, a history of Morgan County.

Madison today is a town filled with progressive, forward-looking citizens, a far cry from the antebellum days when it was necessary to have such town ordinances as "privies must be set away from the Publick Street" and "dead animals must be removed from the premises." But Madison, like Macon and many other places, is concerned with making it possible for the children of the future to have some understanding of those days long past and catch something of the spirit of their ancestors—a spirit that could endure the hardships of that terrible war.

JOURNEY TO THE PRESENT

Almost two months have elapsed since the big valley-wide observance of Confederate Memorial Day at West Point, but I can't erase from my memory the details of that meaningful experience. Mrs. King and I had never seen anything quite like it. It seemed the Chattahoochee Valley people had flooded the town as completely as the water from the river had flooded it a few months before. A big parade flowed through the town. The decorated cars and reactivated West Point Guards and LaGrange Light Guards were led by "Confederate Cavalrymen." There were the Nancy Harts, officials from the neighboring towns, a bicycle corps, bands, bearded gentlemen, and hoop-skirted ladies, complete with police escort.

The success of the parade and the program at the West Point Gymnatorium was due to the cooperative efforts of the Chattahoochee Valley Historical Society, whose president is Mrs. Tom Morgan, and the Pilot Club of West Point, presided over by Mrs. Lillian McCullough. Mr. and Mrs. Shaefer Heard headed the Executive Committee. The Historical Society included the towns of Lanett, Shawnut, Langdale, Fairfax, River View, LaFayette, and West Point.

I was the speaker for the occasion. My old friend Jack Walker, superintendent of the West Point schools, introduced me with more than enough "build-up" to make me feel that I was power-packed and ready to go into orbit. To blow up my ego even higher, lovely young Ellie Belle Spivey, in a beautiful Scarlett O'Hara dress, came down the aisle and presented me with an arm load of red roses tied in a bouquet with a large red ribbon—an old tradition.

I had chosen my topic well in advance and had done as much research on it as time permitted. My address centered on the dramatic story of the capture of Ft. Tyler, 16 April 1865, the last fort of the Confederacy to fall. At the beginning I had alluded to Beauregard's capture of Ft. Sumter four years before and had contrasted the confidence of the Southern Confederacy then with the broken South as represented in Lee's surrender at Appomattox. But I drew a picture of courage and endurance at war's end, exemplified at West Point by Brig. Gen. Robert C. Tyler and his 64 defenders as they beat off the first assault of Col. Oscar H. LaGrange's three regiments.

Gen. Tyler, who had lost a leg at Missionary Ridge, gave his life in defense of the fort that bore his name. After he was killed, the beleaguered garrison fought on as best it could. Even with ammunition gone, the men refused to surrender. When the Union troops reached the ditch surrounding the fort they were met by shells rolled over the parapet, and when they climbed over the parapet they were clubbed with the butts of empty muskets. Col. LaGrange ordered his men to hold fire when he saw that the brave defenders preferred death to surrender. When they buried the dead, soldiers in blue and gray were to sleep forever in the beautiful valley of the Chattahoochee.

I tried to tell those people that day what the Union victory means to us all. I said the Yankees won the war for all Americans by winning the war for the Union. Now Yankees and Confederates sleep together at West Point, and their grandsons live together in the towns and cities of the South today, no longer enemies.

But I pulled out all the stops when I played the note of endurance. Then as Mrs. King and I rode back across Pine Mountain in the night on our journey back to Macon, I gradually, with the help of a practical wife, began to return to reality. I began to reflect upon my speech and also upon the spirit of today's children of the Valley. I was hardly sensitive to it during all the excitement of the day, but I recalled that a number of the leaders of the Memorial Day program had lost a referendum being voted upon that very day. Some of the people had actually been too busy with the activities of the day to save the measure that was being decided at the Court House. As the sun was setting after the flowers had been placed upon the graves of the Confederate and Union dead in the cemetery across the road from the high school, the news came that the town fathers had been defeated. It was an inspiration to me to see the courage demonstrated by those stalwart people.

And as we rode along through the cool of the evening, I recalled the tragic loss they had suffered only a few months before when the Chattahoochee came raging out of its banks and inundated the town and the valley around it. "They mustered a tremendous amount of courage and showed a great deal of endurance in that experience," I said to my wife.

"Yes," she answered in her quiet voice, "we can draw lessons from the present as well as from the past, can't we?"

MEMORIES OF OLD DAYS

What a flood of memories rushed in as I read Irvin McBrayer's story, published recently in the *Atlanta Journal-Constitution*, about the last Confederate flagpole down at Blakely. As a boy I played around that flagpole. Many a night the high school gang—boys, that is—gathered at the Courthouse Square on the green lawn at the base of the old flagpole and sang "In the Evening by the Moonlight." How the old folks would enjoy it; they would sit all night and listen.

I doubt that the old folks listened at all, and surely not all night. But we sang that old familiar song, and many others, until the night was half spent. Some of the boys may have stayed longer, but as for me, I had to get home before an anxious father started out looking for a son who "should be extra careful" about his night life, seeing as he was the Baptist minister's son.

So, it was Councilman Pete Underwood who gave the old pole its "new look," the flagstaff that Peter Howard, his ancestor, had donated to the town a hundred years before. Pete was one of our gang who sang on the Early County Courthouse lawn on moonlit evenings in the good old summertime. Mr. John, Pete's father, raised a fine family, mostly boys. He played the fiddle well and taught his boys to play various instruments. Pete went all out for the trumpet.

Mr. John organized a little church orchestra, which played at our church every Sunday night. Pete played in it, of course, and they let me play the clarinet. I had to do lots of faking because the Italian band leader who sold me the instrument left town after I'd had only one lesson. But being the minister's son, I was tolerated by the group.

Pete did well with his trumpet, blew his way through college with it. After college he led a dance band in Atlanta. I used to listen to his band late on Saturday nights as I sat by my radio up in the Blue Ridge Mountains of western North Carolina, tuned in on WSB. Now Pete is back in his old hometown.

Early County, being in southwest Georgia, was out of reach of Yankee Bluecoats during the Civil War, and Sherman on his march to the sea didn't make a thrust in that direction, not even at Andersonville Prison to release Yankee prisoners. Therefore, we were short on stories of "The War Between the States," as we were taught to call it. World War I was close to us, but somehow did not excite us, and World War II was still on the drawing board. I do not mean to imply that Early County men and boys were indifferent concerning the struggle for Southern independence, not at all. Before First Manassas, even before Big Bethel, Capt. Joel T. Crawford and his lieuenants, Bolling H. Robinson, Virgil T. Nunnally, and Robert T. Bowie, had organized the "Early Guards." They became Company G of the 13th Georgia Volunteer Infantry.

Stories and tall tales were told on the courthouse lawn in those summer evening get-together sessions, but they were for the most part stories of personal conquests and exploits, not war stories of the past century. Sometimes the talk got around to town gossip. Now gossip among a group of boys in a small town at night was not always nice in those days. We would have done better if all our talking had been spent in singing.

After gossip sessions I would walk home—a wiser young man, I thought, than my father, the minister. Little did I know then that he knew more about that town than I did, that he knew the

joys and sorrows of those people better than all of us because
the people loved and trusted him and told him all their troubles.
And he loved them too, all of them. His heart was so big it covered
the entire county and even spilled over into the surrounding
territory. And he tried to make that town a better place for the
children than it had been for the parents.

And did he?

If I could slip quietly down to the old courthouse lawn some
moonlit night and hear the grandsons of my old pals talking, I
would know. I would probably hear better talk, but I doubt that
I would hear better melody than was blended by our gang in
those evenings long ago at the old Confederate flagpole. If Byron
Collier, a fine member of Blakely's present teenage generation
is typical, I would say they exchange more wholesome stories
around the old flagpole nowadays. They pay more attention to
history than we did.

According to Byron the 100-foot pine shaft was erected 16
May 1861, and Thomas Williams and Isaac Layton had a part
in it. Sarah Powell presented the Confederate flag to the Early
Guards, which they raised with a shout. Byron's research shows
that John R. Ransome made a speech of acceptance and then
gave the silken banner to Judge James B. Brown to raise and
lower and raise again, and again, until one day the Yankees
threatened to cut down the pole if the local citizens ever hoisted
the Confederate flag again.

According to young Collier, "Uncle Ben" Fryer stopped a
Union soldier carrying an axe with a threat: "If you strike that
flagpole, you'll be another dead damn Yankee!"

A VISIT TO CHICKAMAUGA

"After Longstreet arrived at Chickamauga with about 11,000 troops from the east to reinforce Bragg, the Confederates broke Rosecrans's right wing and a portion of his center on September 20, 1863, but Thomas, taking up a new position on Snodgrass Hill stood firm—'The Rock of Chickamauga' held his position until the close of the day . . ."

Edgar M. Carden, our guide at Chickamauga, was speaking. The old gentleman who has been reliving Chickamauga for 34 years seemed to take unusual pride in Gen. Thomas who held Snodgrass Hill in the all-day battle. My Civil War history class students, all but one being Southerners, had taken delight in anticipation of a two-day journey to Chickamauga and Kennesaw, two places where the Rebs had won glory. Now our guide was singing the praises of the Yankee general, George H. Thomas. "But, after all," opined one, "this Union general was born in Virginia."

Our guide began,

Here where you stand was enacted a drama of humanity hardly expected in time of battle. It had cost the Federals about 2,000 men to hold Snodgrass Hill, and the Confederates lost almost as many in trying to dislodge them. In the afternoon fire broke out in the underbrush, caused by the flames from the cotton wadding ejected from the muskets. The wounded were in danger of being burned alive. A truce was declared and troops from both sides worked together to rescue them. After their job of mercy was completed they resumed their savage warfare. . . .

Suddenly, lightning began to flash above the tall trees, and we retreated hastily—in our cars—to the Visitors' Center. There we had difficulty pulling one of our party away from a display of 200 guns. Another of our party observed a small boy watching a diorama of Union and Confederate soldiers in formation, ready for a charge. "Which ones are the bad guys?" he asked.

Reluctantly, we left Chickamauga where the Confederates drove the Yankees back to Chattanooga. There they waited for spring and moved again to Georgia.

We reached our motel at Kennesaw in the evening, our minds filled with thoughts of the day's experiences and our briefcases filled with literature and books to help us understand the events that lay between the two big battles: Lookout Mountain, Missionary Ridge, Sherman's departure from Chattanooga, his forcing Johnston from Dalton, the Federal flanking movement at Resaca.

The next morning after breakfast we drove to the museum and met, by appointment, Supt. B. C. Yates. The students were so fascinated with his informal, witty, and informative lecture that the guide and I had difficulty in getting them away from him and on to their tour to the top of Kennesaw. We rode as far as possible, then hiked to the top of the tall mountain. Obviously, Sherman's frontal attack could not have been made against Big Kennesaw. With the guide's help and from our vantage point we could see lying out before us the railroad in the green valley. Beyond it was Pine Mountain, where Gen. Leonidas Polk the fighting bishop was killed, and to the west was Lost Mountain, silhouetted against the blue sky.

"The plan was for Thomas and McPherson to make frontal attacks simultaneously June 27th, Thomas to attack Cheatham on the hill that bore his name and McPherson to assault the Confederate center at the south end of Little Kennesaw."

Our young guide was speaking. He had as much modesty as the superintendent had verve, but he made the Battle of Kennesaw Mountain grow larger and larger until we could see in our imagination the whole valley before us filled with 100,000 troops, stretching for ten miles and hurled against a force half their number.

"The result," said our guide, "was a temporary victory for Gen. Joe Johnston's Confederates. But the fighting Texan, John B. Hood soon would replace the popular leader who had saved his army, and Sherman would resume his movement south."

Our journey was climaxed at the Cyclorama in Atlanta where we saw Sherman victorious over the impetuous Hood. En route to Grant Park we stopped for a two-hour visit at the State Archives where Mary Bryan's entire staff took time to lecture and demonstrate the importance of archives in the study of history.

RENAISSANCE FOR A DAY

You who read this column are accustomed to being carried back 100 years. Today I want you to go with me down a little narrow dirt road in Twiggs County, not 100 years ago but 150. I took that road last Sunday and it carried me back into the past more surely than all the musty records I have read in libraries and archives. The occasion was the sesquicentennial of Old Richland Church sponsored by the Old Richland Restoration League. Mrs. King and another charming lady, the wife of President Rufus C. Harris of Mercer University, went with me.

The weather was ideal. Hundreds of people from everywhere from Jeffersonville to New York City were there. Many of them were dressed in antebellum fashions, some authentic, as was the one worn by an exciting little lady who told me her dress had been in the family for generations and had made appearances at a 50th wedding anniversary and a 100th birthday party. I even persuaded my young daughters to go hear their father speak. They said it was the food that drew them to the place. Children are such kidders!

But for whatever reason, there we were, about a thousand strong, reliving the past, making the quiet woods around the white, columned, dignified old church alive with the chatter of friends and relatives—everybody was kin to everybody—and making the countryside ring with the laughter of children. Indeed, it was a renaissance. It lasted only one day, but for a few hours, the Old South had come alive in the woods.

The kind of renaissance I experienced at Old Richland Church and on the side trips to the quaint and tranquil, but picturesque, Old Southern homes cannot be found on the busy, crowded, paved highways that traverse our state today. Rather, one must turn off the thoroughfares, those long ribbons of concrete where man's inhumanity to man is sometimes tragically demonstrated, if one wishes to see the past.

You must take a side road and breathe a bit of red dust if you wish to find a rebirth of Old South culture, of life at its best, of leisure, of love and friendship, of hospitality, of eating good food and smelling the aroma of coffee on the terrace, of good thoughts and gentle people, of birds catching and imitating the musical notes of young girls' laughter.

Our journey carried us over much of Twiggs County. One side road wound through a pasture filled with Black Angus cattle that resented our intrusion into the ruins that had once been a lovely plantation home. Now that house is beyond repair, and piece by piece it is being demolished until, finally, only the memory of those who can recall playing on the wide shady lawn under the great oaks will identify the spot where it stood. Much of Old South culture is like that old house, fading into the background of a picture that becomes even more crowded with machines that standardize us, master us, and, sometimes, destroy us.

But we followed quiet shady lanes to lived-in houses. We came suddenly upon one in a trim and orderly yard surrounded by a clean white picket fence. Its broad veranda was bordered with lace-like ornamentation. Inside, the visitors filed by the punch bowl in the majestic dining room, and all the while Atlanta newspaper photographers snapped pictures of the "old-fashioned" guests.

Another road led to a home where a music box played German airs, and where a very vivacious and sweet little lady entertained. She held my hand for a picture and stood as close to me as her hoop-skirted dress would permit. She showed us a pitcher and goblet that had been buried during the War Between the States, then recovered after the Yankees had gone home. Another road led to a farm house that resembled a hunting lodge, with its silver cups won by its late owner lining the shelves. The long living/dining room of this house was comfortably furnished in good taste. For you who are trying to identify this place, I shall give you a hint: the dining table is a lazy Susan. And, by the way, the lady of the wedding dress is the daughter of a great Georgia congressman of a generation ago.

We reached the last mentioned place at sunset. The crackle of hickory logs in the huge fireplace gave the room a warmth that symbolized the spirit of our hospitable hostess. But the autumn sun dropping through the trees gave the terrace enough warmth to attract us outside. As we sat upon the broad patio, the conversation was chiefly about the day's events. How full it had been! Macon friends, Atlanta visitors, kinfolks from Perry, all of Jeffersonville it seemed, more kin from Tarversville and other places I didn't know existed. And no one talked about when, how, or why he was going to build a fallout shelter.

PAGEANT AT CHATTANOOGA

Someone said that poets can tell us the meaning of history better than the historians. This may sometimes be true, but in my effort to find something deep and significant in pageants of the Civil War written by poets, dramatists, and musicians I usually come to a disappointing end. This happened to me last summer in Atlanta when I tried to find something more than the obvious and trite in the production of *The Phoenix*. All it said to me was that the mighty city of Atlanta rose from the ashes of war and fire. Perhaps the trouble is with me—can it be that I do not see all there is in the drama?

It happened again this month when I went with my colleagues to the annual meeting of the Southern Historical Association in Chattanooga, Tennessee. The University of Chattanooga, which originated under Northern Methodist sponsorship as U. S. Grant University, produced a Civil War drama for the benefit of the 800 historians gathered there. Written by an English professor, the pageant was entitled "Beyond the Dark Night: A Drama of the Civil War and Reconstruction." Here again I felt let down, cheated because the only lesson it seemed to convey was, to use Robert Penn Warren's words, "power and prestige." Power and prestige are a part of our heritage from the Civil War, but dramas that simply glory in these leave me cold. And when they are played poorly, in an auditorium with opera seats that slant downward, they become extremely tiresome.

This particular pageant had its high moments, however, when one felt rewarded for his patience. Moments such as the hilarious one when Gen. Wade Hampton, a visitor from South Carolina after the war, made a grand, sweeping bow to the assembled Chattanooga citizens of 1877, plus the spectators who filled the high school auditorium, and his moustache fell off!

We were almost in the proper spirit when Gen. Grant and his staff officers stood on stage front and center and viewed the Battle of Lookout Mountain through their binoculars. As the officers called to their general encouragingly of Union advance, one could almost see on the blank wall behind him the armies of Hooker, Sherman, and Thomas driving Bragg off the mountain. Then—and here a day elapsed—Gen. Grant saw Thomas disregarding his orders and pursuing the Confederates to Missionary Ridge and scattering them down the slopes beyond. Grant stormed and stamped his foot, saying he'd fix that so-and-so Thomas for not obeying orders, but the thrill of victory quickly brought a change in his attitude. Thomas was a hero and Grant a victorious general. The curtain closed leaving Gen. Grant, who was standing a little too far out, in front of the curtain—alone! Some Southern Rebels in the audience suggested that they rush upon the stage at that instant and capture the Union general while he was undefended, but before they could act the bearded Grant retreated hurriedly into the wings and to safety.

Under such circumstances it is hard for one to find a serious or deep meaning in Civil War drama. I think, as I have said in this column previously, that there are lessons to be learned from the commemoration of the Civil War. I do not believe we can or should bury the past, but we should do more than clutch, like a small boy clutches his lifeless dog just killed by a passing car, the memories of Union victory or return to the bitterness of Southern defeat, nor should we endlessly mouth the sweet words duty and honor, nor puff up with pride because our Union, welded by the fire of Civil War, enjoys more power and prestige than any other on earth.

I think Civil War dramatists could command more respect if they consulted the historians before the curtain rises on their productions. Having just last year edited Eliza Frances Andrews's *Wartime Journal of a Georgia Girl,* I was amazed to find Garnett Andrews appear in the opening episode of the Chattanooga pageant as one of the citizens of the town in 1856, when I knew he lived in Washington, Georgia. But when four years later, he joined with the Chattanooga fire-eaters to demand secession, it was too much for me. Judge Andrews never favored secession! His sons, one of whom moved to Chattanooga after the war, and daughters defied him, and all fought in their individual ways for the Confederacy, but the Judge never departed from his unionist position.

Heaven forbid that Thalia should disfigure the beautiful face of her sister Clio!

June 24, 1962

In the Form of Retreat

Today marks the end of the first series of essays for this column. The good editor—bless him—has agreed to let me have a vacation for the month of July. It's not that I have run out of ammunition in this four-year war of words, far from it. I am merely doing what Beauregard did at Shiloh, making a strategic retreat to regroup and gather more strength.

The truth is the tired old veteran needs a rest, but don't let Gen. Pope know it, for I hope to make the second attack at Manassas, one of surprise so that we may have success there as we did in that first big battle last year. Whether the *Macon Telegraph-News* is read north of the Potomac or not, the plans for a second attack at Bull Run, followed by Lee's invasion of Maryland at Sharpsburg, should be kept secret. So, will the readers of this column please refrain from mentioning them in any correspondence with acquaintanes behind enemy lines. In any case, I shall be back in August in time to report the outcome of Second Manassas and in September for the big bloody battle of Sharpsburg, or Antietam as the Yankees call it.

During the month of July, I shall be at the Library of Congress, and other libraries nearer home, getting more ammunition for the big battles of words yet to come. My stockpile here at the base of operations is far from exhausted, but a good strategist knows that the source of supply should always be kept active. A number of readers who have responded to my request for letters, diaries, and memoirs have yet to see any parts of them in this column. Such material will be used as time goes on, and it is hoped that much more will be forthcoming. Some who have followed this series have been good enough to phone or write me offering material, and I have failed to follow up your offers. Please be patient with me, and if you have something for me, give me another chance and a reminder.

This column has volleyed forth about 60,000 words since it began to blast away in the battle of words on the Civil War. It has continued without a break for 80 Sundays since 11 December 1960 when it announced, "The *Telegraph* has seceded from the Union." It has reported battles, it has quoted diaries and letters of the soldiers at the front and the folks back home, it has gone on some interesting journeys, and it has covered many topics of interest during the war years of the 1860s. But there are more topics yet to be covered than have already been written. After a few weeks I shall be back with stronger guns, more ammunition, and renewed determination to carry this battle of words to the adversary with full confidence of victory.

Unlike the Army of Northern Virginia under Lee at Richmond and the Army of Tennessee under Joe Johnston in the Atlanta Campaign, who found their supplies getting ever shorter, my supply of words will increase until, finally, we shall overwhelm Grant, Meade, and Sherman, and all their like. And, who knows, we may even talk them out of Vicksburg, Gettysburg, Atlanta, and Richmond.

Seriously, the editor and I never talked about the obligations of the writer in using this space—the obligation to be fair, to be above prejudice. No orders were handed me to avoid using it for propaganda purposes, to avoid using it for promoting "causes" or crusading. I felt complimented to think that none of that was needed, and I have tried to be true to the confidence the editor placed in me by not violating that trust. I think a review of the essays that have appeared in this column will show that my intense pro-Southern writing has been with some degree of sympathetic tongue-in-cheek. I have great admiration for those who fought for the Lost Cause, but I hope my respect for those who fought for the Cause Won has been just as sincere.

The only time I departed from my policy of "no crusading," that is, the only time I deliberately departed with any degree of feeling, was when I wrote pleading for the restoration of Old Wesleyan. That was, I hope, a permissible exception. And I want to say, in closing, that I appreciate all who joined in the fight for that crusade. I think all of us who have any respect for our cultural heritage should take pride in the fact that we were rebels of that lost cause. A word of appreciation should be said for those who led that fight. When the record is read in the years ahead, future generations will rise up and call them blessed.

JOURNEY TO GETTYSBURG

One of the most interesting tours that I made during the summer just passed was a visit to Gettysburg, Pennsylvania. I was visiting my Yankee brother-in-law in our nation's capital. My visit was a combination of work and play, a research jaunt to the Library of Congress with much fun and frolic mixed in at the home of my sister and her husband and children. One day my Yankee relatives took another sister and me to Gettysburg to see the place where the tide of fortune turned definitely against the Confederacy. This excursion, I thought, was in retaliation for a visit on which we had taken our Yankee brother-in-law during one of his visits to Georgia. We had taken him to Andersonville Prison and Cemetery where 13,000 Federal soldiers died. Gettysburg was a pretty fair match for Andersonville, since in that great three-day battle the Confederates' loss was 3,903 dead, about 24,000 wounded and missing. It had taken a few months to run up a total of 13,000 Union dead at Andersonville. Of course, the Federals lost heavily at Gettysburg too. 3,155 killed and approximately 20,000 wounded and missing.

Neither of us, however, saw any humor in it. One just can't joke about that much human sacrifice.

Our day at Gettysburg began at the National Museum, where there is a big electric map showing the entire battle area. There we got a good understanding of the layout of the battle. Sitting on seats high above the big map and listening to the recorded voice of the narrator as he described the events of the three days, with colored lights that flashed on and off to direct our attention to the various places, we could imagine we were watching the actual troops as they advanced and retreated. Culp's Hill lay to the east of where we sat. At Seminary Ridge, to the west, we could see where Pickett, Pettigrew, and Trimble with their divisions, 15,000 strong, were poised under Longstreet's command. To the south of us lay Little Round Top where Longstreet, after having staggered Sickles, failed to take the eminence and thus lost his chance to enfilade the entire Union position. Big Round Top lay a little farther beyond. To the west again we could see the Peach Orchard where Longstreet's assault on Sickles began, and still farther along the horizon stretched Seminary Ridge.

The first day belonged to the Confederates. On 1 July they drove the Federals through the town and back to strong defensive positions on Cemetery Hill and Culp's Hill. Longstreet's corps occupied Seminary Ridge. On the second day Lee opened the attack but Early was driven off Cemetery Hill. On the third day Ewell was driven off Culp's Hill and it was then that Longstreet drove Sickles back towards Little Round Top at the Orchard. Then, Longstreet reluctantly followed Lee's plan by making a frontal attack on the strong Union center. Fifteen thousand Confederates swept down from Seminary Ridge and up Cemetery Hill. "Only 7,800 came back," announced the narrator in a dramatic voice.

All became more clear as we followed the tour route and then recapitulated the whole story at the Cyclorama, housed in the beautiful new National Park Service building. The chief point of interest in the Cyclorama, of course, is Pickett's Charge at The Angle. This took place, as already mentioned, on the afternoon of 3 July. It marked the last attempt of Gen. Lee to destroy Meade's Army of the Potomac. The magnificent picture in the

Cyclorama was painted by the French artist, Paul Philippoteaux. He and his assistants began to study the terrain and interview witnesses in 1881. They finished the work in 1884.

John T. Trowbridge, our roving reporter from Boston who was mentioned in this column previously, was an early visitor to Gettysburg. In the late summer of 1865 he visited the battleground just after the cornerstone was laid for the National Monument. This monument marks the spot where President Lincoln delivered his now famous Gettysburg Address. Trowbridge, at the time, was not enough impressed by the president's address to mention his name. He simply wrote, "The new cemetery dedicated with fitting ceremonies on November 19, 1863, adjoins the old one."

GETTYSBURG MONUMENTS

This column closed last week with a reference to the National Monument at Gettysburg, the cornerstone of which was laid in 1865. It was at the laying of this cornerstone that President Lincoln made his now famous address that closed with these immortal words:

> . . . that we here highly resolve that these dead shall not have died in vain—that this nation, under God, shall have a new birth of freedom; and that government of the people, by the people, for the people, shall not perish from the earth.

The Gettysburg Address is now memorialized in stone on a beautiful circular monument that has Lincoln's words inscribed on one side and a description of the dedication ceremony on the other. In the center on a pedestal is a bronze bust of the author of the clearest and most concise definition of American democracy ever uttered.

There are many more monuments in the Gettysburg National Military Park. One of the most outstanding is the Pennsylvania Memorial. It has statues of officers and bronze nameplates of nearly 35,000 Pennsylvanians who fought on that battlefield. The Virginia monument stands on the spot where Gen. Lee watched the gallant charge of 3 July.

Along the front of the ridge on which the North Carolina monument stands, Gen. Lee marshaled his men for one more supreme effort, only to fail. This monument was sculpted by Gutzon Borglum. Georgians will remember him in connection with one stage of the Confederate Memorial at Stone Mountain, but his real success can be seen on Mount Rushmore, South Dakota, where he carved the heads of Washington, Jefferson, Lincoln, and Theodore Roosevelt. He had earlier done the statue of Lincoln which stands in the rotunda of the Capitol in Washington, D. C.

The newest monument at Gettysburg is the one that holds the greatest interest for Georgians. It is a monument to Georgia's dead who fell there. Gov. Ernest Vandiver, Secretary of State Ben Fortson, Mary G. Bryan, state archivist, and many others dedicated it on 21 Sept. 1961. The erection of monuments to Georgians who died at Antietam and Gettysburg was the result of efforts of the Georgia Hall of Fame Committee of the United Daughters of the Confederacy, of which Mrs. Forrest E. Kibler of Atlanta was chairman. The Antietam monument was dedicated on the previous day.

The Georgia monument at Gettysburg stands only 25 yards from the boundary line of President Eisenhower's farm. It is on the crest of Seminary Ridge. This is the place where the Confederate forces grouped for their attack. It is near the place where Georgia's Brig. Gen. Paul Jones Semmes was killed on the second day of the battle.

So, here where a hundred years ago 3,311 Georgians died, our state now has a simple but beautiful shaft of unpolished Georgia marble. It was designed by Harry Sellers of Atlanta. It is of blue granite, 12 feet high and 3 feet wide. On it one reads the simple inscription:

> *We sleep here in obedience to law.*
> *When duty called, we came;*
> *When country called, we died.*

Gov. Vandiver rekindled the spirit of Lincoln when he said in the dedication ceremony, "We cannot really pay tribute to the dead unless we learn the lessons taught by their sacrifice." The lesson they taught is that Gettysburg symbolizes defeat for no one, but rather victory for all. The British journalist, Arthur Fremantle, writing from the scene of the battle, reports Lee as saying to Gen. Willcox, who was almost in tears over the condition of his brigade, "Never mind, General, all of this has been MY fault—it is I that have lost this fight, and you can help me out of it in the best way you can." After one hundred years, were Lee alive today, he might say, "We are now out of it."

Most Americans now take pride in the victory of Gettysburg, for it is America's heritage—North, South, East, and West.

A JOURNEY TO RICHMOND

With the account of my travels to Gettysburg appearing in the last two issues, this column seems to have evolved into a script for a travelogue. Now I take you to Richmond, and next Sunday I shall report a journey to Mobile. The summer just passed was spent partly in revisiting old historic places and finding new ones. At each place, my family and I concentrated on shrines and edifices that relate to the Civil War. Therefore, I believe these personal tours are appropriate to this column.

The occasion for the Richmond trip was to carry our daughter Jan to the Medical College of Virginia. Mrs. King and I took advantage of the opportunity to look about the city. We passed up St. John's Church where Patrick Henry had his famous "give me liberty or give me death" speech, and the home of Chief Justice John Marshall, and many other places that we had already seen. But we went to the new and beautiful Virginia War Memorial building, a shrine in memory of those Virginians who gave their lives for their country in World War II and the Korean War. The central focus of this marble-columned structure is a majestic monument symbolizing the emotions of Virginia's women who gave up their sons with pride mixed with sorrow. The huge white monument, we noted, was carved from 100,000 pounds of Georgia marble.

The high point of our visit to Richmond was the Centennial Center, which the Virginia Civil War Centennial Commission has built at Eighth and Duval streets, within sight of the Richmond-Petersburg Turnpike. This ultramodern, dome-topped building looks like a flying saucer that has landed bottom up from some distant planet. Ramps curve from the front entrance in two directions to the upper floor and steps descend to the lower floor. The only resemblance this building has to the classical forms that characterized the Old South is the Romanesque dome. That is a slight reminder, however, of Richmond and the Old South's architectural grandeur.

The building is filled with electronic devices and audio-visual gadgets so foreign to anything the generals of that war knew that were they to come see the exhibits they would be completely mystified by it all. As one enters the building one is immediately struck by the mechanical devices. However, there meets the eye full-size pictures of Lee, Grant, Davis, and Lincoln, and John Pelham's battery at Fredericksburg holding off a Union assault for one hour. This "Boy Major" and his wax artillerymen man their smooth-bore cannon near the entrance on the ground floor.

A 35-minute movie, "Manassas to Appomattox," is shown to the visitors on the second level. It is narrated by Joseph Cotton and blends documentaries and live action in a dramatic presentation of the war in Virginia. This movie creates the proper atmosphere for the full appreciation of the exhibits on the first floor.

The purpose of the Centennial Center is to give an overall view of the battles and military campaigns in Virginia. This it does not only by the movie but also by the electronically operated exhibits, and especially by the electric maps depicting the campaigns. The first map covers campaigns of 1861-1862 and the second shows the campaigns of 1863-1865. A third map emphasizes battle areas over the whole state. The narration is tape recorded and is very well done. Each map takes five minutes of viewing time. Visitors listen through an earphone as they watch.

As the voice tells the movement of troops and the course of the battle, the lights flash and projected arrows dart across the map. It is an excellent teaching device. Schools could use such audio-visual aids if they were not so expensive, but it must have cost the Commission a fancv figure to set these machines into operation.

The railroads played an important role in the war as is shown by one of the exhibits. This exhibit also shows the building of pontoon bridges and the use of balloons for aerial reconnaissance.

Perhaps the greatest interest centers around the exhibit of the Crater. This diorama shows the Union soldiers tunneling under the Confederate lines at Petersburg and planting 800 pounds of black powder. It actually simulates the explosion. The Battle of the Crater is one of the most unusual incidents of the entire war. Most visitors who have not already seen the actual crater near Petersburg before seeing the diorama go out to see it after visiting the Centennial Center.

VISITING ON MOBILE BAY

I had never been to Mobile Bay. The opportunity came in the late summer when one of my sisters and I drove our mother to visit another sister who had married and lived in the tourist's haven and fisherman's paradise of Fairhope, Alabama, just across the bay from Mobile. The region is a rich truck farming area, but fishing interested my preacher brother-in-law and me much more. The first morning he had me up at daybreak seining for mullet. The next morning beginning at 2 A.M. the whole town was excited by the announcement of a "jubilee." For some unknown reason, when the fresh water of the Tombigbee and Alabama rivers meets the salt water of the Gulf at certain times and under certain conditions, it sends the fish scurrying toward the shallow water of the sandy shore. We gigged flounder and scooped up crabs simply by wading out knee-deep into the water and spotting them on the sand with the aid of flashlights. Everybody's deep-freeze lockers were filled again. Indeed, they are seldom empty.

But fishing could not hold the historian indefinitely. On the second day when I was being shown the magnificent Grand Hotel at Point Clear, I looked for scars of the Civil War. Of course, I could not expect to find any in the rustic, but marvelous, building now standing on the point where seaplanes land and the hotel's guests and baggage are brought in by boat, for that building dates back only to 1928. The original structure was built in 1843.

The only evidence of the Civil War that I could find in the hotel proper was in the bar. On the wall of that elaborately decorated and richly furnished room hangs a large painting of the "Battle of Mobile Bay," the work of John McGrady. It is a vivid action picture of Farragut's ships, large wooden ones, monitors, and small gunboats engaged in a terrific battle with the Confederate ram *Tennessee* and other boats defending the port city of Mobile. As every student of the Civil War knows, Farragut, lashed to his flagship the *Hartford* and disregarding the torpedoes, forced his way through a rain of shot and shell from the Confederate fleet and gunfire from Ft. Morgan, maneuvering his fleet to victory. But as one looks at the picture one becomes puzzled and finds that history has been contorted by the artist. It is a picture of utter destruction of the Union fleet—clearly a Confederate victory! Miss Moore, our charming guide on the tour, told us the story behind this picture that reversed history. When those who had commissioned McGrady to do the picture pointed out his error, he answered, "It is my picture, is it not; then I shall paint it as I please!"

Though the present magnificent Grand Hotel carries no scars of the war, nearby Gunnison House, in which the hotel personnel live, has a blackened and ragged hole at its right front corner. It is about six inches in diameter. A plaque just under the hole reads: "Compliments of Admiral Farragut—Aug. 5, 1864."

One afternoon, at my suggestion, we rode about the city of Mobile searching out places of Civil War significance. Just as we parked our car on Government Street to pick up information at the nearby Chamber of Commerce, we saw the S. S. *Titan*, a very large cargo ship, being towed in by four tugs. This was a thrilling sight to me, and I could not help thinking of the comparatively small *Tennessee*, which failed to keep Farragut out of Mobile in 1864. If the Confederates had only had something similar, what a different story it would have been, I thought.

Of all the beautiful and historic places in Mobile, the two that attracted me most were Gen. Braxton Bragg's home on Spring Hill Avenue and Adm. Semmes's home next door to the First Baptist Church on Government Street.

Adm. Raphael Semmes, whose long and impressive record of seizures on the high seas during the war was a worthy match for Adm. Farragut's exploits, had been commander of the Confederate raider, the *Sumter*, and later of the *Alabama*. After the war a grateful city presented him an attractive two-story house decorated with iron grill work. Recently this house was presented to the First Baptist Church. Officials of that church have wisely preserved as much as possible the exterior and interior of the house as they utilize it for small weddings and other church functions.

The large white two-story home of Gen. Bragg, with its tall, square columns across the front, sits back deep in an azalea-filled yard of large water oaks. It is not opened to the public, so I can only imagine what the interior looks like.

A JOURNEY TO SAVANNAH

Since for the last three or four Sundays this column has been devoted to my summer travels, I think I should round off October with one final journey. As I walk about the parks and countryside here in Macon looking at the rapturous picture before me, which multicolored leaves make more beautiful than human hands could ever paint, I remember the warm August sun at Savannah Beach. I had taken my class in History 145 on a tour of historic Savannah. History 145 at Mercer University is the study of Georgia history, and we were studying it as it should be studied, by leaving the hot classroom and going out into the open spaces where Georgia history began—to Yamacraw Bluff, to Cockspur Island, to Skidaway, to the beautiful White Bluff of the Vernon River. The sun was hot also in Savannah, but it was a more relaxing heat down on the Atlantic coast where breezes blow through the salt spray of the surf.

We stayed at the DeSoto Hotel—itself an old landmark—and our tours radiated from that point. First, we went out Skidaway Road to Wormsloe on the Isle of Hope, which is just beyond the marshes of Skidaway Narrows. Elfrida De Renne Barrow is the mistress of this 200-year-old estate, which was founded by Noble Jones, her great-great-great grandfather. She had invited us to visit her tree-shaded haven by the sea.

"You will find the gates unlocked," she had written, "be sure to close them behind you as you come in and go out." A beautiful vista met our gaze as we swung open the huge wrought-iron gates and drove down the long, long avenue of water oaks, which with their dripping Spanish moss made a canopy of gray and green above us. The gracious lady welcomed us despite the fact she was convalescing from an operation. She was apologetic, saying she had not been able to supervise the work on the grounds as she should, but everything looked neat and majestic. The trim garden behind the big three-story, white, frame house presented a pretty pattern of color and design. The birds seemed to have been holding a convention there that afternoon; every species must have sent delegates. The expansive wooded areas, God-made, were in contrast to the formal garden and were actually more inspiring. For a detailed history of this relic of colonial culture one should read E. Merton Coulter's *Wormsloe, Two Centuries of a Georgia Family* (Athens, 1955).

We visited many spots that made the colonial period come alive for us, such as the old original cemetery, where the names on the markers and monuments reminded us of the Founding Fathers of our state, and old colonial houses, such as the James Habersham home ("The Pink House"), the Pirate's House, where we had dinner served by young and attractive "Pirates," and the Owen-Thomas House, where we saw draperies and furnishings done in authentic Regency style. But our interest was also in the period of the Confederacy. Since this column appears under the title, "Civil War Centennial," it is fitting that I mention two tours that took us back to that period.

The first of these was White Bluff, or Vernonberg, as it is now officially called—that being the original name of the place where Saltzburgers settled more than two hundred years ago. Most of my students had read my little book, *Ebb Tide As Seen Through the Diary of Josephine Clay Habersham* (Athens, 1958), and were naturally curious to see the locale of the story. "Avon" was the summer home of the mother of Joe Clay and Willie, who

were killed in the same hour the afternoon Sherman defeated
Hood in the Battle of Atlanta. The great grandson of Josephine
Habersham, George Grisfield, who lives next door to the stately
old river home, showed us through the house that had been the
residence of his mother and her sister and brother-in-law, Mr.
and Mrs. Clarence G. Anderson. They are all dead now and the
house stands empty and desolate.

The other tour of Civil War interest was, of course, Ft. Pulaski on Cockspur Island. That old fort, which had been built
and reinforced long before the war, was thought to have been
impregnable, with its seven-foot-thick brick walls and its wide
moat filled with water. And, indeed, it would have been, if the
attackers had not had the use of a new rifled cannon, the Parrott
gun. Mr. Jackson, the superintendent of the fort (which is now
under the National Parks Service), was unsparing in the pains
he took to answer our numerous questions. But he was very
much disconcerted that afternoon because someone the night
before had stolen Col. Charles H. Olmstead's sword that the fort's
young commander had handed to Maj. Charles C. Halpine at the
surrender ceremony, saying, "I yield my sword but I trust I have
not disgraced it."

Our Common Heritage

We come now to the end of our story of the Civil War, which began with the struggle for Southern independence and ended, as Gen. Porter Alexander said, in a union "forged in the white heat of battles." It has taken as long to tell this epic tale as it took to act out that tragic and strange war. This column has chronicled not the war as a whole—that would have been too great an undertaking—but has presented it as it must have affected Macon citizens and as Maconites must have seen it.

This column began in December 1960, a hundred years after Georgia's sister state South Carolina seceded. Then Georgia seceded and helped form the Southern Confederacy. Soon after, Macon people began to hear the drums roll. Drummer boys beat their rat-a-tat-tat as the Floyd Rifles, the Macon Volunteers, and dozens of other companies marched off to Virginia and to-ward the West. The roar of the cannon and the spit of the rifles was too far away for a while to be heard in the Georgia city. Finally, however, the roll of the drums sounded here again, and the roar of the cannon was heard, and the fire from the rifles could be seen. The end came when Gen. James H. Wilson's victorious Cavalry Corps entered the city.

As the war of one hundred years ago has been narrated in this column Sunday after Sunday, I have been conscious of the too striking similarity between events and attitudes during two periods separated by a century. But it is my hope that even as "the white heat of battles" forged a strong, wealthy, victory-minded nation, united by force, so shall classes, sections, and races become even more united and harmonious through mutual respect for law and order and dignity, and that a spirit of goodwill shall prevail in our land. And, since there is a higher law than man-made law, it is my hope that man will climb to that level of justice. This hope is expressed in the knowledge of and in spite of the present tension in the very region through which Wilson's corps marched long ago.

Admittedly, the Civil War proved that fanaticism could win out over statesmanship in a society not mature enough to make democracy work. But that was a century ago. Surely our people have matured enough since 1865 to make democracy work now toward harmony in the areas of section, class, and race through reason even as the nation was welded together through force after Appomattox.

It seems paradoxical to say that good can come out of evil, that the Civil War could result in something beneficial. But if the lesson of reason can be learned by profiting from our past mistakes, that must be considered good. Lessons which the nation can learn from the Civil War are the ability to endure hardships, to master our frustrations, to have courage, to exercise patience, and to clothe ourselves in humility—to accept a Will above and beyond the will of man. Perhaps one of the most important lessons to be learned from the war comes from Lincoln's message to Congress in 1862 when he said, "The dogmas of the quiet past are inadequate to the stormy present. As our case is new, we must think anew and act anew."

Finally, I come back again to the greatness of America. That legacy, left to us by the soldiers of both the Union and the Confederate armies, was inspired by the common purpose of those gallant men who fought, each for what he thought were worthy principles.

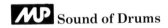 **Sound of Drums**

Designed by Margaret Jordan Brown

Composition by MUP Composition Department

Production Specifications:
    text paper—60 lb. Warren's Olde Style
    endpapers—Strathmore Brigadoon Dondee Blue
    cover—(on .088 boards) Joanna Arrestox A 47440
    dust jacket—100 lb. enamel printed three colors (PMS 288 blue,
        PMS 290 light blue, and PMS 120 light yellow) and varnished.

Printing (offset lithography) by Omnipress of Macon, Inc., Macon,
    Georgia

Binding by John H. Dekker and Sons, Inc., Grand Rapids, Michigan